1988

Milton and the Idea of Woman

Milton
and the Idea
of Woman

EDITED BY

Julia M. Walker

UNIVERSITY OF ILLINOIS PRESS

Urbana and Chicago

© 1988 by the Board of Trustees of the University of Illinois
Manufactured in the United States of America
C 5 4 3 2 1

This book is printed on acid-free paper.

Library of Congress Cataloging-in-Publication Data

Milton and the idea of woman.

Bibliography: p.
Includes index.
1. Milton, John, 1608–1674—Characters—Women.
2. Milton, John, 1608–1674—Political and social views.
3. Women in literature. 4. Sex role in literature.
I. Walker, Julia M., 1951–
PR3592.W6M55   1988   821'.4   87-19075
ISBN 0-252-01486-3 (alk. paper)

To Frederick R. Leenig,
my best friend,
who has long shared with me
an idea of Milton

Contents

Acknowledgments

O F the many debts of gratitude I have incurred while working on this collection, the first acknowledgment must go to Albert C. Labriola and the Milton Society of America (although the former may constitute a fine example of synecdoche for the latter) for giving me the opportunity to organize and chair the 1985 MLA session which began this project. Professor Labriola's unfailing support and extensive suggestions have been of incalculable value to me. Equally valuable was the sound advice of three of my colleagues, past and present: Carol Thomas Neely, who told me not to get involved with this project and who was right; Celia A. Easton and Paul Schacht, who told me that I must finish this project (even if it meant they had to read innumerable drafts) and who were also right. These four head a list of many kind friends and colleagues and Miltonists who offered help and encouragement both practical and metaphysical: Margaret W. Ferguson, Ronald B. Herzman, Michael Lieb, Mary Nyquist, Thomas P. Roche, Jr., Shirley Clay Scott, Anne Shaver, John C. Ulreich, Jr., and Susanne Woods. All of these efforts would have been in vain had it not been for the assistance, efficiency, and tolerance of Gail English and Marie Henry of the SUNY–Geneseo English Department and Ann Lowry Weir and Pat Hollahan of the University of Illinois Press. I would also like to thank my sister, Shirley Walker, for her continuing interest in and support of my work.

My greatest debt is, of course, to the twelve scholars who entrusted to me their fine essays; this is their book and I am proud to have worked on it.

Finally, as the dedication page indicates, not much in my life gets accomplished without the aid and comfort of my friend Fred; thanks, kid.

Geneseo, New York
March 4, 1987

The Idea of
Milton and the Idea of Woman

Presentation

THIS collection had its genesis in the MLA session which I organized in 1985 for the Milton Society of America. When I wrote the initial proposal for the session, my main concern was to keep its focus from sliding into "Milton's Idea of Woman," to keep prominent the title's tacit thesis that Milton had to come to terms with the idea of woman, just as he had to come to terms with the idea of death or the idea of God or with any other force outside himself and inside himself as well. The need for such a session was confirmed when the papers began to arrive—many, many papers, all (even those on Eve and Dalila) evincing what could be called a rhetoric of innovation which figured forth their authors' belief that they were, if not in all cases breaking new ground, at least taking roads less traveled by. And indeed, it is only in quite recent critical history that the possessive relationship between Milton and Idea and Woman has been dislocated by preposition and conjunction. The first fruit of this dislocation was an initially useful but ultimately reductive critical perspective which allows us to see Woman as separate from Milton's Idea, but which finally fails to free Idea from the nexus of social, political, and historical realities. This separation of Woman from Milton's Idea first manifested itself as a sort of reverse witch-hunt, with Milton's "Bogey" being burned again and yet again, having been found guilty— both by textual deed and by intellectual and cultural association—of crimes against Woman. However ultimately reductive this initial period of attack may seem to us now, it served the necessary act of clearing the ground, of getting out of the way the largely emotional reactions generated by Milton's "textual deeds," thereby making way for more detailed and deliberate examinations of those problems springing from Milton's "intellectual and cultural associations." Some excellent work has been done in this area; much remains for us to do.

While I was working on this introduction, one of my students wandered

1

into my office and asked what I was writing. When I told her that I was putting together a collection of essays on Milton and the idea of woman, she exclaimed, "Wow, you're kidding. Well, at least it will be short!" And twenty—even ten—years ago she would have been quite correct, for the critical work on the topic was sparse, predictable, and much of a muchness. But after three hundred years of critics discussing Milton's idea of woman or—worse yet—"Milton's women" with no imaginative space between textual appearance and the readers' perception of reality, the past two decades have seen the development of a crucial critical distinction between the universal concept of woman and Milton's version of that idea. On the face of it, this sounds patently simplistic; but Milton locates his poetic visions of woman so concretely in historical or literary contexts, that Milton criticism, not surprisingly, has further reified these conceptualizations rather than speaking of these "women" as the figuring forth of ideas—of Milton's ideas and of the seventeenth century's ideas. Recent critics, by insisting that we separate Milton's truth from truth itself, have allowed space for further work of a more subtle nature. Because revisionist critics such as Sandra Gilbert have questioned the validity of generalizing Eve or Dalila into Woman, traditional critics such as Diane McColley have been able to analyze these individual portraits of woman as products of seventeenth-century cultural assumptions; because of the recent scholarly explorations of Renaissance attitudes toward the assumptions about women by scholars such as Linda Woodbridge, we may now use Eve and her poetic sisters to examine not only the idea of woman, not only a cultural milieu, but ultimately the poetic imagination of John Milton.

The essays in this collection take these now dislocated nouns—Milton, idea, woman—and examine the spaces between them by drawing in the linkages, sometimes retracing the lines of earlier pens, often finding more direct or precise lines of inquiry, and always being aware of other points of reference beyond and around this triangle.

Typically, one major task of an introduction is to "place" the topic within a broader field of study. The fact that so many contributors to this collection have themselves felt the need to place their arguments within the body of Milton criticism not only relieves me of this task, but also testifies to the validity of a metacritical approach to this topic. The authors of these essays address themselves both to the text and context of Milton's work and to the text and context of Milton criticism. Thus, they speak directly to generations of Milton critics and tacitly to each other. Since the project had its inception in the formation of a public forum on the topic, this ambience of active discourse seems particularly appropriate. Although I could not have all twelve of these scholars at podiums in Chicago, I can provide here an imaginary round table with real arguments at it. Essays by Susanne Woods and Janet E. Halley bracket the collection, framing with arguments which range over the entire canon ten other essays focused primarily (but rarely exclusively) on single works. Rather than summarizing the essays in strict "order of appearance," I prefer to allow—insofar as is possible—these critics to "speak" to one another's main points by organizing a roughly chronological examination of Milton and the idea of woman, from the early poetry to *Samson Agonistes.*

Although the order of Milton's works introduces the topics treated in these essays, the critical approaches of the authors must be grouped differently. Defining Milton's idea of woman by examining the visions and revisions of woman in Milton's sources and in his works proves to be a productive critical strategy. Kathleen Wall explores Milton's adaptation in *Comus* of various myths concerned with female sexuality, while Leah Marcus suggests the records of a 1631 rape case as a contemporary and politically relevant source for the Ludlow *Mask.* Noam Flinker's explication of Milton's references to blind poets and their muses stresses Milton's debt to those darkly enlightened shades; but it is the difference between Milton's portrait of Mary and its biblical source that is the focus of Dayton Haskin's essay on *Paradise Regained;* and Lynn Enterline, in her examination of the Italian sonnets, remarks on their relation to Petrarch's sonnets, a relationship both mimetic and revisionist. Finding Renaissance works which function not as sources for, but as commentary upon Milton's poetry, Diane McColley employs terms from Sidney's *Defense* to discuss Eve as Milton's embodiment of poetry itself, while Marshall Grossman uses sections of *Eikonoklastes* and *Areopagitica* to inform his discussion of Eve's deferred power in *Paradise Lost,* and John C. Ulreich, Jr., sets up the reconciliation of Adam and Eve in *Paradise Lost* as a yardstick for measuring Milton's compassion for Dalila. Complementing these analyses of visions and revisions are Susanne Woods's historically revisionist discussion of Milton's developing idea of female freedom and Janet E. Halley's feminist revisionist discussion of Milton's developing idea of female existence within the bounds of masculine poetry. Within other contemporary critical frameworks, Richard Corum uses Derrida's concept of words written "in white ink" to ascertain the paternity of Milton's Eve; Jackie DiSalvo adapts psychofeminist theories to a reading of *Samson Agonistes;* and Lynn Enterline draws from Jacques Lacan for her discussion of Milton and Petrarch. From the *discordia concors* of these "many accents sweet," we can begin to recognize and appreciate the complexity of the idea of woman as it takes shape in the mind and work of John Milton.

Summary

Three essays, those by Susanne Woods, Janet E. Halley, and Lynn Enterline, contain analyses of Milton's early works. Woods first speaks of the "supremely conventional" viewpoint evinced by *History of Britain* and *An Apology for Smectymnuus* and judges that the early poetry, up to the Ludlow *Mask,* "documents a surprising indifference to questions of gender," while Halley interprets "indifference" as aversion. Halley argues that Milton strives for poetic transcendence as a "strategy for evading dangers imposed by the female figure" and therefore represents this transcendence "in entirely male and genderless terms." Halley's view that the early poems display a "male poetic power and autonomy" achieved by a complete banishment of the female figure from "homosocial sexual poetics" both contrasts with and complements Enterline's belief that, as the poet's "point of entry into male poetic history, the figure of the lady plays the part of a necessary and therefore dangerous supplement to the poetic voice."

Both Halley and Enterline isolate the issues of danger, exchange, and transcendence as central to discussion of the early poetry, agreeing that the female figure represents various dangers for the beginning male poet. Halley employs those theories of Gayle Rubin and Claude Levi-Strauss which locate women in a system of exchange between men, a system "articulating the social relationships that constitute culture," to suggest that Milton's early rejection of the female figure was an attempt to achieve "male poetic power and autonomy." Enterline places Milton in – but not of – the Petrarchan tradition which "brought with it a structure of exchange" by reducing the "figure of the lady to a supplement of the poet's voice." Although this Petrarchan tradition of exchange informs Milton's Italian sonnets, the poet "does more than imply that the text can hear"; he "sets up a series of identifications between male self and female other." Woods, too, believes that Milton has "internalized the current gender roles" in *L'Allegro* and *Il Penseroso,* but sees the results of a "masculinist model [that] is automatic and unselfconscious," finding "no evidence he has given woman's nature any real thought at all." And, while Halley feels that Milton seeks poetic transcendence as a means of escaping the female, Enterline sees the figure of woman as "integral to the male poet's assertion of linguistic transcendence of a utopian moment when the self is one with and in the language." Woods, reacting to the same problems which prompt Halley's and Enterline's remarks, acknowledges Milton's "mixed attitudes toward female authority," but argues that this seeming confusion actually makes sense "because complete consistency of a static sort is inconsistent with Milton's belief in a dynamic and progressive creation."

"In the Ludlow *Mask*," observes Woods, Milton struggles, "really for the first time, with the problem of female freedom." Although freedom always has been a major concern in his early verse and prose, Woods feels that Milton is "less comfortable engaging those ideas when the rational creature he is concerned with is female." Despite this intellectual and poetic discomfort, Milton's "profound respect for human liberty has the ultimate effect of subverting his patriarchal assumptions." Although he does not accept these assumptions unquestioningly, he "has no frame of reference for responding to biblical authority in this matter"—or to cultural authority either, and yet "the dignity and intelligence he gives his female characters strains against the inferior social position in which they find themselves."

One way in which *Comus* evinces both an acknowledgment and a subversion of patriarchal assumptions, according to Kathleen Wall, is the Lady's "whole approach to mores and morality" which has a "patriarchal orientation" residing in her "too masculine, too logical" arguments. Milton adapts the popular Renaissance verson of the Callisto myth, but makes the Lady into a "patriarchalized" Callisto figure. This transformation into a "receptacle of patriarchal virtues renders her virtuous in the masculine sense, but deprives her of the fullest knowledge of her virginity." Wall sees two possible versions of the Callisto myth, the "patriarchalized version" from Ovid and a "matriarchal version" describing the initiation of woman into her own sexuality and her concomitant "acquisition of a psychological virtue of independence." After examining the implications of the myths of Atalanta, of Venus and Adonis, and of Cupid and Psyche for the mask, Wall reaches the same conclusion as Woods—that Milton was stymied by a patriarchal world which rendered whatever strength the Lady gained of little use to her. Milton gives the Lady, Wall concludes, "as much wholeness as she can achieve in a Renaissance context."

Placing Wall's theory that Milton's treatment of the Lady "deprives her of the fullest knowledge of her virginity" into a concrete historical incident, Leah S. Marcus cuts through suggestions of mythic sources to argue that the *Maske Presented at Ludlow Castle* on Michaelmasse Night, 1634, was actually a political and civic "message of sharp criticism" from the earl of Bridgewater, via Milton, to the local officials in the audience. The case of Margery Evans, a fourteen-year-old serving maid raped on Midsummer Eve, 1631, had been referred to John Egerton, first earl of Bridgewater, after it had been mishandled by two local justices of the peace who were influenced by friends of the accused rapist. Marcus conjectures that when Bridgewater attempted but failed to secure a conviction, he then settled the matter privately in the summer of 1634.

Comus, presented in the early fall of that year—far from being merely a private entertainment for family and friends—was significantly performed on "an important state occasion," the night of the earl's installation as lord president of the Council in the Marches of Wales.

Marcus argues that Milton was informed of the particulars of the Evans case either by "the earl himself or one of his associates" and that Milton wove these facts into his *Mask* to confront the members of the council of Wales "with an entertainment which reenacted on a higher social and intellectual plane elements from one of their most significant and troublesome cases of the previous year." Marcus concludes that "the masque offered a stringent challenge to all those officials who served under the earl of Bridgewater's authority—even a veiled threat to the most corrupt of them."

Marcus acknowledges that "Milton himself has frequently been accused of an obtuseness toward women rather like that demonstrated by the judges" who heard the Evans case and who were "unable or unwilling to make the imaginative leap required for empathy with a powerless young girl." But she nevertheless insists that in *Comus* Milton—consciously or unconsciously—produced "a work that displays a rare, unsettling capacity to dismantle the traditional discourse of authority," and therefore "makes that leap, constructing a set of paradigms for the conduct of public office around the womanly figure of Sabrina" and the victim/victor figure of the Lady, a set of human paradigms of justice which comes from a "recognition of not only female but human weakness."

But, even granting the powerful political and social overtones which Marcus foregrounds in the *Mask,* we are left with the reality that Sabrina's justice, however "womanly," is supernatural, not earthly, and Margery Evans's justice—if any—was private (or at best poetic), not public. Milton is still, in Woods's words, "locked into his culture's assumptions of woman's inferior position in the human paradigm."

If woman's position in the human paradigm has a locus classicus, it is in the figure of Eve, which brings us to the discussions of *Paradise Lost.* In this poem, as Marshall Grossman reminds us, "Eve confers upon Adam the title Adam had conferred upon God, and which, interestingly enough, the young Milton had . . . appropriated to himself, 'Author'"—a title which does not, Woods insists, mean that Eve is to Adam as Adam is to God. While Woods and Grossman dispute the place of Eve in this paradigm, Noam Flinker is more concerned with the place of Milton; for it is not of Eve that Flinker speaks in his essay, but of the "other" woman, Urania, and of Milton's "voluntary self-exposure to the nexus between sexuality and inspiration that is mythically presented as lust for the Muses." Flinker's recognition of the "psychosexual" elements of the narrator's invocations of Urania is shared by Janet Halley, although they reach somewhat different conclusions. Flinker believes that a "contrast between the narrator and other lovers in the epic suggests a sensitivity to the feminine consciousness in general and to problems implicit in the relations between the sexes in particular." Halley, on the other hand, feels that—although the "conversation" between Urania and Wisdom constitutes one of only two inversions of Milton's usual "traffic" on the man/woman/man relationship (the other being the "harmonious Sisters" in *Lycidas*)—there is still "a prior masculine understanding or meaning which both incorporates and transcends the mere imagery of the female figure." In the space between these two readings, Richard Corum describes the vision of Urania and Wisdom as "subordinations of previously independent classical goddesses to the hegemony of the father's monotheistic person," as eternally and absolutely obedient daughters, "as models to female character and deportment, and as ideas emanating from the side of the father's head."

Both Flinker and Halley agree that fear colors the narrator's feelings for Urania: the narrator exhibits "simultaneous attraction toward and fear of Urania," observes Flinker, and Milton therefore uses references to other ancient poets to help his narrator "conceal much of his apprehension about his Muse while apparently expressing his admiration"; Halley sees this fear doubled as, "in a single anxious figure, Milton associates a challenge to male primacy and autonomy with a recognition that his poem's language will not necessarily be perfectly referential." (One fear that Milton does not exhibit, however, is that of contradicting himself for, as Flinker points out, the narrator's address to an "explicitly feminine muse" is in direct contrast to Adam's insistence that only "Spirits Masculine" inhabit heaven.)

The idea of woman as a source of both sexuality and poetic inspiration provides a link between this discussion of Urania and Diane McColley's analysis of Eve as "the embodiment of Milton's defense—and, at her fall, his critique—of poesy." Beginning with the caveat "whenever we appropriate the poem for our own textual politics, we exploit Eve as text object," McColley goes on to present Eve not as an allegorical figure, but as a speaking portrait of the artist. "Eve embodies and performs a great many properties and processes that Milton elsewhere attributes to poetry itself, or to himself as poet." Her dreams figure forth the function of imagination, her songs the legendary Arcadian origins of poetry, her temptation and fall the abuse of poetry and the divorce of verse from truth. In fact, argues McColley, Eve's corruption is possible because she has the receptivity of poetic language itself. Taking this idea one step further, Marshall Grossman argues that when Eve "leaves the image of herself to accept the male word," she does so to "become the transmitter of his difference . . . to become *Literature.*" Halley, however, is troubled by the actual source of this literature, of Eve's poetry, and points out that Milton's "historically innovative insistence on female discourse" is obscured by the fact that it is God's wish she articulates when she recounts the replacing of her own image with Adam's.

Richard Corum's essay goes beyond Halley's conjecture that in Eve's speech we hear what God wanted said, to suggest that in Milton's poetry we hear what Milton thought God wanted said, Milton as "son" consciously writing to please a father he fears he will lose. This weights Eve's words with a sort of double intentionality: she voices not just what God wants her to say, but what Milton thought God wanted us to hear her say. Eve is therefore a "vital source, a store of natural and maternal attributes and qualities . . . for which there are no ideas in God's head." Because of Eve, therefore, Milton cannot be entirely successful, according to Corum, since a summary of "the idea Milton's God has of woman" does not "exhaust the subject" of Woman in *Paradise Lost;* there is "a residue: ideas of woman which do not belong to Milton's God" and it is this residue which makes the epic "a fallen poem and of interest to fallen readers." To see this residue "is to recover an invisible 'Milton' inscribed in white ink" lurking "unrepentantly in the text of Milton's rise to ideological perfection." Despite his avowed attempt to carry out "his God's imperial program" by trying to "erase and deny the sexual mother," Milton spends much time and space on the idea of woman. But not, Corum avers, as mother. As Grossman observes, the "Son, like Adam and Eve, lacks a mother," and Eve's promised empowerment as "Mother of the human Race" is deferred beyond the bounds of the poem. Corum argues that Milton begins his "non-discussion" of woman by developing an "iconography of an idea which paradoxically enlarges woman to material passivity by relegating her to some kind of background status." To support this thesis he points to the "fall" of backgrounds designated by female pronouns: "heaven," which is an "inanimate, wholly dependent, will-less, silent background environment for the activity of Milton's God"; "the moon," in which at "a lower, material level woman as background is a planet and a master trope"; "earth," where "woman is colonial territory"; and "hell," where "her widest gates" (4.382) open on "foreign territory" that is "both a political and a sexual threat." Against these backgrounds stands Eve, whose foregrounding is "extremely problematic."

In a discussion that harmonizes with some of McColley's observations about the relationship between Eve and Milton and poetry, Corum suggests that Eve "can do what Milton and Adam cannot do: she can imagine alternatives." This "curious, willful, experimental, witty" Eve—

the Eve we *see* rather than the Eve we hear about—"enjoys, moves, and talks" in a manner which results in her "getting power and pleasure in the space of the father's text of submission" and thus represents to us "the Milton who had not stood blindly and dutifully within the textual space of the father's will" but who ventured out in search of a mother. "Milton's motive for poetry is that he *has* one parent, but *had* two." Corum's explication of *Paradise Lost*'s "white ink" proposes that Milton's "unsubmissive part . . . would have us switch these verbs, and admit that monotheism . . . tragically violates inalienable human rights—Eve's, Milton's, and our own." Corum concludes that "from a nonideological perspective," *Paradise Lost* is important as "sacred history, as manifesto of imperial ideology, as personal confession, as humbly aggressive revision"; but the poem is equally important as an "ideological representation" which becomes "a way of holding on permanently, through white ink, to an idea of woman, and of self, poetry, desire, independence, and freedom which Milton did not want to lose, but had to lose."

Marshall Grossman, on the other hand, questions whether that freedom ever really existed. Grossman believes that the "questions of governance, of equality and hierarchy, of subject and subjection that resonate through Milton's work are all included in the question of woman." Although he does not explicitly disagree with Woods's judgment that a "hierarchy of creation is no hierarchy of value or freedom in Milton's vision," Grossman sees a hierarchy of choice: "the excess ["perhaps / More than enough" (8.536–37)] that is Eve . . . requires a reorganization of the economy of man, and the need of a peer . . . ironically installs a hierarchy." Adam chooses to ask God for Eve, recognizing a lack in himself; Eve, by choosing Adam, creates a lack in the perfection she sees in the pool. "What promise," Grossman asks, "induces Eve to embrace this subjection? A new name." And this new name, he continues, will reverse Eve's "secondary role in creation" when she becomes "Mother of Mankind." Halley contends that Eve is made the "generator of her own signs" so that she will not threaten male relationships, but Grossman suggests that Eve's choice actually facilitates male action. "Within the Miltonic dialectic of sexual difference woman, as mother, is the means of the (re)production of the paternal image, the place on which and in which the father writes his name and reproduces his style." The problems in the poem arise both because Eve's "power" is perpetually deferred and because "she is refractory, possessed of her own style, the mother's style, which must be subordinated under one (paternal) head."

Arguing that *Paradise Lost,* "by virtue of its exhaustive intention, discloses the suppressed and deferred authority of the Mother," Grossman widens his analysis of the reality of that maternal authority by including a discussion of *Eikonoklastes,* so that the "juxtaposition of the two texts will . . . further illuminate the relation of sexual and social difference in Milton's discourse." In *Eikonoklastes* we see the reverse of the equation in *Paradise Lost,* for here the question is the "image and reality of the king" presented with a choice of no fewer than four mothers "Parliament . . . and three papistical women"—his grandmother, Mary Stuart; his wife, Henrietta Maria; and his mother-in-law, Marie de Medici. "Within this economy of mothers, the true king is not Charles, but a role or style created by Parliament." Grossman contends that by placing Charles in "a line of woman-governed governors that extends ultimately to Adam," Milton "makes it clear that Charles's devotion to his queen was at the expense of Parliament," thus foreclosing "any scenario in which Charles and Parliament" could be reconciled and thereby permanently and literally deferring Charles's power on this earth.

"The king thus stands to Parliament as Eve stands to Adam," but Charles, "because he would not subjectify the commonwealth by subjecting himself . . . to parliamentary law," refuses "Eve's bargain." Milton, however, does not. In concluding his arguments, Grossman draws a third parallel of power deferred by choice: "the interplay of subjection and subjectification that marks the marriage of Adam and Eve . . . and the Parliament's violent appropriation of the king's head is (re)played in Milton's account of his own temporal deferral in favor of the Commonwealth's appropriation of his right-handed style." Milton the author, Grossman suggests, was therefore always seeking a poetic "reunification, which is always deferred, always to come, when the 'single defect' is made up and difference has run its course."

In contrast to Corum's belief that the "mother" in *Paradise Lost* must be visible only by her absence and Grossman's suggestions that the power of the mother must be perpetually deferred, Dayton Haskin presents a reading of *Paradise Regained* which stresses the attention which Milton paid to Mary, the mother of the Son. Observing the neglect of Mary exhibited both by seventeenth-century Protestants and by present-day Milton critics, Haskin contends that Milton—who "never deigned to write about superstitious abuses of the Marian variety"—actually depicts Mary as a "model for all disciples, male and female." In a double sense, Mary has been and is a "bearer" of the Word, in both the intrinsically female role of mother and the genderless role of oral historian. By keeping "all these things in her heart" and "pondering them" (Luke 2:19), Mary also takes on the role of textual scholar. "Mary's soliloquy at the beginning of Book 2 shows an exemplary disciple, one who struggles inwardly to interpret her experience in the light of what she has been told by God"; thus Mary is also a "portrait of the responsible reader." In a statement which echoes many of McColley's remarks about Eve, Haskin argues that "Milton presents a Mary who mediates the Word—first to Jesus himself, then to the New Testament writers, and ultimately to Christians in every age. Beyond this, he has painted in her a portrait of the artist." Haskin gives us an interpretation of Mary which blurs "one of the distinctions between male and female roles that we have been accustomed to associating with the English seventeenth century."

Haskin feels that the positive and responsible portrait of woman which we find in Mary is rendered more significant by the discrepancy between the biblical Mary and Milton's mother of the Son. Similarly, John C. Ulreich, Jr., argues that in Milton's revision of the traditional presentation of Dalila, we find significant rewriting of the stereotyped evil woman of medieval commentaries. Speaking directly to McColley's defense of *Milton's Eve,* Ulreich argues that the image of Dalila "becomes problematic precisely to the degree that McColley's case for Eve is successful, inasmuch as Milton's portrait of Dalila seems to suggest a deliberate perversion of just those qualities which make Eve attractive." Woods makes a similar point, remarking that Milton not only gives Dalila "intelligence beyond guile" but also stresses the extent to which "her relation to patriarchal values complicates her choices." Ulreich turns to the reconcilation between Adam and Eve in *Paradise Lost* for an analogue which informs his reading of the scene between Dalila and Samson. When we examine the two scenes in which Eve and Dalila beg forgiveness of their respective husbands, "we see at once the destinies of the two women diverge precisely at the point when Adam's response to Eve changes from rejection to compassion." Eve falls at Adam's feet and is, eventually, tenderly forgiven, while in *Samson Agonistes* one of the most striking qualities of the drama is the "apparent absence of any human connection between the actors; they are always speaking *against* rather than *to* one another, at cross-purposes and at great distance." Ulreich reads Dalila's attempt to touch Samson as a wish, not to "rouse his passion, but to inspire compassion" and feels that—far from being purified by his rejection of Dalila—Samson changes only in becoming more actively destructive. Like Haskin, Ulreich considers Milton's revision of biblical sources a most telling point, suggesting that the marriage of the two characters forces an examination of the issue of marriage, the issue of symbolic incarnation—being one flesh—which is central to Christianity. Calling Dalila's plight "tragic," Ulreich argues that her tragedy "explores the possibility of charity between fallen human beings, in particular as the virtue is (or is not) expressed in marriage," concluding that if marriage is "an image of Christ's redemptive love for those united in his body," then Dalila's "frustrated love of Samson becomes an ironic type of salvation." By placing the "blame" on both characters, Ulreich agrees with Woods's observation that, by the time he wrote *Samson Agonistes,* Milton "has learned where the limits on female agency reside: in culture and individual character, not in gender per se."

Jackie DiSalvo, however, finds culture and gender inextricably enmeshed, as it is gender which determines a person's role in society. Like Ulreich, she judges the poem a tragedy, but a "tragedy of gender of which there is almost none greater." Drawing on psychologists' studies of gender, DiSalvo points out that "in addition to physical aggression, the most consistent psychological disparity between the sexes lies in the far stronger taboos of male self-disclosure." DiSalvo feels this to be at the heart of the poem: "nowhere has the male prohibition been more profoundly explored than in Milton's tragic depiction of a Samson" who suffers because he gave up his "fort of silence to a woman." Although the sexual horror of a woman as man's external and internal enemy is behind Samson's "hypermasculinity," it is not behind Milton's poetry, DiSalvo argues. She contends that Milton's blindness gave him "extraordinary access to the unconscious, and in telling its truths he undermines and expands his own conscious ideologies." Milton is therefore able to represent, in and through the destruction of the characters, a final androgynous vision, the masculine eagle united with the feminine phoenix, a vision "*self* begotten, beyond all contraries of gender, a fully human self."

Commentary

Milton himself argues, in *Areopagitica,* that to accept anything as truth without personal intellectual knowledge, to accept truth on the word of others, however admirable those others may be, is wrong. Milton knew of God and man from studying the truths of others and then analyzing these other truths with his own intellect, making his own truth. In doing this, he retraced the steps of an anciently honorable process of knowing. How then is Milton to acquire a personal intellectual knowledge of woman, woman who has been neither a part of nor a subject of this anciently honorable tradition? Several of the authors in this collection offer explications of Milton's resolution of this problem of knowing in truth: Halley sees it manifested as Milton's fear that his poetry's language "will not necessarily be perfectly referential"; Corum argues that Milton wrote out his ambiguous feelings in white ink; Grossman reads Milton's resolution as an answer to "the question in the text," but an answer which "remains and will remain deferred"; and Woods claims that it is less a resolution than an "original" — and largely continued — "indifference to matters of gender."

Yet another possibility is that Milton saw no need of resolution because he saw—or admitted to—no problem. By his own lights, he was not a "heretick in the truth" on the idea of woman, for he acquired his personal intellectual knowledge of women in the same manner he acquired his knowledge of the classics, of Scripture, of the patristic commentaries: he read them. But, while the classics, the Bible, and the works of the patristic writers were constructed to be known by being read, women were not. When Virginia Woolf wrote in her diary: "I scarcely feel that Milton lived or knew men or women," she was, in this condemnation, using the verb "to know" as Milton himself used it in *Areopagitica.* He tried "to know" by metaphorically reading the women around him and by literally reading the works of other men about women.

Woman is not, like a poem, a "speaking picture" (although the briefest glance at literary history will show that she has long been "read" as such). What Milton saw as text was actually image, idea—an altogether different and more complex entity. An idea cannot be read merely; it must be comprehended, must be subsumed and, in turn, must subsume, a process in which the boundaries of truth can be and are being constantly displaced. To acknowledge such an indefinite relationship between knowledge and truth would have made Milton profoundly uncomfortable. Knowledge of an idea is very different from knowledge of Scripture or history or doctrine. The latter are based on ideas, but they are ideas made manifest, made concrete by the traditional process of knowing, their boundaries now far more clearly defined. They exist in texts and texts are comfortingly accessible to the intellect and to the senses as well as to the imagination. Milton produced texts by processing his knowledge of other texts through his intellect with the aid of his imagination. Woman, however, is not another text, and knowledge of a non-text, of an idea, is knowledge very differently acquired. The difference is not as much one of manner or process as it is one—to borrow Milton's own term—of *degree.*

In Book 5 of *Paradise Lost,* lines 479–505, Raphael's lesson to Adam provides us with a vocabulary worthy of this epistemological distinction. Raphael explains to Adam: "the Soul / Reason receives, and reason is her being, / Discursive, or Intuitive; discourse / Is oftest yours, the latter most is ours, / Differing but in degree, of kind the same" (ll. 486–90). Milton could know in truth through discourse, through texts which are discourse made concrete. But to present woman truthfully, to present her not as a text but as an idea, he could either base his knowledge on intuition, the knowledge of the Angels—a degree of knowledge and authority he would have resisted claiming for himself—or he could admit that he did not, indeed, know in truth. Raphael says that the "time may come when men / With Angels may participate" (ll. 493–94), but one

13

thing Milton *did* surely know was that such time had not yet come. And, although he could defer indefinitely this claim to the knowledge of the angels, he could not defer indefinitely his writing.

For Milton, the lack of intellectual knowledge was the lack of non-heretical truth. To admit that woman could not be known through the intellect, could not be known discursively, was to place her outside the boundaries of truth and thus outside his own writing. To return to my student's remark that a discussion of Milton and women would "at least be short," I suggest that, in as far as was possible, Milton did try to avoid writing about—at least directly and consciously—women. That this was not always possible posed for him an intellectual and artistic dilemma, a dilemma whose only solution would have been the complete revision of his definitions of knowledge and truth. Ironically, because he could know woman only as an intellectual text, not as an idea, woman emerges in Milton's writing only as an idea, not as an intellectual truth.

Poet, scholar, theologian, intellectual, man, John Milton was ill equipped to come to terms with woman as an idea. As we examine the problems and ambiguities discussed by the authors in this collection, we are able to observe the ways in which Milton reacted to this dilemma of knowing in truth. This is not to say that we must make Milton's dilemma our own. Thus it is as image, as idea, that we must read woman in Milton's text. If we take issue with Milton's "mis-readings" of woman as text—if we try to cut the Gordian knot of text and idea, of understanding and fancy, of Reason both Discursive and Intuitive—we are ourselves misreading and missing the heart of a far more intricate epistemological and imaginative complex, the complex which is the work of John Milton.

How Free Are Milton's Women?

SUSANNE WOODS

TRUE liberty, according to Milton, is knowledgeable choice. "When God gave [Adam] reason, he gave him freedom to choose, for reason is but choosing."[1] Choice depends upon the free flow of ideas and presupposes individual responsibility for pursuing and weighing information. "A man may be a heretick in the truth; and if he beleeve things only because his Pastor says so, or the Assembly so determins, without knowing other reason, though his belief be true, yet the very truth he holds, becomes his heresie" (*CPW,* 2:543). Further, the anti-aristocratic Milton assumes an essentially egalitarian meritocracy in a person's ability to develop knowledgeable choice, despite the inevitable number who will reject or misunderstand true liberty, who

> . . . bawl for freedom in their senseless mood
> And still revolt when truth would set them free.
> License they mean when they cry liberty;
> For who loves that must first be wise and good.
> (Sonnet XII, ll. 9–12)

Adam was given freedom to choose. A man may be a heretic in the truth. But what of Eve? May a woman be a heretic in the truth? A man need not be of privileged social class to be "wise and good," but can a woman learn and exercise the truth that would set her free?

Milton's fundamental devotion to religious, civil, and domestic liberty is the cornerstone of his life and art. He has thought long and hard about freedom and is comfortable expounding his views in both prose and verse. He seems less at ease engaging those ideas when the rational creature he is concerned with is female. Far from being a misogynist, Milton was ahead of his time in granting to women a dignity and responsibility rarely conceded in the seventeenth century.[2] His Eve has

15

majesty. His Dalila has intelligence beyond guile. His sonnet to Lady Margaret Ley honors her with the judicial virtues of her father. His divorce tracts cite companionship as the principal goal of marriage and advocate their doctrine "to the good of both sexes, from the bondage of Canon Law, and other mistakes, to Christian freedom, guided by the rule of Charity" (*CPW,* 2:220).

Though not a misogynist, Milton is locked into his culture's assumptions of woman's inferior position in the human paradigm. In *An Apology for Smectymnuus* (1642), for example, Milton describes the importance of male chastity with the gravity of one who takes seriously not only biblical injunctions, but the critical assumption of male supremacy: "I argu'd to my selfe; that if unchastity in a woman whom Saint *Paul* terms the glory of man, be such a scandall and dishonour, then certainly in a man who is both the image and glory of God, it must, though commonly not so thought, be much more deflouring and dishonorable. In that he sins both against his owne body which is the perfecter sex, and his own glory which is in the woman, and that which is worst, against the image and glory of God which is in himselfe" (*CPW,* 1:892). Similarly, his notorious statements in the *History of Britain* confirm current attitudes toward gender roles and female authority. He demurs from the tradition, supported by Holinshed, that the early Briton Queen Martia was herself an important lawgiver: "In the minority of her son Martia had the rule, and then, as may be supposed, brought forth these Laws not of her self, for Laws are Masculin Births, but by the advice of her sagest Counselors; and therin she might so virtuously, since it fell her to supply the nonage of her Son: else nothing more awry from the Law of God and Nature then that a Woman should give Laws to Men" (*CPW,* 5:31–32). Women dressing in men's clothing and fighting as warriors reaps Milton's particular scorn; he rejects the notion outright, even suggesting that the tales about Boadicea were fabricated "to brand us with the rankest note of Barbarism, as if in *Britain* Woemen were Men, and Men Woemen" (*CPW,* 5:79).

Views such as these are supremely conventional and carefully placed to argue a male audience toward the author's position. The anonymous author of a legal handbook for women said much the same thing about women and the law, though toned more sympathetically to a female audience: "(Women only women) they have nothing to do with constituting Lawes, or consenting to them, in interpreting of Lawes, or of hearing them interpreted in lectures, leets, or charges, and yet they stand strictly tyed to mens establishments, little or nothing excused by ignorance" (*The Lawes Resolution of Womens Rights* [London, 1632], Sig. Bv). In his stated abhorrence of women warriors Milton may be having a lingering reaction to the controversy over female cross-dressing, prominent in the 1620s and documented by Linda Woodbridge.[3] In any case, the *History of Britain* contains what may be taken as the standard masculine rejection of women as lawgivers and fear of women in authority.

In the same general period of his career, however, Milton peppered his *Commonplace Book* with approving references to Queen Elizabeth, presented Holinshed's admiration of Queen Martia without comment, and, in *A Second Defence,* interjected a panegyric to Queen Christina of Sweden, who had the wit, learning, and good sense to admire Milton's attack on Salmasius.[4] The panegyric is particularly interesting from a feminist point of view since it constitutes a digression for which Milton was criticized and serves no better purpose than to praise someone who had admired his work. He could expect nothing from the unpopular queen, whom he knew at the time was probably soon to abdicate. Yet he produces an extended praise of her rule and learning and seems at ease with a female ruler and lawgiver whose sex is largely irrelevant. Only once does he draw attention to it, in a positive statement relating her to her illustrious father: "I should say that you are the daughter and only offspring of Adolphus, the unconquered and glorious king, did you not, Christina, as far outshine him as wisdom excels strength, and the arts of peace the crafts of war" (*CPW,* 4, 1:605).

Milton appears to have mixed attitudes toward female authority, despite his famous condemnations. Milton the controversialist reflects current assumptions. In the note-taking privacy of the *Commonplace Book* he is more balanced, and he basks in the praise of a learned queen. Milton's apparent confusion makes sense not only because complete consistency of a static sort is incompatible with Milton's belief in a dynamic and processive creation, but also because the notion of authority is related to autonomy and personal responsibility, both crucial to individual liberty. Knowledge requires sufficient autonomy to pursue it, and freedom requires at least the authority to make choices. It is not surprising that even in his apparently clear statements of his culture's gender hierarchy there may be troubling or contradictory overtones.

Milton's Eve is of course the primary case in point. The issues are much more complex than can be fully addressed here, but even an outline of Eve's position suggests the complexity of Milton's attitudes. On the level of unexamined simple statement she is the human secondary, Adam's unequal helpmate. She may surpass him in beauty, but she is "not equal" to him in the basic elements of human freedom: reason, knowledge, and choice:

> ... what thou bidd'st
> Unargu'd I obey; so God ordains,
> God is thy Law, thou mine: to know no more
> Is woman's happiest knowledge and her praise.
>
> (*PL* 4.635–38)

"To know no more," to cease the pursuit of knowledge at the voice of Adam, may fit comfortably into a Pauline construct of true freedom as accepted, appropriate obedience, as Diane McColley has declared.[5] But Eve does argue what Adam bids, notably in the famous separation scene in Book 9 around which McColley so persuasively centers her study. The conclusion of that argument allows Eve her free choice. Adam's "Go; for thy stay, not free, absents thee more" (9.372) is both a clear statement of Milton's doctrine of free will and the crux of Milton's dilemma with regard to Eve. In the final analysis, Eve is not to Adam as Adam is to God, all Eve's dewy-eyed adoration to the contrary. God is the Creator, while both Adam and Eve are His creatures. God's ordinance is simple and absolute: do not eat of the one tree. Adam's ordinances are subject to time and circumstance, and they are not absolute, but dependent on the mutual freedom of two who may be unequal in some ways, but are equally free and rational.

McColley argues well for Milton's accommodation of Eve's dignity with her stated subservience to Adam. Maureen Quilligan, on the other hand, suggests some loss in that dignity: "In this arrangement of the wife's subjection to her husband there is established not only sexual hierarchy, but a mediated position for the woman with respect to the divine source. *It negates a direct relationship between God and woman*" (italics Quilligan's). She posits that the leveling of other hierarchies led to an emphasis on family hierarchy, "a conservative social move designed to act as a safety valve on the revolutionary energies unleashed by the reformation."[6]

Puritan commentators did place strong emphasis on the family. Robert Cleaver's *A Godlie Forme of Householde Government,* for example, which is firm and explicit on the family hierarchy, went through eight editions between 1598 and 1630. It is nonetheless difficult to believe that Milton could accept an entirely mediated position for women. Adam may be for God only, and Eve for "God in him" (4.299), but she and Adam praise God directly together (4.137–211), and after the fall, Eve is spoken to and responds directly to the Son, here certainly the voice of God whatever Milton's Arminianism (10.157–62). Even more directly, as Michael instructs Adam in preparation for the descent from Paradise, God speaks to Eve in her dream (12.610–11).

Eve's responsibility and freedom remain complex questions which are not finally resolved either by McColley's argument that "in *Paradise Lost* subordination is not inferiority" or Quilligan's interesting speculation that Milton's family hierarchy is his Puritan reaction to social leveling.[7] The tension modern readers continue to feel between Milton's impressive portrayal of Eve's dignity and freedom on the one hand and her stated position according to Pauline doctrine on the other is not likely to go away.

Nor should it. Milton was never comfortable with human hierarchy. The republican who abhorred an aristocratic system that gave authority by happenstance of birth to kings and princes could not be perfectly at ease with a gender hierarchy also dependent on birth. In *The Readie and Easie Way* he is appalled by claims of human lordship: "I cannot but . . . admire . . . how any man who hath the true principles of justice and religion in him, can presume to take upon him to be a king and lord over his brethern, whom he cannot but know, whether as men or Christians, to be for the most part every way equal or superior to himself" (*CPW*, 7:364). As he rejects the broader social hierarchy, he also allows some leeway in the gender hierarchy. Though the husband should ordinarily rule in marriage (as Paul insists), Milton in *Tetrachordon* remarkably concedes that the wife may in some marriages have wisdom equal to or greater than her husband's, and both should in that case yield to "a superior and more naturall law," which is that "the wiser should govern the lesse wise, whether male or female" (*CPW*, 2:589).

Milton's profound respect for human liberty has the ultimate effect of subverting his patriarchal assumptions. He is too thoughtful to accept cultural assumptions without question, yet he has no frame of reference for responding to biblical authority in this matter.[8] The curious result is that the dignity and intelligence he gives his female characters strain against the inferior social position in which they find themselves.

Milton's earliest verse suggests the underlying mind-set that eventually leads to this dilemma. His *Arcades* and Ludlow *Mask*, whose common name of *Comus* says a great deal about the patriarchal critical tradition, show some effort to position female authority and freedom in the problematic cultural milieu. Milton's Eve, as McColley's evidence everywhere illustrates, and his Dalila, to whom I shall turn at the end of this essay, are the fullest embodiments of the uncomfortable limits Milton sees for female freedom.

The early poetry, from *Elegy I* through *Comus*, documents a surprising indifference to questions of gender. Until *Arcades* Milton's references to women are mostly conventional. The bland neutrality of Milton's indifference is startling to one who comes to the subject of Milton and women with the sense of hot debate that has for centuries attached itself to it. Milton has no unusual, much less liberated, ideas about women, but his references usually lack the affective coloring, either of praise or blame, that is common among his predecessors and contemporaries.[9] In *Elegy I,* for example, the virgin surprised by love could as easily be a young man:

> Saepe novos illic virgo mirata calores
> Quid sit amor nescit, dum quoque nescit, amat.

> (ll.35–36)

(Often the virgin, who is surprised by the strange fire within her and has no idea what love is, falls in love without knowing what she does.)

Her lack of autonomy in this situation is as conventional to lover as to lady, and is no doubt a fair description of the London comedies Milton was reporting on to his friend Charles Diodati.

What may be notable here is Milton's association of the female with the comic mode. In *Elegy VI* a woman's music will win the poet to the practice of comedy:

> Perque puellares oculos digitumque sonantem
> Irruet in totos lapsa Thalia sinus

> (ll. 47–48)

(Through a maiden's eyes and music-making fingers Thalia will glide into full possession of your breast.)

The comic is unquestionably a less important mode than the tragic or epic, but it is conventionally appropriate to Milton's youth. Here, as in other elegies to Diodati, women are part of the aura of play that Milton shares with his lively young friend, and part of his dedication to the art of poetry. Whatever Milton's early attraction to personal virginity, there is a young man's lush sensuousness in *Elegy V:*

> Exuit invisam Tellus rediviva senectam,
> Et cupit amplexus, Phoebe, subire tuos.
> Et curpit, et digna est; quid enim formosius illa,
> Pandit ut omniferos luxuriosa sinus,
> Atque Arabum spirat messes, et ab ore venusto
> Mitia cum Pamphiis fundit amona rosis?

> (ll. 55–60)

(The reviving earth throws off her hated old age and craves thy embraces, O Phoebus. She craves them and she is worthy of them; for what is lovelier than she as she voluptuously bares her fertile breast and breathes the perfume of arabian harvests and pours sweet spices and the scent of paphian roses from her lovely lips?)

Similarly, sonnets I–VI (the first in English, the rest in Italian) and their accompanying Italian *canzone* offer conventional if well-wrought expressions of the Petrarchan lover. As did his Elizabethan predecessors, Milton happily equates the inspiration of love with the power to write:

> Whether the Muse, or Love call thee his mate,
> Both them I serve, and of their train am I.

(Sonnet I, 13–14)

His Italian exercises allow him to play in the continental tradition of love poetry:

> Dice mia Donna, e'l suo dir e il mio cuore,
> "Questa e lingua di cui si vanta Amore."

(*Canzone,* 14–15)

(My lady, whose words are my very heart, says "This is the language of which love makes his boast.")

Milton shared with Diodati an enjoyment of the pleasures of youth and affirmed for himself the title of poet. If Italian is the language of love, it is as much because of Diodati's Italian background as it is because of Dante and Petrarch.[10] Female figures may occasionally appear in the verse, but the relationship was with the friend.

The association of female figures with play and with the poet's muse extends to *L'Allegro* and *Il Penseroso*. In the first poem a female mirth is urged to bring "The Mountain Nymph, sweet Liberty." The speaker hopes

> To live with her, and live with thee,
> In unreproved pleasures free.

Liberty here is not quite the great topic of Milton's later work, though she is a cheerful relative. She is essentially a pagan freedom from onerous responsibilities: not license (the pleasures are to be "unreproved"), but rather a free exercise of animal spirits associated primarily with springtime and youth. The mood here is a less ponderous version of the sensuous elegies, and real girls are as remote. In the one glance where a girl is named and presumably human, she is a stock pastoral figure who makes life easier for the boys:

> ... *Corydon* and *Thyrsis* met,
> Are at their savory dinner set
> of herbs, and other Country Messes,
> Which the neat-handed Phillis dresses;
> And then in haste her bow'r she leaves,
> With *Thestylis* to bind the sheaves.

(ll. 83–88)

21

The more sober Melancholy is, like Mirth, a female muse figure. The "pensive nun, devout and pure" serves up contemplative pleasures, including the transcending joys of learned study (ll. 85–92) and church music (ll. 161–66). Like Allegro, she is invoked for the enjoyment of the male speaker, who is the true agent in the poem:

> These pleasures *Melancholy* give,
> And I with thee will choose to live.

(ll. 175–76)

Both poems are about choice, among other things, but choice for a young man with his masculine life ahead of him. His female goddesses are there if he invokes them and they depend on his choices.

Throughout these poems Milton's masculist model is automatic and unselfconscious, filled with the deep assumptions of the time. He has internalized the current gender roles. There is no evidence he has given women's nature any real thought at all.

Milton's earliest efforts to praise female figures both confirm his automatic male supremacy and begin to suggest values in conflict with standard gender roles. The marchioness of Winchester (in *An Epitaph,* 1631) is lauded primarily for her relation to husband and father, with her own unspecified virtues cited as useful in finding her a husband with birth as high as her father's (ll. 2–6, 15–16). *An Epitaph* is a marvelous funeral poem, with an expressive use of verb tenses that combine past and present into an ever-present now, but it says little about the marchioness herself. Later, in 1645, Milton praises Lady Margaret Ley not for the nobility of her birth but for specific virtues of intelligence and judgment. *An Epitaph* was part of the development of a poet's craft; Lady Margaret was a friend.

More revealing of Milton's early values when he gives any thought to characteristic female virtue is the youthful elegy on his niece, *On the Death of a Fair Infant Dying of a Cough.* Whether or not it consoled Milton's sister Anne, the poem suggests the virtues Milton would like to associate with his own family. His speculation on the infant's true nature leads to images he apparently valued from his prolific reading:

> Or wert thou that just maid who once before
> Forsook the hated earth, O tell me sooth,
> And cam'st again to visit us once more?
> Or wert thou mercy that sweet smiling youth?
> Or that crown'd matron, sage white-robed Truth?

(ll. 50–54)

The figure of Astraea ("just maid") is particularly striking. While most of Milton's references to women in the early poems give them little or no agency, Astraea is a powerful representative of judgment and choice. Close to home, Milton's mythic women are perceived in terms of the active liberties he holds so dear.

With *Arcades* and, especially, *Comus* Milton is forced to confront the problem of female agency. While the earlier poems mostly treat women or female figures with a remote and conventional indifference, by and large assuming female passivity, in *Arcades* Milton must write for a great lady, a patroness and cousin of the revered Spenser and a dowager of importance and renown. In *Comus* he must accommodate the same important family, providing roles (in keeping with common mask convention) for some of the earl of Bridgewater's children, including his fifteen-year-old daughter.

Arcades is about the poet's epideictic role as much as it is an actual work of praise. The centerpiece of the short entertainment, the countess dowager of Derby (née Alice Spencer), is honored as a model, inspiration, and glory, whose brightness the poet makes manifest. The spondaic rhythms of lines one, five, and seventeen begin the praise by allowing the poet to point to its object:

$$\acute{/}\ \acute{/}$$
Look Nymphs, and Shepherds look

. . . .

$$\acute{/}\ \acute{/}$$
This, this is she

. . . .

$$\acute{/}\ \acute{/}$$
This, this is she alone

The search for the glorious countess is fictionalized as the free search of both swains and nymphs. Importantly, the young women in the entertainment are granted the same virtue ("as great and good") and free will ("free intent") as the just-mentioned "Swains":

> And ye breathing Roses of the Wood,
> Fair silver-buskin'd Nymphs as great and good,
> I know this quest of yours and free intent
> Was all in honor and devotion meant
> To the great Mistress of yon princely shrine,
> Whom with low reverence I adore as mine,
> And with all helpful service will comply
> To further this night's glad solemnity.

(ll. 32–39)

The last few lines in this passage make it clear that the countess (like Mirth and Melancholy) is a muse figure who aids the agency of the poet, who in turn reciprocates with praise. Unlike Mirth and Melancholy, however, the countess has authority to which the poet chooses to submit ("the great Mistress ... / Whom ... I adore as mine"). She is also a real female presence, as are the "Nymphs" who attend her. *Arcades* is the first exercise in which Milton begins to confront female action, intention, and freedom. It is a slight confrontation, but it helps set the stage for what appears as Milton's muddle over female agency in *Comus.*

The Ludlow *Mask*'s central character is the Lady, played by the earl of Bridgewater's daughter Alice, granddaughter and namesake of the countess dowager of Derby. Milton's artistic choice for honoring this young relative of the sage and serious Edmund Spenser was to set her in the very Spenserian wood of this world, filled with confusions and presided over by an archimago, Comus. The bacchanalian magician's well-filed tongue and powers of illusion render appearances in the wood suspect. As in *The Faerie Queene,* only virtue can make it past the deceptions. Appropriately for a young woman just on marriageable age, Milton gives Lady Alice the particular virtue of chastity, one he himself valued and had thought carefully about. In addition, chastity was both the first criterion for the good maid and wife, and also a virtue with grand literary reverberations from Book III of *The Faerie Queene.*[11]

Although the enchanter Comus has "power to cheat the eye with blear illusion" (l. 155), the Lady is cautious. Lost at night in dark woods, and proper to one who judges by the intellect rather than by the eyes, she relies on what she hears rather than what she sees. Even there she is careful: "This way the noise was, if mine ear be true" (l. 170). She distrusts the "thousand fancies" (l. 205) that besiege her frightened imagination, and asserts her faith in God and in her own virtue. Her famous invocation to "pure-ey'd Faith, white-handed Hope / And thou unblemisht form of Chastity" (ll. 213, 215) has raised some critical eyebrows over the centuries. It should not have. Apart from asserting Lady Alice's preeminent marriageability, the invocation to Chastity is surely a direct reference to Britomart's very active virtue of personal integrity in *Faerie Queene* III. It will also be recalled that for Spenser charity, in the allegorical person of Charissa (I.x.29–31), was a matron, not a maid.[12]

From the beginning of *Comus* the Lady is given judgment and the active virtues appropriate to her, a considerable sophistication of Milton's handling of female character. Chastity is by no means restrictively female (see the earlier citation from *An Apology*), nor is it mere physical restraint. The Elder Brother's paean to chastity (ll. 420–27) affirms it as an internal and purposive dignity and power, while the Lady's choice of this active virtue allows her to see through the machinations of wickedness and gives her freedom even in the face of stronger physical power. The Elder

24

Brother reassures the younger: "Virtue may be assail'd but never hurt, / Surpris'd by unjust force but not enthrall'd" (ll. 589–90).

The Lady's exercise of her freedom nonetheless remains problematic. Cautious as she is, she is initially deceived by Comus, and by his false speech as well as false appearance: "Shepherd, I take thy word, / And trust thy honest offer'd courtesy" (ll. 321–22). The deception is only temporary. With more evidence she is well able to see Comus for what he is and to remain untouched by his threats: "Thou canst not touch the freedom of my mind / With all thy charms" (ll. 663–64). Her eventual response to Comus's temptations comes not from any belief that he will be swayed but as an affirmation of her own freedom:

> I had not thought to have unlockt my lips
> In this unhallow'd air, but that this Juggler
> Would think to charm my judgment, as mine eyes.
>
> (ll. 756–58)

Comus has "nor Ear nor soul to apprehend" the logic that would "unfold the sage / And serious doctrine of Virginity" (ll. 784, 786–87). If Comus were fit audience, the Lady concludes, she would rise to heights of eloquence on her chosen course of virtue (ll. 792–99). But he is not fit to be persuaded, and must be routed by force. The brothers "rush in with swords drawn" and drive Comus and his company away.

Up to this point both the problems and the triumphs the Lady encounters are largely indifferent to her sex. She has a characteristic virtue, chastity, that is appropriate to her and her gender but by no means exclusive to it. Her virtue is assaulted, and she not only stands firm but actively asserts it in the face of guile and force. The providential appearance of her brothers, aided by the Attendant Spirit (played by Henry Lawes), confirms her choice and routs her oppressor. But the Lady is not physically freed. She remains bound to her chair by Comus's enchantment which, like Busirane's over Amoret in *Faerie Queene* III.xii, can only be undone by the enchanter. This confuses the question of the Lady's freedom, even allowing that freedom of mind is vastly superior to mere physical mobility. In *Comus* movement and action are emblems of liberty on its most mundane level, and the Lady's freedom is incomplete until she regains her physical liberty. She has stood fast, exercised her virtue, and relied on Providence. Yet (perhaps in part for reasons of stagecraft or casting) she must wait to be freed from her chair by the virgin water nymph, Sabrina. This effected, the Attendant Spirit leads her and her brothers to their parents and the grand party celebrating the earl of Bridgewater's accession to the Lord Presidency of Wales.

Sabrina signals the *Mask*'s subtheme of transformations. As Comus

25

(son of Circe) sought to transform through and to vice, so, conversely, Sabrina's virtue has transformed her from threatened virgin to virginal nymph, beyond the power of human wickedness and into the role of Chastity's handmaiden. The Attendant Spirit's epilogue alludes further to famous transformations—Hyacinth, Adonis, and most notably Psyche as the bride of "Celestial *Cupid*" (ll. 1004–8). The Attendant Spirit concludes by urging mortals to "Love Virtue, she alone is free" (l. 1019) and will lead to the ultimate transformation from earth to heaven. There is coherence and a charming didacticism in all this, but it slides away from the problem of the Lady's restricted agency.

In sum, the Lady in *Comus* is free to choose virtue and hold steadfast to it in the face of temptation and threats. The effect is to keep intact the freedom of her mind, though her body is confined. Heaven's reward is to send her brothers to a rescue which turns out to be only partly successful. Her physical freedom remains contingent, in this case on the agency of the Attendant Spirit. Lawes, the mask's composer, is an authorial figure. Sabrina, who draws her authority from the *Metamorphoses* tradition, may be the efficient cause of the Lady's release, but the Attendant Spirit who calls up Sabrina is the true begetter of the Lady's complete freedom, and indeed of the whole *Mask,* including the final presentation of children to parents.

As in *Arcades,* it is ultimately the author who releases the "free intent" of the characters and reveals virtue and the virtuous glories of the participants. To a certain extent a mediating role by the author through the author's mediating characters is well within the tradition in which Milton works. No central figure of *The Faerie Queene* (except, interestingly, Britomart) accomplishes a quest without a mediating influence, usually that of Prince Arthur. In each Spenserian case the character contributes to his own predicament and cannot free himself. Red Cross Knight drinks of the enervating well; Guyon descends to the Cave of Mammon. In Book V Artegall's failure to enforce proper justice against the Amazon Radigund enthralls him to her, and his rescuer, who comes also to restore the Amazon nation to the rightful rule of men, is none other than Britomart. Spenser's figure for Chastity is much more active than Milton's Lady. The Lady has in no way contributed to her peril yet she remains physically bound.

In part the difference between Britomart and the Lady can be attributed to different times and purposes. Spenser was writing for and under Queen Elizabeth, Milton for the new lord president of Wales and under cultural injunctions against female authority that had no ruling queen to mitigate them. In part, though, the Ludlow *Mask* shows Milton struggling, really for the first time, with the problem of female freedom. While it is true the Lady retains the more important mental freedom, she is no Samson to whom that must be everything. Throughout his life Milton believed that right choice led to and required right action. His apparently passive reaction even to his own blindness, "They also serve who only stand and wait" (Sonnet XIX), gave way quickly to a different consolation. Milton will not complain of blindness, but "still bear up and steer / Right onward" (Sonnet XXII, ll. 8–9). In *Comus* Milton insists on the Lady's freedom but has some sense that it is limited. The limits are not defined. They are simply overriden by authorial manipulation.

In *Paradise Lost*, as McColley has shown, Milton seeks to accommodate the contradiction between Eve's inequality and her freedom by making the choice of obedience to Adam an active virtue in itself.[13] Submission does not necessarily lower. Everywhere in *Paradise Lost* Milton makes clear that disjunctive thinking (either high or low, ruler or ruled) is largely Satanic. The Son's obedience to the Father is true freedom and dignity rather than the reverse, and Abdiel's choice to obey God and not rebel is the heroic choice. As in *Lycidas,* characters in *Paradise Lost* routinely sink in order to rise.

A hierarchy of creation is no hierarchy of value or freedom in Milton's vision.[14] The harmony of heaven outlines different roles for various grades of angels, and all of creation praises God in its manifold variety. The one troubling note in placing Eve in this scheme is that she is of the same order of creation as Adam. If her position as "daughter of God and Man" meant that she did obey unargued, *Paradise Lost* would simply confirm Milton's claim in *Christian Doctrine* that the biblical institution of marriage "consisted in the mutual love, delight, help and society of husband and wife, though with the husband having greater authority" which "became still greater after the fall" (*CPW,* 6:355). Yet the importance Milton places on human freedom, and the insistence on Eve's freedom and dignity, continue to allow in *Paradise Lost* a tension between these simple descriptions of authority and the attitude expressed elsewhere in *Christian Doctrine:* "The first and most important point [in marriage] is the mutual consent of the parties concerned, for there can be no love or good will, and therefore no marriage, between those whom mutual consent has not united" (*CPW,* 6:368).

Paradise Lost remains a heroic attempt to integrate the subtle potential for contradiction in statements such as these. Its success is remarkable, and modern feminists should in fairness acknowledge Milton's effort to give woman full dignity, freedom, and agency in a male supremacist environment. But the portrait of Eve, however splendid, is not likely to have lasting appeal to a modern feminist sensibility. The portrait of Dalila, on the other hand, speaks much more directly to the limits on female freedom and comes close to confronting the dilemma of an intelligent and attractive woman in a patriarchal world.

Dalila is not free, despite what Milton clearly establishes as her capacity for rational choice.[15] Mary Ann Radzinowicz has argued brilliantly that Dalila's Philistine historical relativism, not some innate female illogic, renders her incapable of understanding Samson's Jewish values. As a result, "Samson was ill-married to an incompatible person" according to Milton's own extensively documented theory of marriage. "His rejection of her therefore actually symbolizes the tempering, reordering, and reharmonizing of his inner personality. The total episode constitutes a dialectic concluding in the re-establishment of personal freedom."[16] The freedom is Samson's. Dalila remains trapped by her Philistine belief that success validates action. In this trap, she is bewildered by Samson's rejection of her offer to free him from his physical prison: "This Gaol I count the house of Liberty," he tells her, "To thine whose doors my feet shall never enter" (ll. 949–50).

Dalila is also trapped by the patriarchy, and there is some evidence that Milton was aware of it. Without exculpating Dalila's guilt, Milton portrays her as caught between husband and fathers, a woman who has internalized patriarchal attitudes and yet strains against them. Her treachery was real and wrong, but her choices were made more complex not only by her Philistine relativism but also by the interaction of both internal and external patriarchal demands on her will and sense of responsibility.

She blames her betrayal of Samson's secret on common assumptions of female weakness:

> . . . it was a weakness
> In me, but incident to all our sex,
> Curiosity, inquisitive, importune
> Of secrets, them with like infirmity
> To publish them, both common female faults.
>
> (ll. 773–77)

Like Eve's distortion, after the fall, of the separation scene before the fall, Dalila charges Samson with greater responsibility because of his greater strength and authority.

Dalila's patriarchal assumptions also infuse contradictory arguments in which she ignores her feminine weakness and claims a manlike strength. "The Magistrates / And Princes of my country came in person" (ll. 850–51) to argue patriotic and religious responsibility, against which Dalila could (she says) only silently counter her love of Samson.

> . . . at length that grounded maxim
> So rife and celebrated in the mouths
> Of wisest men, that to the public good

Private respects must yield, with grave authority
Took full possession of me and prevail'd.

(ll. 865–69)

Samson's response, that a wife must leave "Parents and country" (l. 886), is true for Jewish values, and for Milton's. Dalila's values are less clear. The choice she makes is a wrong one but there is no reason to think she does not believe it to have had moral content. She associates her personal preference with her love and sexual enjoyment of Samson, which she loses in her treachery. Dalila's love is defective both in her desire to possess and govern Samson and in her misunderstanding of the companionship values of marriage. Even so, her passion is real, and her effort to regain Samson is, in its own terms, sincere. She argues well from her premises. It is those premises that Samson rejects, and his own values that the confrontation allows him to rediscover and reassert.

Dalila's freedom is limited by the basic demands of the patriarchal system. She must obey her fathers, and she must obey her husband. As Samson affirms, when fathers and husband are in conflict, the right choice is to obey the husband (ll. 885–88). In trying to get what she wants (enjoyment of Samson on her own terms), beyond husband and fathers, she makes the wrong choice and loses Samson altogether. Her culpability is clear, but her relation to patriarchal values complicates her choices and the definition of female freedom as proper obedience is strained in *Samson Agonistes*. Dalila, like Eve, is a strong character beyond the simple manipulation of culture or of author. Unlike the Lady in *Comus,* she has agency of her own. Milton has learned where the limits on female agency reside: in culture and individual character, not in gender per se.

One of Dalila's more desperate statements is particularly suggestive of Milton's complex vision: "In argument with men a woman ever / Goes by the worse, whatever be her cause" (ll. 903–4). Radzinowicz dismisses this complaint as being in "the pettish terms of the inadequate feminist."[17] There is more to it, however. Dalila is using it, as she uses so much of her argument, to try and gain Samson's sympathy. It is on the one hand merely the device of the strong and intelligent woman who has learned that a simpering presentation of "poor little me" often works better than an assertion of her own strength. Yet the statement is also true. Its proof is the Chorus's misogyny (ll. 1010–60), which both Radzinowicz and Camille Wells Slights have shown is not Milton's own.[18] Women's wiles are so dangerous, with her "Capacity not rais'd to apprehend / Or value what is best / In choice, / but oftest to affect the wrong" (ll. 1028–30), that the only solution is for man to exercise what the Chorus believes is his God-given "despotic power" over woman. The very outrageousness of this solution, from the perspective of Milton's lifelong devotion to human freedom, casts a glow of validation on Dalila's petulant complaint.

To answer the question in this essay's title: Milton's women are not as free as his men, but they remain as responsible for their actions. Milton comes to this position not out of misogyny but out of an original indifference to matters of gender, informed and complicated by cultural and biblical attitudes toward women. So much is obvious. What is less obvious is Milton's struggle to provide women dignity in the terms he most values—in their freedom to choose virtue—while allowing for Pauline assumptions that limit female autonomy, belittle their reason, and deny them the right to test their ideas in a public setting. It is no easy task and the results, in Eve and Dalila, betray some discomfort with the received wisdom of male supremacy. Eve has a mind of her own, both before and after the fall, and that in itself is no sin. Dalila, a famous villain in the misogynist's canon, is an intelligent and even sympathetic adversary for heroic Samson. Milton's male supremacy is that of his time, but it is, like the author himself, much more subtle and complex and moves always in the direction of greater liberty.

NOTES

1. *Areopagitica,* in *Complete Prose Works of John Milton,* ed. Don M. Wolfe et al., 8 vols. (New Haven: Yale University Press, 1953–82), 2:527. All citations from Milton's prose will be from this edition; when convenient, they will appear in the text as *CPW.* All citations from Milton's poetry will be from Merrit Y. Hughes, ed., *John Milton: Complete Poems and Major Prose* (Indianapolis: Odyssey, 1957).

2. As recent critics have amply confirmed. See especially Barbara K. Lewalski, "Milton on Women—Yet Once More," *Milton Studies,* 6 (1974), 4–20; Heather Ross Asals, "In Defense of Dalila: *Samson Agonistes* and the Reformation Theology of the Word," *JEGP,* 74 (1975), 183–94; and Diane Kelsey McColley, *Milton's Eve* (Urbana: University of Illinois Press, 1983).

3. Linda Woodbridge, *Women in the English Renaissance* (Urbana: University of Illinois Press, 1984), pp. 139–271.

4. *CPW,* 1:425, 483, 492; 4, 1:602–6.

5. McColley, pp. 51–57 and passim.

6. Maureen Quilligan, *Milton's Spenser: The Politics of Reading* (Ithaca: Cornell University Press, 1984), pp. 224, 225.

7. McColley, p. 35.

8. Milton's reliance on Paul is evident throughout his work, particularly in *Christian Doctrine* (*CPW,* 6). Although Milton was generally skeptical of secular assumptions on social and political matters, his very definition of Christian liberty assumes the primacy of the New Testament and absolute authority of the

Gospels (*CPW*, 6:521–41), which abrogates Mosaic law but assumes Pauline doctrine on the relative authority of the sexes.

9. Woodbridge, in virtually every passage she cites from controversy or from fiction, documents the emotional coloring that commonly overlays references to women.

10. William Riley Parker documents the special quality of Milton's relationship with Diodati in *Milton: A Biography* (Oxford: Clarendon Press, 1968), pp. 59–60.

11. Suzanne W. Hull documents the primacy of chastity in directions to Renaissance women, in *Chaste, Silent and Obedient* (San Marino: Huntington Library Press, 1982), pp. 31, 65, 81, 162, 173–74, 180, 189, 195.

12. In this regard, it is interesting that Milton's one known reference to his mother cites her "acts of charity" for which she was "celebrated throughout the neighborhood." He also comments that she was "a woman of purest reputation" (*CPW*, 4, 1:612).

13. McColley, pp. 56–57.

14. See, for example, the vision of creation in Adam and Eve's morning hymn (5.153–208) and God's evaluation of angelic natures (6.687–94), followed by the Son's joyful obedience and move to battle (6.723–26). See also God's rejection of the Satanic belief that descent is humiliation (3.303–19).

15. Camille Wells Slights, in *The Casuistical Tradition in Shakespeare, Donne, Herbert, and Milton* (Princeton: Princeton University Press, 1981), notes that the casuistical paradigm, a technique for examining cases of conscience, "pervades almost everything that Milton wrote" (p. 247), and that "unlike the Chorus and Manoa, Dalila formulates her judgments as cases of conscience" (p. 275). As a result, her reasoning powers are foregrounded rather than obscured. "Samson does not speculate on women's incapacity for rational thought and moral choice. On the contrary, his denunciation of Dalila assumes that she is capable of and hence responsible for her moral choices" (p. 278).

16. Mary Ann Radzinowicz, *Toward "Samson Agonistes": The Growth of Milton's Mind* (Princeton: Princeton University Press, 1978), p. 48.

17. Radzinowicz, p. 40.

18. Radzinowicz, pp. 41–42; Slights, p. 278.

"Myself / Before Me":
Gender and Prohibition in Milton's
Italian Sonnets

LYNN E. ENTERLINE

EARLY in a career marked by successive poetic self-definitions, Milton chose to imitate and to modify the Petrarchan love sonnet as a way of defining his poetic voice. Declining to follow the example of earlier English Petrarchanists, Milton represents himself as poet not in the language of his country but in the language of his poetic models. In addressing himself as poet-to-be to a beloved lady—a figure already canonical for poetic address—he represents himself to her in Italian. The *Canzone* draws attention to the aspiring poet's choice of language as an important issue both for the present sequence of sonnets and for his future career: asking him to defend his momentary dalliance in the language and poetic tradition of another country, the poet's friends remind him that

> ... "Altri rivi
> Altri lidi t'aspettan, ed altre onde
> Nelle cui verdi sponde
> Spuntati ad or ad or a la tua chioma
> L'immortal guiderdon d'eterne frondi."
>
> (ll. 7–10)

(Other rivers / Other shores await you, and other waves, / On whose green banks an immortal reward of eternal leaves / Is putting forth shoots now, even now, for your locks.)[1]

The *Canzone* invites us to ask why Milton names himself in a foreign language as a poet who in the future will return to his native tongue.

By writing love sonnets and a *canzone* in Italian, Milton poses in his own way the problem of the poet's relation to language and gender, a problem that pervades Petrarch's *Canzoniere*. A psychoanalytic approach to these texts, in particular one that makes use of the writings of Lacan, offers a way of reading the issues of self, language, and gender in relation to one another. Lacan's writing and the rereadings he inaugurated develop Freud's most radical claim—that neither the ego nor sexual identity is natural or unified. Self and sexual identity are, rather, normative fictions we construct and continually reproduce in the process of becoming speaking members of organized society. A psychoanalytic reading of poetic representation thus would examine the shaped and shaping social text from which the lyric voice speaks: by taking imaginary and symbolic determinations into account, we may better understand the symptoms and the historical resiliency of patriarchy, a cultural system that has survived many class and political structures. The feminist critic would question the logic of the "vast social connivance" that Lacan designates, a connivance that makes the woman the "privileged site" of desire and prohibition.[2] An analysis of the erotic investments of male love poetry of the Renaissance in terms of the psychic and symbolic effects of patriarchy may first help us understand the tangle of erotic issues and power relations that a specific poetic moment reveals and then help clarify some of the ideological determinations of a society that has received, read, and canonized that moment.

Milton's various innovations in his Italian poems suggest that he sought to modify traditional definitions of gender and poetic representation, to imagine a new relation between male poet and female beloved. By reading the linguistic and fantasmatic issues raised and mutually implicated in these poems, this paper aims to assess the cost of Milton's utopian voice. To delineate the cultural determinations constraining his attempt, however, we must first address the parameters of representation in the poetic tradition he chose momentarily to adopt. The Petrarchan tradition of love poetry that Milton takes up in these poems brought with it a structure of exchange that could not help but influence the direction a new poet would take if he aspired to establish a voice within that poetic mode. Contrary to each new love poet's announced role as servant and celebrant of his particular lady, the Petrarchan tradition became a canon of poetry in which men represented women for other men. The structure of the tradition *as* a tradition reduced the figure of the lady to a supplement of the poet's voice. Through her, he made himself a poet; through her he established a place for his voice within a male poetic tradition. One poet responded to the text of a previous poet through the figure of the beloved yet unattainable lady, inscribing a homoerotic subtext that works like the one Freud reads in exchanges of dirty jokes. A woman's resistance, Freud writes, her "inflexibility is . . . the first condition for the development of obscene speech. . . . The ideal case of resistance of this kind on the woman's part occurs if another man is present at the same time . . . gradually, in place of the woman, the onlooker, now the listener, becomes the person to whom the obscenity is addressed. . . . "[3] Such a joking conversation relies on an ambigious structure, as does the more decorous poetic conversation of the Petrarchan tradition—the woman occupying both a central and a marginal position, providing first the condition and then the conduit for male discourse.

One acute reader of the *Canzoniere*, John Freccero, points out that in the relation between male poet (laur<u>o</u>) and female beloved (laur<u>a</u>), Petrarch's cycle makes Laura's role supplementary to his poetic project: the lady as historical referent seems to disappear before the lady as signifier.[4] Delineating without interrogating the same triangular relation in the *Canzoniere* that Freud finds in the dirty joke, Freccero concludes that when the laur<u>o</u> seeks to achieve self-definition from the "brilliant surface" of the "pure signifier" laur<u>a</u>, the only residue of signification left between the two signs is another male poet, Dante. Freccero offers this analysis, however, without considering the implications of the peculiar double logic of the "mere" supplement. Essential to an enterprise larger than the one of adoration her poet announces, the supplementary lady becomes the linguistic figure without which the poet as lover could not produce his poetry, without which he could not establish a place for himself in the history of other male poetic achievement. Be she Laura, Delia, Stella, or Milton's lady without a name, the logic of a canon of love-poetic cycles addressed to women requires that the poet as lover add the representation of her presence to the representation of his own if he seeks to present his voice to himself, to realize his nature as author. She becomes representable, in fact, to the extent to which she eludes him. Her absent presence and her difference mark the space that generates desire and the struggle for poetic self-presentation. The poet as lover continues to be grateful to her even as she exceeds his grasp: her very distance allows him, by means of representation, to fill a lack in himself he could not fill on his own. The traditional structure of a cycle of Petrarchan love poems brings with it an abasement before "the lady I cannot have" who is at the same time "the lady without whom I cannot have myself."

As the poet's figure of address, means of self-representation, and point of entry into male poetic history, the beloved *donna* plays the part of a necessary and therefore dangerous supplement to the poetic voice.[5] An exchange that both requires and represses the feminine presents a complex issue of the relation between language and gender when it takes place between two (or more) poetic texts, for the opacity of poetic language, in contrast to the generally functional clarity of conversation, puts into the foreground the problem of the self's mediation in language. To make himself a poet, a Petrarchan love poet tries to present himself to himself and to the world by re-presenting a figure that is already a representation of a representation from the poetry of his male predecessors. Such a sonnet cycle enacts a drama of self-alienation through previously established codes of representation, an eccentric strategy for self-presentation that undermines the fiction that a self could ever present itself to itself as such. The Petrarchan canon establishes unstable if poetically generative poles, masculine self and presence defining itself against and within the feminine other and linguistic representation. This unstable strategy threatens to undermine as soon as it produces the illusion of an authentic ground for the self-presenting male voice. The parameters of representation and historical tradition exact a price: the poet represses his "beloved" the very moment he exalts her.

Milton takes up the issue of how the poetic self defines itself in language as the subject matter of the *Canzone,* a poem that purports to account for and to defend his project. Several young friends surround the poet, laughing, and ask,

> . . . "Perchè scrivi,
> Perchè tu scrivi in lingua ignota e strana
> Verseggiando d'amor, e come t'osi?"
>
> (ll. 3–5)

(Why do you write, / Why do you write in a language unknown and strange, / Writing verses of love, and how do you dare?)

Milton answers the question not in his own voice but in the voice of the song, which he personifies by apostrophe:

> Canzon, dirotti, e tu per me rispondi:
> Dice mia donna, e 'l suo dir è il mio cuore,
> "Questa è lingua di cui si vanta Amore."

(Song, I will tell you, and you answer for me: / My lady says, and her speech is my heart, / "This is the language of which Love boasts.")

The conventional language of Petrarchanism brings with it this rhetorical device: direct addresses by the poet to the poem itself in the last stanza pervade the *Canzoniere.*[6] Recent studies of apostrophe in Romantic poetry suggest that this figure attempts to project a face capable of hearing and speaking onto the inanimate world and, by implication, onto the poetic text.[7] Petrarch's apostrophes also project the capacity for hearing and speaking, but without imagining a detour into the world: he gives a responsive face directly to his own visible text.

When Petrarch closes a song by apostrophe and quotation, as Milton does in the *Canzone,* he makes it clear that the poem is imagined to be quoting the poet's words. Petrarch usually addresses the poem, "Canzon," issues an imperative or makes a suggestion, ("di," "digli," or "tu puoi ben dire"), then supplies the words, in quotation marks, that he thinks will be useful if someone in the future should ask the poem a question.[8] The variations Milton introduces into the concluding Petrarchan apostrophe foreground rather than suppress the assumptions behind that figure, stressing both that the text can hear his address and that the quotation marks in the last line set off the poem's own "spoken" answer to it. The quotation functions simultaneously as a response to the apostrophe and to the question that inaugurates the *Canzone.* Milton's concluding gesture differs subtly but crucially from Petrarch's in a number of ways. Rather than issue an imperative immediately followed by a quotation, thus putting his words directly into the poem's mouth, Milton shapes an address that passes through several mediations emphasizing an exchange of voice and of agency. Not only does he address the poem, "Canzon," but he also says he will speak to it ("dirotti," "I will tell you"). He thus draws attention to his gesture of speaking to the text by saying he is about to speak while in the middle of doing so. He then imagines the poem—now a listening "you" to the poet's speaking "I"—both to have a voice and to be able to "answer" on his behalf ("tu per me rispondi," "you answer for me"). While the language of the apostrophe and response in this poem encourages the confusion about whose "speech" is being quoted in the final line, the line that separates the apostrophe from the reply in quotation marks complicates matters further: in it, the lady's speech also enters the *Canzone.* The last three lines leave tantalizingly unclear whose speech the quotation marks mark—the poet's as he speaks to the poem, the poem's as it answers his address, or the lady's as she directs her lover. Petrarch's apostrophe and quoted remarks, while imagining a time in the future when his voice and the poem's might signify in unison, never include the lady's speech. To add her speech to his or to his poem's would bridge the necessary gulf that distances the poet from Laura.[9]

Milton's conclusion explicitly develops a meaningful and successful relation between poet and text as vocal address and response. These same lines, however, simultaneously intensify the problem of Petrarch's exile from language: it is precisely the foreign language in which the quoted remark answers the question that motivates Milton to write the poem in the first place.[10] The *Canzone* answers both the apostrophe and its opening question in a language every bit as "unknown and strange" as the language that prompted the question, "why do you write in an unknown language?" The poem answers in the language that, in the third sonnet, Milton acknowledges is "not understood by my own good people" ("dal mio buon popol non inteso" [III.9]).

The figure of apostrophe as *prosopopoeia* proposes a meaningful circuit of spoken communication between the speaker and the object that the speaker endows with a face capable of responding. By projecting voice onto a written text as Petrarch's apostrophes did before him, Milton attempts to elide the difference between voice and the materiality of the written word. By writing a *canzone* that answers the apostrophe by quoting the "speech" of a foreign tongue, as Petrarch did not do before him, Milton attempts to recuperate through voice the signifying strangeness of a poem written in the very language at issue for its foreignness. The apostrophe that ends Milton's *Canzone* makes explicit what that figure implies for the poetic voice by directly staging the problem of voice and signification. Taking a foreign language as the subject of the *Canzone,* Milton then turns that foreignness into the poem's own performance. The apostrophe and its quoted answer imagine a voice that means inherently, that achieves its meaning even through the opacity of foreign signification. The verb *dire,* a verb that appears three times in the last three lines, reinforces the apostrophe's attempt to familiarize the poem's material signifying strangeness ("*dir*otti . . . *Dice* mia donna, e 'l suo *dir* è il mio cuore"). A chorus of voices asserts that meaning is immanent in the spoken form of the foreign text.

The self-consciously Italian text, its apostrophe, and its quoted reply thus mark the dynamic of the poet's struggle for poetic self-presentation: by means of a signifying idiom identified as foreign to his voice, the poet tries to present his "heart." When he does so, that interior self turns out to be constituted by the "unknown and strange language" that represents it. By projecting voice onto the text and intertwining his own with it, Milton actively embraces the reversibility of voice and text that Paul de Man elucidates as the threat latent in prosopopoeia's "symmetrical structure."[11] Rather than find the possibility of exchange with foreign signification threatening, the "I" foregrounds that foreignness in order to celebrate it as its own. This concluding apostrophe both sets up and works to deny the difference between foreign language and immanent meaning, between text and voice, for the sake of the integrity of the living "heart" of the poetic self.

Milton assumes a foreign language in order to assert his union with that language and also to mark an itinerary that will lead him through an alien language back to his mother tongue. Both his choice of language and his closing rhetorical figure in the *Canzone* render the linguistic dilemmas of the *Canzoniere* acute and bring into the foreground what Lacan would claim, as speaking subjects inscribed in the Symbolic, we push into the background: the "speaking-being's" simultaneous precipitation in and alienation from language. The highly self-conscious Italian poems of an English poet directly pose the problem of the effects on the speaking subject of the alterity of preexisting signification, written or spoken. Lacan reads in Freud a theory of the self's "radical eccentricity from itself," where the fiction of coherent subjectivity emerges as the subject continually positions and repositions itself in relation to others within a field of signifying differences and deferrals already determined.[12] Milton's *Canzone* shows a self already constituted in one Symbolic system reenacting an earlier scene of self-positioning. Trying to present himself to himself, the poet creates a voice from the language and erotic-poetic tradition of another country. What Lacan will stress, however, is that while every subject must articulate a place for itself in the relations of gender and language, this very finding of a place from which to speak is at once enabling and alienating. The "speaking-being" will continue to produce fictional syntheses of subjective coherence within the Symbolic and Imaginary matrices of representation in order to try to resolve its discordance with its own material reality.

The insistent repetition of the verb "dire" in the last three lines imbricates the poet, the poem, and the lady in the faculty of speech, the three entangled utterances constituting the poet's "heart": "Canzone, *dir*otti . . . / *Dice* mia donna, e 'l suo *dire* è il mio cuore." These last lines represent the poetic voice and lay claim to coherent interiority ("il mio cuore") by incorporating in it not only the text of a foreign language but also the "speech" of the other gender. If we look at the language and allusions in Sonnet III, "Qual in colle aspro," we find the figure of the woman yet again integral to the male poet's assertion of linguistic transcendence, of a utopian moment when the self is one with and in language. The third sonnet makes this relation between the subject and language an erotic problem as well and raises the question of the effect on the speaking subject of culturally organized distinctions between genders by alluding to and changing a very old story: the encounter between Diana and Actaeon.

Several allusions to the *Canzoniere* in Milton's third sonnet help to define the poet's relation to language, the references revising Petrarch's poetics of lament, exile, and fragmentation.[13] Milton's declaration at the turn from octave to sestet, "Canto . . . / E 'l bel Tamigi cangio col bel Arno" (I sing . . . And the beautiful Thames I change for the beautiful Arno) (III.9–10) alludes to Petrarch's famous sonnet, "Quella per cui con Sorga o cangiato Arno" (She for whom I have changed the Arno for the Sorgue) (308). In the sonnet of changed rivers, Petrarch quickly shifts from the subject of spatial dislocation to explore his erotic and linguistic exile. In his new landscape, the poet confronts language's deceit: words remain a radically inadequate means to attain or to express desire. He laments his continuing failure to describe love and Laura accurately: "Da poi più volte o riprovato indarno ... pinger cantando ... " (Since then many times I have tried in vain ... to paint her picture by singing) (ll. 5–7). When faced with the never-ending but poetically productive task of bridging the erotic and linguistic gulf between himself and Laura, the poet concludes, "passion, inspiration and art" all fail ("ivi manca l'ardir, l'ingegno et l'arte" [l. 14]).

Closely echoing the entire first line of Petrarch's sonnet, Milton's allusion to the conceit of changing rivers as a synecdoche for changing place suggests that he accepts and repeats the earlier love-poet's spatial and linguistic exile. But Milton's sestet alters the Petrarchan predicament by alluding to and altering other lines from Sonnet 308. In his sonnet's turn, Milton takes up the Petrarchan issue of the linguistic act, his "Canto" echoing Petrarch's "cantando." Rather than "singing in vain," however, ("indarno ... cantando" [308.5–7]), Milton claims to sing in a different country because "love *never* turned anything *in vain*" ("cosa *mai* volse *indarno*"). The relationship between the poet and the words that never adequately represent Laura becomes in Milton a relation no longer futile. Sonnet III defines as futile only the act of refusing to write.

The sonnet echoes yet another poem from the *Canzoniere,* an allusion that sets this utopian story of a self coincident with language in an erotic frame of reference. The *Canzone*'s image of a plant sprouting "eternal leaves" for the poet on England's shores reappears: Milton compares his "new flower of foreign speech" ("il fior nuovo di strania favella" [III.7]) to the foreign, beautiful little plant watered on the hillside ("l'erbetta strana e bella" [III.3]). If Petrarch achieved his poetic laurel ("lauro") from "Laura," Milton shapes his poetic plant from the fact of his lady's foreignness. The way in which it grows refers back to the *Canzoniere:*

> Qual in colle aspro, al'imbrunir di sera
> L'avezza giovinetta pastorella
> Va bagnando l'erbetta strana e bella ...

(III.1–3)

(As on a rugged hill, at the darkening of evening / A local, young little shepherdess / Goes to bathe the strange and beautiful little plant ...)

An unusual diminutive, "pastorella" occurs only once in the *Canzoniere:* the Diana-Actaeon madrigal (52). Milton's "pastorella" evokes the action of the madrigal, for his shepherdess sets out to bathe the foreign plant ("Va bagnando ... " [l. 3]) as her predecessor had also set out to bathe something:

Non al suo amante più Diana piacque
. . . .
ch'a me la pastorella alpestra et cruda
posta a bagnar un leggiadretto velo
ch'a l'aura il vago et biondo capel chiuda . . .

(52.1–6)

(Diana did not please her lover more . . . than did the cruel little mountain
shepherdess please me / as she is set to bathe a pretty little veil / that hides
her beautiful, blonde head from the breeze . . .)

Comparing himself to Actaeon in the woods, Petrarch puts a veil between
himself and Laura as Diana, imagining a sign that prohibits him from
seeing her nakedness. The covering veil thus distinguishes him from
Ovid's Actaeon: he sees Laura's veil rather than Laura's body, but the
sight of her behind her veil pleases him, he claims, as much as the sight
of the naked goddess, Diana, pleased Actaeon. The symbol of Laura's
veil works to evoke various possible readings. Suggesting linguistic representation as well as the impossibility of linguistic representation,[14] the
covering veil that hides Laura from the poet's sight also turns an image
of a fetishized object into a symbol for the prohibition that makes fetishes
possible.

If Actaeon's dismemberment represents the fear underlying this visual
encounter with the naked female body, a psychoanalytic account of the
fear would explain its traumatic or "wounding" effect on the psyche as
the result of the deferred or "nachträgliche" nature of the experience.
What specifically characterizes Freud's understanding of sexuality, and
what constitutes the condition for psychic trauma and repression, is the
time lag, the delay between experience and understanding. As Jean
Laplanche and J.-B. Pontalis point out, "It is not lived experience
. . . that undergoes a deferred revision but, specifically, whatever it has
been impossible in the first instance to incorporate fully into a meaningful context. The traumatic event is the epitome of such unassimilated
experience."[15] The wounding effect of retrospective understanding, where
a later scene triggers the memory of an earlier, unassimilated one that
has not yet even acquired the status of event — so that the danger seems to
arise from within the self rather than from without — helps to explain the
tenacious and deep-seated effects that cultural representations of sexuality can have on the psyche. An already inherited paternal matrix of
representation privileging the binary division between presence and
absence enables the boy to read the female body in a specific way. He
comes to understand her body, to read the sight of it both as a "lack" and

as the precise referent of the previously unspecified paternal threat. The inherited Symbolic order organizes the experience both as an experience and as meaning, thus enabling the boy to tell the castration story.

Both Petrarch's madrigal and Ovid's narrative stress prohibition. Casting water over Actaeon's head, Ovid's Diana warns the transgressor that he will be prohibited from speaking: "nunc tibi me posito visam velamine narres, / sit poteris narrare licet" (You would now tell the story of me seen before you, my robe put aside, if it were permitted that you be able to tell it).[16] Petrarch condenses the lengthy Ovidian narrative of transgression and prohibition into a single image, the covering veil, an image that prevents him from seeing what Actaeon had seen. Psychoanalytic writing sees the object of a fetish as a representation that works simultaneously to symbolize and to repress the memory of precisely this trauma, when a boy reads the different body before his eyes as castrated and believes that difference to be the outcome for his own body should he violate the cultural prohibition.[17]

The Ovidian subtext of Actaeon's visual transgression and enforced silence in Petrarch's allusion to Actaeon thus implies two kinds of threat for the male poet: the threat of bodily dismemberment and the threat of loss of voice.[18] This nexus of problems—dismemberment and loss of voice—disappears from Milton's sonnet when the poet refuses to admit Actaeon's visual transgression or Petrarch's prohibiting, fetishized veil into the allusive fabric of the sonnet. Rather than washing Laura's prohibiting veil, Milton's *pastorella* waters a beautiful, foreign plant. His tongue then sprouts the flower of poetic utterance:

> Così Amor meco insù la lingua snella
> Desta il fior nuovo di strania favella . . .

(ll. 6–7)

(So love on my slender tongue / Arouses the new flower of foreign speech . . .)

Alluding to two scenes of visual transgression, the sonnet does not, however, describe the exchange between the poet and his beloved as a visual one. We find no verbs of seeing. Between feminine and masculine figures we find rather a relationship of contiguity transformed into interiority, an oral rather than a specular exchange. The erotic metaphor of Love arousing a flower on the poet's tongue imagines a scene very different from that of the poem's two subtexts. The threat to the poetic voice in Petrarch's allusion to Ovid vanishes as Milton rejects threatened dismemberment and silence for interior abundance and production of voice. In modifying Petrarch's Diana-Actaeon madrigal by effacing its prohibiting veil, Milton denies the possibility of a censoring agency. The threatening dynamic of visual transgression and censorship revealed in the Diana-Actaeon madrigal helps to explain the logic of Petrarch's mourning and his "poetics of fragmentation"[19] but seems not to pertain to Milton's third sonnet.

In addition to the oral imagery of the flower of foreign verse on his tongue, the third sonnet's feminine adjectives and diminutives describe a relation between male and female quite different from the dynamic of visual transgression, separation, and dismemberment depicted in the Petrarchan and Ovidian subtexts of the poem. The language of Sonnet III sets up a series of identifications between male self and female other. Several adjectives bridge the male and female principles: the foreign beauty, his "pellegrina bellezza" of the fourth sonnet (IV.6), encourages a plant as unfamiliar and beautiful as she, "l'erbetta strana e bella," to grow on the hillside (III.3)—which, in turn, is compared to the flower of foreign speech growing on her lover's tongue ("il fior nuovo di strania favella"). Not only does his foreign flower remind us of his foreign beauty, but the poet's tongue becomes a feminine "slender" tongue: "la lingua snella" (III.6). The adjective "snella" does not appear often in the *Canzoniere.* Petrarch describes the topography surrounding the lady as slender ("freschi rivi e snelli" [219.4]) or parts of Laura herself as slender ("da più bei piedi snelli" [348.7]) but never describes himself or his poetry in this way. Feminine diminutives also link the male voice to his feminine principle: the giovin*etta* pastor*ella* waters a plant, the erb*etta,* that Milton equates with the "flower" growing inside on his own "slender tongue."

The change from Laura's covering veil to the flower of poetic production refuses prohibition and at the same time the adjectives and diminutives refuse the division between genders. Alluding to and overturning a tradition of rigid distinctions between genders, Sonnet III identifies male subject with female object, making her exterior foreignness his interior plenitude so that the two genders no longer seem to be defined adversarially as they are bound to be from the advent of paternal prohibition. An oral fantasy of incorporation represents the female object as not yet object—a fantasy we must examine more closely in relation to the Petrarchan predicament of mourning and fragmentation. These two modes of representation have more in common than at first sight would seem to be the case.

Petrarch's poetics of exile produces a lament, a *planctus,* repeated over three hundred fragmented, "scattered" lyric poems ("rime sparse"). In addition to representing himself as the eternally weeping lover, Petrarch also announces his own unworthiness as part of his self-defining strategy: he opens the poetic cycle by confessing his former mistakes ("giovenile errore") and his "shame" before the eyes of the public.[20] Freud describes melancholia as a failed attempt to achieve a dialectical resolution of mourning. In melancholia, the "shadow of the object falls back upon the ego" so that the subject reads a loss in the world as a loss within the self.[21] The melancholic thus loses self-esteem and at the same time betrays a curiously narcissistic pleasure in talking continually about his own abjectness. The condition of melancholia, it seems, enacts another version of an already familiar structure that also exceeds dialectical resolution: the Lacanian "stade du miroir."[22] Knowing its body only in fragments, the *infans* launches itself "in a fictional direction," assuming a representation of its bodily integrity by means of external information, attempting to achieve a dialectical synthesis with its specular image. Material reality, however, exceeds any such final resolution. The unresolved dialectic of melancholia lays bare the lie of a coherent inner self, articulates the alienating fiction of the "I" that is Lacan's account of subjectivity. Citing as examples of self-knowledge Hamlet's self-accusations and his assessment that all men deserve whipping, Freud remarks, "we only wonder why a man must become ill before he can discover a truth of this kind."[23] The memory of fragmentation, bodily and vocal, that melancholia evokes haunts the lamenting, self-accusing, and "scattered" voice of the Petrarchan lyric.

The affect of Milton's sonnets differs markedly from that of Petrarch's. Instead of an unworthy lover lamenting the loss of his lady, Milton declares himself a simple and candid man worthy of his lady's love ("Giovane piano, e semplicetto amante . . . io certo a prove tante / L'ebbi fedele, intrepido, costante," "a candid young man, and a simple lover . . . In many ordeals I have proven . . . faithful, fearless, and constant" [VI.1–5]). Milton refuses to consider his lady lost or to denigrate himself. In Sonnet V, for example, Milton posits the possibility of his separation from her, beginning the poem with the Petrarchan notion of self exiled from self (V.1–6). He then reworks the initial predicament and the figurative language of the poem so that by the last line we find that *her* sun has become *his* dawn. The poet resolves potential division in language of return, plenitude, and joy: tears last only "Until my dawn returns, filled with roses" ("Finchè mia Alba revien colma di rosa" [V.14]). In contrast to a Petrarchan scene of nocturnal lamentation, this sonnet never indulges in the self-accusation that Freud identifies as characteristic of melancholia.[24]

Refusing to mourn by taking pleasure in his own shame, and in the third sonnet refusing a sign of prohibition, Milton links the two genders, producing an oral image that proposes a fantasy of taking inside, of "incorporation." But the fantasy of incorporation, as examined extensively in the writing of Nicolas Abraham and Maria Torok, stages yet another kind of lament—a silent, unacknowledged, but still "eloquent" lament that also attests to the continuously operative but nonetheless unresolved dialectical processes of the speaking subject.[25] A fantasy of denial that "refuses to know the true sense of loss," that forecloses the possibility that the subject ever had anything to lose,[26] incorporation literalizes loss as a lost object in order to keep it inside, to bypass a conflict the subject cannot solve.[27] An hallucinatory and recuperative strategy, incorporation marks the failure of what they initially posit as a successful mechanism of inclusion, "introjection."[28] Torok proposes the distinction by examining Sandor Ferenczi's definition of introjection, a thinking early in the history of psychoanalysis of the mediation between narcissistic love and the love of objects. She quotes Ferenczi: introjection is a "mechanism permitting the primitive auto-erotic interests to open out . . . by including the objects of the exterior world in the 'I.'" Developing the psychoanalytic premise that self-love provides the condition for any other loving investment, Ferenczi suggests that insofar as a subject loves an object, it adopts that object as part of itself.[29]

Torok then distinguishes introjection, a process whereby the "I" is expanded, from its failure, the fantasy of incorporation, by considering the effect of loss: "Loss, whatever form it takes, always works as a prohibition, and will constitute an insurmountable problem for introjection. In compensation for lost pleasure and a failed introjection, the subject installs the prohibited object in the interior of the self."[30] In literalizing the metaphor of the open mouth that characterizes introjection, incorporation mimes introjection by fantasizing ingestion in the absence of the object.[31] Such a fantasy has a narcissistic vocation, since, by "refusing the verdict of the object and of reality,"[32] incorporation requires no libidinal reorganization. Born of a prohibition that it acknowledges only in evasion, that it skirts without ever transgressing, incorporation can only repetitively commemorate a desire riddled with a contradiction it cannot resolve.[33] This strategy of denial carries within it another prohibition—an interdiction against signifying that as a subject formed around prohibition and loss, one is, in fact, unconsolable.

The poetic figures and modifications of previous texts in these Italian poems betray a repeated attempt to negate by incorporation the loss attending accession to language and to a place in the division between genders. Milton revises the Diana-Actaeon subtext, excluding paternal prohibition and the adversarial, oedipal divide between male and female, but at the same time he also signals a crucial psychic connection between femininity and language in the wish to restore them both together, inside. Evoking only to evade the otherness of signification and the feminine by condensing the two in the *Canzone*, the poetic voice denies the materiality of signification and the necessity of separation from the feminine by apostrophe: the language of this trope figures his interiority, "il mio cuore," as constituted by her speech, "il suo dir." And again in the third sonnet, we find interior plenitude asserted by a voice that takes the feminized and feminizing "flower of foreign speech" inside as its own.

Throughout Milton's Italian sonnets, the poetic voice overturns or denies the possibility that he ever lost the figure of the lady in the first place. Her exterior enters his interior at the same time that the plant of foreign utterance grows up on the poetic tongue. We might compare the oral image of interior plenitude in the third sonnet with the other traditional figure for femininity in the fifth, the rose, that multiplies and "fills up" the poet's room at dawn, again replacing self-division with joy ("mia alba . . . *colma* di rosa" [V.14]). In contrast to Laura, the beloved *donna* of these poems has no name. As giving a name is the quintessential poetic act, the omission is remarkable: she never acquires enough difference from the poetic voice to receive one. The supplementary figure of the beloved in the Petrarchan tradition becomes a supplement to Milton's poetic voice in a different way. The poet does not require the representation of her gender in its absence or difference from his own. Rather, he incorporates that figure, refusing to acknowledge she ever had the status of an object apart from the self. Denial or foreclosure rather than resolution, Milton's enabling fantasy of incorporation allows a utopian vision of the poetic self at the expense of any status for femininity apart from that self.

The incorporating voice of the Italian sonnets appears again, I believe, in *Paradise Lost*. In the opening meditation on its own creative act, Milton's voice would control both genders, again fantasizing a taking inside. Borrowing much of his descriptive material for chaos and the idea of chaos as the stuff of poetic creation from the opening lines of Ovid's *Metamorphoses*, Milton gives chaos his own distinctive stamp by giving Ovid's neutral matter a gender, by making of it a maternal principle. The epic voice models itself on the "wild Abyss" of chaos, the "Womb" of nature, would use her as the matter of its own poetic fecundity (2.910–11). Summoning the Spirit that is his muse, the poet places himself in apposition to chaos, a vessel ready for an ordering principle:

> . . . Thou from the first
> Wast present, and with mighty wings outspread
> Dove-like satst brooding on the vast Abyss
> And mad'st it pregnant: What in me is dark
> Illumine . . .
>
> (1.19–23)

This epic voice that negates separation by incorporating the feminine represents its character, Adam, as embodying a similarly double nature.

When God first draws Eve from Adam's side in Book 8, she withdraws from him, giving us an Adam who, for a moment, sounds like a love-poet in the Petrarchan tradition:

> She disappear'd, and left me dark, I wak'd
> To find her, or forever to deplore
> Her loss . . .

(8.478–80)

Unlike Petrarch, however, Adam pursues her, woos her, and wins her. Father of mankind *and* bearer of Eve, Adam then exclaims to God, "I now see . . . My self / Before Me," thus incorporating Eve into an imaginative extension of his own subjective interiority (8.495). When Adam later leaves Paradise hand in hand with his wife, Milton identifies the two genders as one in a studied oxymoron: though two people and two sexes, Adam and Eve take "thir solitary way" out of Eden (12.649). The utopian song can deny "loss of Eden" by refinding a "paradise within" and by identifying the mother and father of mankind. This epic voice would incorporate femininity into itself as much as does its character, Adam, and as much as does the voice of the Italian love poems.

NOTES

1. All quotations are from *John Milton: Complete Poems and Major Prose,* ed. Merritt Y. Hughes (Indianapolis, 1957). Translations are mine. For translations of Petrarch's verse, I have consulted Robert M. Durling's translations in *Petrarch's Lyric Poems: The Rime Sparse and Other Lyrics* (Cambridge, Mass., 1976).

2. As quoted by Jacqueline Rose in *Feminine Sexuality,* ed. Juliet Mitchell and Jacqueline Rose (New York, 1982), p. 39. The two seminars in which Lacan discusses the issue directly, "L'Envers de la psychanalyse," Le seminaire XVIII, and "Les non-dupes errent," Le seminaire XXI, are still unpublished typescripts. While Lacan agrees with Freud that we will always find a triangular structure at work in any subject's accession to culture and to the Symbolic, he warns that we cannot then claim that this structure refers to any particular, historical organization of the family. The third term in the oedipal struggle is, for Lacan, precisely that—a term, an agency that fathers have happened to have come to fill in the historically specific configurations of most of European society. Patriarchal determinism becomes a problem of reading too literally. The "Law-of-the-Father" breaks the dyadic and potentially incestuous relation between mother and child, but to believe that the signifier of "The Phallus" refers to any real father is to fall into an ideological trap: it would be a mistake, Lacan claims, to define the oedipus complex as "natural, rather than normative" (*Feminine Sexuality,* p. 69). In "Is the Oedipus Complex Universal?" (*m/f,* 5–6 [1981], 85, trans. Ben Brewster), Moustafah Safouan stresses that for Lacan, this third term in the triangle is an arbitrary one: "nothing of itself requires that this [position] should be embodied

46

by the father as such." See Jacqueline Rose's introduction for a thorough and provocative discussion of the implications and possibilities of Lacan's work for feminist criticism (*Feminine Sexuality,* pp. 27–57).

3. Sigmund Freud, "Jokes and Their Relation to the Unconscious," in *The Standard Edition of the Complete Psychological Works of Freud,* trans. James Strachey, 24 vols. (London, 1974), 8:99–100.

4. John Freccero, "The Fig Tree and the Laurel," *Diacritics,* 5 (Spring, 1975), 34–40. The *Canzoniere,* Freccero argues, attempt to produce an "auto-reflexive poetics" contrary to Augustine's poetics of allegory. Petrarch tries to reify his signs, to produce a linguistic "fetish" that at first complements but ultimately supersedes the thematic idolatrous reification of the lady. Freccero analyzes the strategies of representation and signification in the *Canzoniere,* showing how Petrarch tries to shape his signifying voice out of the rhetorical conceit of the lady. The trope of the lauro/laura becomes a reified sign that no longer points outside the sonnet cycle it subtends. Caught up in the tradition's logic of the lady's mere supplementarity to the poetic voice, Freccero offers a semiotic analysis that, subtle as it is, leads to a conclusion whose cultural logic this paper seeks to interrogate: "I have spoken repeatedly of Petrarch's attempt to exclude referentiality from his text. His success, of course, was only relative. Not only is referentiality intrinsic to all language, but also there towered behind him the figure of Dante, to whom all love poetry, especially in Italian, would forever after be referred, if only by contrast . . . " (p. 39). By concentrating on Augustine's theological and Dante's poetic discourses as subtexts for Petrarch's voice, Freccero makes the problem of the erotics of the love-poetic self one of texts and ideas alone. We might object to the presuppositions of his argument along the same lines as Althusser objects to those of source criticism in general: such criticism imposes limits such that the critic "regards the history of ideas as its own element, maintains that nothing happens there which is not a product of the history of ideas itself and that the world of ideology is its own principle of intelligibility" (*For Marx,* trans. Ben Brewster [London, 1977], pp. 56–57).

5. See Jacques Derrida, *De la grammatologie* (Paris, 1967), pp. 203–34, particularly "Ce dangereux supplement," for his analysis of the logic of supplementarity of writing in Rousseau's *Confessions.*

6. Petrarch's apostrophes to his song appear in the following: 23.161; 28.107; 37.113; 50.71; 53.99; 71.106; 72.76; 73.91; 119.106; 127.99; 128.113; 129.66; 135.91; 207.92; 237.38; 264.127; 268.80; 323.73; 325.11; 331.61. All citations and quotations are from Francesco Petrarca, *Canzoniere,* ed. with intro. by Gianfranco Contini (Turin, 1968).

7. For three different discussions of apostrophe, see Paul de Man, "Autobiography as De-facement," *MLN,* 94 (1979), 919–30; Jonathan Culler, *The Pursuit of Signs* (Ithaca, 1981), pp. 135–54; and Cynthia Chase, " 'Viewless Wings': Intertextual Interpretation of Keats' Ode to a Nightingale," *Lyric Poetry: Beyond New Criticism,* ed. Chaviva Hosek and Pat Parker (Ithaca, 1985), pp. 208–25.

8. In 53.99ff. Petrarch writes, "canzon . . . vedrai / un cavalier . . . / Digli: 'Un che non ti vide . . . ' " ("Song . . . you will see a knight . . . Say to him: 'One who

has not seen you . . . ' ."); in 119.106ff. he tells the poem what it should respond when asked about its obscurity: "Canzon, chi tua ragion chiamasse oscura, / di' 'Non o cura . . . ' " ("Song, say to whoever calls your reasoning obscure: 'I don't care . . . ' ."). For further examples, see 37.113ff.; 128.113ff.; 135.91ff.; 323.73ff.; 331.61ff.

9. The closing apostrophe of sonnet 37 affords an excellent moment to compare with Milton's. The distance between Petrarch and Laura and the poet's self-portrait in this poem owe much to the exiled Ovid's opening address to his text in the *Tristia:* about to send his poem off as an emissary to Rome to beg for leave to return from exile, Ovid delivers an apostrophe to his book as the only means he will have to touch the feet of the person whom he is addressing. Ovid's "loca grata," Rome, becomes Petrarch's "il dolce loco," the place where Laura is. For Laura's speech to enter the poem would violate the space of exile ("'l duro esilio," l. 37) that characterizes the poems of the *Canzoniere:*

> Canzon, s'al dolce loco
> la donna nostra vedi,
> credo ben che tu credi
> ch'ella ti porgerà la bella mano
> ond' io son si lontano;
> non la toccar, ma reverente ai piedi
> le di' ch'io saro la tosto ch'io possa,
> o spirito ignudo od uom di carne et d'ossa.

(Canzon, if in that sweet place / you see our lady, / I believe that you believe / that to you she will stretch out the hand / from which I am so far away; / do not touch it, but reverently at her feet / tell her that I will be there as soon as I can, / either a naked spirit or a man of flesh and bone.)

Petrarch posits distance both between himself and his text ("credo ben che tu credi") and between himself and the lady ("ond' io son si lontano") within this circuit of poetic apostrophe and address. Compare the language of Ovid's opening apostrophe, where his *liber* will be the metonymic means by which the exile may come back to Rome and throw himself at the feet of the person whom he would address:

> Parve nec invideo sine me, liber, ibis in Urbem:
> Ei mihi quod domino non licet ire tuo.
> Vade, sed incultus, qualem decet exulis esse.
> . . . .
> Vade, liber, verbisque meis loca grata saluta.
> Contingam certe quo licet illa pede.

> (*Tristia* I.1–16)

10. See Giuseppe Mazzotta, "The Canzoniere and the Language of the Self," *Studies in Philology* (1978), 287ff., for an extensive reading of the nature of Petrarch's linguistic exile.

11. Paul de Man, p. 928. De Man suggests that the dimension of language as inscription, as indeterminably significative, poses a "latent threat" that particu-

larly "inhabits prosopopeia, namely that by making the death speak, the symmetrical structure of the trope implies, by the same token, that the living are struck dumb, frozen in their own death."

12. See, for instance, Lacan's "L'instance de la lettre dans l'inconscient ou la raison depuis Freud," in *Ecrits* (Paris, 1966), pp. 493ff., and, more generally, "Le stade du miroir comme formateur de la fonction du Je" and "La chose freudienne" for a sense of the full force of Symbolic and Imaginary matrices of representation on the subject.

13. Mazzotta, "*Canzoniere* and the Language of the Self," and Nancy Vickers, "Diana Described: Scattered Women and Scattered Rhyme," in *Writing and Sexual Difference,* ed. Elizabeth Abel (Chicago, 1980).

14. See Freccero, p. 39, for a reading of Laura's veil as the traditional symbol for the relation of sign to referent and Mazzotta for a reading of the implications of the impossibility of such signification.

15. Jean Laplanche and J.-B. Pontalis, *The Language of Psychoanalysis,* trans. Donald Nicholson-Smith (New York, 1973), p. 112.

16. Ovid, *Metamorphoses,* ed. Frank J. Miller (Cambridge, 1977), III. 192–93. Translation mine.

17. Freud, "Fetishism," in *The Standard Edition,* 21:147–58. "[The fetish] is not a substitute for any chance penis, but for a particular quite special penis that had been extremely important in early childhood but was afterwards lost. That is to say: it should normally have been given up, but the purpose of the fetish precisely is to preserve it from being lost. To put it plainly: the fetish is a substitute for the woman's (the mother's) phallus which the little boy once believed in and does not wish to forego—we know why."

18. Mazzotta, examining the madrigal in relation to Ovid's story of Actaeon, discusses it in terms of the loss of voice. Nancy Vickers, "Diana Described," reads the poem, the scattering of the "rime sparse," and the scattering of Laura's body as so many beautiful fragments, as symptoms of castration anxiety. While Vickers makes an important point about the anxiety motivating such poetic scattering, she faces an impasse in thinking of the trauma as instantaneous, in suggesting that the female body is naturally and immanently "intolerable" to the male child (p. 103). When considering the complicated issue of woman's difference, feminist criticism must try not to think of such lived experience as unmediated but rather try to distinguish carefully between a visual encounter and the interpretive matrices representing that encounter—interpretive networks that are the condition of the possibility of the event being perceived as an event and of the possibility of its narration.

19. Mazzotta's phrase, p. 274.

20. Petrarch looks back on his "primo giovenile errore," when he was the "favola" (the laughing-stock) of the crowd (1.1–11). One can find many variations on the theme of Petrarch's unworthiness. In particular, sonnet 364 offers the most telling contrast to Milton's confident lover. Milton hopes in III that he will be as "good a terrain" for God as he is for the shepherdess that waters his plant/tongue; Petrarch also views his relation to God as an extension of his relation to Laura

but, after her death in particular, that relation becomes one of unworthiness and shame rather than hopeful deserving (i.e., "i' conosco 'l mio fallo et non lo scuso," "I know my fault and do not excuse it" [364.14]). Some of the many other instances of self-rebuke or shame: sonnets 67, 201, 207, 224, 264, 355.

21. Freud, "Mourning and Melancholia," in *The Standard Edition*, 14:237–58.

22. Lacan, *Ecrits*, pp. 92–97.

23. Freud, "Mourning and Melancholia," in *The Standard Edition*, 14:166.

24. Compare Milton's fifth sonnet to Petrarch's sonnet 234, "O cameretta." Describing himself in his room at night, his "lagrime notturne" ("nocturnal tears") are a fountain of shame that he hides from the dawn ("che 'l di celate per vergogna porto," "which in the day I keep hidden for shame" [l. 4]). The flight of the self from the self never seems to end, "Ne pur il mio secreto e 'l mio riposo / fuggo, ma piu me stesso . . . ," "Nor do I flee my secret place nor my rest, but I flee more from myself . . . " [ll. 9–10]). Rather than waking to a dawn returning with renewed joy, Petrarch mentions only the fearful possibility of waking to find himself alone: "tal pauro o di ritrovarmi solo" (l. 14).

25. Nicolas Abraham and Maria Torok, *L'Ecorce et le noyau* (Paris: Aubier Flammarion, 1978), especially "Deuil ou Mélancholie, Introjecter-Incorporer," pp. 259–75. I am grateful to Milad Doueihi for bringing this work to my attention and for making many helpful suggestions while this paper was in progress.

26. Ibid., p. 261.

27. See Derrida's account of the contradictory strategy of incorporation in his essay, "Fors" (a preface to *Cryptonymie: Le Verbier de l'homme aux loups,* by Nicolas Abraham and Maria Torok [Paris: Aubier-Flammarion, 1976], pp. 9–77), esp. pp. 70–73. "This is not a solution, rather the opposite of one, but it allows for the easing of the conflict (by feigning its internalization) between the aggressiveness and the libido which are directed toward the Object. . . . [T]he process of incorporation into the Self provides an economic answer to the loss of the object. . . . I pretend to keep the dead alive, intact safe (save) inside me, but it is only in order to refuse, in a necessarily equivocal way, to love the dead as a living part of me, dead *save in me*, through the process of introjection, as happens in so-called 'normal' mourning." (Translated by Barbara Johnson, *Georgia Review,* 31 [1977], 64–116.)

28. Torok points out the possible collapse of a distinction between introjection and incorporation at an "archaic level" of the formation of the subject in "Maladie du deuil et fantasme du cadavre exquis," in *L'Ecorce et le noyau,* p. 238 (first published in *Revue Française de Psychanalyse* [Paris, P.U.F., 1968, no. 4]). She writes that at a pre-oedipal level, a fantasm of ingestion in the absence of the object also characterizes the "*introjection* of the oral libido" which should constitute the archaic "I." Derrida notes both the necessity and the eventual impossibility of maintaining such a distinction: "one could be tempted to see a simple polarity, a polarized system (introjection/incorporation) rather than the intractable, untreatable rigor of their distinction. But . . . one has to be sensitive to the sometimes massive, spectacular opposition between tendencies in a bipolar mechanism, in all the compromises and negotiations it permits. And these tendencies can only be

analyzed by starting out with a rigorous dissociation, even if the purity of such a dissociation remains in fact only a theoretical ideal" ("Fors," trans. Barbara Johnson, p. 73). See also p. 102 in "Fors" for a reading of the fragility of this distinction particularly with respect to accession to language.

    29. Torok, in *L'Ecorce et le noyau,* p. 235.

    30. Ibid., p. 237.

    31. Ibid., p. 238.

    32. Ibid., p. 237.

    33. Torok, p. 237: "Let us not forget that [incorporation] was born of a prohibition it bypasses without truly transgressing."

A Mask Presented at Ludlow Castle: The Armor of Logos

KATHLEEN WALL

F IVE classical sources tell the myth of Callisto, a votive of Diana who was raped by Zeus one day as she wandered alone and unprotected in the forest.[1] In Ovid's version, Zeus spied her when he came to earth to survey the damage done by Phaeton's disastrous ride in his father's chariot. Thinking that this independent-looking young huntress might not be exactly friendly, he disguised himself as Diana and approached the girl, gaining her trust this way until he "revealed himself by a shameful action." She became pregnant, was cast out of Diana's band of virgins, gave birth to Arcas, and was finally transformed first into a bear and later into the Great Bear constellation. Apollodorus credits Zeus himself for her ursine transformation, claiming that he felt this was necessary to hide his unfaithfulness to Hera.

The myth found its way from the classical sources into the medieval and Renaissance tradition via interest in "the matter of Rome" that formed part of so much fifteenth- and sixteenth-century literature. It is contained in three important translations of Ovid's *Metamorphoses,* those done by Caxton, Golding, and Sandys.[2] Three other writers made it part of their own "matter of Rome" narratives; hence it appears in Caxton's translation of Raoul Lefevre's *Recuyell of the Historyes of Troye,* William Warner's *Albion's England,* and Thomas Heywood's play, *The Golden Age.*[3] In these works, the rape of Callisto is introduced as part of Jupiter's early career as soldier and king. Finally, there is an odd little narrative called *The Barley-Breake, or a Warning for Wantons,* written by a person who calls himself or herself merely "W. N., Gent."[4] It is a moral tale about a flirtatious girl whose father, wishing to keep his daughter pure, tells her the story of Callisto, as if this were the proper story to tell young women who are on the verge of promiscuity.

This myth makes its most important appearance in Renaissance literature as the foundation of Milton's *Mask Presented at Ludlow Castle.* It is
certain that Milton was familiar with the myth, not only because he knew
his Ovid in classical and Renaissance sources, but because it is referred to
directly within his work, as Osgood has noted in *The Classical Mythology
of Milton's Poems.*[5] When the Lady's brothers begin to search for her, they
wish for guidance from the "star of Arcady," the star into which Zeus
transforms Arcas in Ovid's version of the myth. Even a cursory examination of the masque's situation reveals the strong influence of the myth
upon both plot and imagery.

Like Callisto, the Lady of the *Mask* is a young virgin alone in the forest
who is vulnerable because she is separated from her companions. Although
the Lady's companions are male—probably because Milton's commission stipulated the employment of the two young Egerton boys in the
performance—the young men have decidedly feminine appearances: the
Lady tells Comus that their faces are "smooth as Hebe's."[6] They also
discourse at length, and with some pretense of knowledge, upon female
virtues and vulnerabilities as if they were indeed analogous to the band
of Diana.

Like Callisto, the Lady is sexually threatened—in this case with seduction by Comus, a magician described as "Grandson of the Sun" who has
made his home in the wood in which the young people wander. These
woods seem to belong to him, as the forests of Arcady once belonged to
Zeus; there Comus conducts his rites and performs his magic. When he
hears the Lady's song, he is immediately attracted to her. But afraid of
frightening her, he adopts a disguise, hoping to gain enough trust to
convince her to drink of his magic potion, which will not only loose
animal passion in her but also literally transform her into an animal:
"Into som brutish form of Woolf, or Bear, / Or Ounce, or Tiger, Hog, or
bearded Goat" (p. 87, ll. 69–70). When he cannot seduce her, he "rapes"
her by freezing her with his magic wand, temporarily depriving her of
control over her fate. While these correspondences identify the myth of
Callisto as the one which informs Milton's *Mask,* it is the differences
between the original forms of the myth and the form given it in the
masque that provide us with interesting insights into Milton's ideas
about the feminine.

Although Comus resembles Zeus in his control of the forest, his desire
to seduce a young virgin, his taking on of a disguise, and his magical
ability to turn people into animals, there are a number of ways in which
he differs from the figure in Ovid's *Metamorphoses.* Comus contrives to
look like a harmless shepherd instead of taking on the appearance of the
goddess. But Milton expresses the feminine aspects of the original dis-

guise by giving Comus a female nature and orientation. While Zeus pretends to be Diana, Comus actually worships the goddess, dancing to the moon "in wavering Morrice" (p. 89, l. 116), declaring himself the priest of various moon deities, and speaking, in the goddess's stead, as a proponent of earthly fecundity. He shuns the sun, the traditional symbol of Zeus, symbol of logic, rationality, and Puritanism, but is, like the goddess, at home in the night. Even his magic potion is said to cure the "drouth of Phoebus" (p. 87, l. 66), that is, to counteract the effects of the planet symbolic of reason and law. In addition, many of Comus's characteristics come from his mother, Circe, who in Renaissance iconography is considered the enslaver of man's animal passions. Circe turned the crew of Odysseus into swine, but she also directed Odysseus to the underworld for badly needed instructions and warned him about the dangers of Scylla and Charybdis: her ability to direct Odysseus through the threatening elements of his homeward journey suggests that she is a guide to the dark side of the soul, both its passions and its dangers.

Like the Lady of the Beasts and his mother, Comus represents the passional side of human nature. His magic potion is credited with the power to change men into animals, not only by transforming their countenance, but by removing the rational side of their nature altogether. The Attendant Spirit accuses him of removing, with men's "human count'nance," their "express resemblance of the gods" (p. 87, ll. 68–69). With the gain of sensuality comes the loss of their rational powers: his

> . . . pleasing poison
> The visage quite transforms of him that drinks,
> And the inglorious likenes of a beast
> Fixes instead, unmoulding reasons mintage
> Character'd in the face.
>
> (p. 104, ll. 525–29)

Comus also considers himself a priest of Hecate and Cotytto, two aspects of the Great Goddess. The licentious orgies performed in Cotytto's name are similar to those of Comus; the rituals associated with her are performed in the interests of the earth's fertility; it is this cause that Comus himself professes when he argues with the Lady. Hecate is described by the Attendant Spirit as some evil witch, but she was originally the triple goddess herself, a beneficent deity in many respects, and frequently associated, like Diana, with the moon.

Comus, then, is hardly associated with the sun and a rational, logical orientation. That role is saved for the Attendant Spirit, a messenger of Jove who has come to "save" the Lady and return her to her father. The Attendant Spirit is something of a new addition in Callisto narratives: he essentially represents a different side of the Zeus figure of Ovid's myth. Like that character he descends, from "Jove's Court" to the "smoak and stirr" of the forest. And like Zeus at the end of the myth, who perceives that Callisto is in danger and saves her from death, the Attendant Spirit "stoops to her," to the Lady, to "save" her and return her safely home. In spite of his role as savior, he nevertheless bears some resemblance to Comus in that he too takes the disguise of a shepherd. The name of the shepherd, Thyrsis, whose appearance the Spirit has taken, connects the Spirit with Bacchus, and hence with Comus.

In a sense, then, Milton has split his Zeus figure in two, giving us the seductive and the apotheosizing components of the original figure in two distinct characters. We could understand this act as a division of the characters into "good" and "bad" components that shows the effect of the transparent overlay of Christianity, which may slightly alter the myth's configuration but which does not undermine its meaning. Stronger than Milton's desire for moral clarity, however, is a desire to explore the implications of a confrontation between two discrete and even opposite qualities of human nature: the animal and passional, represented by Comus, and the rational and godlike, represented both by the Attendant Spirit and the Lady herself.

Whereas woman is traditionally identified with the moon and with Eros, man with the sun and with Logos, the Lady's character is extraordinarily rational, and the iconography associated with her makes a number of references to the sun. Her logical, conservative character is revealed in her opening speech, which finds her following the sounds of Comus's band, while at the same time disapproving of the "ill manag'd merriment" and the "wanton dances." She is both lost and alone, yet she is not frightened, thinking of night, in imagery both benevolent and Christian, as "grayhooded Eev'n / ...a sad Votarist in Palmers weed" (p. 92, ll. 187–88). When fancies do begin to plague her imagination, she squelches them with the comforting thoughts of virtue:

> The vertuous mind, that ever walks attended
> By a strong siding champion Conscience.—
> O welcom pure-ey'd Faith, white-handed Hope,
> Thou hovering Angel girt with golden wings,
> And thou unblemish't form of Chastity,
> I see ye visibly, and now believe
> That he, the Supreme good, t'whom all things ill
> Are but as slavish officers of vengeance,
> Would send a glistring Guardian if need were
> To keep my life and honour unassail'd.
>
> (p. 93, ll. 209–19)

The Lady's reasoning seems, in practical terms, circular; she believes that she will remain chaste *because* she is chaste. Comus's own reaction to both the Lady's presence and her song reveals that the protection of chastity is equivocal. For unlike the typical Zeus figures, Comus is attracted to her not because she is beautiful, but because she is chaste, not because she is vulnerable, but because she seems so sober and self-certain. Thus he follows her footsteps because their chasteness calls him; he is entranced by her song because it indicates something holy, because it is the antithesis of the songs of licentious Circe. Comus declares that he has never heard songs quite like this: "But such a sacred, and home-felt delight / Such sober certainty of waking bliss / I never heard till now . . . " (p. 95, ll. 261–63).

Her elder brother appears to repeat essentially the same argument, except that the image which introduces his discussion—that of the need for the star of Arcady as guide—is an image which immediately belies his conclusion. Once chaste, always chaste is *not* the moral of Callisto's story. Hence, there seems to be a tremendous naiveté to the elder brother's declaration that she is physically safe because she is virtuous:

> . . . but yet a hidden strength
> Which if Heav'n gave it, may be term'd her own:
> 'Tis chastity, my brother, chastity:
> She that has that, is clad in compleat steel,
> And like a quiver'd Nymph with Arrows keen
> May trace huge Forrests, and unharbour'd Heaths,
> Infamous Hills, and sandy perilous wildes,
> Where through the sacred rayes of Chastity,
> No savage fierce, Bandite, or Mountaneer
> Will dare to soyl her Virgin purity,
> Do ye believe me yet, or shall I call
> Antiquity from the old Schools of Greece
> To testifie the arms of Chastity?
> Hence had the huntress Dian her dred bow
> Fair silver-shafted Queen for ever chaste,
> Wherewith she tam'd the brinded lioness
> And spotted mountain pard, but set at nought
> The frivolous bolt of Cupid, gods and men
> Fear'd her stern frown, and she was queen oth' Woods.

(pp. 100–101, ll. 418–45)

The nymph with her arrows, "tracing the forests," is Callisto, who is not, however, invulnerably "clad in compleat steel." The images of the star of Arcady and the nymph tracing the forests both point to the myth of Callisto, implying that the judgments of the Elder Brother and the

Lady are thoroughly wrong. But the final image, that of Diana, the virgin goddess, suggests a way in which they are not altogether naive. For Diana was not always considered physically chaste; Neumann and Walker, among others, argue that her physical virginity is a patriarchal virtue.[7] Moreover, Callisto is, in fact, the Arcadian cult name for Diana; the bear into which Callisto is transformed is the goddess's totem animal.[8] Indeed, we know that certain rites which initiated women into their sexuality incorporate many of the elements of the myth. In these rites, woman symbolically gives up her sexuality to the goddess (hence Zeus is disguised as Diana) but it is ceremonially taken by a representative of the god.[9] In certain Athenian ceremonies, young women danced as bears before they left the place of initiation for the real world.[10] The object of such ceremonies is what Mary Ester Harding terms psychological virginity, which is manifested in a woman's independence, her ability to be one-in-herself.[11] Thus it can be argued that there are two possible aspects of this myth, the patriarchalized version given by Ovid which overtly deals with rape and exile, and the matriarchal (for want of a better word), a version which describes a woman's initiation into her sexuality and her acquisition of a psychological virtue of independence.

Thus it can be argued that the Lady and her brother are not altogether naive, for each considered chastity to be a frame of mind. The brother claims that she will be protected by "Wisdom's self," which

> Oft seeks to sweet retired Solitude,
> Where with her best nurse Contemplation
> She plumes her feathers, and lets grow her wings
> That in the various bustle of resort
> Were all to ruffl'd, and sometimes impair'd.

> (p. 99, ll. 375–79)

It is impossible not to see the Platonic image of the feathered soul embedded in this description; the fact that self-knowledge and chastity are juxtaposed is precisely the point.[12] Thus the Elder Brother suggests that her chastity is not, then, merely a physical entity but a matter of knowledge, a frame of mind.

The Lady's emphasis on her frame of mind is demonstrated in her argument with Comus. He threatens to "rape" her with his phallic wand; she replies, "Thou canst not touch the freedom of my minde" (p. 110, l. 662). He then feels it necessary to remind her that she has a body as well and that she must not treat it harshly by forbidding it the "refreshment after toil." She shifts the argument back to the mental sphere by confronting him with his dishonesty and arguing that if he is false, so are the gifts he offers. He replies by appealing to her senses and by arguing that the whole natural world is there only in relation to its inhabitants, wanting them to use it, and, by analogy, that her beauty and virginity also have meaning only if they are used.

Critics of the masque have thoroughly analyzed these arguments, but have failed nevertheless to discern any fixed notion of chastity in the work, largely because they assume that Milton was working in the allegorical mode, and hence that the definition of chastity proposed in the masque involves essentially Christian virtues. Mythic criticism of the masque, however, suggests that chastity is not a moral concept, but a psychological one. Not only does the Lady emphasize throughout that she is more concerned with the freedom of her mind than the ownership of her body, but while arguing with Comus, she invokes chastity in a surprising way when she claims that she is protected by the "sun-clad power of Chastity." The moon is the orb associated with Diana and the Christian notion of chastity; the sun usually symbolizes knowledge, Logos.

By understanding chastity in terms of the Callisto myth, we can account for the paradoxical nature of the Elder Brother's arguments, his naiveté about his sister's physical safety, and yet the proven correctness regarding the power of his sister's chaste frame of mind. We also see more clearly how it is that the Lady can refute Comus's attractive arguments, for he is talking not of some abstract religious doctrine but of the woman's very concept of herself as her own person, not a bit of beauty to be "us'd."

It is this point in the masque that frequently alienates readers who would be sympathetic with the Lady. Often they cannot understand her unwillingness to see the attractive side of Comus's arguments, and accuse her of being precious and prudish. But what if the Lady *had* given in to Comus's arguments, as those who term her "prudish" suggest she should have? Chastity was important in the Renaissance; without that one virtue, all a woman's other virtues were as nothing; with it, Ruth Kelso points out, a shrew might be thought a good wife. The consideration of Renaissance men was, of course, a practical one: only a chaste wife can assure a man that his heirs are really his own. Still suspected under the aegis of Eve, Renaissance woman was expected to prove all her virtues through this one restriction.

Even could the Lady have considered drinking from Comus's sensual cup and experienced the transformation into an animal, could she, in the context of Renaissance society, have achieved Harding's version of psychological virginity? The inevitable answer is no: she has been so indoctrinated into the patriarchal notion of *sun-clad* chastity that she cannot conceive of any other. The sun, of course, symbolizes the patriarchal orientation she exhibits in her arguments, the patriarchal concept of *physical* chastity which replaces the older, matriarchal notion of psychological virginity. In a sense, she does the best she can by remaining unmoved, and independent in that sense, by being her own person, even if that person does not acquire, as she might have in another context, the wholeness indicative of a virgin in the matriarchal sense.

When the Lady rashly tells Comus that he cannot, whatever he does to her body, touch the freedom of her mind, she *professes* that mind is most important. But the transformation of Callisto shows this to be untrue. When Zeus or Hera changes Callisto into a bear, her mind is left untouched and free. Yet it is Callisto's supposedly free mind which causes her to wander toward Arcadia in search of human company; what she meets instead is her death. Clearly one message of the myth is that in a patriarchal culture, physical virginity is important. The positive matriarchal symbolism of the bear, Diana's totem animal, is not powerful enough to overcome man's fear of the animal in himself and in fellow humans, whether the creature is met in the sacred precincts or in the forest. As if aware of Callisto's fate, the Lady does not—in spite of the professed importance of a free mind—allow Comus to have her body, for she is aware of her culture's real priorities as opposed to those she professes.

But this answer generates another question: if physical virginity is the issue here, why does the Lady insist that Comus cannot touch the freedom of her mind? Is that a specious argument? Certainly the myth of Callisto, as well as the status of women in the Renaissance, suggests that this is untrue. I think rather it emphasizes the patriarchal orientation typical of the Lady's whole approach to mores and morality. Certainly she is wrong, but it is the particular way that she is wrong that is interesting. Her argument errs not by being too feminine, too emotional, too illogical, but by being too masculine, too logical.

Comus, on the other hand, seems to be more interested in making the Lady's body part of his revelry, yet he does not, like the typical Zeus figure, simply take what he wants. He does not want to rape her, he wants to *initiate* her, to persuade her to choose his matriarchal vision over her patriarchal one. His very alliance with Circe, Cotytto, and Hecate shows him as a priest of the ancient goddesses— one quite fit to perform the initiation ceremonies Harding describes. The Lady is unable to give in to the experience because of her very "masculine" patriarchal frame of mind, one which she cannot transcend. Consequently Comus must find some other way to achieve the desired result—an initiated woman—without the usual means: sexual intercourse. Comus's wand, an appropriately phallic prop, freezes the Lady, putting her beyond his control. Harding says, after all, that the object of initiation is to free a woman from her *need* of a man, and this is precisely the effect his wand has. It even puts her beyond rescue by the Attendant Spirit.

The masque's ending is the complete turnabout of the myth: instead of being reviled and exiled, the Lady is rescued, not by a male Zeus figure but by Sabrina, who resembles a local aspect of the Great Goddess. She is noted somewhat paradoxically (but in a way often characterizing patriarchal goddesses) for her physical virginity and for her contribution to fecundity among the local shepherds who pay tribute to her. Instead of denouncing the Lady, as Diana did Callisto at the sacred bath, Sabrina brings from her stream a virginity-renewing liquor. By having Sabrina rescue her, Milton emphasizes the extent to which the Lady must depend upon the feminine for guidance.

The Lady is saved by the feminine, not destroyed by it, because she has adhered to the rules enforced by women to protect themselves from the disdain of the patriarchy. Also, the Attendant Spirit's inability to save her, in spite of what he knows, indicates the feminine quarter from which the Lady must draw strength and knowledge to achieve wholeness. Comus's rape with the phallic wand forces the Lady to look to the feminine for help, and it is this which gives her as much wholeness as she can achieve in the Renaissance context.

Being saved by Zeus typically indicates the extent to which a woman's status is dependent upon that given her by man, and this is reflected in the masque. For the fact remains that the Lady inhabits a patriarchal world, so that while Sabrina saves her, the Attendant Spirit presents her to her parents. Since her maidenhead is intact, he credits her with having withstood temptation.

What is curious is that the Lady has nothing to say once the spirit has "rescued" her. It would seem that, in a position where she had to fight her own battles, she was more than adequately equipped with strength, courage, and language, but that these qualities are repressed once she is returned to the normal world. Her experience with Comus has allowed her to test herself. Her subsequent wordlessness suggests that her strength is, however, not much use to her in the patriarchal world; that it is, in fact, either demanded or taken for granted.

We ultimately see that the two versions of the myth are part of the dramatic conflict of the masque. Not only is Milton exploring the conflict of Eros and Logos embedded within the myth, he is also contrasting its matriarchal and patriarchal manifestations. Comus intends to offer the Lady an initiation, but the Lady is too afraid of being raped to allow herself the opportunity. She is not being precious, she is being practical, but Milton nevertheless views her practicality as a limitation.

The Attendant Spirit, in contrast, offers the Lady an entirely different vision of any eventual union she should make—for we must remember that the real Lady Alice is doubtless meant for a more reasonable relationship: marriage.[13] Those "happy climes" toward which the Daemon flies contain the "golden tree" given to Hera as a wedding present. The golden apples of that tree tempted Atalanta to give up her virgin freedom and marry Hippomenes. Like both Diana and Callisto, Atalanta was a great huntress who was militant about her virginity. Her determination to remain virgin is reflected in her consultation with the Delphic Oracle on the subject of a husband. Apollo, Ovid tells us, responded to her question by saying: "You have no need of a husband, Atalanta. You should avoid any experience of one. But assuredly, you will not escape marriage, and then, though still alive, you will lose your own self."[14]

The parallels between Atalanta and Callisto are strong. Both virgin hunters, they are metamorphosed into animals, a lion and a bear, when men dominate them. The difference is that Atalanta agrees to marry Hippomenes after he wins the race by diverting her attention with the golden apples. Atalanta's experience has a message for the Lady who, like both Callisto and Atalanta, values her virginity, who has been threatened with transformation into an animal, and who, it is likely, will be bound for marriage.

Atalanta gives in to her husband when he is moved by an "untimely urge" to make love to her. In effect, she allows him to control her sexuality and does indeed lose her own self as a result. She functions as a monitory image for the Lady, who might take the Christian notion of chastity too literally and unwillingly allow a husband the favors which she would not allow Comus. To do so would be to merely repeat the very experience she refused with Comus. The context of marriage does not make the giving up of one's volition any less a loss of self and integrity.

The myth of Atalanta is related by Venus to Adonis in the *Metamorphoses;* shortly afterwards, Adonis is wounded by the boar. Here one encounters one of these uncanny correspondences (which Jung called "synchronicities") characteristic of myth, when one realizes that the Daemon's next reference to myth in the epilogue is to Venus and Adonis. Hence we see both the appropriateness of allowing the Hesperian tree to recall Atalanta's story, and the implied relationship of the Atalanta and Venus myths. Let us assume that, like the myth of Atalanta, that of Venus and Adonis is about the dangers of a permanent union, for Milton has changed the original myth to suggest permanence: here Adonis waxes "well of his deep wound." Venus told Atalanta's story to Adonis as a warning to avoid "every kind of wild beast which does not turn tail and flee" (Ovid, p. 244). But of course he does not avoid them, and so receives the wound which, in the masque, merely saddens the Assyrian Queen. The animal imagery suggests that Adonis's animal passions ran wild, rather than being governed by the superior knowledge of Venus. This is true to Renaissance thought in a very prosaic way; for women, when they were not being damned for their unchasteness, were credited with a superior, guiding virtue. So that while the Atalanta myth describes a woman's loss of herself via the submission of her sexuality to the demands of the male, the myth of Venus and Adonis shows a future relationship not quite so grim: Venus loses control over Adonis only temporarily, and while she is saddened and deeply affected by his wound, she loses nothing of herself.

The final scenario from mythology presented by the Attendant Spirit as he ascends to his home is the myth of Cupid and Psyche, which Lawrence called the myth of "woman becoming individual, self-responsible, taking her own initiative."[15] Psyche does not originally know who her lover is, but accepts at first a lover she cannot see and therefore does not know. This lack of knowledge, Erich Neumann suggests, symbolizes Psyche's acceptance of the sexual domination of Eros:

> For with all its rapture is this existence in the sensual paradise of Eros not an unworthy existence? Is it not a state of blind, though impassioned, servitude, against which a feminine self-consciousness—and such is the matriarchal attitude of the feminine—must protest, against which it must raise all the arguments that are raised by the sisters? Psyche's existence is a non-existence, a being-in-the-dark, a rapture of sexual sensuality which may be fittingly characterized as a being devoured by a demon, a monster. Eros as an unseen fascination is everything that the oracle of Apollo . . . has said of him, and Psyche really is his victim.[16]

The myth suggests that real love, the kind of love that will inspire the undertaking of impossible tasks, comes only through knowledge, for we are told that only when Psyche sees her lover does she fall in love with Love. This moment of knowledge also marks the change from passivity to activity in Psyche's attitude. Neumann further suggests in his commentary that Psyche's helpers, insofar as they symbolize or indicate the masculine aspects of her character, show that she comes to know the masculine side of herself. Such knowledge, Harding tells us, allows her to be one-in-herself; only then, in this myth of marriage, is Psyche willing once more to subordinate herself to the male god.

The ascent of the Daemon which is paralleled in these three references to myth is not, as Woodhouse points out, a movement from the area of nature to that of grace,[17] and Tillyard's observation that it introduces a new theme, that of marriage, is only partially correct.[18] Instead, the three myths—that of Atalanta, evoked by the Hesperian tree; that of Venus and Adonis; and that of Cupid and Psyche—represent the range of experience, in ascending order, which the Lady may find when she marries.[19]

This ascending sequence is part of the updating of the Callisto myth for Renaissance woman. Psychological virginity, along with the philosophical orientation which it implies in Milton's work, is still the goal for the independent woman, yet being one-in-herself is largely an intellectual quality, as it is embodied in Lady Alice's ability to argue so logically and persuasively. But just as such virginity cannot be achieved through anything even remotely similar to a night of sacred prostitution in the temple, so it must include the reality of marriage. The age demanded chaste brides; it also demanded that women marry. As Ruth Kelso points out, the Renaissance lady is educated for marriage; outside that social structure she has no identity.[20] The woman who would retain her inner independence in the context of marriage must not follow in the steps of Atalanta, a Callisto figure whose fate is not any different for her marrying. To do so is to repeat the experience with Comus within the legalities of marriage.

In a sense, then, Milton offers Renaissance woman two workable prototypes. For the married woman there is the example of Psyche. For the unmarried maiden there is his disguised Callisto, whose mind and virtue protect her body, who nearly achieves psychological virginity through the assertion of her masculine exercise of logic and reason, her sun-clad chastity. Callisto has, in a sense, been patriarchalized. Completely feminine and completely whore in the works of Lefevre, Warner, and Heywood, her transformation by Milton into a receptacle of patriarchal virtues renders her virtuous in the masculine sense, but deprives her of the fullest knowledge of her own femininity.

NOTES

1. The five classical sources that recount the myth of Callisto are Hesiod, the *Homeric Hymns and Homerica*, trans. Hugh G. Evelyn-White (New York: Macmillan, 1914), p. 69; Apollodorus, *The Library of Greek Mythology*, Book III, trans. Keith Aldrich (Lawrence: Coronado Press, 1975), p. 71; Hyginus, *Poetica Astronomica*, Book II, in *The Myths of Hyginus*, trans. and ed. by Mary Grant (Lawrence: University of Kansas Press, 1960), pp. 181–82; Ovid, *Metamorphosis*, trans. Mary M. Innes (Harmondsworth: Penguin, 1955), pp. 61–64; and Pausanias, *Description of Greece*, trans. J. G. Frazer, vol. 1 (London: Macmillan and Co., 1913), p. 419.

2. William Caxton, ed., *The Metamorphoses of Ovid*, 1480, rpt. as vol. 1 of *The Phillips Manuscripts* (New York: George Braziller, 1968); Arthur Golding, trans., *Shakespeare's Ovid*, ed. W. H. D. Rouse (London: Centaur Press, 1961), pp. 45–46, ll. 539–44; George Sandys, trans., *Ovid's Metamorphoses Englished, Mythologiz'd, and Represented in Figures*, 1632, ed. Karl K. Hulley and Stanley T. Vandersall (Lincoln: University of Nebraska Press, 1970), pp. 91–92.

3. Raoul Lefevre, *The Recuyell of the Historyes of Troye*, trans. William Caxton

1503, ed. H. Oskar Sommer (1894; rpt. London: David Nott, 1973); William Warner, *Albion's England* (1612; rpt. New York: George Olms Verlag, 1971); Thomas Heywood, *The Golden Age,* in *The Dramatic Works of Thomas Heywood,* vol. 3 (New York: Russell and Russell, 1964). All of these works were extremely popular.

4. W. N., Gent., *The Barley-Breake, or a Warning for Wantons* (London: Simon Stafford, 1607; rpt. in *Early English Books,* 1475–1640, Ann Arbor: University Microfilms).

5. Charles Grosvenor Osgood, *The Classical Mythology of Milton's Poems* (New York: Henry Holt and Co., 1900), p. 18. Under the "Callisto" entry, Osgood merely catalogues Milton's reference to the "star of Arcady" in the masque; he makes no effort to relate the reference to the whole mythic fabric of the work.

6. John Milton, *A Mask Presented at Ludlow Castle,* in *The Works of John Milton,* ed. Frank Allen Patterson, vol. 1, part 1 (New York: Columbia University Press, 1931), p. 96, l. 289.

7. Barbara G. Walker, *The Woman's Encyclopedia of Myths and Secrets* (San Francisco: Harper and Row, 1983), pp. 58–60, and Erich Neumann, *The Great Mother,* trans. Ralph Manheim (Princeton: Princeton University Press, 1963).

8. Walker, pp. 58–60.

9. M. Esther Harding, *Woman's Mysteries, Ancient and Modern,* (1935; rpt. New York: G. P. Putnam's Sons, 1971), p. 137.

10. Marija Gimbutas, *The Gods and Goddesses of Old Europe* (Berkeley: University of California Press, 1974), pp. 196–200.

11. Harding, p. 102.

12. See John Arthos, "Milton, Ficino, and the Charmides," *Studies in the Renaissance,* 6 (1959), 265. Exploring the Platonic echoes in the *Mask,* John Arthos concludes that Milton's concept of chastity is similar to the kind of self-knowledge implied by Plato's "sophrosyne," which Ficino describes in the epitome to his translation of *The Charmides* as "the light that drives out darkness and helps us to escape the potions of Circe that would transform us into beasts." Arthos points out that "Socrates . . . develops the meaning [of sophrosyne] stage by stage, as reverence, as working for oneself, as doing good, and finally, as knowing oneself."

13. E. M. Tillyard, "The Action of *Comus,*" in *A Maske at Ludlow: Essays on Milton's "Comus,"* ed. John S. Dieckhof (Cleveland: Case Western Reserve University Press, 1968), p. 54.

14. Ovid, p. 240.

15. *The Collected Letters of D. H. Lawrence,* ed. Harry T. Moore (New York: Viking, 1962), vol. 2, p. 615.

16. Erich Neumann, *Amor and Psyche: The Psychic Development of the Feminine: A Commentary on the Tale by Apuleius,* trans. Ralph Manheim (New York: Pantheon Books for the Bollingen Foundation, 1965), p. 74.

17. A. S. P. Woodhouse, "The Argument of Milton's *Comus,*" in *Milton: "Comus" and "Samson Agonistes,"* ed. Julian Lovelock (London: Macmillan, 1975), pp. 61–66.

18. Tillyard, p. 55.

19. Ibid.

20. Ruth Kelso, *Doctrine for the Lady of the Renaissance* (Urbana: University of Illinois Press, 1956), p. 24.

Justice for Margery Evans:
A "Local" Reading of *Comus*

LEAH S. MARCUS

M ARGERY Evans was an illiterate fourteen-year-old servingmaid who, according to her own testimony, was accosted by the roadside in Herefordshire near the Welsh border on Midsummer Eve, 1631, by one Philbert Burghill and his man, raped, robbed, and left at the edge of a village with the warning that she would be killed if she told anyone what had happened.[1] Ignoring the threat, she gave hue and cry, pursued her attackers to a nearby town, and accused them in the presence of numerous witnesses, whereupon she was thrown into jail, without formal charge or the possibility of bond. We have no way of knowing how often such apparent reversals of justice occurred in seventeenth-century England. Surviving records show relatively few convictions for rape, although in the Welsh border country where Margery Evans was attacked, the abduction and ravishing of young virgins was alleged by contemporaries to be commonplace.[2] What makes Margery Evans's case different from others which may have existed is that we have such detailed information about it. The girl was by no means silenced by her imprisonment. Despite her youth and poverty, she appealed for redress to King Charles I and her appeal was heard. His majesty's privy council eventually called upon John Egerton, first earl of Bridgewater, lord president of the Council in the Marches of Wales, to make inquiries into the case.

The earl of Bridgewater took his task quite seriously. Although he was by no means convinced of the truth of her charges, at least at first, he proceeded in an efficient and fair-minded way to disentangle the web of conflicting testimony surrounding the alleged crime, to keep his skeptical underlings in the council of Wales from prejudging the case against her, and to try to ensure her a speedy and impartial trial. Indeed, it is only through his meticulous preservation of the major documents, now part of the Bridgewater Collection at the Henry E. Huntington Library, that we know of the case at all, or of his attempts to obtain justice for Margery Evans.

Beyond its inherent interest, however, the case of Margery Evans is worth our attention for the light it casts on the milieu of John Milton's "MASKE PRESENTED At Ludlow Castle, 1634: On *Michaelmasse night, before the* RIGHT HONORABLE, IOHN *Earle of Bridgewater, Vicount* BRACKLY, *Lord President of* WALES, And one of His MAIESTIES most honorable Privie Counsell."[3] In recent years, critics have been taking increasing interest in the "occasion" of Milton's masque—the immediate political and social circumstances surrounding its performance. The masque was not just a private family celebration, but a political event: part of a ceremonial structure marking the earl's formal installation as lord president of the Council in the Marches of Wales, a judicial body and also the central government's chief administrative unit in Wales. Ludlow town officials were invited to the festivities. So, unquestionably, were officials of the council of Wales itself.[4] What follows is a "local" reading of *Comus*—an exploration of the impact the masque is likely to have had upon council officials who were part of its original audience. The parallels between the Margery Evans case and elements of Milton's masque are significant enough that, for anyone in attendance with particular knowledge of the case, they would have been difficult to evade. For administrative officials of the council of Wales, particularly its chief officers in permanent residence at Ludlow, Milton's masque would have carried a sharp message of criticism. Their laxity and prejudice in the Evans case had been a perversion of justice—a virtue, like courtesy, which belongs as much to "lowly sheds" as to the "Courts of princes" (p. 89). Seen in terms of its 1634 "occasion," Milton's masque becomes a mirror for the judges of the Council in the Marches of Wales: it shows them their own failings by recasting elements of the Evans case in terms of the earl's own family, allowing the judges in attendance to measure their principles as demonstrated in their conduct of the case against the principles in action in the masque.

I

Margery Evans's petition to the privy council is dated August 21, 1633. At that point, the case was already more than two years old. According to her petition, she had been attacked in June, 1631:

> being then about fourteen yeeres of age and travailing out of Hereford Shire into Brecknocke Shire [she] was by the way overtaken by one Philipp [Philbert]

67

Burghill, and John Williams both on horsebacke; and the said Burghill after some questions would haue had the peticioner to ride behind him, on his horse which shee refused to doe, wherevpon the said Burghill vsed many threatening wordes. But not prevaying, hee alighted from his horse with his Sworde drawne, and caused the said Williams to alight, and put the peticioner vpon his horse, whence shee removed her selfe to the grounde three tymes, but in the ende shee was inforced by the said Burghill to ride about a quarter of a mile, where shee alighted and would haue escaped. Then the said Burghill called to Williams to staie her, who caught fast holde on the peticioner and delivered her into the said Burghills handes saieing, Master doe not lett her goe againe, wherevpon the said Burghill did there most inhumanlie and vnchristeanly seize vpon the peticioner and forceablie defloured and ravished her being then not aboue fourteen yeeres of age as aforesaid, and alsoe tooke awaie frome her a bundle of Clothes, a purse and four shillings sixpence in money, Renting and tearing her wascoate and apron in peeces, and afterwordes the said Burghill Compelled your peticioner to ride vpon the same horse to a village called the Bage aboute one mile and a halfe thence distante, and at the townes ende left her vowing her death with his sword in his hand drawne if shee should discover what had passed betweene them.[5]

At this point most victims would probably have held their peace, but Margery Evans did not. She raised "Hue & Cry," overtook the two men in a nearby town called The Hay, Breconshire, and charged them both with "Rape & Fellony" in the presence of the town bailiff and numerous others. Instead of arresting Burghill and his man, however, the bailiff took Margery into custody. He and others attacked and "sore" wounded her and threw her into jail; Burghill procured a warrant from the two local Justices of the Peace—Thomas Price and Sir Henry Williams—to keep her there, and she was released only in the Quarter Sessions twenty-five days later. She was never charged or given a chance to post bond.

After her release from prison, Margery Evans took the enormous step of appealing for justice to King Charles I. She came from a poor family and seems to have had no powerful allies. Nevertheless, her story was compelling enough to precipitate the creation of a special Commission of the Peace, by whom in 1632, "vpon the Testimony of Divers Wittnesses the Said Burghill & Williams were both Found guilty of the Rape & Fellonie." These witnesses included four men who had encountered Margery Evans after the attack as she ran "howleinge and cryinge" along the highway to catch her assailants. One of the witnesses rode her into town, another rode ahead to detain Burghill and Williams until she got there, and heard her charge the two men with robbery and with doing her a "worse turn." He also testified that the bailiff used the young girl "very roughly," pushing her before him toward the town jail (EL 7384,

p. 1). Three women visited her in prison: her sister, a casual acquaintance, and a midwife. They deposed that when they came in, Margery was weeping and leaning her arm upon a table board; she talked despairingly and refused the money one of them offered her. The midwife examined her for evidence of rape, observed that she was torn and bruised, and judged that she had indeed been ravished (EL 7381, 7385). There seems to be little doubt that Margery Evans was telling the truth: that was the conclusion of the royal commission, and the conclusion we modern readers of the 1632 materials are also likely to reach. Although Burghill and his "Adherentes" had threatened her with death, she went down according to the instructions of the attorney general to prosecute Burghill and Williams at Hereford Assizes, March, 1633, only to see her case vanish into air. "Burghills frendes soe prevailed" that the indictment was thrown out by the grand jury at Assizes and never came to trial (EL 7383). She finally appealed to the privy council in 1633 because she was convinced that she and her aunt Elizabeth Evans, who was prosecuting on her behalf, could not get justice against Burghill and Williams in Herefordshire or Breconshire.

The first evidence we have of the earl of Bridgewater's involvement in the case appears in a note from the privy council appended to her 1633 petition. The earl was directed to take some course "For the Releeffe of the Peticioner, and For punisheing of the offendours, if vpon Further Examination of the Busines, there shall be Found Iust Cause for the same" (EL 7383). Charles I's privy council had recently taken up the problem of corruption and undue influence in the courts, and the earl of Bridgewater was a member noted for his special interest in legal matters and fair-mindedness in disentangling them; in addition, he had already been appointed president of the council of Wales. That body had legal jurisdiction over both Breconshire and Herefordshire and was required to "examine, search, and represse" all felonies, including rape, committed within its jurisdiction.[6] So Bridgewater was the logical person to investigate Margery Evans's allegations. In "*Comus* and the Castlehaven Scandal" Barbara Breasted has reminded us that the earl's family had only shortly before been embroiled in a notorious case of its own. His wife's brother-in-law, the earl of Castlehaven, had been tried by the privy council for rape and sodomy, convicted, and executed in 1631. Breasted implies that the Castlehaven affair may have tarnished the reputation of the whole family.[7] But the choice of Bridgewater to handle the Evans case suggests that they were under no particular cloud. Just the opposite may have been true: the dignity with which the earl had dealt with that painful situation may have particularly recommended him as an impartial judge of other similar cases.

When Bridgewater received Margery Evans's petition in 1633, he had no compelling reason to believe her story. He did not have any of the depositions taken in 1632. Nevertheless, from London he quickly set wheels in motion at Ludlow. By September, only two weeks after the petition had been referred to him, Margery Evans's father and aunt had appeared at Ludlow, but Margery herself and the 1632 witnesses had not. The earl's main Welsh associate and confidant while in London was a man named Tymothy Tourneur, who held a judicial post nearby. But Tourneur was not much help in this particular case. For him, the fact that only the father had appeared to testify showed the groundlessness of Margery Evans's claims. He wrote Bridgewater, "Now my Lord I am suspicious the yonge wench is put on by hir Aunt one Elizabeth Evans named in the peticion, a woeman I heare of light conversacion hir husband by hir owne confession lately hanged for felony." The earl's associate seems to have forgotten the important legal principle, reaffirmed in the Castlehaven trials, that a woman's loose life or connections are immaterial to the issue of rape.[8] For Tourneur, it was improbable that a rapist would carry his victim along with him for any distance; Burghill had seduced her, then abandoned her, upon which she had concocted the rape story in order to get revenge or make a bit of money (EL 7386). Margery Evans and her unsavory aunt were merely bothersome distractions from more important business, and the earl's interest in the case, inexplicable. Nevertheless, he states that the council of the Marches "to shew their diligence & desire to discouer the truth" had sent out a request for information from the 1632 commissioners.

During the next several months, the earl of Bridgewater kept up a constant pressure for further investigation of the case. His subordinates at Ludlow grumbled politely and expressed their doubts, but managed a "shew" of diligence; they seem never to have developed much enthusiasm for their task of discovering the truth, and the actual efforts they made were apathetic at best. As early as September 10, 1633, in fact, they seemed to have hoped that their duties in the matter were done: a formal letter signed by Sir John Bridgeman, Chief Justice of Chester and the most powerful man on the council of Wales, along with the three other officials required to be in permanent residence at Ludlow, informed the earl that they had already done what they could. Margery Evans had brought charges of false arrest before them already in November, 1631; a commission had been formed to examine the case and the defendants had denied all charges, "sithence which tyme the plaintiff hath noe further proceeded in her suite" (EL 7387). But what the official letter neglected to mention was that Sir Henry Williams, one of the justices Margery Evans had wished to prosecute for false arrest, was himself a member of the council of Wales, so that her failure to proceed was almost certainly a result of fear or continuing intimidation. Given that obvious possibility, the official letter was more a whitewash than a "shew" of diligence. Sir John Bridgeman followed it up with a private letter of September 20 assuring the earl that "vpon perusall of the bookes at the Counsell I find much more clamour than truthe" (EL 7388).

But Bridgewater himself took a different view of the matter, for within a month, we find, twelve witnesses—four of the six 1632 deponents along with eight others—had appeared before the council, almost certainly by direct order of the earl.[9] New interrogations were undertaken before members of the council at Ludlow on October 9 and 10, and a copy has survived among the earl's papers. It is a vague and puzzling document, full of contradictory evidence, for some of the witnesses had radically altered their testimony since 1632. The two men who had helped Margery Evans catch up with Burghill and Williams both stuck to their stories. Significantly, however, in their 1633 statements we find no mention of the violence done her by the bailiff of the Town of Hay, although the fact that he had used her "very roughly" had figured prominently in one of their 1632 depositions.

There is also considerable uncertainty in the 1633 depositions about what Burghill had actually been accused of. According to the Sergeant of the Mace who had held Margery Evans overnight, she claimed only that Burghill had robbed her, "throwne her downe & *endeauoured* to ravish her [italics mine]"; his seventeen-year-old son and another witness corroborated this statement. On the other hand, two other witnesses claimed that "Margery Evans did giue out in speeches that she was ravished & robbed" (EL 7395, pp. 3–4, 6–9). But the most damaging shift was the complete alteration in the story told by the midwife. She had been the plaintiff's "expert" witness in 1632 and had corroborated the physical evidence of the rape. In 1633 she still admitted she had visited Margery Evans in jail, but claimed that she "did not see any hurts or woundes vpon her" (EL 7395, p. 3). The shift in her testimony, along with the uncertainties produced by town officials of The Hay as to the actual crime Burghill and Williams had been accused of immediately after the fact, made what had been a clear case against the two in 1632 inconclusive by 1633. The 1633 interrogations produced major evidence in Margery's favor: her sister Anne testified that both Burghill and Williams had eventually confessed the rape to her. Since in the 1633 depositions the nature of the crime was unclear, however, Anne's evidence was suspect. She could, in sisterly fashion, have lied to help Margery's case (EL 7395, p. 2).

Not unsurprisingly, Ludlow officials found in the 1633 depositions "litle or nothing of weight" (EL 7389). When Elizabeth Evans asked to see the documents, she was refused. Fearing that the case had again reached an impasse, on November 13, 1633, she dispatched a new petition to the earl of Bridgewater in London beseeching him to examine all the evidence, including the earlier 1632 depositions, with his own eyes. By this time, we can sense, the earl was becoming weary of the business. His subordinates were ready to drop it altogether and he himself had as yet no particular reason to trust the plaintiffs. Nevertheless, as Elizabeth Evans had hoped he would, he doggedly pursued the truth. He wrote a note to himself at the bottom of her petition dated 15 November, 1633, and stating, "These Allegacions for ought appeareth to me may be as well false as true. Yet I haue geuen order to haue the clerke of the Assises (if he be in towne) to come unto me; that I maye the better enforme my selfe of the Latter parte of this Petition." And, at the bottom, "Keepe this" (EL 7391).

Within a week, much useful information had come in. Tymothy Tourneur discovered that Thomas Price, the justice who had thrown Margery Evans in jail, was either Burghill's relative or his very close friend and, Tourneur admitted, "I find none there [at The Hay] willing to examine a rape against Burghill." Although the defendant's reputation was none of the finest, Tourneur was almost laughably reluctant to consider him capable of the crime with which he was charged: "The man (as I heare) is reputed to be of evill behavior but not of soe highe a straine as felony vnlesse he may come somewhat neere a rape" (EL 7394).

Sometime during November or December, the earl also received copies of the 1632 depositions and was therefore able to see for himself the devastating shifts in testimony between 1632 and 1633. As his later conduct in the matter made clear, he then became convinced of what he had probably suspected all along: Margery Evans had indeed been denied justice as a result of Burghill's powerful influence in Hereford and Breconshire. Some witnesses had probably been intimidated or bought off; others, especially town officials of The Hay, who were obliged to get along with their own justices of the peace and bailiff, had probably agreed among themselves to suppress evidence which might lead to the charge of false imprisonment.

The Evans case, then, was a particular example of a more general political problem. The justices of the peace of the Counties of the Marches—the four English counties under the jurisdiction of the Council in the Marches of Wales—and also many of their colleagues within Wales itself, were reputed to be unusually given to placing family and friends above the law, and even members of the council itself were not immune to this failing. Local officials also bore strong resentment against the council of Wales on the grounds that it diluted their own authority. The council was one of the so-called prerogative courts established by royal decree to supplement the common law and ecclesiastical courts, and an affront, in the view of its enemies, against local autonomy, an illegal infringement upon an ancient system of law.[10] But in the case of Margery Evans, local autonomy had produced a miscarriage of justice. The earl of Bridgewater had been charged by the king with strengthening the council and forging it into an agent for judicial reform. Reform was clearly needed: Tourneur's letters to the earl refer cryptically to cases of judicial malfeasance within the court of the Marches, a tricky and dangerous matter which the earl would have to approach with caution, but in which he was clearly determined to proceed.

While the earl was maneuvering against corrupt officials at Ludlow, he was also being showered with petitions from Elizabeth Evans, whose legal expenses had run her deeply into debt. She asked for a court-appointed lawyer since her own had quit, and pleaded to be kept out of debtors prison until the case was concluded. Both petitions were granted. And by February 28, 1634, the earl was ready to report the rape case for trial. Philbert Burghill was actually thrown into jail, and the case brought to trial in Hereford, probably at Lenten Assizes, March, 1634. It is likely that the earl of Bridgewater offered the judge at Assizes, Baron Thomas Trevor, some private words of circumspection about the damaging power of the defendant, for we find that Trevor went far beyond the bounds of ordinary impartiality in order to counteract Burghill's influence and secure a conviction.

But after so much time and effort a conviction was still not to be had. Our report of the trial comes from Elizabeth Evans's own undated account: "At the Last Assizes at Herefford Philbert Burghill gent. and one Williams his man were indicted for a rape and felonie Committed vpon the said Margery and the said Burghill appeared was araigned and the Bill formed and the matter appeared soe odious to Baron Trevour Judg there that hee caused Burghill to bee taken from the barr to the Gaole and in open Assizes, saide hee should not come thence till hee came to be hanged. Yet Neverthelesse the Jury upon life and death acquited him to the Admiration of the Judge and the whole Court" (EL 7403). We can imagine the almost unbearable frustration his acquittal must have caused all those concerned with the prosecution. Although Elizabeth Evans may have magnified the response of the "whole Court" out of her own sense of outrage, it seems clear that Judge Trevor and other officials regarded the plaintiffs' evidence as decisive. Perhaps the jury was put off by Trevor's melodramatic attempts to instill horror; more likely, they voted as they did out of intimidation or misplaced loyalty.

But that dramatic scene was not the end of the matter of Margery Evans. Having escaped hanging, Burghill sought revenge for the indignities he had suffered and preferred a bill against Margery, Elizabeth, and others in the Court of Star Chamber. Elizabeth again petitioned for help. Since this suit was a clear case of harassment and Bridgewater was a member of the Star Chamber, he was surely able to get it quashed according to her desire by certifying to the Lord Keeper his "honorable opinion touching the said matter" (EL 7401).

But there had still not been justice for Margery Evans. In her final petition, Elizabeth mentions that the defendants in her suit for false arrest had begun to send letters "vnto her, and her friendes thereby pretending that they have much desired a finall end." Having seen what the earl's power could accomplish, they were now anxious to reach some accommodation. She also notes that the earl had offered to settle the case himself in person when he next came to Ludlow, "for the good of all parties therein" (EL 7401). And that is probably what happened. The earl was in residence at Ludlow by early July, 1634. Then, if not earlier, he probably gathered all those concerned to settle the matter as fairly as he could. Such a solution would have been quite characteristic of him. He was reticent by nature and tried to avoid open confrontations, preferring to use his power indirectly and get his way by quiet and adroit maneuvering. Elizabeth would certainly rather have had public vindication in court. But the case must have been settled at least to the plaintiff's partial satisfaction, for there appear to have been no more petitions. It would have gone quite against Elizabeth's adamant nature to have given up her long struggle before at least some of her goals had been achieved. And it would have been equally unlike the earl and his usual meticulousness to have allowed a matter which had assumed such political importance to go unresolved. It is possible that the matter was still pending at the end of September, 1634, when the earl was formally installed as lord president of the Council in the Marches of Wales. But it is more likely that during the summer before his installation he had managed to achieve at least some measure of justice for Margery Evans. He had also served notice on the members of his own council of Wales and the justices of the peace and other county officials under his wide jurisdiction that his own notions of justice were considerably more stringent than some of theirs.

II

Comus used to be viewed as "essentially private and personal," a rather intimate entertainment for the Egerton family, "some of them watching it and others performing in it."[11] But the evening of the earl's installation as lord president of the Council in the Marches of Wales is not likely to have afforded much time for privacy and intimacy. The night of *Comus's* performance was an important state occasion. The newly reconstituted council of Wales over which the earl was to preside had been greatly expanded and new members may well have formally assumed office that Michaelmas Night along with the earl himself. Furthermore, Michaelmas was a holiday traditionally associated with public administration, justice, and the law. It was the day on which rents and various types of contracts came due, on which autumn court sessions were opened, and on which magistrates and other local officials assumed the burdens of office.[12]

As William B. Hunter, Jr., noted ten years ago, *Comus* is shaped to reflect the major themes of the liturgy for its festival occasion. The collect for the feast of St. Michael and All Angels beseeches God for angelic succor and defense like that offered by Milton's Attendant Spirit; the epistle recounts St. Michael's battle with Satan from the Apocalypse, a cosmic prototype for the lesser struggle against Comus and the spirits of darkness in the masque.[13] The gospel for the day is Matthew 18:

> At the same time came the disciples unto Jesus, saying, Who is the greatest in the kingdom of heaven? And Jesus called a little child unto him, and set him in the midst of them, And said, Verily I say unto you, Except ye be converted, and become as little children, ye shall not enter into the kingdom of heaven. Whosoever therefore shall humble himself as this little child, the same is greatest in the kingdom of heaven. And whoso shall receive one such little child in my name receiveth me. But whoso shall offend one of these little ones which believe in me, it were better for him that a millstone were hanged about his neck, and that he were drowned in the depth of the sea. (Matt. 18:1–6)

This text has obvious applications to the three children of *Comus,* implications also for the masque's theme of the humbling of those who sit in judgment. But in the lessons proper for Michaelmas, the subjects of law and public administration are considerably more prominent. Milton's masque looks forward to the lesson for Evensong in its praise for the earl of Bridgewater. That text moves from children to fathers, particularly fathers in positions of political authority: "Let us now praise famous men, and our fathers that begat us. The Lord hath wrought great glory by them through his great power from the beginning. Such as did bear rule in their kingdoms, men renowned for their power, giving counsel by their understanding, and declaring prophecies: Leaders of the people by their counsels, and by their knowledge of learning meet for the people, wise and eloquent in their instructions" (Ecclus. 44:1–4). As Hunter has noted, Evensong was very likely celebrated some time after the performance of the masque, so that the closing passages of *Comus* which honor

the parents through the successful trial of the children would lead naturally into the liturgical lesson.[14]

Even more important for our purposes, however, is the lesson proper
for Matins, which offers a portrait of the man fit to "sit on the judges'
seat" and "declare justice and judgment" (Ecclus. 38:33): "But he that
giveth his mind to the law of the most High, and is occupied in the
meditation thereof, will seek out the wisdom of all the ancient, and be
occupied in prophecies. He will keep the sayings of the renowned men:
and where subtil parables are, he will be there also. He will seek out the
secrets of grave sentences, and be conversant in dark parables. He shall
serve among great men, and appear before princes: he will travel through
strange countries; for he hath tried the good and the evil among men"
(Ecclus. 39:1–4).

Comus is itself a "dark" and "subtil" parable which reaches beyond the
literal in a number of directions, and I would not want to argue that all
interpretation of the work must be based on a reconstruction of its "local"
significance at Ludlow in 1634. On the other hand, I would urge that
such reconstruction has just as strong a claim to our attention as more
"detached" and universalist approaches to the work—particularly given
that the very possibility of our attaining such interpretive generality is
more and more being called into question.[15] Milton's masque is steeped
in passages from the liturgy which invite a measuring of actual judges
and administrators against an ideal of judicial office. On Sept. 29, 1634,
members of the council of Wales in attendance at the Ludlow performance were confronted with an entertainment which reenacted on a higher
social and intellectual plane elements from one of their most significant
and troublesome cases of the previous year—a case in which they had
forgotten their role as protectors of the downtrodden and had neglected
the "little ones" in favor of the powerful, in which they had shown small
capacity to read "dark" evidence or to try "the good and the evil among
men" before proceeding to judgment.

Like many other holidays, Michaelmas was celebrated with a period of
ritual inversion, a "lawless hour" when ordinary social rules were
suspended and masters and servants exchanged places. That ritual pattern is enacted in *Comus.* The Lady is confronted with a situation very
much like that faced by Margery Evans, whose case had absorbed so
much of the earl's and the council's attention in the year before the
masque. The part of the Lady was performed by an earl's daughter while
Margery was only a servingmaid, but the two were nearly the same
"tender age," Margery fourteen at the time of the assault and the Lady
fifteen at the time of the masque's performance. As Margery Evans had
been, the Lady of *Comus* is traveling westward through the lonely and

dangerous border country from England toward Wales. Like Margery Evans, she finds herself alone, although her solitude, unlike Margery's, is temporary and accidental. Like Margery Evans, she is accosted by a seducer who is well established in his territory with a network of local connections: Burghill had powerful friends; Comus has his own court and an obedient retinue of monsters. Both encounters are associated with a time of holiday license and misrule. Margery Evans was ravished on a Midsummer Eve, a festival celebrated much as Mayday Eve was, with sex-play and rowdiness in the forest. We may wonder whether Burghill saw himself merely as carrying on the time-honored traditions of Midsummer when he encountered Margery Evans by the road. Comus's action is associated with Michaelmas Eve, a time which had its own traditions of disorder and lawlessness, but the masque's menacing revelry suggests Midsummer celebration as well. Wakes and morrises in the forest like those of Comus and his crew were more characteristic of Midsummer, when Margery Evans was traveling, than of Michaelmas Eve, when the Lady of *Comus* is.[16]

Of course Comus's attempted seduction is orchestrated very differently than Philbert Burghill's had been. Burghill began by questioning Margery Evans and trying to coax her to ride along with him, using force when words failed to gain him his object. Comus is considerably more subtle, as befits the Lady's station and sophistication. He lures her to his palace through lies and "bleare illusion," appearing to her in the guise of a simple shepherd. But he too must eventually resort to force, immobilizing her in her chair when she attempts to escape. The Lady is not raped—the parallel with Margery Evans breaks down there. But she is placed in an atmosphere of seemingly gratuitous sordidness and increasing sexual menace. Comus likens her first to a near victim of rape— Daphne fleeing Apollo (p. 137). Then, along with the "cordiall Iulep heere / that flames, and dances in his christall bounds" (p. 139), he offers her a chance to surpass "love-borne Hellena," an actual victim of abduction who complied with her abductor. But when it becomes evident that his sugared language has failed to move her, he takes a harsher tone which suggests the possibility of physical aggression against her: he vows not to "suffer" her "meere morrall babble" further (p. 157) and touches the cup to her lips—seemingly in an effort to compel her to drink.[17] At that moment her brothers and the Attendant Spirit enter, the brothers break the glass and disperse the seducer's retinue, but Comus escapes (as, alas, did Burghill) and the Lady remains "in stonie fetters fixt, and motionlesse" (p. 159).

Our sense of the full sordidness of the Lady's situation comes only at the moment she is freed from it, when Sabrina describes the "marble

venom'd seate / smeard with gums of gluttenous heate" (p. 173) in which
the Lady has been imprisoned. The precise meaning of these lines has
been a matter for much controversy lately, but most readers seem to
agree that there is something distinctly seamy about them: Milton's
vagueness, if anything, heightens the atmosphere of sexual innuendo by
allowing our imaginations to work on the images he provides.[18] There
have been various attempts to account for the poet's strategy here, among
them Barbara Breasted's suggestion that Milton designed the masque as
a cleansing ritual which deliberately elicits comparison with sordid
details of the Castlehaven scandal of 1630–31 in order to demonstrate the
Egerton family's purity, their refusal to assent to pressures like those
which had destroyed their relatives.[19] But for officials of the council of
Wales attending the Ludlow performance, the Margery Evans case would
have provided a much more immediate and devastating analogue to the
action of the masque. The Lady is not ravished, as Margery Evans had
been, but she is placed in a position of similar powerlessness, trapped
and surrounded with defiling substances, and brought into involuntary
association with a pollution she despises. Her fate is not that of a victim
of rape, but her predicament is morally identical. A young aristocrat of
obvious and unquestioned innocence appears in a position analogous to
that of a mistrusted servingmaid, and the effect is to open up the whole
question of volition in cases of physical compulsion. In light of the Evans
affair, Milton's masque becomes a strenuous exercise in legal and moral
judgment.

If Comus had sexually assaulted the Lady while she was in his power,
would the assault have compromised her innocence and virtue? If the
earl of Bridgewater's colleagues on the council were to judge the Lady by
the same standards they had applied to Margery Evans, the answer
would be yes. Those who reviewed the case seem to have made the
age-old but illogical assumption that a young girl who has been attacked
must in some way have provoked the encounter, and must therefore share
the blame. But one of the key points in the Evans case was "the disagreement of the woman at the tyme of the act . . . soe that the issue is not vpon
th'external Act whether it was done or not but whether it was in the
patient voluntary or compulsary" (EL 7399, p. 1). The Lady argues,
similarly, that she is guiltless so long as she has reserved her mental
assent. Although the enchanter can "immanicle" her "corporall rind," he
cannot "touch the freedome" of her "mind" (p. 136). It is worth noting at
this point that the Lady's specific praise for virginity (the "sage / And
serious doctrine of Virginitie," [p. 155]), as opposed to chastity, appears
only in the 1637 version of Comus, by which time the masque's immediate
Ludlow occasion would have faded from people's minds, and its audi-

ence expanded to encompass numerous readers with no knowledge of the Evans affair. In 1634, the central issue in *Comus* is not virginity, but chastity, a virtue which does not automatically perish along with the loss of virginity, even in cases of rape, despite the assumption of some in power at Ludlow that it did. In making hue and cry and demanding justice against her violators, Margery Evans had implicitly assumed the separability of virginity and chastity, and had been thrown in jail for her pains, her charges ignored or turned against her. But the eloquent appeal of the Lady—particularly *this* Lady, the daughter of the lord president of the Council in the Marches of Wales—is less easy to ignore. She has assumed the position of one of the powerless, and her voice becomes their voice. She challenges her listeners to abandon their stereotyped view of rape victims in particular, but her words expand to echo and interpret afresh the gospel message for the day. Those holding high office at Ludlow are reminded that he who comes to the aid of a child, or any of the similarly mute and powerless, is serving no less a person than God himself, and that failure to render such assistance is an offense against the Lord: "Whoso shall receive one such little child in my name receiveth me. But whoso shall offend one of these little ones which believe in me, it were better for him that a millstone were hanged about his neck, and that he were drowned."

In her rebuttal of Comus, the Lady carries the revolutionary implications of the gospel text even further:

> If every Iust man that now pynes with want
> had but a moderate and beseeminge share
> of that which leudly-pamper'd luxurie
> now heap's vpon some fewe, with vast excesse
> natures full blessinge, would be well dispenst
> in vnsuperfluous even proportion.

(p. 153)

This speech seems to convert the "leveling" of holiday inversion into a principle for social reform. Indeed, recent historians and anthropologists have have suggested that ritualized holiday overturn of the normal social hierarchy may at times have helped to precipitate reform rather than simply reinforcing a status quo.[20] Whether or not we are willing to take her language as advocating a permanent readjustment of the social hierarchy, the Lady's words do call attention to the gospel for the feast of Michaelmas and its injunctions for the abasement of the powerful. In terms of the masque's emphasis on law and administration, her arguments suggest, at the very least, that anyone concerned with "greatness" should "humble himself" as a little child, place himself imaginatively in the position of those he is to serve, and model his dispensing of justice upon the example of nature herself, who meant her "full blessings" to be allotted in "even Proportion," not lavished on a privileged "few" and withheld from others equally or more deserving.

Comus offers a prototype of such judicial humility in the quiet figure of Sabrina. She is a supernatural being, but so curiously modest and unassuming in Milton's portrayal that we may be tempted to overlook her historical connections with judgment and the law. Sabrina carries many associations pertinent to the larger political task the earl of Bridgewater faced in Wales, as well as to the more limited subject of rape. According to standard accounts, she had herself been the guiltless product of a forced sexual relationship, her mother a hostage of war, the daughter cast into the flood despite her own innocence, and transformed into the goddess of the Severn. Even as a goddess, she encountered the problem of rape: according to one contemporary retelling of her story, her nymphs were so frequently ravished by satyrs emerging from Dean Forest that she finally had to appeal for help to Neptune.[21] Like the earl of Bridgewater, she has been tempered for her "office" of helping "ensnared chastitie" by a difficult past that has taught her empathy for such victims. The earl of Bridgewater's colleagues may or may not have remembered Sabrina's traditional association with rape, but the most experienced of them were well aware of her significance as a political symbol. As the River Severn, Sabrina spanned the border between England and Wales; she was also a famous judge who presided over border disputes. Her political role in contemporary mythography was very much like the actual role of the Council in the Marches of Wales in that she mediated between a central authority and local officials—there are interesting analogues between the masque's portrayal of Sabrina and legal briefs prepared by the earl and officials of the Council in the Marches of Wales as part of their defense of council jurisdiction.[22] It would be foolhardy to argue that Sabrina must be interpreted as a figure for the earl of Bridgewater himself, but that is very likely the way she would have been taken by council officials viewing the masque. And again, the effect would have been strongly admonitory. Sabrina's talents and special strengths are precisely those that all the judges involved in the Evans affair with the exception of the earl himself had very notably lacked. She thus offers a paradigm for the proper handling of such cases, and for the doing of justice in general—an example not of censoriousness, but of compassion, offering the victim not judgment but grace. She is above all constructive: her quiet ministrations give the Lady not merely formal vindication, but a reaffirmation of her integrity and self-worth.

There is an essential radicalism about this "local" 1634 *Comus*. A "noble Peere of mickle trust, and power" charged with the governing of a vast territory inaugurates his term in office with an entertainment that displays his own daughter in a situation of leering sexual jeopardy, like that of a lowly servingmaid. The Bridgewater family had suffered in the past from an involuntary association with sordidness and sexual violence. They had been forced into a recognition of their—and everyone's—vulnerability to such associations through the Castlehaven affair. The ability to tolerate a basic kinship with the less fortunate is a virtue particularly appropriate for Michaelmas and its gospel lesson of humility. By allowing his daughter to be placed in the symbolic position of one of the powerless, the earl of Bridgewater demonstrated his willingness to humble himself even as he called his subordinates to task. The masque offered a stringent challenge to all those officials who served under the earl of Bridgewater's authority—even a veiled threat to the most corrupt among them, men like the justices Thomas Price and Sir Henry Williams, who had openly flouted the law to protect Burghill and themselves. According to the gospel for the day, such offenders deserved to be cast into the depths of the sea—suffer for their guilt a fate like that Sabrina had suffered in her innocence. But despite the undertone of warning, the masque's overriding purpose, like Sabrina's and like the earl of Bridgewater's in his usual conduct of business, is constructive. The judges in the audience on Michaelmas Night, 1634, at least those who cared enough to consider themselves good judges, and who in the previous months had yet obstructed or failed to further the tedious case of an ignorant fourteen-year-old girl who had complained of rape and robbery, would have gone away from the masque considerably chastened. A new legal term at Ludlow—the Michaelmas term—was about to begin under the authority of the council's new president, and with the earl of Bridgewater, the masque's praise of him and his family suggests, there would commence a new order of rectitude. As the judges of the Council in the Marches of Wales took up their busy round of trials, depositions, and other related matters, they would be afforded an immediate opportunity to act upon what they had learned on Michaelmas Night and rededicate themselves to the impartial discovery of truth.

How are we to locate the poet John Milton in terms of this "local" interpretation of his masque? He had excellent sources of information about the earl's interest in reform, his quiet struggles against conservative elements in the central government, and his larger goals for Wales.[23] But we have no evidence beyond that provided by the masque itself that Milton knew of the Evans case, and cannot therefore argue with certainty that Milton *intended* the powerful "local" meaning that the masque would have carried for Ludlow officials on Michaelmas, 1634. My own inclination is to believe that Milton did know what he was doing—the correspondences between the case and the masque seem too striking to have been arrived at through mere chance. But it is equally possible that the earl himself or one of his associates suggested some of the masque's major motifs without necessarily giving the poet full information about the case. There are many other cases of official collaboration in the seventeenth-century masque. One of the earl's close associates and political allies had, for example, taken a major role in the planning of the 1634 production of *The Triumph of Peace*.[24] What Milton himself may or may not have intended in *Comus* is far less significant than what he actually produced—a work that displays a rare, unsettling capacity to dismantle the traditional discourse of authority. Milton himself has frequently been accused of an obtuseness toward women rather like that demonstrated by the judges of the council of Wales, who were unable or unwilling to make the imaginative leap required for empathy with a powerless young girl. In *Comus,* Milton makes that leap, constructing a set of paradigms for the conduct of public office around the womanly figure of Sabrina, whose strength in the undoing of injustice comes in part from her recognition of not only female, but human, weakness.

NOTES

1. I owe special thanks to the Henry E. Huntington Library, where I received a research fellowship to work on the Bridgewater materials, and to the Research Board of the University of Illinois for a travel grant. This article is a condensed and much revised version of my earlier "The Milieu of Milton's *Comus:* Judicial Reform at Ludlow and the Problem of Sexual Assault," *Criticism,* 25 (1983), 293–327. My thanks to the editors of *Criticism* for permission to reprint segments of the original article.

2. See J. S. Cockburn, "The Nature and Incidence of Crime in England 1559–1625: A Preliminary Survey," in *Crime in England* 1550–1800, ed. J. S. Cockburn (Princeton: Princeton Univ. Press, 1977), pp. 55, 58; and Suzanne Gossett's survey of other evidence in "'Best Men are Molded out of Faults': Marrying the Rapist in Jacobean Drama," *ELR,* 14 (1984), 305–27. For rape and abduction in Wales and the border country, see G. Dyfnallt Owen, *Elizabethan Wales: The Social Scene* (Cardiff: Univ. of Wales Press, 1962), p. 47.

3. John Milton, *A Maske: The Earlier Versions,* ed. S. E. Sprott (Toronto: Univ. of Toronto Press, 1973), p. 37. I have quoted the 1637 title page, because it gives the most elaborate exposition of the occasion. Further quotations from the masque will be from the Trinity and Bridgewater versions in Sprott, and will be indicated by page number in the text.

4. On the public nature of the masque and the attendance of local officials, see John Creaser, "'The present aid of this occasion': The Setting of *Comus,*" in

David Lindley, ed., *The Court Masque* (Manchester: Univ. of Manchester Press, 1984), pp. 111–34. For previous work on aspects of the masque's occasion see John D. Cox, "Poetry and History in Milton's Country Masque," *ELH*, 44 (1977), 622–40; William B. Hunter, Jr., "The Liturgical Context of *Comus*," *ELN*, 10 (1972), 11–15; James Taaffe, "Michaelmas, the 'Lawless Hour,' and the Occasion of Milton's *Comus*," *ELN*, 6 (1968–69), 257–62; Maryann Cale McGuire, *Milton's Puritan Masque* (Athens: Univ. of Georgia Press, 1983); and David Norbrook, *Poetry and Politics in the English Renaissance* (London: Routledge and Kegan Paul, 1984), chaps. 8–10, pp. 195–284. There is also valuable work still in manuscript, especially William S. Miller, Jr., "The Mythography of Milton's *Comus*" (Ph.D. dissertation, University of California at Berkeley, 1975) (I am indebted to Stephen Orgel for this reference).

5. HEH EL 7382. All my quotations from the 1633 petition to the privy council are from this page; further quotations from the Bridgewater collection at the Huntington Library will be indicated by manuscript number (and where necessary, page number) in the text. For quotations, I have expanded contractions and occasionally added punctuation to aid readability. All quotations from the Bridgewater collection are made by permission of the trustees of the Henry E. Huntington Library, San Marino, California.

6. Quoted from the printed version available in Rymer's *Foedera*, 2d ed., XIX (London: for J. Tonson, 1732), 350. See also EL 7571.

7. See Barbara Breasted, "*Comus* and the Castlehaven Scandal," *Milton Studies*, 3 (1971), 201–24. In n. 18, p. 222, Breasted suggests even that the two-year gap between the earl's appointment to the presidency of Wales and his actual taking of office may have been caused by the earl's or the privy council's embarrassment over the Castlehaven affair. On the scandal, see also Rosemary Karmelich Mundhenk, "Dark Scandal and the Sun-Clad Power of Chastity: The Historical Milieu of Milton's *Comus*," *SEL*, 15 (1975), 141–52; and William B. Hunter, Jr., *Milton's Comus: Family Piece* (Troy, N.Y.: Whitson Pub., 1983).

8. See the account of the trial in T. B. Howell, ed., *A Complete Collection of State Trials*, III (London: Hansard and Longman, 1816), col. 414.

9. In her petition dated Nov. 13, 1633, Elizabeth Evans states that she had appeared at Ludlow "by your Lordships order" (EL 7391); since she was the plaintiff and the most anxious to continue the case, it is likely that the witnesses were also ordered to appear.

10. The standard works on the council of Wales are Penry Williams, *The Council in the Marches of Wales under Elizabeth I* (Cardiff: Univ. of Wales Press, 1958); and for our period, Caroline A. J. Skeel, *The Council in the Marches of Wales*, Girton College Studies II (London: Hugh Ries, 1904); this study is a bit superficial in its examination of documentary evidence: see also the information in A. H. Dodd, *Studies in Stuart Wales*, 2d ed. (Cardiff: Univ. of Wales Press, 1979), esp. pp. 44–62; Dodd, however, portrays the earl and the council in a very negative light. On council jurisdiction see also J. S. Cockburn, *A History of English Assizes*, 1558–1714 (Cambridge: Cambridge Univ. Press, 1972), pp. 35–38. There is also a wealth of material in the Bridgewater collection.

11. David Wilkinson, "The Escape from Pollution: A Comment on *Comus*," *Essays in Criticism*, 10 (1960), 32–33.

12. Taaffe, p. 259.

13. See Hunter, "Liturgical Context," pp. 13–15. I have used the 1634 Book of Common Prayer and for biblical quotations the Cambridge Pitt Brevier edition of the King James Bible. As Hunter notes, all those in attendance at the masque would also attend church on Michaelmas; the lessons would therefore be quite fresh in the audience's minds.

14. Hunter, "Liturgical Context," p. 15.

15. For recent Renaissance examples of the questioning of "universalist" interpretation, see Jonathan Dollimore and Alan Sinfield, eds., *Political Shakespeare: New Essays in Cultural Materialism* (Ithaca: Cornell Univ. Press, 1985); and John Drakakis, ed., *Alternative Shakespeares* (London: Methuen, 1985). I cannot explore the theoretical issues within the confines of the present essay, but would argue that the critical relativism that is becoming dominant in Shakespeare studies is equally applicable to the case of John Milton, despite his strong authorial voice in many of his works, a voice that is itself constructed out of various contingent and historically determined forces.

16. Except, of course, that their revelry is associated with harvest. For Michaelmas customs, see Taaffe and for a hostile contemporary account of Mayday and Midsummer lawlessness, sexual license, and their ill effects, see [Henry Burton], *A Devine Tragedie Lately Acted, Or . . . Gods judgements upon Sabbath breakers* (n.p., 1636). According to contemporaries, both sylvan holidays caused a rise in the bastardy rates.

17. I am following John Shawcross's general line of interpretation in "Two Comments," *MQ*, 7 (1973), 97–98. I am indebted to my friend and former colleague Michael Lieb for suggesting the reading, and for encouraging me to expand my understanding of how the issue of rape may relate to the masque.

18. See the lively exchange of views in *MQ* beginning with J. W. Flosdorf, " 'Gums of Glutinous Heat': A Query," *MQ*, 7 (1973), 5; continuing with Shawcross and Stanley Archer, " 'Glutinous Heat': A Note on *Comus*, l. 917," *MQ*, 7 (1973), 99; Edward Le Comte, "By Sex Obsessed," *MQ*, 8 (1974), 55–64; Shawcross's response, pp. 56–57; and Jean-François Camé, "More about Milton's Use of the Word 'Gums,' " *MQ*, 9 (1975), 51–52.

19. See Breasted, pp. 201–5.

20. See Barbara A. Babcock, ed., *The Reversible World: Symbolic Inversion in Art and Society* (Ithaca: Cornell Univ. Press, 1978), pp. 13–36; and Natalie Zeman Davis, "Women on Top: Symbolic Sexual Inversion and Political Disorder in Early Modern Europe," reprinted with minor revisions in Babcock, pp. 147–90, from Davis, *Society and Culture in Early Modern France* (Stanford: Stanford Univ. Press, 1975); see also her chapter "The Reasons of Misrule," *Society and Culture*, pp. 97–123.

21. See Milton's *History of Britain*, ed. George Philip Krapp, in *The Works of John Milton*, X (New York: Columbia Univ. Press, 1932), pp. 15–16; Drayton, *Works*, ed. J. William Hebel, IV, *Poly-Olbion* (Oxford: Blackwell, 1933), pp. 128, 137;

and Jack B. Oruch, "Imitation and Invention in the Sabrina Myths of Drayton and Milton," *Anglia*, 90 (1972), 60–70.

22. Drayton, *Poly-Olbion*, pp. 98–99, 107, and 137. For the jurisdictional dispute see the sources in n. 10 above, especially Skeel, pp. 133–44; my discussion in *The Politics of Mirth: Jonson, Herrick, Milton, Marvell, and the Defense of Old Holiday Pastimes* (Chicago: Univ. of Chicago Press, 1986), chap. 6, "Milton's Anti-Laudian Masque"; and "Milieu," n. 1 above. There is a connection between Sabrina's function of "bridging the waters" and the earl's name Bridge-water which naive allegorists among the audience might have found significant.

23. See my extended discussion of the earl in *Politics of Mirth*, chap. 6.

24. That associate was William Noy. See Stephen Orgel and Roy Strong's account of the planning of the masque in *Inigo Jones: The Theatre of the Stuart Court* (Berkeley: Univ. of California Press, 1972), I, 63–66.

Courting Urania:
The Narrator of *Paradise Lost*
Invokes His Muse

NOAM FLINKER

I N his various invocations to Urania, the narrator of *Paradise Lost* presents a statement about his attitude toward the Muse which includes a series of metaphors with striking psychosexual elements. Although at first the narrator makes no attempt to indicate either the name or sex of Urania, he eventually does provide this information and in so doing approximates the psychic stance of a lover courting his beloved. The narrator's request for inspiration from Urania thus partakes of many of the hopes, fears, and desires that ordinarily characterize the emotional disposition of a lover. The following account of his relations with the "Heav'nly Muse" begins by analyzing his presentation of the sexist behavior of Satan and Adam (during a temporary lapse) in order to suggest how far such prejudice is from the mind of the poet himself. There follows an examination of a series of classical allusions to ancient blind poets and prophets who were all traditionally involved with one or another aspect of the feminine spirit. After a final methodological digression into psychoanalytical literary criticism, it will be possible to return to *Paradise Lost* and demonstrate just how and why the narrator courts his Muse.

A contrast between the narrator and other lovers in the epic suggests a sensitivity to the feminine consciousness in general and to problems implicit in the relations between the sexes in particular. Satan's incestuous affair with his daughter Sin provides the most striking instance of manipulative masculinity based upon Petrarchan rhetoric. The narrator describes Sin as a "Snakie Sorceress" sitting "Fast by Hell Gate" (2.724–25).[1] Satan then addresses her with less than courtly delicacy: "What thing thou art, thus double-form'd," he asks and concludes that he has never seen "Sight more detestable then . . . thee" (ll. 741, 745). Sin reminds him of times past when she was "deemd so fair / In Heav'n" (ll. 748–49), "shining heav'nly fair, a Goddess arm'd" (l. 757). In the following description of her incestuous affair with Satan, Sin deliberately presents herself as a lovely heroine who "with attractive graces won / The most averse" (ll. 762–63), that is, Satan himself. The result, of course, was that

> Thy self in me thy perfect image viewing
> Becam'st enamour'd, and such joy thou took'st
> With me in secret, that my womb conceiv'd
> A growing burden.
>
> (ll. 764–67)

Satan's response to this tale oozes with the self-centeredness of the courtly lover paying false compliments to his lady for his own selfish purposes:

> Dear Daughter, since thou claim'st me for thy Sire,
> And my fair Son here showst me, the dear pledge
> Of dalliance had with thee in Heav'n, and joys
> Then sweet, now sad to mention.
>
> (ll. 817–20)

Sin presents herself as an active heroine who wins rather than tempts her lord. Her horrible description of how her son, Death, raped her (ll. 790–95) makes her appear most unfortunate. Perhaps there is some irony here since the rhetoric of Sin's speech appeals on an emotional level that ignores the reasons for her physical condition, obviously a measure of her moral state. Much more blatant, however, is the hollowness of Satan's response. The contrast between his initial view of Sin ("thing . . . double-form'd . . . detestable") and his corrected comments ("Dear Daughter . . . fair Son . . . joys / Then sweet") reveals him as manipulative and conniving as well as lying and insincere. Satan as courtly lover, in love with his own perfect image, Sin, is the real villain in this passage, and part of his villainy stems from his selfish treatment of the female.

Adam as lover is less egotistic and manipulative than Satan, albeit not without implicit shortcomings. Under pressure he unconsciously allows himself to imitate Satan's rhetoric. Thus, after the fall, it is Eve who first realizes the futility of their "mutual accusation" with no "self-condemning" (9.1187–88). Adam initially responds in terms that reflect strident and exaggerated notions of male supremacy. His irrationality directs him and he uses misogynistic commonplaces to attack Eve in such a way as to make himself sound slightly ridiculous:

> O why did God,
> Creator wise, that peopl'd highest Heav'n
> With Spirits Masculine, create at last
> This noveltie on Earth, this fair defect

> Of Nature, and not fill the World at once
> With Men as Angels without Feminine,
> Or find some other way to generate
> Mankind?
>
> (10.888–95)

Eve, however, begs his forgiveness nonetheless, and "soon his heart relented / Towards her" (10.940–41). Alastair Fowler points out that Adam's "almost comical multiplication of griefs accords with his present despair, but hardly with M[ilton]'s own more rational view." Adam's "culpable sentiments and erroneous opinions"[2] present him as a foolish man who prefers to take refuge in the clichés of misogyny rather than examine himself closely. Diane Kelsey McColley has recently contrasted traditional medieval and Renaissance antifeminist platitudes with similar materials in *Paradise Lost* and shown that "by shifting these commonplaces from their usual position in drama and commentary—that is, in descriptions of Eve before the Fall—to the speeches of fallen and despairing Adam, Milton exposes their distortions."[3] Only after Eve has brought him back to his senses by begging forgiveness does Adam abandon his somewhat ridiculous rhetoric and call for an end to their bickering:

> But rise, let us no more contend, nor blame
> Each other, blam'd enough elsewhere, but strive
> In offices of Love, how we may light'n
> Each others burden in our share of woe.
>
> (10.958–61)

This is the admirable Adam, but we cannot forget his recent foolishness, especially in the heroic light of Eve's emotional maturity.

In direct contrast to Adam's insistence that only "Spirits Masculine" inhabit heaven, the narrator of *Paradise Lost* addresses a Muse who is explicitly feminine.[4] Although he eschews such fallen modes of approaching Urania as the Petrarchanism of Satan or the momentary misogyny of Adam, the narrator makes no effort to avoid alluding to sexual tension in general or to his own masculinity in particular. As he adopts a series of metaphors that link inspiration and sexuality as part of his way of appealing to Urania, the narrator must be in close contact with fallen role models for would-be lovers. This is not to discount the admirable aspects of the prelapsarian Adam, but rather to insist upon the poet's awareness of less savory patterns of behavior. His exclusion of prostitution, *amour courtois,* and Petrarchan modes of courtship is presumably no less applicable to his own involvement with Urania than to the sleep of the "Blest pair":

                              not in the bought smile
Of Harlots, loveless, joyless, unindeard,
Casual fruition, nor in Court Amours
Mixt Dance, or wanton Mask, or Midnight Ball,
Or Serenate, which the starv'd Lover sings
To his proud fair, best quitted with disdain.

                                        (4.765–70)

The Petrarchan or courtly lover who rarely treats his beloved as an individual with real emotions but prefers to see her as an extension of his own ideas, needs, and ideals is thus condemned in *Paradise Lost.*

Prelapsarian sexuality in Eden is crucial to the spirit of the epic. Straightforward treatment of Adam and Eve's activities in "thir inmost bowr" underlines the mutual nature of ideal love according to the narrator:

                         into thir inmost bowr
Handed they went; and eas'd the putting off
These troublesom disguises which wee wear,
Strait side by side were laid, nor turnd I ween
Adam from his fair Spouse, nor *Eve* the Rites
Mysterious of connubial Love refus'd.

                                        (4.738–43)

These lines define the narrator's position with regard to propriety and lovemaking. The emphasis, as in Milton's divorce tracts, is on the rapport between the two. Adam and Eve go "handed" into the bower after their evening prayers and proceed to "the Rites / Mysterious of connubial Love." That is, sexual intercourse is part of their general conversation and its spiritual intensity. The "Rites" suggest a closeness to God as well as themselves without detracting from the fundamental fleshliness of the experience. Of course, it is true that Adam, not Eve, initiates them, so that man's hierarchical superiority is implicit, but both of them seem concerned with the mutuality of their actions. Adam does not turn away from Eve nor does she refuse. In one sense, both of them are somewhat passive here since their actions are described in terms of what they do not do. Implicit is the assumption that by not turning away from Eve, Adam must have initiated "the Rites" which she did not refuse. In the context of the seventeenth century, it is striking to find such willingness to envision near equality for even idealized relations between the sexes.

His presence as observer in the text about lovemaking in the bower is indicative of the narrator's own delicacy in such matters. He knows enough about the details of the scene to tell us that "Handed they went" (l. 739) but has to guess ("I ween" [l. 741]) about the "Rites / Mysterious of connubial Love." That is, he is explicitly present in the text but much less obviously a witness in Eden. Such delicacy carries over to his own relations with Urania. By praising the mutuality of Adam and Eve's prelapsarian love, he is commenting on how he ought to relate to the feminine spirit that inspires him. He wants to be as direct and open as possible about the purity and propriety of sexuality ("Hail wedded Love" [l. 750]) and yet he must not insist too stridently on his own inspired participation lest he overstep his bounds and anger his Muse. He thus settles for textual rather than real presence in the bower, just as his metaphors about inspiration suggest sexuality, but only obliquely.

By inverting the Petrarchan model of a fleshly woman as source of poetic inspiration, the narrator of *Paradise Lost* presents inspiration in the guise of a feminine spirit. Whereas for Petrarch Laura was a specific woman who inspired him to write verse, Urania, while feminine, is hardly flesh and blood for Milton's narrator. She signifies the inspiration itself, and yet she does so in language and allusions that ascribe to her a femininity which resembles that of a Beatrice if not of a Laura. That is, the narrator alludes to a range of perceptions about the psychosexual relations between poet and inspiration which the reader can attempt to unravel in search of the full statement about inspiration and the making of an epic poem.

One of the narrator's more conspicuous qualities is his simultaneous attraction toward and fear of Urania.[5] He first asks her to "Sing" (1.6) and then invokes her "aid to my adventrous Song" (l. 13). This careful, formal address is followed by a request for instruction, illumination, and support from a Spirit that would seem to link the "Heav'nly Muse" with God. In Book 3 we learn that the Muse has taught the narrator "to venture down / The dark descent, and up to reascend, / Though hard and rare" (ll. 19–21). Thus far the narrator's presentation of inspiration seems quite straightforward. Then, however, he speaks of nightly visits to "Thee Sion and the flowrie Brooks beneath" (l. 30) and mentions his constant recollection of various blind poets and prophets of the ancient world:

> nor somtimes forget
> Those other two equal'd with me in Fate,
> So were I equal'd with them in renown,
> Blind *Thamyris* and blind *Maeonides,*
> And *Tiresias* and *Phineus* Prophets old.

$$(3.32–36)$$

These ancient figures help the narrator to conceal much of his apprehension about his Muse while apparently expressing his admiration. Roger H. Sundell sees the lines as "troublesome." He points to lack of "precision" in the passage and even goes so far as to "doubt whether the speaker does in fact recall properly the fate of Thamyris."[6] The relevant echoes and traditions that these ancient blind poets and prophets should suggest are problematic. To some extent, the narrator may seem to be less than clear about his point, but this is probably deliberate. His choice of the relatively obscure name Maeonides for Homer may be an indication of an attempt to deter the casual reader. That is, the "troublesome" quality of these lines can be read as a ploy on the part of the narrator, which puts off some readers in order to "fit Audience find, though few" (7.31).

Investigation of the background here reveals a pattern somewhat disguised by the obscurity of both Thamyris and Maeonides, just as it throws light upon the relevance of Tiresias and Phineus beyond the simple fact of their blindness. Each of the four ancients is associated with complex interrelations between inspiration and light on the one hand and sexuality on the other. The narrator is very concerned about the audacity of his request for inspiration and realizes that his ancient predecessors courted a great deal of danger on their various quests for poetic or prophetic achievement. By failing to distinguish between the four, he establishes ironic tensions between the surface association of blindness that they each call up and the less well known background details of their various personal histories.

Thamyris of Thrace provides the narrator with a model of fallen and unsuccessful poetry bound up with lust. Eustathius, bishop of Thessalonica, whose twelfth-century commentary on the *Iliad* Milton might have used,[7] provides the following information about Thamyris in commenting upon Homer's reference to the mythical poet: "Thamyris, son of Philemon, a Thracian of surpassing beauty, was first stricken with shameful desire. He, being most accomplished in song, strove with the Muses, stipulating that should he win, he might have sexual intercourse with all of them, and should he lose, they could deprive him of whatever they wished."[8] When the Muses won the contest, they took Thamyris's eyes, destroyed his voice, and maddened him for their reward. Pausanias provides a rationalist's interpretation of the significance of this Thracian's fate in a passage that is particularly relevant to Milton: "My view is that Thamyris lost his eyesight through disease, as happened later to Homer. Homer, however, continued making poetry all his life without giving way to his misfortune, while Thamyris forsook his art through stress of the trouble that afflicted him."[9] As a poet, then, Thamyris was unsuccessful in continuing to compose after his blindness, as opposed to Homer, who did. In addition, at least part of the poet's presumption was his lust for the Muses, punished with blindness and a loss of inspiration.

This allusion in the invocation to light encourages the reader to

contemplate that which the narrator insists he never forgets: Thamyris
and Maeonides (Homer). A series of ironies informs these references.
The careful reader must wonder why it is that these two obscure names
are singled out for such exalted mention. Beneath the surface is the
distinction between the two made by Pausanias. Although the narrator
makes no attempt to differentiate, he must be aware of the differences,
especially with regard to inspiration, poetic productivity, and sexuality.
By including both poets as worthy of emulation, the narrator may be
suggesting that he would combine the productivity of Homer with the
sexuality of Thamyris but the balance between these models is not
explicitly indicated.[10]

The blind prophets, Tiresias and Phineus, add models of spiritually
enlightened men whose physical blindness was accompanied by inner
vision not available to ordinary mortals. Both of them were also in
dangerous conflict with varying aspects of the feminine principle. Tiresias
lost his vision as a direct result of offending an angry goddess in terms of
sexual propriety (Juno according to Ovid, Athena in Callimachus).[11]
Phineus was blinded by Zeus for revealing the secrets of the gods. He was
also plagued by the Harpies, horrible feminine creatures who took away
his food whenever he wanted to eat and left a terrible stench on whatever
they did not finish. Like Sin, the Harpies represent the feminine principle at its most repulsive. Phineus, their victim, suffered at their hands
because of his indiscretion in revealing heavenly secrets. Apollonius
Rhodius makes it clear that Phineus learned his lesson before the Argonauts saved him from his tormentors. Phineus had the gift of prophecy
"and he reverenced not a whit even Zeus himself, for he foretold unerringly
to men his sacred will."[12] When the Argonauts finally arrived and offered
to save Phineus from the Harpies, he told them of their future but was
suitably careful not to reveal too much. The Harpies had taught him that
"not everything is it lawful for you to know clearly; but whatever is
heaven's will, I will not hide. I was infatuated aforetime, when in my
folly I declared the will of Zeus in order and to the end. For he himself
wishes to deliver to men the utterances of the prophetic art incomplete,
in order that they may still have some need to know the will of heaven"
(p. 123 [2.311 ff.]).

As with Homer and Thamyris, the fact that the narrator wishes to be
"equal'd" with Tiresias and Phineus adds to the impression that these
ancient blind men represent different aspects of a poet willing to risk
incurring the wrath and remorselessness of an inspirational feminine
spirit as a necessary part of spiritual endeavor. As the narrator proceeds
to invoke the inspiration of his "Heavenly Muse," he alludes to the
dangers he risks, lest she attack him in ways similar to those of Athena,

Juno, and the classical Muses. He is willing to explore a full range of sexual attitudes within himself in considering his Muse, from the lust of Thamyris to the accidental voyeurism of Tiresias to the indiscretion and subsequent victimization of Phineus. The potential threat of the feminine spirit is part of the narrator's consciousness as he asks for enlightenment but trembles at the risk. Just as he already shares the fate of blindness that characterizes all four of the ancients, the narrator wishes to share the fame and success of Homer, the dreams of Thamyris, and the prophetic skills of Tiresias and Phineus. The obscurity of the references to Thamyris and Maeonides parallels the darkness of their blindness, while the full knowledge of who they were corresponds to the narrator's hope for poetic success. The prophetic component of the reference suggests that the narrator also wants the clairvoyance of Tiresias along with Phineus's hard-won consciousness of just how much it is permitted to reveal so that he can "deliver to men the utterances of the prophetic art incomplete."

Contemporary psychoanalytic theory suggests a technique for reconstructing the narrator's experience with his sources of inspiration. In a simultaneously provocative and forbidding article translated as "The Unbinding Process," André Green speaks of a process whereby a writer "converts certain representations into the written word. But he hides the point from which these representations originate, and delivers only those he is willing to transmit through the scriptural process."[13] For Green, the psychoanalytical critic must then unbind the literary text in search of the "nucleus of truths" (p. 19) hidden by the writer. Green's object, however, is beyond the public realm of a literary text and somewhat closer to what he calls "a nonliterary reality" (p. 21). He would have only professionally trained analysts venture beyond the literary into "the practical field of psychoanalysis" (p. 12). Nevertheless, Renaissance "faculty psychology," such as that used by Adam to explain Eve's dream, provides a means of applying some elements of Green's methodology without the tools of modern psychoanalysis. Such a technique is useful for explaining the narrator's allusion to the blind poets and prophets of classical antiquity in particular, and his attitude to sexuality and inspiration in general.

Adam's attempt in Book 5 to comfort Eve after her Satanic dream presents commonplaces of Renaissance thought about what modern psychology calls the unconscious. He explains

> that in the Soul
> Are many lesser Faculties that serve
> Reason as chief; among these Fansie next
> Her office holds; of all external things,

Which the five watchful Senses represent,
She forms Imaginations, Aerie shapes,
Which Reason joyning or disjoyning, frames
All what we affirm or what deny, and call
Our knowledge or opinion; then retires
Into her private Cell when Nature rests.
Oft in her absence mimic Fansie wakes
To imitate her; but misjoyning shapes,
Wild work produces oft, and most in dreams,
Ill matching words and deeds long past or late.
Som such resemblances methinks I find
Of our last Eevnings talk, in this thy dream,
But with addition strange: yet be not sad.
Evil into the mind of God or Man
May come and go, so unapprov'd, and leave
No spot or blame behind.

(5.100–119)

Robert Burton summarizes seventeenth-century psychological theory in a similar way: "*Phantasy,* or imagination ... is an inner sense which doth more fully examine the species perceived by *common sense,* of things present or absent, and keeps them longer, recalling them to mind again, or making new of his own. In time of sleep this faculty is free, and many times conceives strange, stupend, absurd shapes.... In *melancholy* men this faculty is most powerful and strong, and often hurts, producing many monstrous and prodigious things.... In Poets and Painters, *imagination* forcibly works, as appears by their several fictions, anticks, images.... In men it is subject and governed by *reason* or at least should be."[14]

An important distinction between this theory and the views of a more modern psychology such as Freud's is the role of "reason" as a conscious censor. For Milton there was no need or desire to repress "Fansie" but only the requirement that the conscious mind govern it. The "Wild work" of Fansie could thus, for example, have all of the sexual energy of Thamyris as long as the narrator did not allow his awareness of these feelings to affect his consciousness of what is pure and proper. While Thamyris lusted after the flesh of the Muses and failed to satisfy his passion, Homer treated his sources of inspiration with epic decorum and was able to create despite his blindness. The narrator of *Paradise Lost* had to tap all his sources in a decorous manner that would bring him his inspiration without rejecting the approach of Thamyris, or even the experiences of Tiresias and Phineus. We can read his desire to equal the renown of the four as a subtle statement about his own binding of a "nucleus of truths" about the sexual and spiritual elements of inspiration hidden in ancient tradition which the reader must unbind to understand the basis of the relationship with Urania.

Although the sexual aspects of the metaphor of inspiration in *Paradise Lost* have been discussed by various scholars,[15] the significance of this material to the narrator's relationship with Urania has not been treated explicitly. While, in John Shawcross's words, the poem "simulates an act of generation,"[16] its narrator undergoes a sublimative experience as he encompasses a Thamyran interest in sex with his Muse and the dangers of prophecy into a more Homeric emphasis on inspiration where sexuality is a motivating force integrated into the spiritual mode. The blind narrator treats a series of tensions between ordinary natural experience and the transcendent intensities of the spirit. The blindness that he laments becomes a means of reaching out to the celestial world that he could not perceive with "mortal sight":

> Thus with the Year
> Seasons return, but not to me returns
> Day, or the sweet approach of Ev'n or Morn,
> Or sight of vernal bloom, or Summers Rose,
> Or flocks, or heards, or human face divine;
> But cloud in stead, and ever-during dark
> Surrounds me, from the chearful wayes of men
> Cut off, and for the Book of knowledge fair
> Presented with a Universal blanc
> Of Natures works to mee expung'd and ras'd,
> And wisdom at one entrance quite shut out.
> So much the rather thou Celestial light
> Shine inward, and the mind through all her powers
> Irradiate, there plant eyes, all mist from thence
> Purge and disperse, that I may see and tell
> Of things invisible to mortal sight.
>
> (3.40–55)

Loss of light in blindness or "ever-during dark" leads via night to a heavenly light somehow "happier farr," just as the epic as a whole traces a pattern whereby the paradise that is lost is, with the grace of the Son, recovered within man's soul. The narrator's experience thus parallels that of Adam.

The route from blindness to heavenly or "Celestial light" is traversed by the narrator with the guidance of Urania. She appears to him at night and he ascribes much of the credit for his song to her:

> If answerable style I can obtain
> Of my Celestial Patroness, who deignes
> Her nightly visitation unimplor'd,
> And dictates to me slumbring, or inspires
> Easie my unpremeditated Verse.
>
> (9.20–24)

Urania brings the "Celestial light" to the narrator at night and thus clarifies the spiritual potential of all creation. Although "night" is often associated with Satan and his domain in *Paradise Lost*, the unfallen can assign a very different valence to that which Belial describes as "the wide womb of uncreated night" (2.150). Before retiring to "thir inmost bowr" (4.738) Adam and Eve pray to God in a paraphrase of Psalm 74.16: "Thou also mad'st the Night, / Maker Omnipotent" (4.724–25). Night and light are not opposites but rather different aspects of God's creation. It is fallen experience that introduces dualism into the universe and much of the justification of the "wayes of God to men" (1.26) is a vision of the potential unity in the cosmos despite the divided nature of postlapsarian reality. The narrator combines "Celestial light" with Urania's nightly visits which are not entirely distinct from Thamyris's desire for the Muses.

The application of the ancient poetic-proleptic model for inspiration is, of course, to be found in the narrator's relationship with Urania. Here too, the "Wild work" of Fansie which might suggest an explicitly sexual reading of the nightly visitations, must be "unapprov'd" by Reason and then reapplied in a sublimated form. The mythic allusions to the four blind ancients help to establish a psychological struggle within the narrator that is best understood as the wise shaping of the unconscious or Fansie by his artistic "reason" which recognizes the importance of sexuality and wishes to govern or mold this "Wild work" (5.112) into an acceptable artistic experience. Just as the invocation to light in Book 3 juxtaposes ordinary and celestial light, so sexuality for Thamyris has to be sublimated into inspiration by Urania to achieve its proper valence. This is reinforced by the sexual aspects of vision for the Renaissance. According to William Kerrigan, "the word 'propagation' referred to the multiplication of the visual image in the spatial continuum between the object and the eye — seeing was making love to the world."[17] This kind of natural seeing was thus sublimated by the blind narrator into an intense relationship with a feminine Muse who allowed him to replace the physical with the spiritual.

The narrator's inner progression from "Day" to "Celestial light" and from Thamyris to Homer and Urania is also parallel to the basic movement of Milton's epic from a prelapsarian paradise to "A Paradise within

thee, happier farr" (12.587). Milton's speaker alludes to a process akin to
Freudian sublimation in which Thamyran lust and Homeric inspiration
are combined with Christian piety and vision to achieve the inspiration
of Urania. The reader's unbinding of the narrator's text can retrace this
process without venturing out of literary discourse into the domain of
psychoanalytical practice.

As the creator of a text about the significance of inspiration for writing
epic poetry, the narrator of *Paradise Lost* suggests that sexuality is part of
an anti-Petrarchan strategy that reverses some of the basic assumptions
in the Italian tradition about poetry and courtship. In particular, this
involves the inversion of the topos of woman as source of inspiration
which so often can become part of a sexist technique for seduction. Thus
instead of an actual woman providing the means of inspiring her lover to
creative productivity, the psychosexual roots of the sublimation process
are presented to the reader to encourage an imitation of the narrator's
own successful search for inspiration in the production of his poem. In
order for this to happen, it is necessary to lay bare the traditional mythic
sources that link sexuality and poetic endeavor to recreate the sublimative
process for the narrator. This requires the unmasking of Thamyran lust,
Tiresian voyeurism, and Phinean indiscriminate delivery of prophetic
utterance as part of the poet's voluntary self-exposure to the nexus
between sexuality and inspiration that is mythically presented as lust for
the Muses, seeing the nudity of Athena, or unerring prophecy of Zeus's
will. Whereas the sexual interest of the Petrarchan poet in a particular
woman led via a sublimative process to a poetic production which was in
turn a plea for the lady's sexual favors, Milton's narrator courts Urania in
order to transfer the powers of sublimated inspiration from her mythical
sources into his poem. The Petrarchans made inspiration a means of
aspiring to sexual seduction. Milton had his narrator open himself to a
full range of mythic sexuality in order to intensify his inspiration.

NOTES

1. All citations from Milton's poetry in my text are to *The Complete Poetry of
John Milton,* ed. John T. Shawcross, rev. ed. (Garden City, N.Y.: Doubleday and
Co., 1971).

2. *The Poems of John Milton,* ed. John Carey and Alastair Fowler (London:
Longmans, Green and Co., Ltd., 1968), p. 972.

3. Diane Kelsey McColley, *Milton's Eve* (Urbana: Univ. of Illinois Press,
1983), p. 29.

4. This theme is mentioned in passing by Marcia Landy ("Kinship and the
Role of Women in *Paradise Lost,*" *Milton Studies,* 4 [1972], 7) as part of her

discussion of "the basic notions of masculinity and femininity which are to pervade *Paradise Lost.*" Although she associates "the male principle . . . with 'absolute rule,' the feminine with 'submission,'" she does admit that "'Inspiration' is female" but makes no attempt to relate this to her previous statement that "for Milton the poet is male, 'creator' and 'author.'" She refers to the four blind ancients, but ignores their crucial relationship to femininity: "furthermore past poets are exclusively masculine, as the quotation [3.35–36] indicates, reinforcing the masculine creative principle." Maureen Quilligan's *Milton's Spenser: The Politics of Reading* (Ithaca: Cornell Univ. Press, 1983) treats the gender of the Muse in terms of the problem of the fit reader (pp. 218–26). Professor Quilligan's interest is in a recurrent motif in Milton's poetry to the dismemberment of Orpheus, and its relationship to the reader of *Paradise Lost.*

5. Cf. Michael Fixler's discussion of "this numinous dread" in "Milton's Passionate Epic," *Milton Studies,* 1 (1969), 184. B. Rajan puts it delicately in "Osiris and Urania," *Milton Studies,* 13 (1979), 229: "Though the light is the source of all singing, there is a presumption in singing of the light."

6. Roger H. Sundell, "The Singer and His Song in the Prologues of *Paradise Lost,*" *Milton and the Art of Sacred Song,* ed. J. Max Patrick and Roger H. Sundell (Madison: Univ. of Wisconsin Press, 1979), p. 75.

7. Although the Columbia edition of Milton's works includes a series of references to Eustathius in Milton's "Marginalia" (*The Works of John Milton,* 18 [New York: Columbia Univ. Press, 1938], pp. 277, 281, 282, 285, 287, 292, 294, 295, 299, 303, 305), Maurice Kelley and Samuel D. Atkins have thrown considerable doubt on the validity of the assumption that these marginal references in works by Pindar and Euripides can be ascribed to Milton. They challenge the Pindar annotations in "Milton and the Harvard Pindar," *Studies in Bibliography,* 17 (1964), 77–82, and question the one remaining reference in Euripides in "Milton's Annotations of Euripides," *JEGP,* 60 (1961), 684. Thus Harris F. Fletcher's assumptions about Milton and Eustathius are, perhaps, open to question: "Eustathius' Homer seems to have been well known to Milton before he read Pindar intensively, as the references to it, which show thorough familiarity with that colossal edition, point toward its acquisition either before Cambridge or very early in his residence there" (*The Intellectual Development of John Milton,* 2 [Urbana: Univ. of Illinois Press, 1961], p. 287). Nevertheless, the edition would have been available to him even if he did not own it. Jackson Campbell Boswell's *Milton's Library: A Catalogue of the Remains of John Milton's Library and an Annotated Reconstruction of Milton's Library and Ancillary Readings* (New York: Garland Publishing, Inc., 1975) lists Eustathius with a question mark (item 578, p. 98). It would appear then, that if Milton did not write the notes in his Euripides or own the copy of Pindar now at Harvard, he could at least have been familiar with the materials referred to by the real annotators.

8. Eustathii Archiepiscopi Thessalonicensis, *Commentarii ad Homeri Iliadem Pertinentes,* ed. Marchinus van der Valk, 1 (Leiden: E. J. Brill, 1971), p. 462 (298.38–41). Sixteenth-century editions of Eustathius were published in Rome and Basel and many of them included a volume with an index by Matthaeus

Devarius, the nineteenth-century copy of which is more readily accessible today than the original Renaissance editions (*Index in Eustathii Commentarios in Homeri Iliadem et Odysseam* [Lipsiae: J. G. Weigel, 1828]). The entry for Thamyris in Devarius's index directs the interested reader to the above passage. Thus a Renaissance scholar with considerably less erudition in Greek than Milton need not have read all of Eustathius to gain access to his comment on Thamyris. I am indebted to Ms. Chava Boyarin and Prof. Robert Sider for the translation of the Greek.

9. *Pausanias: Description of Greece with an English Translation,* tr. W. H. S. Jones and H. A. Ohmerod (1926; rpt., London: Wm. Heinemann Ltd., and Cambridge: Harvard Univ. Press, 1966) II, 357 (IV [Messenia], xxxiii.7).

10. Cf. William Kerrigan, *The Sacred Complex: On the Psychogenesis of "Paradise Lost"* (Cambridge: Harvard Univ. Press, 1983), pp. 170–81, for a discussion of the relation between Muse and mother which I find relevant to Thamyris. Kerrigan's brilliant psychological treatment of Milton and his epic includes a comment on Orpheus that is also true of Thamyris, another "Thracian bard": "the overwhelming fact about the Thracian bard, so obvious that we have tended not to see, is that his mother is his Muse" (p. 178). According to Eustathius, Thamyris was the son of Eratos, one of the nine Muses (*Commentarii* . . . , vol. 3 [Leiden: E. J. Brill, 1979], p. 107 [817.32]). Thus his lust for the Muses was, among other things, incestuous and oedipal. Part of the resolution of the oedipal complex in Milton's narrator must therefore include incorporating Thamyris into his sense of self.

11. Ovid, *Metamorphoses,* 3.316–38; Callimachus, "Hymn Five: On the Bath of Pallas," in *Callimachus: Hymns and Epigrams,* tr. A. W. Mair (1921; rpt. Cambridge: Harvard Univ. Press and London: Wm. Heinemann Ltd., 1960), esp. p. 121.

12. *Apollonius Rhodius: The Argonautica,* tr. R. C. Seaton (1912; rpt. London: Wm. Heinemann and New York: G. P. Putnam's Sons, 1919), p. 115 (2.178 ff.).

13. André Green, "The Unbinding Process," *NLH,* 12, (Autumn, 1980), 24–25.

14. Robert Burton, *The Anatomy of Melancholy,* ed. Floyd Dell and Paul Jordan-Smith (New York: Tudor Pub. Co., 1927), pp. 139–40 (I.i.2.7).

15. E.g., John T. Shawcross, "The Metaphor of Inspiration in Paradise Lost," in *Th' Upright Heart and Pure: Essays on John Milton Commemorating the Tercentenary of the Publication of "Paradise Lost,"* ed. Amadeus P. Fiore (Pittsburgh: Duquesne Univ. Press, 1967), pp. 75–76; Michael Lieb, *The Dialectics of Creation: Patterns of Birth and Regeneration in "Paradise Lost"* ([Amherst]: Univ. of Massachusetts Press, 1970), pp. 44–46; Kerrigan, *Sacred Complex,* pp. 157–92.

16. Shawcross, "Metaphor of Inspiration," p. 83.

17. William Kerrigan, "The Fearful Accommodations of John Donne," *ELR,* 4 (1974), 357.

Eve and the Arts of Eden

DIANE McCOLLEY

NEAR the end of Book 4 of *Paradise Lost,* we come upon a multilayered image. Innocent Adam and Eve, in the innermost, flower-decked, awe-encircled bower, sleep in one another's arms. Squatting by Eve, Lucifer turned Satan turned toad pours poison into her ear in the form of "Vain hopes, vain aims, inordinate desires / Blown up with high conceits engend'ring pride." Standing over Satan, the archangel Ithuriel, searcher-out of truth, touches him "lightly" with his spear, causing *him* literally to be "blown up"—as is fitting for the father of gunpowder—into his own shape, an inadvertent frog-prince or reverse Orgolio, for "no falsehood can endure / Touch of Celestial temper, but returns / Of force to its own likeness" (4.807–19).[1]

The literalness of Satan's exposure by the literalization of conceits; his explosion at the touch of truth; Milton's literal reading of Genesis; and his attention everywhere to the letter of language—etymology, metaphoric roots and branches, connotations spelled and dispelled, links of sense (as image) with sense (as significance)—beg us to reconsider the modern notion that the meaning of literature has little to do with the words. Ithuriel, with his more vocal companion Zephon, has been instructed to "Search through this Garden; leave unsearched no nook" (4.789). He is therefore a *figura* of the reader, and his searching and disclosing comments on the critic's calling, which is to search every nook of the poem and, using the tempered spear of interpretation "to [which] must be added industrious and select reading, steady observation, [and] insight into all seemly and generous arts and affairs,"[2] to free the text to do its work.

Ithuriel's spear contrasts to Satan's, also presumably of celestial temper, but misused to prop the "uneasy steps" of "unblest feet" (1.295, 238): a figure of limping prosody on unhallowed grounds; and Satan's spear contrasts also to Moses' rod, which struck water out of rock, and Aaron's, which flowered. It becomes the wand he holds before his pseudo-decent steps while he is disguised as an inquisitive cherub, which like Comus's charming rod can only disable. It is a staff of unlife.

Satan throughout is a cautionary kinetic emblem for the act of interpretation. We can use the spear of criticism to free the text, or we can pour venom, distempers, phantasms, and high conceits into it. "Throughout," William Kerrigan comments, "Milton associates Satan with violence to inward parts."[3] And whenever there is a rape of the text, Eve gets the worst of it. Whenever we appropriate the poem for our own textual politics, we exploit Eve as text object. She is the receptacle of our inordinate desires, sexual frustrations, marital discontents; vain hopes, yearning dreams, unattained ideals; patronizing tolerance for her pretty, wifely officiousness, her feminine whims, her bustling household economy, or whatever we think we do well to put up with in those around us; matronizing resentment for the endowment of less dignity than Adam's and less power than God's; acclaim for poaching God's sole reminder that "it is he that hath made us and not we ourselves"; anger for millennia of hierarchic thinking; helplessness. It is part of the poem's work to elicit these feelings so that we can recognize them and take due action. But it is an even larger part to help us recognize and love goodness, of which unfallen Adam and Eve are both brimfull. How is it that we find so much fault with them and miss so much grace? If we let our modern habit of looking for base motives obscure their goodness, their "Truth shall retire / Bestuck with sland'rous darts, and works of Faith / Rarely be found" (12.535–37). The cure is to exercise a principle of interpretation Milton calls "*candor:* whereby we cheerfully acknowledge the gifts of God in our neighbor, and interpret all his [her] words and actions in a favorable sense"—unless he [she] attempts to "seduce or deter us from the love of God and true religion."[4] The antidote for "sland'rous darts" is the celestial temper of Ithuriel's spear.[5]

Those actions which enter into a woman, rather than issue out of her—let us hope Milton thought—defile not. The action that issues out of Eve in Book 9 and ushers in murder, war, cruelty, malice, fraud, disease, and death contrasts utterly to the acts that issue out of her before that choice is made. We see in her the ability to make it, but unless we see in her also the ability to choose joy we turn food to wind and lose the means Milton offers to repair the world we know and the selves we are as he says his and our aim is.[6]

There is a curious lack of faith in, and even desire for, undefiled joy in the modern world, a sense that a life of rampant blessedness would somehow be less interesting than one providing opportunity for, or tolerance of, or warfare against, every vice. For Milton sin was defect and inanition. People who think that perpetual paradise (or what may be regained of it) would be dull must not only be undelighted by sensuous and erotic pleasures, as Joseph Summers and Edward Le Comte and others have richly declared,[7] but must not much care for music, gardening, angels, children, ethically considered scientific inquiry, the glory of the Lord, the funniness of animals, good government, good care of the whole earth, or conversation of the most felicitous reciprocity, dense with poetic shoots. Adam and Eve have plenty to do and be, without "vain hopes, vain aims." Yet it seems to me that on the whole more attention has been paid to Satan than to Adam and Eve and more to what is wrong with Eve and Adam than to what is right with them. And one of the things that is right with them is that they are splendid artists, blithely engaged in acts that are pregnant with all the arts that do not hurt the earth, nor the community, nor the soul, but, contrariwise, enhance them all: poetic speech, music, the rudiments of dance and dramatic play, and, in the form of horticulture, all visual and fruitful beauty-making. God's sculpturing of Adam and Eve, and the jewel-tones of his Garden, wrought with the luminous detail of a van Eyck painting (4.236–66, for example) portray God as Artifex and his human images as artists, as all of these Edenic arts show them to be. In all of them, Eve takes at least equal part with Adam, and often she takes the lead. Does the fact that Eve's questing imagination is subsequent or rather precedent to Adam's tempered reasoning, both needs it and feeds it, make it any less vital to the poet who intends his song to soar above the Aonian mount?

I should like therefore to consider Eve's part in the arts of Eden, beginning with what I perceive as her role as the embodiment of Milton's defense—and, at her fall, his critique—of poesy.

While Eve in Book 8, attended by graces and amoretti, visits bud and bloom that "touched by her fair tendance" gladlier grow, Adam attempts to tell a not very sympathetic "Interpreter Spirit" how he feels about her. She is a handmade present from God, his "last, best gift," but God may have subducted "more than enough" from *him.* He is in charge of her, but he is "transported." He knows that her mind is "less exact," yet "Greatness of mind and nobleness their seat / Build in her loveliest," yet these things "subject not"; their union is "Harmony" (8.528–605). Their courting dance patterns forth similar transpositions: "she turned . . . I followed her . . . she . . . approved . . . I led her." Heaven and earth also join to approve: Heaven sheds "selectest influence," Earth gives "sign," airs fling rose, fling odors from the spicy shrub, "the amorous Bird of Night" sings spousal (8.507–19).

The pattern echoes an analogous equi-vocation and union in *Of*

Education: "Logic" (which is also "well-couched") will "open her contracted palm into a graceful and ornate rhetoric...To which poetry would be made subsequent, or indeed rather precedent, as being less subtile and fine," ("less exact") "but more simple, sensuous, and passionate," and decorum will teach "what religious, what glorious and magnificent use might be made of poetry, both in divine and humane things." That equivocation in turn echoes Sidney: "For poesy must not be drawn by the ears; it must be gently led, or rather it must lead; which is partly the cause that made the ancient-learned affirm that it was a divine gift."[8]

Milton may have felt much as Adam did, as he couched his argument in the amazing beauty of his sensuous verse—or hers who brought it nightly to his ear. The relation between the "less winning soft" but "manly" grace and wisdom of his stern fable and the delight of verse "adorn'd / With what all Earth or Heaven could bestow" (4.479–90, 8.482–83) is a delicate marriage. The marriage of Adam and Eve tropes its reciprocities. As you can see, I find Milton's poesy and his *istoria* to be "one flesh."

Eve embodies and performs a great many properties and processes that Milton elsewhere attributes to poetry itself, or to himself as poet. These properties belong both to poesy, or the art and craft of making poems, and to poetics, or the *gnosis* and *praxis* of interpreting poems, since for Milton one Spirit "who can enrich with all utterance and knowledge" touches both. Milton did not write tracts called *Poetics* or *A Defense of Poesy*. But Eve, the special carrier of fancy, which is both subsequent and precedent to understanding, figures forth Milton's own art. The images associated with her and her work are conventional metaphors for poetry. Her accounts of her creation and of her dream manifest the function of imagination in discerning and choosing good. Her bucolic songs of praise are allied to the legendary Arcadian origins of poetry and to Milton's youthful intention to follow those "who never write but honor of them to whom they devote their verse, displaying sublime and pure thoughts, without transgression."[9] Her temptation and fall represent the abuse of poesy by a politic libertine and the divorce of verse from truth: Satan has replaced his limping feet with redundant coils, making intricate seem straight (9.504, 632), and by erecting his argument on a false base debases poetry to propaganda and devises reductive criticism. Eve's final going forth rejoined to Adam and refreshed by propitious dreams mimes the renovation of the imagination that art can provide and its reunion with reerected reason, so that humankind may carry seeds of goodness even into a world of woe.

In considering Eve as poesy I do not wish to allegorize her or her

work, but to see her as a speaking portrait of the artist. One of the habits
of mind that Milton revises in *Paradise Lost* is that allegorizing of Scripture that makes Adam reason, mind, or soul, Eve passion, sense, or flesh,
and the Garden abstract moral virtue.[10] Adam and Eve are each whole
human personages developing in all the ways humans do in relation to
each other and to God, nature, angels, art, and experience; and the
Garden burgeons and beckons as gardens do, needing and repaying real
care.[11] However, in those manifold relations, Eve especially figures forth
poetic graces and poetic imagination, the work of the faculty of fancy,
which shapes the representations of the senses into significant forms
(5.104–5), as poems do.

It is her work that most startlingly metaphors the poetic process:
startlingly, because no one else had shown Adam and Eve working before
the Fall, much less imagined Eve singularly engaged in acts of creative
stewardship and design as a regular part of her life, producing—like
illuminated texts—"thick-wov'n Arborets and Flow'rs / Imborder'd on
each bank, the hand of *Eve*" (9.436–37).[12]

In the Renaissance, the art of poesy was habitually troped by the art of
gardening. *Anthology* means either knowledge of flowers or flowers of
knowledge. Titles of collections proliferate Arborets and Flowers: *Poetical
Blossoms, The Garden of the Muses, A Hundredth Sundry Flowers, The Arbor
of Amity, Underwoods, A Posy of Gilliflowers, Hesperides, A Paradise of Dainty
Devices, A Bower of Delights, The Shepherd's Garland, Flosculum Poeticum*, to
name a few. Puttenham and Shakespeare use the trope of gardening for
the relation of art to nature; Spenser describes contrasting bowers that
epitomize degenerative and regenerative art; Herbert, Donne, and Marvell
wreathe poetical garlands.[13] Sidney says that "Christ vouchsafed to use
the flowers" of poetry[14] and later Christopher Smart would say that
"flowers are peculiarly the poetry of Christ."[15] Herbert writes "And so I
came to Phansies Medow strow'd / With many a flower" and, in "The
Flower," "now in age I bud again . . . and relish versing."[16] Milton himself
calls his yet-unwritten poems "no bud or blossom," joins other poets to
strew the laureate hearse of Lycidas with flowers cast by the Sicilian
muse, offers "some Flowers and some bays" of verse to the marchioness of
Winchester, makes his Genius a keeper of Arcadian groves, and like
Herbert compares the return of his poetic inspiration, in Elegy V, to the reviving earth in spring, who twines her hair with flowers powerful to charm.

Eve is specifically responsible for buds and blossoms in *Paradise Lost*
(8.40–47, 9.424–33, 11.273–81). Even though Adam and Eve were joined
and enjoined by God to dress as well as keep the Garden, it was unheard
of before Milton to show them gardening, and especially to make Eve a
gardener even more committed and original than Adam, and so a figura

of the poet's own work; and equally unheard of to join her in naming the creatures by having her name the flowers (11.277): *naming*, until then, had been Adam's prerogative.[17] It implies knowing, and so being able to aid, the natures of God's creatures. And the natures of flowers are of some consequence in *Paradise Lost.* On "the bright consummate flow'r / [That] Spirits odorous breathes" depends all nurture: "flow'rs and their fruit, / Man's nourishment, by gradual scale sublim'd . . . give both life and sense, / Fancy and understanding, whence the soul / Reason receives, and reason is her being, / Discursive, or Intuitive" (5.481–88). Raphael is being quite literal. Flowers work up to fruit, fruit nourishes the bodily senses, those feed fancy and understanding, and these reason. The crossing over from body to spirit, if such a distinction may be made at all, occurs at the bridge of fancy. But flowers are consummate as well as prevenient, their "spirits odorous" a figure of prayer and they of poetry, which is both subsequent and precedent to reason, nourishing the soul and nourished by it.

Anyone who tries to write, or even read, may recognize in Eve's naming, nursing, propping, pruning, watering, selecting, supporting, and adorning the actions of this work that "under our labour grows" (9.208) and in her plea for freedom and a little solitude a condition she shares with Milton in his solitary lucubrations and independent-minded literary practice.

The analogy between Eve's art and the poet's own is like the sun: obvious to all eyes, and so sometimes not regarded. Almost everything she does or says before the Fall allies her to Milton's craft in some way. Her first speech is about looking into a mirror. When poetry is not a garden, it is often a mirror: a *Speculum Humanum*, a *Mirror for Magistrates*, a *Muses' Looking-Glass*, a "mirror held up to nature to show virtue her own feature, scorn her own image."[18] But Milton cautions us against using poetry only as a mirror. Eve, stretched on the flowery bank of Eden's mirror, at first sees only herself, as we too are prone to do, but when she knows that the reflection is her own image she (not unhesitatingly) joins her fanciful nature (but Milton has exalted fancy to conjunction with understanding) to Adam's wise one. Janet Knedlik has characterized Satan's mental state as an "utter inability to imagine . . . that he could be truly changed by anything external to himself."[19] The fallen angel is, indeed, unable to imagine freshly at all; he merely projects his present states or deconstructs what others imagine. His undelighted broodings frame Eve's tale of her mirror and of her choice to let herself be enlarged by someone outside herself. (This virtue of openness to enlargement is also the source of her vulnerability, and of the text's. She will later credulously allow herself to be reduced by someone outside herself, as interpreters may reduce the text in their commentaries.) In choosing to be enlarged, Eve does not "exist to, for, and from herself," as Christine Froula thinks she ought to do,[20] but she does not feel herself impaired or breached by her expansion until Satan fathers upon her a poetic of Eve for Eve's sake. Every character in the poem has the choice of being fostered or not by "God's uncontroulable intent,"[21] as does the poet; and the reader has the choice of being nourished or not by the incalculable enlargements the poem offers.

Eve personifies poesy in her work, in the imagery associated with her, and in the method of her vocation. She identifies the voice that calls her from her mirror simply as "a voice." Adam says she was "Led by her Heavenly Maker, though unseen, / And guided by his voice" (8.485–86). But the narrator speaks of the day "the genial Angel to our Sire / Brought her" (4.712–13). Did Milton nod? Or does the *equi*vocation echo Milton's *in*vocation of both the Holy Spirit and the Celestial Muse?

Led by God or his messenger, Eve is divinely wrought and brought, but not fixed and finished: God gave man, as Raleigh says, to be his own painter.[22] As a wife she is, like a Muse, or a poem a-making, incalculable, surprising, much beyond expectation, notable for having a will of her own. Adam learns that his image or other half is not *just* his image, has much to give, can enlarge and change *him,* is not for him (though she becomes for Satan) a text object to be possessed and exploited but a nigh-overwhelming bliss, almost too beautiful to bear, like "amourous delight" or Monteverdi's music or Milton's poem. She needs, as Adam will say fancy does, Reason well erect if harmony, not only solo voice and audience, is to survive; but she is also an erector of reason; his, but not all his, as Milton says his poesy is not all his, but "Hers who brings it nightly to my Ear" (9.47).

Eve's divine origin and calling put her at the crux of present discourse about poetic authority and the nature of inspiration. In her exchange with Edward Pechter in *Critical Inquiry,* Christine Froula says with some asperity, "Mr. Pechter apparently imagines that I take the Holy Spirit to be an actual entity."[23] The exchange delineates a watershed in literary studies between those who treat poems strictly as historical artifacts and those who find that art and language can be numinous. If Milton's Holy Spirit—whom he asks to "raise and support" his poesy as Eve stoops to support her roses—is a fiction, it pretends to confer a preposterous authority. But if his invocations report experiences of God tested on his own pulses, they claim no poetical prelacy, but an access Milton insisted was equally available to all who seek it, however great or humble their tasks.

Milton again intimately links Eve to his own calling in a love song to Adam that echoes his invocations by its form and imagery: especially the image of the nightingale, whom in his first sonnet Milton had adopted as his poetic emblem. In his invocations, Milton wanders night and morn "where the Muses haunt / Clear Spring, or shady Grove, or Sunny Hill" (3.27–38)

> Then feed[s] on thoughts that voluntary move
> Harmonious numbers; as the wakeful bird
> Sings darkling, and, in shadiest Covert hid
> Tunes her nocturnal note.
>
> (3.37–40)

Eve sings her nocturn as she and Adam move hand in hand toward a bower collaboratively wrought by God and Eve, whose "thickest covert was inwoven shade" of those most poetical flowers, laurel and myrtle, and whose nuptial bed Eve has decked with flowers and garlands. Her song "with thee conversing I forget all time," lauds "All seasons and their change":

> Sweet is the breath of morn . . .
> . . . . sweet the coming on
> Of grateful Ev'ning mild; then Silent Night,
> With this her Solemn Bird and this fair Moon,
> And these the Gems of Heav'n, her starry train:
> But neither breath of Morn, when she ascends
> Nor charm of earliest Birds, nor rising Sun
> On this delightful land, nor herb, fruit, flow'r
> Glist'ring with dew, nor fragrance after showers,
> Nor grateful Ev'ning mild, nor silent Night,
> With this her solemn Bird, nor walk by Moon,
> Or glittering Star-light, without thee is sweet.
>
> (4.640–56)

Eve's speech, with its gracious, dancelike measures,[24] repeats the rhythms and imagery of Milton's own state: less happy than hers, except when, like her, he is touched and enlightened from beyond himself.

> Thus with the Year
> Seasons return, but not to me returns
> Day, or the sweet approach of Ev'n or Morn,
> Or sight of vernal bloom, or Summer's Rose,
> Or flocks, or herds, or human face divine . . .
> So much the rather thou Celestial Light
> Shine inward. . . .
>
> (3.40–44, 51–52)

Before they enter the bower, Eve and Adam say a prayer that begins "Thou also mad'st the Night." Those archetypal critics who see Eve and femaleness associated with darkness and the moon and think she must therefore inevitably fall must read that prayer differently than I do, and Milton's relation to the Muse who brings his poem "Nightly" to his ear. And Eve's question, just after her song, about the stars—"for whom / This glorious sight, when sleep hath shut all eyes?"—is, similarly, often alleged as egocentric questioning of the divine economy, and so a foreshadowing of her fall. But an interest in stars is the province of Urania, the Muse of astronomy and of Milton, who links "harmonious numbers" to cosmic harmony. And Eve's question elicits from Adam a brief defense of the arts as he celebrates "celestial voices" with "heavenly touch of instrumental sounds / In full harmonic number joined / [that] lift our thoughts to Heaven" (4.682–86).

Just as remarkable as Milton's giving Eve a part in naming is the fact that in their unfallen conversations he gives Eve and Adam almost an equal number of lines. He neither makes Adam the dominant proprietor of Edenic language, nor Eve either a figure of the female vice of loquacity— even in her conversation with the Serpent—or an emblem of the virtue so often exhorted to women, silence, except when she refrains from interrupting her husband's eager after-dinner inquiries of a communicative space-traveler. In their unfallen conversations, she has almost an equal voice—217 lines to Adam's 230—a semitone, one might say, apart. Their verbal conversation is "meet" in innumerable interinanimating ways: hers more adventurous, playful, sweet, charming, questioning; his graver, explanatory, sequential and consequential upon hers. Each is sufficient in both reason and spontaneous grace, but in proportion due; together their words resonate like part music, to the enhancement of both.

When Raphael arrives and Adam requests a feast, Eve's reply (5.321–30) recapitulates Milton's claim of spontaneity in his art and his statements about decorum and "various style." She then considers "What choice [things] to choose for delicacy best, / What order, so contriv'd as not to mix / Tastes, not well join'd, inelegant, but bring / Taste after taste upheld with kindliest change" (5.333–36). The passage, thick with puns, calls attention to its own language. "Contrive" derives from *Tropos*, style or figure of speech; "inelegant" means, literally, not choice: from *eligere*, select; "kindliest" hints at "the kindly fruits of the earth"[25] and at the decorum of poetic kinds. Milton, also long choosing, also gathers, orders, tempers, changes, and disposes kinds in answerable style.

In her dream, Eve experiences in fancy the operations of evil without doing evil, as the poet must do to depict evil without being corrupted by it; and Adam's explanation of the relations of reason and fancy (5.100–121) makes fancy both subsequent (or subordinate) and precedent (or provident) to reason, which is but choosing. When she goes off to practice the art of gardening as usual, having persuaded Adam not to let the Foe destroy their artistic liberty, she is much like the poet who continues to sing though "with dangers compast round, / And solitude; yet not alone ... " (7.27–28) as long as the Spirit whose Temple is the upright heart is with her, and like poetic imagination, whose stay not free absents it more.

But, as Sidney says, "that which being rightly used doth most good, being abused doth most harm. . . . For I will not deny that a man's wit [or a clever fallen angel's] may make poesy infect the fancy with unworthy objects."[26] Satan is nearly rapt from his evil by Eve in naked innocence figuring forth good things; instead he infects her fancy, and she Adam's, and "So is that honey-flowing matron eloquence apparelled, or rather disguised, in a courtesan-like painted affectation ... with figures and flowers extremely winter-starved."[27] Satan divorces the signifier from the signified, makes words an autonomous language-game in which he feigns a trivial and tyrannical patriarch; and he psychologizes the inclination for forbidden fruit and its alleged power that he has projected into Eve as a "need." Language becomes an instrument for deception and exploitation, an implement of rape, rather than an instrument for the pleasure of discovering and nurturing goodness. Eve, thus abused, poisons Adam; Adam, thus diseased, whores Eve; the result is fratricide.

"But what, shall the abuse of a thing make the right use odious?"[28] It is not Eve's imaginative freedom that causes her wild work, but her corruption: a corruption made possible by the receptivity that is, like that of poetic language, a rich virtue when rightly used. As a part of the process of her regeneration, her fancy is the faculty that receives separate divine attention, in a healing dream that reconnects the fancy to the Word. As Adam and Eve set forth from the Garden with the task of erecting the infected will and taking goodness in hand, neither is subsequent or precedent. Like Sidney's art and nature, and like Milton's shaping intent and shapely text, Adam and Eve go forth hand in hand, bearing the seeds of an infinite progeny.

The metatext of Ithuriel's spear, wherein we are invited by kinetic mimesis to stand as angelic interpreters or squat as Aristophanic land-frogs, is surrounded by concentric scenes all of which also touch in some way on the nature and uses of imagination. Most of them also present to ours with great delicacy and intimacy the mutuality of paradisal marriage. In the nearest sphere, before Eve's dream, she and Adam make love festively, by connubial rites, and after it by honesty and solace. In the next, they pray. Before their evening prayer, Adam discourses on the nature of their work, and after their morning prayer they set out to do it.

In the evening, Eve says or sings a love song to Adam, and in the morning Adam says or sings a love song to Eve. Before that, they entertain a fallen angel unawares, and after, they entertain an unfallen one awares. And, lest anyone in Milton's audience think any of the arts intrinsically irreligious, *both* angels indulge in feigning along the way. Satan sits like a cormorant—who are a dime a dozen and all sit the same way—and misreads the Garden without delight. Raphael arrives as a phoenix—of whom there is only one—feigning in play, for sheer pleasure, gaz'd on by all the fowls, and reads God's book of creatures with charity and candor. Raphael sails on steady wing, upheld by buxom air, in contrast to Satan's sudden sprawls: one artist hand in hand with nature, the other opposed and subject to fatuous falls (2.927–42, 4.194–204, 5.266–74).

These concentric passages contain every sort of imaginative exercise, with Eve's dream and Adam's explanation of what imagination was made for at their center. They demonstrate that no art or pleasure is forbidden that does not deceive, exploit, or enslave, and that imagination can be an antidote against evil as well as a means to apprehend goodness. Ithuriel's action discloses Satan, as the dream itself might have done, to free Eve; the poison Satan pours into her ear might have been a mithridate against further nocence. And that pattern recapitulates the poem. In it, Milton gives us innocent goodness in all its rich and various beauty; he shows it blighted; he shows it beginning to be restored; and he hands us the threads of continuance.

Framing the dream, Milton embodies creativity in the two most interesting and intimate of human mutual activities, sex and prayer. The fact that the prayer may be sung further links the two, for procreativity and creativity had in the Renaissance firm philosophical connections, especially with regard to music.

The question is still sometimes belabored whether unfallen Adam and Eve, in the vulgar phrase, "had sex" in *Paradise Lost.* The problem is that if Paradise is in good working order, everything including Adam and Eve is presumed fertile, so that every sexual union should produce issue: those "more hands" that Adam and Eve, artists and gardeners, metonymically look forward to. But if conception had occurred before the Fall, Cain would have been born without original sin. There are several objections. According to Genesis, Cain was conceived after the expulsion. Even if we read Genesis 4:1 retrospectively, we are left with the difficulty that the murder of Abel is surely the archetypal effect of the archetypal sin. If it were not, Cain's sin would have stood "in the following of Adam," as the Ninth Article of Religion puts it, rather than "the fault and corruption of the Nature of every man, that naturally is engendered of the offspring of

Adam; whereby man is very far gone from original righteousness." Milton is quite clear about rejecting the Pelagian heresy that denies the corporate nature of sin.[29] Therefore, Cain was not conceived in the course of the nuptial embraces Milton's Adam and Eve enjoy in their flower-decked, nightingale-serenaded bower (4.736–75).

This either-or dilemma—that either Eve and Adam remained virgins and only embraced allegorically, as the Fathers thought, or Cain was conceived in Paradise—Milton apparently regarded as a false one. The idea that every divinely sanctioned sexual act produces offspring is classical, not scriptural. Every sacrosanct rape by a pagan god begets a hero, or a troublemaker, but the mothers of scriptural heroes—Isaac, Samson, John the Baptist—often had to wait through years of married barrenness to bear them. If Adam and Eve had not fallen, Eve would probably have been bloomingly pregnant most of the time, and each child a new burgeoning microcosm of tenderness, beauty, wit, talent, and unexpected views. But although she might produce a child every solar year, I see no reason to suppose that Eve was not connected to the cycles of the moon or that there might not have been a period of sheer amorous delight before the first conception, in aid of the other purposes of marriage Milton lists first[30] and in preparation for the beginning of new life.

Nevertheless, wedded love is the "true source of human offspring," a "perpetual Fountain of Domestic sweets" in that way as well as in the multifloriate pleasures of erotic mutuality; and in his apostrophe to it, Milton with his celestial spear dispels the vain imaginings of prurient hypocrisy. This passage is balanced, on the other side of the dream, by Adam's aubade and his discourse upon good and bad uses of imagination, concluded with a kiss of peace.

In the two scenes before and after the dream, Adam and Eve turn toward each other. In the two scenes before and after that, they turn together toward God to pray. Since in the act of prayer Adam and Eve become poets and singers, they are *figurae* of the unfallen artist and *exempla* of the regenerate one, inventing and performing the genre that Sidney calls "that lyrical kind of songs and sonnets: which, Lord, if He gave us good minds, how well it might be employed, and with how heavenly fruit, both private and public, in singing the praises of the immortal beauty, the immortal goodness of that God who giveth us hands to write and wits to conceive; of which we might well want words, but never matter; of which we could turn our eyes to nothing but we should ever have new budding occasions."[31]

Although I have argued lengthily that Eve was right to defend the exercise of creative freedom even if it meant being sometimes on her own and at risk,[32] I do not want to overstress her separate and singular talents.

Eve as monody is a fresh and astonishing creature of her author, but Adam and Eve as harmony are the core of the world. The art form in which that harmony most fully resounds is their evening (4.724–35) and morning (5.153–208) prayers.

Milton's warm-toned drawing forth of Adam and Eve together in prayer before the Fall is almost without precedent; but glimmers of such a life appear in a few rare visual depictions. An engraving by Nicholaes de Bruyn, after Maerten de Vos, illustrates the Admonition; but Jan Theodor de Bry's version of the same original has as its inscription the first verse of Psalm 117: "O praise the Lord all ye peoples, praise him all ye nations," all nations being incipient within Adam and Eve.[33] And an illustration bound into English Bibles in the mid-seventeenth century identifies a similar image as the Institution of the Sabbath.[34] Original righteousness, though not as popular as original sin, is at least acknowledged in these unusual representations, which are part of the early seventeenth-century impulse that Milton's account of richly joyous Edenic activity brings to its fullest consummation.

Mutual spontaneous prayer—two people together visibly and audibly opening their souls to God—is perhaps the most intimate and risky of human activities. It almost inevitably increases love, and in baring themselves to the Spirit, the pray-ers bare themselves in "holy rapture" to obvious, vulnerable growth of soul. If you add music—and, echoing the Prayer Book rubrics, Milton tells us that the prayers of Adam and Eve are either "pronounced or sung"—the opportunity for heavenly interchange is redoubled. Milton's yoking together of the act of prayer and the act of love, "whatever Hypocrites austerely talk," is perfectly natural, and is supported in the case of sung prayer by Renaissance theories of music. For the eternal verities of pitch and measure link music mathematically to the mystic Dance of the cosmos and to the divine forms in the mind of God, and so set the affections in right tune. And, for Galileo and Kepler, the pleasure of music was akin to the pleasure of lovemaking. For they saw musical proportions as corresponding to the "proportion due" of male and female. In one of his letters, Kepler, explaining the geometry of music, says, "Non puto me posse clarius et palpabilius rem explicare, quam si dicam te videre imagines illic mentulae, hic vulvae." Galileo said that the interval of the fifth produces "such a tickling and stimulation of the cartilage of the eardrum that, tempering the sweetness with a dash of sharpness, it seems delightfully to kiss and bite at the same time," and Kepler that "the progeny of the pentagon, the major third and the minor third, move our souls, images of God, to emotions comparable to the business of generation."[35]

The mutuality of their love and the goodness of the whole creation

form the theme of the evening prayer of Adam and Eve, when "both stood, / Both turn'd, and under op'n Sky"—which Raphael will call God's Book—"ador'd / The God that made both Sky, Air, Earth, and Heav'n / Which they beheld, the Moon's resplendent Globe / And starry Pole" (4.720–24). The exactness of "resplendent" images their own relation to God as Artifex and that of the creation for which they speak. The moment is the more dramatic when we recall that in Vondel's version of the story, Adam *leaves* Eve in order to pray, "and in my solitude / Give thanks to [God] for thy companionship," thus allowing Satan to find Eve alone.[36]

The abrupt beginning, "Thou also mad'st the night," suggests a psalm-verse that could have begun their earlier unrecorded morning prayer, "This is the day that the Lord hath made; we will rejoice and be glad in it" (118:24): one appointed for Easter and so known to Milton in numerous jubilant settings. Here, Adam and Eve rejoice in each other and in their coming children.

Their morning prayer is both more liturgical and more explicitly connected with Milton's work as a poet. It is an "unmeditated" canticle based on the Song of the Three Children from the apocryphal portion of the Book of Daniel, which is the morning canticle in the Book of Common Prayer called the Benedicite, and on Psalm 148, said or sung at Evening Prayer on the thirtieth and thirty-first of every month. Both sources call upon all of nature, from angels to cattle to creeping things, to praise the Lord. They reappeared in the metrical psalters set to authorized church tunes, bound into sixteenth- and seventeenth-century prayer books; in numerous harmonized versions of these printed for home use; and in entirely different translations and settings such as George Wither's, set for two voices by Orlando Gibbons,[37] and George Sandys's, set by Henry Lawes "to new Tunes for private Devotion: and a thorow Base, for Voice, or Instrument" and published in 1637, shortly after Lawes's collaboration with Milton on the *Mask Presented at Ludlow-Castle*. Lawes also published selected psalm settings "for three voices and a thorow-Base" with an equal number by his brother William as a memorial to him, prefaced by commendatory poems including Milton's sonnet to "Harry . . . that with smooth air couldst humour best our tongue," in 1648: the same year that Milton contributed a series of metrical psalms in which he uncharacteristically confined his muse to the common meter needed for the common tunes. Lawes's two-part settings are singable by anyone and his viol, or wife, or child, or any two or more people; other settings provide a range of musical difficulty and interest reaching to the polychoral polyphony of the Chapel Royal.

Psalm-singing was a major national pastime in Milton's day.[38] Nearly all of his first readers would have some experience of it—not only in the hearing, but in the doing—to bring to their reading of the canticles of Adam and Eve. They, of course, are accomplished artists, but even the singing of simple harmonies available to the youngest or newest singer can give a taste of the pleasure and sense of communion that psalm-singing affords. Milton suggests that sung prayer, spontaneously embellished in various style, is one of the inexhaustible felicities of unfallen or regenerate life; and he illustrates its possibilities by incorporating the effects of music into words, as his admired Mazzoni observes in Dante,[39] a process that is the inverse of the Renaissance composer's practice of incorporating the effects of words into music.

Some of the musical treatment of words that informs Milton's verbal treatment of music may be found in Adrien Batten's setting of Psalm

117,[40] the psalm attributed to Adam and Eve by the inscription of de Bry's representation of them praying before the Fall. Batten's word-painting includes close weaving of four vocal lines (which would have required an amicable Cain and Abel for the inner parts), each voice having a comfortably small range, to achieve the serene harmonies suitable to the text; use of moderate polyphony on "all ye nations"; tender and beseeching harmonic changes on "merciful kindness"; strong unanimity on "for his truth endureth"; and melisma extending "forever and ever." As is usual in Renaissance music, one must ignore the bar lines and time signatures and attend to the ways the musical line is responsive to the words: within the steady pulse of "strictest measure even" the phrasing shifts back and forth between common or earthly time, in twos and fours, and triple or "perfect" time on words naming the attributes of God. "His merciful kindness" enters in triple time; "is ever more and more towards us" reverts to common time; "the truth of the Lord" is in triple time; but the two kinds of time, the earthly fours and the heavenly threes, flow together as fluidly as temporal and eternal activities may be supposed to do in Eden.

Milton's hymn is, we might say, the proposed archetype of the scriptural hymns it spontaneously elaborates. Adam and Eve are not, like the Three Hebrew Children, in a fiery furnace; but they have just had their first taste of evil, in Eve's dream, and we the readers have spent two books in hell and more in the hell of Satan's self. The three children in the fiery furnace, refreshed by a wind an angel brings, can still praise fire. And as we are refreshed by the wind of the Spirit that blows through these joyful lines, we are also aware of the misuse the fallen angel makes of the creatures they invoke. He has used the sun and a treetop as spying posts, entered the Garden through mists and exhalations, and winged and walked the earth as a bird, a tiger, a lion, and a toad; he will become a snake that lowly creeps: all "not nocent yet." And like the Psalmist, Adam and Eve, in their closing petition, recognize the need for "God's merciful kindness."

The imagery of their song partakes of textural and prosodic as well as thematic musical interest. The recurrent figure denoted by the words "Circle," "Circlet," "crown," "Sphere," and "Perpetual Circle" links earth's creatures to the cosmic mystic dance and suggests the "perfect measure" that in Renaissance notation is denoted by a circle. But the measure varies, like Batten's, to suit the words: Within the steady pulse of decasyllabic lines, if you count only the major stresses, God is described in triple time, as

Unspeakable, who sit'st above these Heavens.

"In these thy lowest works" shifts back to iambs. Angels have varied meters, then at line 164 we are back to earth decidedly in fours:

On Éarth join áll ye Créatures to extól

Hím first, hím last, hím midst, and without énd:

with three firm stresses concerning God within the line. The five wandering fires get more regular pentameter, and "His práise, who out of Dárkness call'd up Líght" gets three primary stresses. The four elements that in quaternion run get four-beat lines until the exhortation to ceaseless change, in which they vary. "Hail universal Lord" invites three accents; and the concluding lines move from earthly to heavenly time in a way that prosodically restores the tranquillity for which they plead.

Rather than rhyme, there is a closely woven harmony of similar sounds: dawn, morn, prime; praise, rise, sky, flies; frame, then, seem. Often this close weaving is onomatopoetic, providing verbal tone painting: "Ye Mists and Exhalations that now rise"; "wet the thirsty Earth with falling showers"; "Fountains and yee, that warble, as ye flow, / Melodious murmurs"; the swoop of "ye Birds / That singing up to Heaven Gate ascend" (and how pleasant to know that Adam and Eve knew their Shakespeare); the syncopation of syntax against line at "mix / And nourish all things, let your ceaseless change / Vary. . . . "

In the act of prayer, Adam and Eve become poets and singers, and so figurae of the poet and of the mutual spontaneous prayer Milton preferred to a fixed liturgy: both poet and worshipper should be freely responsive to the indwelling Spirit, though they may use established genres within whose structures spontaneous art can always find new budding occasions. As Milton's celestial patroness "inspires / Easy [his] unpremeditated verse" (9.23–24), so for Adam and Eve "neither various style / nor holy rapture wanted they to praise / Their Maker, in fit strains pronounced or sung / Unmeditated; such prompt eloquence / Flow'd from their lips, in prose or numerous Verse, / More tuneable than needed Lute or Harp / To add more sweetness" (5.146–52). Imagine doing that. Could anything be more engaging than the mutual, spontaneous production of poetry and song, made possible by shared rapture and established structure? Milton leaves it to our imaginations to figure out how two people linked in happy nuptial league can unanimously compose spontaneous songs, even when blessed with union of mind "or in [them] both one soul": whether by antiphonal verses or mutual infusion by the celestial muse;[41] but no doubt in Paradise, even more than in Sidney's Arcadia where improvised poetic exchanges often occur, such acts of spontaneous composition would be endlessly diverse and interesting. If the Fall had not interrupted their courses, Adam and Eve—prime artists with God's image and the Holy Ghost fresh within them—might have continued to compose in various style, increasing voice parts as their tribe increased to something like—on grand occasions—Michael Praetorius's setting of the Benedicite, which begins with two voice parts— Adam and Eve as it were—and increases to five hundred voices, human and instrumental, gathering in all the voices of creation with copious opportunities for word-painting, all these voices growing more delicately harmonious as they increase, while the refrains expand to cosmic resonance and the word "Domino" receives increasing tenderness.

In spite of its Venetian origin, I see no reason why Adam and Eve should not be imagined or we encouraged to make such music; Milton had no objection to letting "the pealing Organ blow / To the full voic'd quire below, / In Service high and Anthems cleer, / As may with sweetnes through mine ear, / Dissolve me into extacies / And bring all Heav'n before mine eyes."[42] Unfallen or regenerate, the whole human family might "join thir vocal Worship to the Choir of Creatures wanting voice" (9.198–99) as secretaries of God's praise. Surely to do so in the various style, the fluid responsiveness, and the exfoliation of the life of words characteristic of Renaissance music and of Milton's verse proliferates endless pleasures and by literally joining hearts to heaven nourishes *this* resplendent globe.[43]

NOTES

1. Quotations from *Paradise Lost* are from the edition of Merritt Y. Hughes (New York, 1962).

2. From *The Reason of Church Government Urged Against Prelaty,* in *The Student's Milton,* ed. Frank Allen Patterson (New York, 1930), p. 526. All quotations from Milton's prose are from this edition, hereafter cited as *SM.*

3. William Kerrigan, *The Sacred Complex* (Cambridge, Mass., 1983), p. 245.

4. John Milton, *De Doctrina Christiana,* in *SM,* pp. 1070 and 1066.

5. Perhaps I should mention that at the time of writing this section I had not read John Guillory's interesting (and puzzling) emblematic use of Ithuriel's spear as poetic principle in *Poetic Authority: Spenser, Milton, and Literary History* (New York, 1983), pp. 148–51.

6. John Milton, *Of Education,* in *SM,* p. 726.

7. Joseph Summers, *The Muse's Method* (London, 1962); Edward Le Comte, *Milton and Sex* (New York, 1978).

8. John Milton, *Of Education,* p. 729; Sir Philip Sidney, *An Apology for Poetry,* ed. Forrest G. Robinson (Indianapolis, 1970), p. 72.

9. John Milton, *An Apology for Smectymnuus,* in *SM,* p. 549.

10. J. M. Evans discusses allegorical readings in *"Paradise Lost" and the Genesis Tradition* (Oxford, 1968), pp. 69–99. Milton selectively retains many connotations from these readings, but discards implications that set nature against spirit or mythologize Adam and Eve. For a contemporary allegorizing treatment of the Genesis story see Troilo Lancetta's *Scena Tragica d'Adamo e d'Eua* (Venice, 1644).

11. On the abundant significance of literal gardens and gardening in relation to literature, philosophy, and religion in the English Renaissance, see Charlotte F. Otten, *Environ'd with Eternity: God, Poems, and Plants in Sixteenth and Seventeenth Century England* (Lawrence, 1985).

12. "Hand" as handwork may pun on "hand" as handwriting or "character."

13. George Puttenham, *The Arte of English Poesie* (London, 1589), pp. 308–13; Shakespeare, *The Winter's Tale* 4.4; Spenser, *The Faerie Queene* II.12 and III.6; Herbert, "A Wreath"; Donne, "La Corona"; Marvell, "The Coronet."

14. Sidney, p. 51.

15. Christopher Smart, *Jubilate Agno,* l. 506, in the edition by W. H. Bond (London, 1954), p. 106.

16. George Herbert, "The Pilgrimage" and "The Flower," in *The English Poems of George Herbert,* ed. C. A. Patrides (Totowa, 1975), pp. 151 and 172.

17. In the visual arts, however, Eve is sometimes present at the naming; see for example *A Thirteenth Century Breviary in the Library of Alnwick Castle,* intro. Eric George Millar (Oxford, 1958).

18. *Hamlet* 3.2.

19. Janet Knedlik, "Medieval Metaphysics and Temporal Process in Milton's *Paradise Lost,*" a paper presented at the Nineteenth International Congress on Medieval Studies, Kalamazoo, 1984.

20. Christine Froula, "When Eve Reads Milton: Undoing the Canonical Economy," *Critical Inquiry,* 10 (Dec., 1983), 328.

21. *Samson Agonistes* 1754.

22. Sir Walter Raleigh, *The History of the World* (1614), p. 35.

23. Christine Froula, "Pechter's Specter: Milton's Bogey Writ Small," *Critical Inquiry,* 11 (Sept., 1984), 173. Professor Froula's work is an extraordinarily honest exhibition of the intention to read *Paradise Lost* from the point of view of a feminist sociology of religion, asserting for example that "Adam fashions a god that is invisible *to Eve* in order to master her" (p. 173).

24. In a broad sense (not the technical, prosodic one) Eve's poem is a *rondeau,* which originates in dance; and it perhaps suggests the form of a round dance in which the partners circle in opposite directions, then return to join together.

25. From the Litany, prescribed to be used at least three times a week, in the Book of Common Prayer.

26. Sidney, p. 59. Milton echoes Sidney's words, with regard to marriage, in *Tetrachordon, SM,* p. 673: "what doth most harm in the abusing, used rightly doth most good."

27. Sidney, p. 81.

28. Sidney, p. 60.

29. Milton, *De Doctrina Christiana,* 1.11.

30. That is, "a mutual help to piety" and "to civil fellowship of love and amity; then, to generation . . . ," Milton, *Tetrachordon,* pp. 657–58.

31. Sidney, p. 80.

32. In *Milton's Eve* (Urbana, 1983), especially chap. 5.

33. The engraving by de Bruyn is part of a creation series available in the Print Room of the Reiksmuseum, Amsterdam (inv. no. A22380). The de Bry (with the inscription, backwards, in French) is in the Museum Plantin-Moretus, Antwerp, Cat. nr. I/B635, and is reproduced in F. W. H. Hollstein, *Dutch and Flemish Etchings, Engravings, and Woodcuts, ca.* 1450-1700 *(Amsterdam,* 1949-*),* 4:27.

34. William Slatyer (compiler) and Jacob Floris Van Langeren (engraver), STC 22634.5. Photograph reproduced by permission of the British Library.

35. Both Galileo and Kepler are quoted in D. P. Walker, *Studies in Musical Science in the Late Renaissance,* Studies of the Warburg Institute, 37 (London and Leiden, 1978), pp. 32 and 53–54.

36. Joost van den Vondel, *Adam in Ballingschap* (1664), trans. Watson Kirkconnell, in *The Celestial Cycle* (Toronto, 1952), p. 462.

37. George Wither, *The Hymnes and Songs of the Church* (London, 1623).

38. For an account of this movement see Nicholas Temperley, *Music of the English Parish Church* (Cambridge, 1979), chap. 3.

39. Giacopo Mazzoni, *On the Defense of the Comedy of Dante: Introduction and Summary,* trans. Robert L. Montgomery (Tallahassee, 1983), p. 58.

40. Batten (1591–1637?), "O Praise the Lord," from John Barnard's *First Book of Selected Church Musick* (1641), available in a modern edition by Anthony Greening in *The Oxford Book of Tudor Anthems,* compiled by Christopher Morris (Oxford, 1978).

41. Possible performances of this passage have been suggested by Joseph H. Summers, in *The Muse's Method: An Introduction to "Paradise Lost"* (Cambridge, Mass., 1962), pp. 75–83, and Louise Schleiner, *The Living Lyre in English Verse from Elizabeth through the Restoration* (Columbia, Mo., 1984), pp. 134–36.

42. *Il Penseroso* 161–66, in *SM,* p. 29.

43. This essay was written with the help of a grant from the Research Council of Rutgers, the State University of New Jersey. A portion of it is reprinted, with permission, from *Milton Quarterly.*

In White Ink:
Paradise Lost and Milton's
Ideas of Women

RICHARD CORUM

> ... frescoes translating
> violence into patterns so powerful and pure
> we continually fail to ask are they true for us.
>
> —A. Rich

THERE are different ways of having an idea, so it is helpful to have limiting cases. To stand in history as a mortal perceiver is to have limited, finite ideas of things. In ordinary usage we would say that we have concepts, mental representations open to change. Moreover, since the things we perceive are also subject to change, these referents change as much as our concepts and our language change. Thus in this kind of semiotic system it is customary to expect that there will be gaps between concepts and words, between signs and their referents, and usual too to recognize that these gaps are necessary, neutral, or beneficial in some circumstances, destructive and lethal in others.

The ideas of Milton's omniscient God are, however, radically different from common ones because they are neither limited nor subject to change. As the persons and things represented by the ideas and word of Milton's God are capable of change, a gap frequently opens between a divine sign and its referent. But because it opens as a result of the referent's choice, not of God's, such a gap angers Milton's God sufficiently enough that if it is not closed immediately by penance the referent will be excluded forcibly from the domains of Milton's God and in time obliterated. In this canon law, or ideological model, a divine idea is a pattern or image persons and things cannot afford not to fit. Thus in the universe of Milton's God, where mortals cannot escape being the referent of a divine idea of themselves, men and women have compelling reasons to recognize that knowledge of God's ideas is basic to their survival.[1]

Moreover, since the idea that Milton's God has of man includes an obligation on man's part to shape his subordinates to the measure of a divine idea, a man's survival depends in part on fulfilling certain obligations to women and children. He must make clear, distinct, and accurate representations of God's ideas available to his subjects. And he must back up his representations with his own responsible example. He must translate himself and his subjects into perfect referents for his God's Word, whether with persuasive education or with discipline and punishment. If, after all of this, his subjects choose to differ, then the responsibility for this difference falls, like the stones of a Philistine temple, on their own heads, as they would fall on his were he to differ.

From a conservative ideological perspective, *Paradise Lost* is a catalogue of orthodox representations which fulfills a divine responsibility. Through Milton's English, Milton's God satisfies his obligations to his English subjects. He has published—has made public—his expectations, and he has shown through a sacred narrative, a sacred history, the consequences of measuring up or not measuring up to these expectations.

The first half of this paper takes seriously the canonical nature of Milton's epic undertaking. It details the idea Milton's God has of woman, an idea victorious over common ideas in heaven, and soon to be so everywhere else. In theory this should exhaust the subject. There should be no residue, as common ideas have no role to play in *Paradise Lost* other than representing error. But there is a residue: ideas of woman which do not belong to Milton's God, but are not rooted out and destroyed—ideas which, were they not invisible, would keep *Paradise Lost* from passing cleanly through the eye of the needle. This residue makes Milton's epic to some extent, however small, a fallen poem, and of interest to fallen readers. To see it is to see the side effects, in poet, poem, ideological system, and one's own psyche as reader, of trying to banish finite, nonideological processes of conceptualization from an imperial order of things. To see it is to recover an invisible "Milton" inscribed in white ink who hides unrepentantly in the text of Milton's ideological perfection. The motive for apprehending this other Milton is not condemnation, nor disrespect; rather it is to disclose those features of the natural, vernacular, historical, finite Milton which an ambitiously obedient Milton has labored to erase.[2]

If we credit Milton's invocations and agree that Milton's God is the authorial consciousness who wrote, Urania a kind of neural medium which transmitted, and Milton himself the voice who dictated *Paradise Lost* to the female hands which put it on paper, then we can start at the top of Milton's corporate enterprise and examine his idea of woman by investigating his God's idea of woman: " . . . in him all his Father shone Substantially expressed" (3.139–40).[3]

I. In her most ideal manifestation, woman is heaven and, as heaven woman is an ideal home country: an inanimate, wholly dependent, will-less, silent background environment for the activity of Milton's God: "heav'n open'd wide Her ever-during gates" (7.206). Despite the sexual implications of a political image ("open'd wide"), this home country, as maternal matrix, has no sexual or genetic relationship to the father's generation of sons. Milton's God is not sexual: "this day I have begot," he says, "whom I declare My only Son" (5.603–4). Nevertheless, heaven's other action is also a maternal act: "and heav'n gates Poured out by millions her victorious bands" (2.996–97). Among the millions she figuratively births, however, there are no daughters:

> O why did God,
> Creator wise, that peopled highest heav'n
> With Spirits masculine, create at last
> This novelty on earth, this fair defect
> Of Nature, and not fill the world at once
> With men as angels without feminine,
> Or find some other way to generate
> Mankind?
>
> (10.888–95)

Nor are these male angels sexual in any material sense. Their love and sexuality, if it is sexuality at all, is a metaplatonic union "of pure with pure Desiring; nor restrained conveyance need As flesh to mix with flesh, or soul with soul" (8.627–29).

II. At a lower, material level woman as background is a planet and a master trope. On the second day of creation a portion of the "Bright effluence of bright essence increate" (3.6) of Milton's God is materialized as a female "light Ethereal" and "spheared in a cloudy tabernacle" (7.243). On the fourth day Milton's God creates the sun: "A mighty sphere he framed, unlightsome first, Though of ethereal mold" (7.354–57). And then, in a passage which anticipates the creation and education of man, and the sacrament of communion, "by far the greater part" of "light Ethereal" he took,

> and placed
> In the sun's orb, made porous to receive
> And drink the liquid light, firm to retain
> Her gathered beams, great palace now of light.
>
> (7.360–63)

After this firm, porous orb has been set in the east as "Regent of th' day,"

> ... less bright the moon
> But opposite in leveled West was set
> His mirror, with full face borrowing her light
> From him, for other light she needed none
> In that aspect.
>
> (7.375–79)

Unlike man, woman is not given light; she can only reflect it. As a mirror she can index male power, and sexuality, but she can have no rival store of her own. Unless she is his mirror she will be dull, dark, and uninspiring. Male light, however, is real—"liquid"—and storable. It is a basis for power, and a source for political and economic exchanges with other, lesser males: "Hither [to this sun] as to their fountain, other stars Repairing, in their golden urns draw light" (7.364–66).[4]

III. At third best woman is colonial territory, earth. At this distance from the imperial center, woman becomes valuable when she is transformed into an ideal space for the imperial male, whether a procreative vessel to nurture his seeds, a serviceable nursery environment to care for, support, and satisfy him throughout his life, or a political and economic space for him to rule and profit from as father, monarch, or deity. The intent is to mimic as closely as possible the female functions and benefits of the home country. Consider, for example, the day God's word brings forth grass from the earth:

> He scarce had said, when the bare earth, till then
> Desert and bare, unsightly, unadorned,
> Brought forth the tender grass, whose verdure clad
> Her universal face with pleasant green.
>
> (7.313–16)

The father's word transforms a doubly bare woman into something rich and valuable, and a large part of her new value derives from the fact that as an inanimate, vegetable object she has proven to be absolutely responsive to male imperatives.[5]

IV. At worst, as background, woman is a foreign territory who, from Milton's point of view, performs lethal parodies of her environmental functions for an adult male lover and ruler other than Milton's God: "hell shall unfold, To entertain you ... , her widest gates, And send forth all her kings" (4.381–83) is both a political and a sexual threat. That Milton figures all background women who have adult, royal lovers—i.e., heaven and hell—synecdochially by their "gates" suggests the degree to which independent or rival control of the "gates" of a woman's eyes, ears, mouth, and sexuality is a threat to imperial rule.

From the point of view of Milton and his God, the necessity and advantages of turning woman into a home or colonial territory are, of course, numerous and obvious, with possession, wealth, security, maternal care, and sexual availability, however repressed, among the most prominent.[6] Such control creates an imperial space from which powerful and threatening differences can be excluded, particularly a space from which the eldest and sexually mature son can be exiled as a mutinous rebel if he is not willing to be an obedient colonial regent.[7] Exclusions at home set the pattern abroad. For an emperor not to vanquish his foreign rivals, making the "gates" of their territory subject to the authority of his erected standard, would be to take the risk of letting a foreign territory's differences foment anger, opposition, disobedience, warfare, castration, adultery, as when "Bellona storms, With all her battering engines bent to raze Some capital city" (2.922–27).[8] Far preferable in Milton's mind to these terrible consequences of failed masculine control — these efforts by unchecked woman to raze the chief signifiers of male power, the ruler's capital city and his steadfast wife — is the image Milton draws elsewhere of this earth as a woman resting peacefully "upon her center, poised" and ready for male insemination, male command (5.579).[9]

Up to this point I have been tracing the iconography of an idea which paradoxically enlarges woman to material passivity by relegating her to some kind of background status. Confusing the patriarchal economy of these ideal sex and gender distinctions, however, is the fact that woman does not remain in the background. On the contrary, she constantly and persistently foregrounds herself, just as other female things — poetry, the mind, or *langue,* for example — are also constantly foregrounded as poem, idea, or *parole.* What this individuation means is that female spaces are populated at their imperial centers not just by Milton's God, his sons, or his rival, but more problematically by women.

  I. At her best again in heaven, woman, foregrounded, is not an independent entity nor an angel but an abstract, eternally asexual personification of the father's divine attributes: "Urania . . . and Wisdom [her] sister" (7.10), "Virtue in her shape how lovely" (4.848), "harmony divine so smooths her charming tones" (5.625–26), and, perhaps, the "light Ethereal" of creation's second day (7.243). As subordinations of previously independent classical goddesses to the hegemony of the father's monotheistic person, as models of female character and deportment, and as ideas emanating from the side of the father's head, these daughters are eternally perfect in their "love" and absolute in their "obedience."

  II. At a lower level foregrounded woman is a presexual and temporary personification of a material background environment. Like a servant, she comes into being as person when she is needed. And once she accomplishes her task, she goes back immediately to being landscape. In other words, Milton transposes the heavenly model for foregrounding woman — abstract idea emanating from the mental landscape of Milton's God — to the material world (if we can assume that he is not projecting a private or, say, a classical model onto heaven). In *Comus,* for example, Sabrina figures herself forth momentarily from the river of which she is goddess in order "to undo the charmed band Of true virgin here distressed" (ll. 904–5).[10]

III. At third best is Eve, whose emergence as a woman is extremely problematic.[11] As she is neither an idea in God's head nor a nymph safely immured in the landscape, as she can make choices, and is sexual, Milton's defenses are numerous. Eve emanates from the landscape of Adam's body, and is joined on earth to Adam in an androgynous relationship which will rise to heaven at the expense of Eve's identity, since if as "man" they get there "they" will have become a male angel.[12] Satan tells her that she can become a goddess, but he is lying. The best she can hope for in heaven on her own is to be a personified abstraction, an idea, in the mind of Milton's God. Indicative, too, of her problematic status is the fact that as soon as she becomes a person, she must be subordinated immediately to male dominion. Having Adam's "head" added to her part of "man's" androgynous body translates her from independent, curious, imaginative person into the background, and depersonalizing states (in both senses) of "wedded" wife, androgyne, and subject:

> With that thy gentle hand
> Seized mine, I yielded, and from that time see
> How beauty is excelled by manly grace
> And wisdom, which alone is truly fair.
>
> (4.488–91)

Following parental injunction, this "native" has moved from "outside" to "inside" the empire. And the imperial practice of backgrounding woman, defined as civilization, has been legitimized.

What is sacrificed here for imperial control is Eve's curiosity, her sense of playfulness, her delight in shapes and colors, her developing sense of herself, and her need to validate herself in her own terms. In nature's liquid mirror, she would see that she is of worth, and she would come to understand that she is worthy of her own affection and esteem as she is. Moreover, her own abilities would have been sufficient to get her away when this pool becomes inadequate to her developing needs. This does not mean that she will refuse an education, only that she needs to learn as well by trial and error, by experimentation, by creative use of her imagination. She does not need to have the "gates" of her eyes, ears, and sexual body placed under male sovereignty, nor her person diminished by a patriarchal idea of woman. In sum, she must have a head as well as a room of her own.[13]

IV. At worst foregrounded daughter is mere biology, a legion of adulterous women — Eve, Sin, Astaroth, Astoreth, the Syrian damsels (1.448), the night hag (1.453), and the "bevy of fair women" from the tents (11.582), among others — who have transferred their mirroring dependencies to authorities and lovers other than Milton's God. Consider Sin's account of her role in her man's life:

> but familiar grown,
> I pleased, and with attractive graces won
> The most averse, thee chiefly, who full oft
> Thyself in me thy perfect image viewing
> Becam'st enamored.

> (2.761–5)

Unable to be an obedient "daughter" mirroring the light which the father invested in Lucifer, Sin can only be the dark and rebelliously lustful body of Satan's deformed self-perception projected into narcissistic psychic space as the pool in which Satan's disfashioned self is emblematically figured:

> Before the gates there sat
> On either side a formidable shape;
> The one seemed woman to the waist, and fair,
> But ended foul in many a scaly fold
> Voluminous and vast, a serpent armed
> With mortal sting.

> (2.648–53)

Since Sin's "gates" have been barbarically inseminated, since they reflect the energies of natural passion rather than the austere form of divine love, they do not generate children of light, but hordes of "unlightsome," uncivilized, native children — "hell hounds," to use Milton's phrase. The ideological point is that unchristian women are things of chaos, that fathers and sons rivalrous to Milton's God are by definition ignorant, expendable, and for the most part ethnically dark, and that the only viable solution to their troublesome presence as the rulers of a foreign territory is a military one.[14]

This is the gender structure of the new regime. What has been left out, of course, is the gender structure of the old regime — the gender structure which, breeding opposition and rebellion, was erased, from heaven at least, with Satan's expulsion and defeat. To fill in what has been left out is to recognize how thoroughly Milton's God depends on an imperial technology of power which reached Milton through Tudor bureaucracy and monastic Catholicism from imperial Rome and the Ottoman empire.[15] I begin, however, with a set of narrative models.

From Milton's point of view the father's ideal imperial position—the new regime—is to be alone and asexual, with one obedient and only begotten son, a number of absolutely "obedient" daughters, a loyal home territory as one's "wife," a peaceful and well-ordered colonial empire, and the means to protect everything of value from the nomadic barbarians beyond the walls. For a son the best situation in this regime is to be the only begotten heir of this emperor, to be brought up without a natural mother in a maternally organized palace, and when mature to serve the father in a home office, or, next best, if necessary, to serve in the colonies, but in either case to remain unmarried.

For the imperial father the next best, and nearly the worst, situation—as in the old regime—is to have a wife and many sons, to watch the wife and sons grow rebellious, to suffer the loss of a newly won colonial territory to a mutinous alliance of a third of his sons and a dangerous foreign rival under the leadership of his oldest and sexually mature son, and, despite the defeat of this son by his younger, obedient, and asexual son, to need local help in carrying out his imperial ambitions in this colony against strong native resistance.

It is, of course, the translation of the old regime into the new one which creates the best situations for those "sons" of the emperor who, like Christ, Adam, and Milton, were not born into the original and sexual royal family. Needing loyal public servants to replace his own either nonexistent or untrustworthy sons, or the perhaps even less trustworthy sons of his nobles, the Ottoman shah takes "unlightsome" but promising young men from their natural parents and homes in the provinces and brings them to the royal enclosure at Constantinople. He adopts them, and thereby supplies them with a new father—the shah himself—and a new corporate "mother": the court itself, the country, the religion, the imperial enterprise, the shah's idea of woman. In this educational space, or in some displaced, colonial replica of it such as Eden, the father, through intermediaries like Raphael and Michael, educates and civilizes these provincial sons. He pours his light into psyches made porous to receive it. He deprives these sons of contact with their natural parents, and then, when they are educated, places them in positions of administrative or military responsibility at home, or abroad in the colonies.

What makes *Paradise Lost* a particularly problematical text is that

Milton is writing all these narratives simultaneously, leaving out not only large segments of each of them but also the temporal, spatial, and generic markers which would allow us to separate them into distinct stories. As generations of deconstructive critics have observed, with Dr. Johnson foremost among them, the result is a vast confusion of eternal, conceptualized spirit and temporal, narrative matter.[16]

Consider one well-known example of this confusion, a crux in *Paradise Lost* where a simile has been an embarrassment to divinity and consistency. God's angelic border patrol has found Satan pestering Eve while she is sleeping. When this patrol of loyal soldiers begins "to hem [Satan] round With ported spears," it appears

> as thick as when a field
> Of Ceres ripe for harvest waving bends
> Her bearded grove of ears, which way the wind
> Sways them; the careful ploughman doubting stands
> Lest on the threshing-floor his hopeful sheaves
> Prove chaff.

(4.980–85)

Why is God doubting his own troops, and why in the posture of a ploughman? My argument is not just that existing explanations of this crux are less than satisfactory, but that they are so because the terms which the epic provides cannot explain this simile.[17] The crux exists because the text cannot afford to explain something which it also cannot leave out, and cannot in this case because it must locate the origin of evil somewhere other than in God himself. Thus to read this crux requires independent terms, terms that can fill in the missing pieces, terms that recognize that a new regime is writing an older one out of existence, but leaves a trace of the old regime to show the cause of its problems, and to justify the takeover.

In the new regime's terms the simile makes no sense at all. If God is asexual light and the single parent of adopted sons then his word created this field, brought forth corn, and it was good wheat. By extension, if God filled his angels with his liquid gold, they are loyal; if not, they are chaff. The field, heaven, is a passive object: she did her part, can, in fact, do nothing that is not done to her. Free will is nonexistent: the sons, swayed or not swayed, have no say in deciding what they do. Nor is this God dealing with persons; in his mind he is simply storing grain, and getting rid of chaff. One advantage is that the agricultural metaphors perhaps ease the conscience of those who want to make distinctions, which tyranny ignores, between things and people, between political opposition and criminal behavior.

According to the narrative structure and agricultural implications of this simile, however, God is a sexual husband, a ploughman, whose sexual wife, a field, not only has genetic influence, but also can make independent choices about her lovers. The point of linking his sons with their mother as corn to field is therefore either to displace anxiety about his own purity and creative mastery on to her or to question her adequacy, difference, or fidelity. In his mind a third of this woman's sons have already proven themselves chaff, so he has reason to be anxious about the other two-thirds. By extension, a monarch is evaluating potentially disloyal or inadequately trained home or colonial forces. Perhaps, despite his imperial self-image, he is no better than a ploughman: barely in control of his own people, less so of his colonies, and even less so of the winds of historical change.

Looking from this double perspective, it seems that Milton's simile records a moment after the birth of the new regime. The sexual ploughman who was not in control either of his wife or a third of his sons has already taken steps to become an asexual God of light wholly in control of everything in heaven. As readers we encounter the simile expecting the latter God already established but instead we find the former one solidifying his power. We also expect a wholly subordinated and backgrounded, inanimate, and asexual institutional woman, field/heaven, but we get a sexual, foregrounded person, wind/rebel, as well.

"Wind," then, is literally the crux of the matter. She provides Milton with a source of evil, not a direct presence, but, as the "Ceres" simile suggests, an indirect one standing ominously at the "head" of a chain of causation which reaches Milton through Adam, Adam through Eve, Eve through Satan, and Satan through that part of his mother which, like the mortal part of Milton's mother, was not brought under imperial control. She is the ultimate source of angelic and human disobedience; she is the power opposed to the power of Milton's God. Uncertainty about her nature and identity is unavoidable because several scenarios are possible. Either God's exiled and rebellious wife has corrupted some of her royal sons genetically, or her actual presence in exile may still be powerful enough to sway them. However, if "field" represents the new and submissive institutional mother, then the point is that she may be no match for the emotional ties by which her "sons'" natural, provincial mothers might sway them. If, on the other hand, "field" and "wind" are the same person, then the backgrounded, imperial mother has been split into a submissive aspect, field, and a repressed but subversive aspect, wind. In this case this double she sways some of her sons but not others.[18]

In any case the crux occurs because Satan's mother, though hidden under a trope, has been effectively left out of the text except as a kind of unacknowledged logical premise buttressing Milton's imperial ideology. But she sets a precedent; it is her absence from imperial space which the epic program of Milton's God extends to all other sexually fertile women. Eve, for example, enjoys a contraceptive, nonreproductive, and in several respects incestuous kind of dependent sexuality as Edenic wife, but when she becomes an independent, sexually mature woman, when the gates of her senses have been inseminated by Satan's rivalrous and fertile word, God bans her from Eden as he has banned Sin from heaven. The question to ask, then, recognizing that the background-foreground, agricultural-human representational techniques Milton relies on throughout *Paradise Lost* have broken down in this simile, is why Milton and his God must erase or ostracize the actual wife and sexual mother?

To understand that the natural, sexual mother with her horde of common ideas is responsible for all but the best of the scenarios I have sketched in above is to realize that, from the divine father's point of view, there is no more place for such a woman in the imperial program to which Milton has to maintain allegiance than there is, say, for Cleopatra in Caesar's program. The price of having a powerful, independent woman share one's rule, if not equality, is competition, plurality, difference, or, if not these, resentment, anger, revenge. Such a yoke compromises the imperial father's self-image, and confidence, limits his dissemination of light, qualifies his mastery, shows up his omniscience: if we are to trust this simile, no man, including God, finally has any real knowledge concerning a woman's genetic contribution to his sons, which is why the adopted son educational process is essential to an imperial bureaucracy. In the presence of natural woman every male is a "careful ploughman doubting."

To understand why the natural, sexual mother needs to be hidden or negated by the son is to see what it costs an adopted son of the shah to have such women in his life. He is a material, tainted or potentially tainted, suspect: at least a third of his genetic material is not the divine father's. He has two natural parents, and at best he has to earn his way as the shah's adopted son; if the shah is in any sense a careful ploughman he will sit and wait to see if his son will prove wheat or chaff, doing nothing more, perhaps, than educate him, an inpouring he may be too unporous, as a result of having had a mother, to receive. In sum, with a natural mother the son sinks from being resplendent spirit to mere mortal seed in the Edenic womb with only Raphael to help him advance.[19]

But if, as his God's imperial program is designed to do, Milton's new poetic regime must erase and deny the sexual mother, he must also include her in the text as an invisible presence, as an excess who is named "the wind," and whose sister is named Chaos. These two ungovernable biological and historical forces of change Milton links wholly with the sexual mother who consistently upsets the father's imperial control, the perfection of his sons, not to mention the consistency of Milton's epic. It is this woman, who is not background nor foreground nor even Satanic, but simply "before," "other," and "outside"—as the adolescent Eve was at the liquid plain—who is the raw material from which Milton must create a civilized wife and a subject territory. Or, to put this in heroic terms, she is the colonial project, the epic task, and the never-ending problem with whom the adopted son has to cope in his imperial post as bureaucrat, educator, or soldier.

The reason for Milton's superimposed, contradictory narratives, and for the background-foreground, animate-inanimate split in his imperial representation of woman is extra-imperial woman, whether she is named Chaos, wind, error, or Sin. This problem requires a solution. The solution one learns as an adopted son at court is mastery, control: to imitate, improve, and extend the father's aging, or failing, his inadequate or simply inexplicably withheld mastery at backgrounding, controlling, subordinating.[20]

Unlike his God, the adopted Protestant son must deal with actual women. His filial status obliges him to reproduce the divine father's image and imperial system through sons. Thus mastery of "natural" woman, of field and, he could hope, the wind, becomes an art of personal and cultural survival. The point of turning Eve, at the "liquid plain" and again after her fall, into the "Mother of Mankind" is not so that she will have many children, but so that she will produce multitudes of that imperially inscribed and ideologically pure entity, man—the one *parole* which Milton's God's *langue* desires to speak.

The colonial son knows that if his Eve is unclean, unsubjected, uncivilized, she cannot help but add genetic information (characteristics, that is, and not just material body) to, or subtract it from, a man's program of self-replication. Or worse, she will bear the illegitimate children of dark, native, and uncivilized rivals. The result of either contamination, like the results of any failure of an imperial ideology's never-ending battle against biology and history, is obvious: such an Eve would engender deformed, mutinous children "in bulk as huge As whom the fables name of monstrous size Titania, or Earthborn" (1.196–98). She would give birth to uncivilized "fables"—that liquid-plain genre in which she would see her unimperial self-image and hear it named by herself as a thing of value. As "Titania" suggests, she would reproduce herself as daughters.

To prevent such calamities, the principal labor of the heroic man whose mind has been freed from common ideas and uncivilized background environments known as cave, tribe, wilderness, field, barbaric mother, or alien lover, is to author the body of woman, making her, as he makes his poem, into nothing more than material, nothing more than a pure reproductive matrix for his replication of his imperial and subject "self." He knows that Eve will replicate himself if she is pure or is made pure. And to make her pure, she must be "castrated," and then, once her own head is removed, she must be given a new one by a patriarchal program of phallic supplementation. She cannot be allowed, as she is not allowed at the "liquid plain," to develop independence. Rather, she must be denied the rights and privileges of what Lacan calls the "phallus." She must not be allowed to stay in the "Imaginary" world of "smooth wat'ry image" and dream on her own. She must be subjected to Adam's dominance; she must accept his right and need to replace her image with "his" own, to have her dependent upon him and his knowledge, and to explain her dream in his symbolic, imperial terms.[21]

Milton's idea of woman was in part dictated and in part grew out of the father's ideas of other female "bodies": mind ("the mind through all her powers ... "), reason, flesh, nature, language, poetry and the arts, appetites and passions, children, society and its institutions, culture, virtues and graces, and the entire non-Christian world. Thus mastery over and purification of this extended female body is an additional inescapable, ceaseless, and necessary heroic labor for the regent son and inspired poet who has been warned that "apt the mind or fancy is to rove Unchecked, and of *her* roving is no end" (8.188–89, my italics).[22] However, he knows that when he has finally checked the endless roving of these female bodies, he, his mind, text, and civilization will stand as substantial expressions of his father's and his father's fathers' ideas in a perfect genealogical succession emanating from the mind of the new regime's God. Having come forth from the fallen and unclean body that is the old regime's mortal, foreign, vernacular, and biological mother, such a man will not suffer the torment of being trapped in or dependent upon that rotting *material* flesh on judgment day.

There is a risk. Psychic circumscription of a woman, as of colonial territories, though it keeps Eve submissive to a male head external to herself and to male control of her gates, and thus dependent, is a problematical venture. As Eve's dream, and her later self-subordination to the imaginative word of Adam's political and erotic rival, Satan, suggests, a subject woman's dependency is transferable, and to a certain extent it is also self-repairing. To put this in political terms is to argue that Milton's text of perfect mastery is broken by the patriarch's and colonialist's inescapable dilemma. The analogs are Lear and Prospero. Either Milton and his God arrest the development of their daughters, wives, obedient sons, and territories in a dependency stage, thereby running the risk, or rather the inevitable fact, of rivals, betrayals, mutiny, and rebellion. Or they allow their alleged dependents a mirror stage (which paradoxically prevents them from being mirrors), permit their subsequent development, accept their resulting independence, their inevitable rewriting of the Word, and renegotiate their several kinds of intercourse at a considerable cost to their monopoly and to their expectation of absolute control, infinite supply, and constant satiation.

Milton's situation is clearly a difficult one. The required solution, control, creates a vicious circle. Mastery pares woman down to a controllable, inanimate object, a narcissistic mirror. It creates a creature with whom one cannot discourse, an echo starving in the hills, and leaves an enormous excess of self, and potentiality for self, on the cutting-room floor, excess that is officially worthless but, on the contraband market, is of such great value that a strong woman, despite whatever fiction of submission or obedience, will refuse to give it up, reclaiming it, as Eve does, in an act of rebellion; an excess of such considerable attraction and worth, moreover, that strong men, against every orthodox ambition, look so tenaciously for it in their memories, and through entanglements with unmastered and unattenuated secular, classical, artistic, or foreign women that, like Samson, they get ensnared again and again in seeking that pearl which they have cast aside and lost. It is not accidental, I am suggesting, that *Paradise Regained* is about one son who does not, and that *Paradise Lost* and *Samson Agonistes* are about three sons who do, get involved with fallen women.[23]

This vicious circle reaches further. Mastery would also pare down Milton's poem and consciousness, his emotional capacities and historical, material self so that they too might stand as perfect icons in God's Edenic studio, their classical devices and subject matter, their ideas, passions, actions, and memories as rubble about their feet, their adolescent "mornings," like Eve's, cast down as waste upon the floor. But again, the more poem or mind or self is mastered, the more they, too, like Eve, betray the speech of their imperial author in an uncheckable rebellion against the patriarchal word.

With this orthodox, patriarchal idea of woman, this labor of mastery, this loyalty to his God at the price of his absent and exiled mother, sister, brother, and self, the Milton who finished the late poems seems to have had little difficulty. How could he and survive? How could he and succeed? To have received God's light into his unlightsome but porous, biological self has considerable advantages. It means that *Paradise Lost* will be an imperial monument, though also an increasingly large grave-yard of dead and dying common ideas. It gives him adopted son status, places him in a privileged enclosure, guarantees an imperial inheritance. It allows confidence that the paternal order of things will never change, makes the past and future known entities. It assuages his fear of things being out of control, his fear of being judged and found wanting, his fear of not knowing what was going to happen. It legitimizes his narcissistic identification with his God, and it keeps him from having to worry about alternatives, or from having to dream about other and different worlds. It allows him to sacramentalize the aggressive and acquisitive forces of repression and oppression, to write a text of revenge against every-thing he could not control. It allows him to be a Raphael laboring to make woman, poem, and reader mirrors of his iconic, narcissistic self. It allows him to be Michael, a right arm helping his divine father remove the rivalrous head of his natural father, Charles I. It allows him to imagine a perfectly submissive Eve, to write a text in which the fiction of her submission becomes a fact, a text in which he in his chariot of brilliant words is victorious at last over woman's refractory behavior.

But the Milton who enjoyed these advantages, and who wrote these late poems, seems also to have found such an idea, such a loyalty, and such a posture of superiority problematic. This other Milton knew that he had not always been the heroic son, that he had held onto the natural mother, that he had ideas of woman which were not divine father's, that, like Adam, he had felt passion and not just love for woman, that he had dismissed his father's wisdom which alone is truly fair, that he had been entangled in female charms. He knew that, like Satan, he had raged against the father's power, the father's restrictions, and the father's indif-ference to the son's need not to be infantilized. Moreover, he knew that he had written poetry contrary to his father's idea of poetry, poetry that mirrored the dark and cratered particularities of his mortal self rather than the father's light, poetry that had mirrored curiosity and play, courage and rebellion rather than sublimity and submission. Milton had not wanted *Paradise Lost* to be a sinful mirror projecting itself out from the side of his mortal head. He had not wanted to listen, though listen he did, to Orpheus's Muse—she who could "not defend Her son" from the Thracian women's "savange clamor," "she [like Eve's] an empty dream" (9.34–39). But he knew that as a text of man's disobedience *Paradise Lost* reflected the image of his own disobedient self. He had long sat with a mess of porridge when he should have been looking to his inheritance, and, coming to his inner senses, he knew he had to confess and do penance for what he now had to recognize as misperception, as slowness, as failure, as pleasure. To fail to confess and do penance was to be Satanic, doomed. Yet to confess publicly was painful; worse, it would undermine his authority and his image. And so *Paradise Lost, Paradise Regained,* and *Samson Agonistes,* though imperial texts, can also be said to be private confessional texts, admitting under the covering and displacing trope of sacred story the failures of the private life.

Consider, for example, the matter of Adam "fondly overcome by female charms," and this remarkable passage where Adam mistakes "a bevy of fair women . . . In gems and wanton dress" for decent and interesting women:

> . . . to the harp they sung
> Soft amorous ditties, and in dance came on:
> The men, though grave, eyed them, and let their eyes
> Rove without rein, till in the amorous net
> Fast caught, they liked, and each his liking chose;
> And now of love they treat till th' ev'ning star,
> Love's harbinger, appeared; then all in heat
> They light the nuptial torch, and bid invoke
> Hymen, then first to marriage rites invoked;
> With feast and music all the tents resound.
> Such happy interview and fair event
> Of love and youth not lost, songs, garlands, flow'rs
> And charming symphonies attached the heart . . .
>
> (11.582–95)

A parallel: unfallen Eve looked for play and love in her "liquid plain," so fallen Adam, brought to this, does likewise, looking at this play and love on this "plain" (11.580). And perhaps a reassuring parallel: as Eve corrected by a bodiless voice, so Adam corrected by Michael: "Of goddesses, so blithe, so smooth, so gay, Yet empty of all good wherein consists Woman's domestic honor and chief praise" (ll. 615–17).

It would be speculative, of course, to go beyond parallels and the bourgeois morality of a rising Protestant class to regard this scene of "lost" youth as a disguised autobiographical confession, a penitential repudiation of Milton's own youthful erotic errors, perceptual or otherwise. But to hide a text of memory (positively valued in the singular) within a text of doctrine (condemned in the plural) would demonstrate to the father just how completely this prodigal son had perfected in himself and in his poetry the paternal image, the paternal idea. Moreover, would it not help extenuate Milton's errors to show that they were also Adam's, and thus a hereditary remnant of the old regime, not merely a personal or willful deviation?[24]

We have been discussing the success of Milton's efforts to take possession of his God's inheritance by proving submission, in part, to this God's idea of woman, but surely the point to make first is that had Milton succeeded at his self-heroicizing task we should have found him and his poems far less interesting and problematical. As it is, we do find Milton important and interesting, and though this is not necessarily proof that he failed at the heroic ambition he inherited from his God, it does suggest that the part of him which is of permanent interest to us is the part that temporized, the part that failed to measure up to his God's idea of him as man and poet, the "invisible" part which his mother—as field, wind, Chaos—contributed to his character and art.

Of the significant ways in which the genetic contribution of Milton's mother subverts patriarchal ambition, the least subject to denial is Milton's brief for, as opposed to his confession of, his past. The text we have is also a text of aggressively subversive power. It risks rewriting a monarch's idea of monarchy by temporarily translating king and judge into a father who will allow his children a time and a history during which they might correct their misdemeanors or persist in their felonies. Milton is confessing to a misdemeanor in order to deny that he has committed a felony, and though this plea for temporary permission to have had an idea of woman and self different from his father's may seem weak, Milton's strategy is in fact bolder. It shows God inventing, asks him to invent, praises him for having invented, threatens to expose him as tyrant if he does not invent an idea that supplements the established order of things. Put in contemporary terms Milton's concept of adolescence allows Milton's God to accept temporarily the biological fact that children, like poems, have more than one parent. "Understand," Milton is saying to his God, "that I had a mortal mother, a mortal body, and therefore could not have perfectly reflected your image in the pool of my flesh at birth. Nor could my mother have been a virginal echo of your wish and will." In short, Milton is protecting himself, he is asking for something, forcing assurances, and his limited victory is that he makes it possible for an angry monarch who decreed that the mother's "genes" would be nonexistent to understand that her "genetic" material is an inescapable part of a child's historical identity, though not, he is arguing, a permanent or irremediable part of that identity.[25]

What makes *Paradise Lost* of interest from a nonideological perspective is its status as sacred history, as manifesto of imperial ideology, as personal confession, as humbly aggressive revision. It is important to understand these consequences of empire. But as important are the invisible spaces Milton creates within his iconic monument which allow him to keep his lost youth and his exiled mother. Ideological representation itself, that is, becomes a way of holding on permanently, though in white ink, to an idea of woman, and of self, poetry, desire, independence, and freedom, which Milton did not want to lose but had to lose. That the battles in *Paradise Lost* are fictional battles allows them to be both won forever and in a sense never won.[26]

To put the larger effect of the contribution of Milton's mother to *Paradise Lost* in the terms of my implicit analogy, Milton was a party to a custody fight. In this fight the parent with vast power, status, education, privilege, and wealth had exiled the other parent into deprivation and oblivion. Then, years later, he sent his oldest, rival, and natural son, biology, falling after wife and mother in an effort to keep himself in endless power in the person of his "maternal," younger, and asexually begotten son, theology, whom he forbade to grow up—"maternal" because this son, uncontaminated by the mother, would be the "wife" the actual wife had failed to be. In such a situation, considering how dangerous it was for Milton to hold onto any part of his mother or of his older and rebellious half-brother, and recognizing how burdened *Paradise Lost* is with courage, caution, and various confusions of sexuality and gender, we can most easily gain access to the rival ideas of woman Milton has permanently inscribed *within* the father's idea by the mechanisms of displacement and denial if we ask what the principal woman in *Paradise Lost* represents. It is this woman who stands in the text as Milton's icon, as a secret cache of nostalgic remnants of the excluded other, and as a conscious defense against any such collection of charged traces.

There is every reason to think that Milton believed his character, Eve, to be a true representation of a historical woman and the things this woman did. This had to be the case: the heroic Milton had to be able to say that he had written a text of true knowledge. Nevertheless, to pursue Eve along Milton's textual path does not bring us up truth's high hill to greater factual knowledge of a woman who is perfectly other. Rather, climbing this hill brings us to ourselves, to our codes for, and to our representations of, actual women, and, for our purposes here, to those pieces of his unsubmissive self which Milton hid, by transference, in his Eve—in the "fictional," secular, and classical materials, the excess, that is, which Milton added to the relatively bare and unadorned Eve of his biblical and theological sources.[27]

As this hiding technique is not unique to Eve, it is necessary first to see how it works more generally in *Paradise Lost* as a mode of ambivalence. To split off and then to project his own rebellious prodigality onto Satan, and his patriarchial rage onto God, irrespective of his need to condemn, protect, appropriate, or legitimize either, was Milton's way to preserve *all* of himself permanently by representing this "all" in a text and its characters. To displace his rebellious prodigality so that it could be safely condemned and destroyed in the distant, Satanic other is also to keep it, to preserve one's attraction to and identification with it. Similarly, to return to the father the rage which was received from him is to hate this gift as intrusion and demand, and to persist in this hatred no matter how much such a gift is also appreciated and needed.

In this field of ambivalence Eve enters as a compromise cipher who acts out in a minor, temporary mode Satan's absolute political refusal to negotiate those economic and psychological exchanges whereby the child must trade the mother, and the mother's part in his adolescent self, for the divine father's inheritance. Thus, while Adam sits dutifully receiving inspiration at the knee of the father's servant, Eve is allowed to wander about imagining things, both in order to rule Eden and to get out of it, which are two versions of one desire: to give up dependency upon the father, and to appropriate his autonomous powers and privileges. Eve, "Undecked save with herself, more lovely fair Than wood-nymph, or the fairest goddess feigned" (5.380–81), is the natural, pagan, imaginative half of the Adamic poet who has promised to bend himself to the hopeless labor of being a pure, Christian, and laureate poet.

What is important about Eve, therefore, is that she can do what Milton and Adam cannot do: she can imagine alternatives, she can be dressed in classical poetic devices—"She as a veil down to the slender waist Her unadorned golden tresses wore Disheveled" (4.304–6), she can appropriate, however temporarily, the father's prerogative to author her own life and circumstances, and she can do these things over and against the self-castrating and self-infantilizing consequences of Adam's and Milton's obedience. Curious, willful, experimental, witty, capable of imaginative flight, sexual excitement, and courage—is it not clear that she enjoys, moves, and talks as a way of getting power and pleasure in the space of the father's text of submission? And thus, because she can represent the Milton who had not stood blindly and dutifully within the textual space of the father's will, and the Milton who also was not irretrievably Satanic, Eve is Milton's assurance that much of the self he once had and of the poetry he had written would and yet would not be translated instantly and forever either into serpent, ashes, and a hiss, or into a perfect icon of obedient and mimetic perfection.

Like all of Milton's characters, each of whom is, to some extent, a projected and displaced part of Milton's person or behavior, actual or imagined, past or present, Eve allows a ritually self-fragmented, self-dismembered Milton to scatter his memories across a landscape of heroic obedience where these memories are symbolically maintained as presence even as they are being annihilated as rivalrous excess: "These lulled by nightingales embracing slept And on their naked limbs the flowr'y roof Showr'd roses, which the morn repaired" (4.771–73).[28] To extend the method of this piece to the whole is to argue that *Paradise Lost* inscribes within its sacred history a biography of Milton's relations with women. Thus it includes his passion—"Commotion strange . . . weak Against the charm of beauty's powerful glance" (8.531–32); his "misplaced" devotion—"as with new wine intoxicated both They swim in mirth" (9.1008–9); his masculine, sexual pride—"For never did thy beauty since the day I saw thee first and wedded thee, adorned With all perfections, so inflame my sense With ardor to enjoy thee, fairer now Than ever" (9.1029–33); his inability to win arguments under pressure even though it means loss—"Go; for thy stay, not free, absents thee more" (9.372); his sense of loss—"O Eve"; and shattered happiness—"and all the faded roses shed." Such is the power of subversive pleasure to be one with and at the same time to trope the scene of obedience.

That his complex idea of Eve allows Milton to maintain a kind of psychic integrity, not to mention a kind of psychic equilibrium, despite ritual "dismembering" is just one aspect of Eve's usefulness in Milton's text. Once she is opened as a self-referential memory place this pandoric Eve cannot be kept from helping Milton leap across the distances of displacement and over the walls of repression to gain access to fragments of a lost self and to the altogether forbidden other—those women, and the experiences and expectations accompanying them, whom Milton has lost but is determined not to lose, even though he must lose them, a second time. Once disclosed, that is, Eve insists on becoming herself in all that self's multiplicity.

Eve, in short, is a rival source, a store of natural and maternal attributes and qualities that are unwanted and unvalued in heaven, attributes and qualities for which there are no ideas in God's head. Although Eve's difference and value are acknowledged implicitly by Milton, they are also openly asserted, cost what it may either to his security or to the consistency of his text. For Adam, who in theory gets his light solely from his God, to say at Eve's "birth" that the as-yet-unsubordinated Eve "disappeared and left me dark" (8.478) is momentarily to shatter the ideological structure of Milton's epic by locating, in what should be a mirror, a light that cannot be God's. Nevertheless, it is this brilliant Eve, "not far off, Such as [Milton] saw her in [his] dream" (8.481–82), whom Milton must pare down and transform into a mirror; it is this Eve whom he must also preserve as she is "or for ever to deplore Her loss, and other pleasures all abjure," including the pleasure of being his divine father's approved son.

What *Paradise Lost* gave Milton in addition to an imperial inheritance, making submission bearable, was an invisible means by which he could endlessly defer having to give up his mother's and his divine father's repressed ideas of woman, self, sexuality, and existence. And such is the power of Milton's desire, that once it is inscribed in white ink within his God's Word, that Word, for all Milton's submissive rigor, finds itself voicing a polyphony of rival, ambivalent, anguished, and nostalgic imperatives, whose tropes no hermeneutical methodology to this day has been able to silence.

As Milton's critics, we, too, have had conflicting ideas of Eve. She has been the obedient minion of our patriarchal will, and she has been a rapidly diminishing, temporary, and yet textually endless sanctuary space for our most tenaciously held conscious and unconscious private memories. So my question is, What do we do with the alternative idea of woman which we find in this text? Do we simply participate in its doublenesses, its deferrals, its fetishized maintenances, its inescapable trials, and its dependency?[29] Or do we break the dependency, lift the repression, recognize the displaced and disseminated pieces of woman and self, cancel the hyperboles, erase the extreme polarities of innocence, corruption, praise, and condemnation, reduce our previously necessary narcissistic rage and voyeuristic obsessions, and thereby allow alternative ideas of woman to oppose Milton's father's "true" and "beautiful" idea?

For women readers, how could Eve not be an icon to be decisively rewritten by the very persons whom Milton had cherished in his doubly treasonable, doubly lethal way? For men readers the choice is either to stand with those who have worked to extend a patriarchal idea of woman throughout an infinite male universe as unalterable, orthodox truth, or to ally oneself with those who have struggled to reduce this patriarchal structure of imperial signification to a concept in the minds, and in the practice, of one's predecessors, however brilliant or influential.

Either choice is expensive. To remain in the world of Milton's God, as Milton's method with Eve indicates, is to keep striking a constraining and disfiguring alliance between the displacements and recuperations dependency requires. The psychic cost of remaining dependent upon Milton's God is, however, to go blind: to save a little, idealized bit (Eve) of the repressed and mortal other as a way of saving little, idealized bits of ourselves is to refuse to recognize and, more important, to use those aspects of ourselves and the other which we have excluded, condemned, or disowned.[30] By this path one's material self, like "Milton's," is textually torn asunder for the sake of a perfect self-image. But to take the other option requires the costs and gains of having to acknowledge one's material, historical self, its other parent's "genetic" existence, its need for an adequate rather than an imperial education, not to mention having to acknowledge the injustices and damages to self and alien societies, to women and children caused by the orthodoxy of Milton's God. As Virginia Woolf reminds us,[31] the disenfranchised, uneducated, and dependent, actual woman had her imperial place, and thus she also had her rages, her needs for revenge, her untutored noises. She had tempted her children to her darkest side; she had fueled the insane rebellions of her first born and Satanic sons; moreover, she had broken the father's fictions, laws, hearts. She often did seem to have nothing but a horde of vermin issuing forth from below her waist. And given all of this, she did seem to require being unsexed, cleansed, imprisoned, purified, burnt. But despite these man-made terrors that lay beyond the patriarchal enclosure, despite these encouragements to set sail for an imperial Rome, Milton is holding on to his absent mother and forsaken lover, and not merely as a regressive prelude to disowning them. Rather let us think with Empson that Milton has preserved them as a pearl within the bitter drink he is pouring down a usurping monarch's throat, an action he is spurred on to finally by the terrible absoluteness of their absence, their loss.

Long before *Paradise Lost* was written, Milton had lost both of his "parents." He had been forced to give up his mother, her "fancies" and "her prime," in order to keep his tyrant father's love and inheritance. He had lost his father because he had been unable to relinquish his memory of and desire for his mother's love and presence. Thus he had lost two paradises: he had lost this earth, and he had lost as well an empire not to be found on this earth about which he could only dream. And though we read the text of a prodigal son who knows exactly what he must do to repair the imperial loss and regain the father, what we also read is an extraordinary effort by an orphan to regain his other parent, his siblings, himself, his other and original home. Both ambitions are futile, and tragically misguided. Futile, because both losses are irreparable and imaginary; tragic, because in his long show of treasonable love and loving submission there is no healing grief. As there is no work of mourning—only an impossible labor of desperate reparation and covert nostalgia—there can be no fresh woods or pastures new, or at least none here, though elsewhere with the absent father is clearly the textual space in which Milton's hopes must forever lie.

In conclusion, Milton's motive for poetry is that he *has* one parent, but *had* two. What I have tried to do in this "writing" of *Paradise Lost*'s white ink is to suggest that the unsubmissive part of him would have us switch these verbs, and admit that monotheism, a narcissistic translation of parenting into a regressive, sadomasochistic dependency upon the "kidnapped" son's endlessly grateful submission, tragically violates inalienable human rights—Eve's, Milton's, and our own.

NOTES

I am indebted to Stephen Orgel for a conference paper, "Prospero's Absent Wife," presented at Renaissance Woman/Renaissance Man: Studies in the Creation of Culture and Society, Yale University, Mar. 12, 1982, and for his helpful comments on this paper. A faculty fellowship from Dartmouth College, and the valuable support of my colleague, David S. Kastan, are also gratefully acknowledged.

1. For lack of space I am ignoring the complicated issue of whether a Neoplatonic godhead can contain negative ideas or ideas of absence. From Milton's text it seems clear that such ideas exist in Milton's God's consciousness as a mote in the eye to be expelled or as a vacuum to be filled.

2. Jacques Derrida, "White Mythology: Metaphor in the Text of Philosophy," *New Literary History*, 6 (1974), 11. I am particularly indebted to Gary F. Waller's "Deconstruction and Renaissance Literature," in *Assays: Critical Approaches to Medieval and Renaissance Texts*, vol. 2, ed. Peggy A. Knapp (Pittsburgh: University of Pittsburgh Press, 1982), and to the following: Derrida's discussion of a text as "an assemblage" of "different threads and different lines of sense or force" in *Speech and Phenomena*, trans. David B. Allison (Evanston: Northwestern University Press, 1973), p. 132; William Empson, *Milton's God* (London: Chatto & Windus, 1961); M. M. Bakhtin, *The Dialogic Imagination* (Austin: University of Texas Press, 1981); and Roland Barthes, "The Death of the Author," in *Image-Music-Text*, trans. Stephen Heath (London: Fontana, 1977), p. 146.

3. All citations are from *The Complete Poetical Works of John Milton*, ed. Douglas Bush (Boston: Houghton Mifflin Co., 1965).

4. In theory woman is imagined as an essentially inanimate *tabula rasa*, or wax surface, or mirror, which takes the impression of the man or men she is with. In civilized company she, like the full moon, will be civilized. To move from the civilized center and its regent son out past the margin and periphery is to fall from being one to another kind of mirror. If in between, as Eve is between Adam and Satan, as Milton is between his classical and biblical sources and genres, as Milton's reader is between Milton's text of subversive mutiny and his text of obedient submission, or as the earth is between day and night, woman becomes a reflection of each, fair above but foul below where she literally has lost man's phallic light:

> If earth industrous of herself fetch day
> Travelling east, and with her part averse
> From the sun's beam meet night, her other part
> Still luminous by his ray.

(8.137–40)

5. Milton uses figures of nature and earth to signify the ideal natural behavior of woman as maternal background. His personifications of time, on the other hand, signify maternal woman's social graces, appearance, and deportment as functions of male presence: "Morn, her rising" is sweet with Adam present, but without him is not sweet (4.641); "evening . . . Had in her sober livery all things clad" (4.599) under divine tutelage; "night with her will bring Silence" (7.105–6) inside the imperial enclosure. The point is that the most conventional of Milton's tropes express, or reflect, ideological doctrine.

6. In psychological terms colonializing the mother or a territory is a way for the asexual son or colonial regent to divide and conquer his parents or a territory. By desexualizing the mother, and by displacing the sexual father with an asexual, imperial, and invisible divinity with whom he identifies, he can replace this sexual father in the mother's affections. In this way, by silencing her sexuality and by removing the actual father who satisfied it or by filling, in an asexual way, the vacuum the actual father and his kind of sexuality had filled, the asexual son will get the love, care, attention, and power he desires. She presumably will get the kind of son-lover she wants, and he will dispose of anyone who has a different effect on the mother or wife or territory, anyone, that is, who has a passionate or sexual rather than, say, a sublime or aloof effect. "I scarcely feel," Virginia Woolf wrote in a 1918 diary entry, "that Milton lived or knew men and women; except for the peevish personalities about marriage and the woman's duties," cited in Sandra M. Gilbert, "Patriarchal Poetry and Women Readers: Reflections on Milton's Bogey," *PMLA*, 93 (1978), 368–82. See also Alice Miller, *The Drama of the Gifted Child* (New York: Basic Books, 1981).

7. To take an instance from English history, Elizabeth knew, when she commissioned Essex, that Ireland was not large enough to keep him from becoming a mutinous, adult rival. No doubt she would have known that an India, if she had one, would simply have inflated his ambition all the more. So, as Gaza was for Samson, Ireland was the place to hem him in and test him. She stood by, a "careful ploughman doubting," as did Samson's God, to see which way the wind would sway him — Essex proving chaff, Samson becoming wheat under his God's millstones.

8. To oppose chaos and night as natural, physical forces, or war as a destructive terror, is one thing, but to personify them as alien, ethnically inferior, aged, and in two cases female political opponents shows Milton's God imitating the imperial tyrant's refusal to distinguish between persons and things, political opposition and criminal behavior, a strategy evident in the absolute equation of Satan's political rebellion with everything that is evil. Such terms as "Bellona," "Chaos," and "Nature's fardest verge," no matter how conventional, have here the effect of turning the indigenous population and the existing cultural practices of foreign territories into dark and inanimate matter. The point of this kind of personification is to discredit a sex, and to depopulate a territory for occupation by its new colonial ruler or inhabitants.

9. Neither Milton nor his sources had an answer to the problem of why his God had not already reduced every existing piece of foreign territory to such a

submissive posture other than the question-begging need for heroic labor, on the part of God's subjects, to extend the empire.

10. In *Paradise Lost* Milton's prophetic speaker seems to have something like this same appearance-disappearance technique in mind when, after finishing his "presumptuous" labor of drawing empyreal air as "an earthly guest" in "the heav'n of heav'ns," he begs Urania to "return [him] to [his] native element" lest he fall (7.12–16).

11. Being foregrounded is also risky for Eve, because exposing a powerful woman in this way is one traditional way to eliminate her as a threat to imperial hierarchy. Consider, for example, one reason why Virgil foregrounds, in the person of Dido, the female landscape and landscape-abstraction obstacles, Scylla, and Circe, which test Homer's Odysseus. To embody these natural forces in an independent, royal woman capable of subordinating Aeneas to her rule necessitates, but more important enables, her destruction as a political rival, and as an immoral person. Moreover it guarantees her return, albeit as ashes, and Aeneas's, as imperial master, to their native elements, nature and empire.

12. For an alternative point of view on the issue of Milton's androgyny, see in particular Marilyn R. Farwell, "Eve, the Separation Scene, and the Renaissance Idea of Androgyny," *Milton Studies*, 16 (1982), 3–20.

13. See Christine Froula, "When Eve Reads Milton: Undoing the Canonical Economy," *Critical Inquiry*, 10 (1983), 321–47.

14. By metonomy, all gates under independent, foreign, or rebellious control are lethal, issuing forth death of one kind or another: damnation for pagan chieftains, catalogued as Satan's crew, who refuse to convert to Christianity; mortality to those who listen, as Adam does, to discourse generated from impressions entering through the gates of Eve's and his own senses; death to those sons, like Samson, who stray beyond the gates of the imperial enclosure into a foreign woman's sexual embrace.

15. Milton says he is writing an "argument Not less but more heroic" than pagan literature, its subject matter ("stern Achilles" or "Juno's ire"), and its devices (9.13–15, 18), but to begin tracing the political textuality traversing *Paradise Lost* is to see how thoroughly inscribed in Milton's God's presence is the presence, too, of Roman imperial practice. See, among other helpful studies, Edward N. Luttwak, *The Grand Strategy of the Roman Empire* (Baltimore: Johns Hopkins University Press, 1976). The Janissary model is outlined by Norman Itzkowitz, *Ottoman Empire and Islamic Tradition* (Chicago: University of Chicago Press, 1980). For a discussion of this practice in Inca civilization, see John Howland Rowe, "Inca Policies and Institutions Relating to the Cultural Unification of the Empire," in *The Inca and Aztec States*, ed. George A. Collier et al. (New York: Academic Press, 1982). Cf: Freud's discussion of the displaced child in *Moses and Monotheism* (New York: Vintage Books, 1939), pp. 10ff. From a longer agricultural perspective, imperial educational programs are one chapter in the history of hybridization; from an even longer cultural perspective they are one of the many "greenhouses" (such as religions, cities, universities, professions, military encamp-

ments, monasteries, administrative bureaucracies, and, among others, literature) which civilizations use to nurture nature.

16. The traditional explanation of these rival narratives, accommodation theory, is that the historical narrative makes the eternal one accessible to us. This theory fails, however, on three grounds. The eternal narrative *as an idea* is already wholly accessible to us: Milton has clearly signified it. The theory itself lacks a principle of selectivity: it cannot explain why what is in the text is in or why what has been left out has been left out, except to repeat after Milton, "be lowly wise." It fails to show that the combination leaves us without an adequate theory of responsibility, or of crime, or therefore of narrative.

17. For alternative readings of this simile see, among others, William Empson, *Some Versions of Pastoral* (Norfolk, Conn.: New Directions, 1950), p. 172, and Christopher Ricks, *Milton's Grand Style* (Oxford: Oxford University Press, 1963), p. 129.

18. In support of this identification of wind and rebellious woman, consider that for Wyatt, among others, trying to capture the wind in a net metaphorically sums up the futility and stupidity of thinking one will be able to master a powerful and independent sublunary woman: "I leave off therefore, Since in a net I seek to hold the wind," ll. 7–8 of "Whoso list to hunt," *Collected Poems of Sir Thomas Wyatt*, ed. K. Muir and P. Thomson (Liverpool: Liverpool University Press, 1969).

19. Having had a mother also means that one must be born, that one must leave Eden through her mortal gates hand in hand to take one's place in the reproductive, biological world where children have two parents and geneological chaos reigns. Politically speaking, it means that as soon as one is educated, either at colonial school or at court, one will again be expelled—one will have to leave heaven's "ever-during gates" and labor in the colonies, where one will experience, like the son on the cross, the painful revenge of one's natural fathers, or, like Orpheus dismembered, his head adrift on the flood, the rage of one's natural mothers.

My debt here is to William Kerrigan's work on Milton's family situation and its implications, especially Aubrey's report that Milton's blindness was inherited from his mother: "blindness," Kerrigan writes, "was in one important way a maternal inheritance descending from the line of Eve.... From the limitless strength of the Father [Milton] could solicit a 'Celestial Patroness' free from the taint of earthly mothers—a mother who will not disillusion." *The Sacred Complex: On the Psychogenesis of "Paradise Lost"* (Cambridge: Harvard University Press, 1983), p. 180.

20. The code of mastery in an imperial hierarchy is that one is male to those one dominates, female to those one submits to. Ancient Night, for example, is male when he is ruling his domains, but domesticated by God's creative power he turns into a woman: "night with her will bring silence" (7.106). Likewise Satan, defeated, turns into a serpent which is Sin's "part averse" and the creature whose head Milton's God crushes in punishment for its part in Eve's adultery. For an

interesting discussion of male castration anxiety as it relates to a seventeenth-century "womanish man" and "manish woman" pamphlet controversy and to Milton, see Margaret Ferguson's "Milton and Women on the Outskirts of Canonical" (forthcoming).

21. Jacques Lacan, "The Mirror Phase," *New Left Review*, 51 (1968), 71ff.; Rosalind Coward and John Ellis, *Language and Materialism* (London: Routledge and Kegan Paul, 1977), pp. 109ff. The difference between the mirror stage, where Eve would see her image, and dependency, where she would see only Adam's, is that when constrained by the Adamic image she cannot develop her own capacities, or any confidence that she has capacities other than Adam's. The larger fear is that "if the mother is not contained then semiotic riot is the result." I quote Catherine Gallagher's "Response" to Neil Hertz, "Medusa's Head: Male Hysteria under Political Pressure," *The End of the Line: Essays on Psychoanalysis and the Sublime* (New York: Columbia University Press, 1985), p. 196.

22. In the category of language I am including institutions like the press and the theater, areas, that is, where censorship becomes, in the father's eye, a legitimate mode of "cleansing" bodies. See Jonathan Goldberg's study of discourse and power in *James I and the Politics of Literature* (Baltimore: Johns Hopkins University Press, 1983).

23. Nor is it coincidental, considering the numerological significance of the number 9, that 9.999, the moment of Adam's fall, reads: "But fondly overcome with female charms," an obsessive motif writ small at numerous points throughout the epic—Japhet's "fair looks ensnared mankind" (4.719), for example; large in Raphael's admonition on Adamic passion; and at length of Samson, drawn "awry enslaved With dotage, and his sense depraved" by female charms (*SA* 1040–42). Given this preoccupation one can argue that being overcome, whether by sensual charms or argumentative persuasion, both versions of military defeat, is more of a fall than eating, in that this defeat, this foreign penetration of one's self, shifts one's oral attention from imperial to foreign and forbidden fruit. Moreover, it is precisely this failure that Abdiel and the Christ of *Paradise Regained* successfully resist, heroic because they overcome temptation. Of course the other side is that one wants to be overcome by one's God: Donne's assertion to his God, for example, that he "never shall be free, Nor ever chaste, except you ravish me." "Holy Sonnet 14," ll. 13–14, *John Donne: The Compete English Poems*, ed. A. J. Smith (Harmondsworth: Penguin Books, Ltd, 1971).

24. A text of fear and duty is, of course, only one inflection of this scenario: surely the imperial father's iconic text would argue love as Milton's motive for confession and happiness as his reward. It is the anxious and ambivalent son whose nostalgia is indirect and subversive. Cf. Stephen Greenblatt's discussion of subversion and submission in *Renaissance Self-Fashioning* (Chicago: University of Chicago Press, 1980) and in "Invisible Bullets: Renaissance Authority and Its Subversion, *Henry IV* and *Henry V*," in *Political Shakespeare: New Essays in Cultural Materialism*, ed. J. Dollimore and A. Sinfield (Ithaca: Cornell University Press, 1985), pp. 18–47.

25. This is just one of this monarch's new ideas. Others follow: of a deity

capable of mercy, and of woman as nourishing maternal matrix and submissive wife, ideas opposed to the older, monastic views that found God merely just, and woman so irreparably unclean that father and son had to be divorced from her as thoroughly and as quickly as possible. Whether Milton is insensitive to the implications of such "new" ideas for his claims of his God's divine eternal omniscience and perfection, or is simply avoiding this issue of divine change, or generously implying that fallen man has only just now got his deity right must remain a moot point. In any case these two patriarchal ideas of woman are absurd from the point of view of biology because they create a false difference between male and female genetic material. This makes Milton's argument anachronistic in the sense that he reads adolescence, time, women, and history as being radically different from life, men, and consciousness, which he regarded as being a priori and permanent.

26. Also moot is the question of how conscious this holding on was, and the issue of whether, and if so how, we can answer such a question.

27. I have in mind Stanley Fish's iconic discussion of the "unreliable" text Milton writes in order to entrap the unwary reader. Of the critics other than William Empson who have asked why there is so much excess and "waste" in a text so iconic in ambition, and why it is given such prominence, Fish's argument is perhaps the best known: Milton puts all the rich and beautiful adolescent trinkets about the door of the cave where the invisible icon stands, so that those of us who are like Stephano and Trinculo can mistake this inherently imaginary, material "trash" — Eve's watery image, for example, or Satan's massive weapons — if we will, for what is truly real, namely, the symbolic structure of the adult Father's law. See *Surprised by Sin* (Berkeley: University of California Press, 1971).

28. My debt here is to Nancy J. Vickers, "Diana Described: Scattered Women and Scattered Rhyme," *Critical Inquiry,* 8 (1981), 265–80.

29. The paradox is that the more omnipotent one conceives oneself or one's God as being, the more dependent one in fact has become, so that to have a fantasy of total omnipotence is to be dependent upon everything exterior to the self. For Milton to project omnipotence upon the father is, ironically, to create a fantasy in which God is wholly dependent, if not upon Milton, then upon his other son, Christ, and his church, as Milton's battle in heaven would suggest.

30. Milton seems to have read his own blindness as punishment, and as a mark of maternal contamination. In this way, of course, loss is recuperated as a sign of election, as a difference separating Milton from the mother's body. Thus a mechanism is established whereby every other absence or loss — of youthful passions and opportunities — can be recuperated as a mark of divine adoption, as a signification of divine grace.

31. Virginia Woolf, *A Room of One's Own* (New York: Harcourt, Brace & Jovanovich, 1957).

Servile / Sterile / Style
Milton and the Question of Woman

MARSHALL GROSSMAN

Wo Es war, soll Ich werden.[1]

The object of the drive is to be situated at the level of what I have metaphorically called a headless subjectification, a subjectification without
a subject, a bone, a structure, an outline, which represents one side of
the topology. The other side is that which is responsible for the fact
that a subject, through his relations with the signifier, is a subject-
with-holes (sujet troué). These holes came from somewhere.[2]

1

IN *Paradise Lost*, it is Adam who poses the question of woman, and
poses it decisively; for it is his question that brings her into being. The
newly created Adam is able to name all that he sees with the exception of
God, whom he calls synecdochically by an attribute, "Author of this
Universe" (8.360). The question of woman begins as a question asked of
the "Author" that requires the able namer to call into being precisely
what he does not see. For this task he employs a periphrasis: "But with
mee / I see not who partakes" (8.363–64).[3] Thus woman enters Milton's
creation as a lack, as the part-taker Adam does not see. Without Eve,
whom, throughout this account of her creation, he will give only the
generic name "Woman," Adam has everything, "all," and can enjoy
nothing: "In solitude / What happiness, who can enjoy alone, / Or all
enjoying, what contentment find?" (ll. 364–66).

After successfully negotiating God's "trial" of his ability to express the
divine Image (ll. 440–41), Adam receives divine assent, "I, ere thou
spak'st, / Knew it not good for Man to be alone" (ll. 444–45), and
assurance: "What next I bring shall please thee, be assur'd, / Thy likeness,
thy fit help, thy other self, / Thy wish, exactly to thy heart's desire"

148

(ll. 449–51). What follows is a dream in which the part is taken from his left side, and the partaker "form'd and fashion'd."[4]

> Under his forming hands a Creature grew,
> Manlike, but different sex, so lovely fair,
> That what seem'd fair in all the World, seem'd now
> Mean, or in her summ'd up, in her contain'd
> And in her looks, which from that time infus'd
> Sweetness into my heart, unfelt before,
> And into all things from her Air inspir'd
> The spirit of love and amorous delight.
>
> (8.470–77)

The interplay of "all" or "nothing" invoked to assert the need of a partaker is reinscribed within the fancied creature. "All" is contained and summed up in her.

When Adam wakes to find his dream come true, he speaks at once to creator and creature, naming she-who-partakes with him, with man: "Woman is her Name, of Man / Extracted" and she differs from the rib she was and is in one salient way: she may be seen. Standing before the fleshed vision of his flesh, the visible incarnation of his bone, Man shall leave Father and Mother to find himself, "one Flesh, one Heart, one Soul," a wish, exactly to his heart's desire (ll. 494–99). Adam's desire to view his own rib becomes comprehensible when we consider that the lack he sees in creation, "the one who partakes with me" is quite literally himself. Prior to the creation of Eve, he is the one thing in Eden that he cannot behold. Recognizing that he has no proper analog among the beasts, he turns correctly to God, whose image he is, but also recognizing his unbridgeable difference from God, he insists on another of his kind so as to make himself visible to himself, so as to realize and remedy his always already defective human nature:

> Thou in thyself art perfet, and in thee
> Is no deficience found; not so is Man,
> But in degree, the cause of his desire
> By conversation with his like to help,
> Or solace his defects. No need that thou
> Shouldst propagate, already infinite;
> And through all numbers absolute, though One;
> But Man by number is to manifest
> His single imperfection, and beget
> Like of his like, his Image multipli'd,
> In unity defective, which requires
> Collateral love, and dearest amity.
>
> (8.415–26)[5]

Adam makes his desire the fleshly image of his word. He speaks to it (her) so as to possess that interior and excessive rib, which lies concealed in his side until it appears before him as Eve. What had been the dark perception of the empty place occupied by Adam's body moves into the sunlight carrying "Heav'n in her Eye" (l. 488), and Adam exclaims this is I, "My self / Before me." But this visible projection of his heart, soul, rib (חַיִּם, life), when she speaks, becomes her own "I" to his eye, not Adam's "I" but another, "Manlike, but different sex." When he confronts this other who is not himself, Adam's previous vocabulary of containment, his plan to partake of all with his partaker, is disrupted. Gazing on this other, who is and is not himself, has the effect of purloining the very self from which its part was taken. He had hoped to hold Eve in his eye but instead feels himself drawn, as it were, through that beholding eye into this something that exceeds an object.[6]

Thus before he completes the conversation with Raphael, of which this creation narrative is a part, Adam will rewrite his perceived autonomy of man and woman, containing "all" within their partaking, as an anxiety concerning the autonomy of woman, in whom man is contained; that is, an anxiety over an inside that has somehow gotten outside, a part that has become independent, amputated:[7]

> transported I behold,
> Transported touch; here passion first I felt,
> Commotion strange, in all enjoyments else
> Superior and unmov'd, here only weak
> Against the charm of Beauty's powerful glance.
> Or Nature fail'd in mee, and left some part
> Not proof enough such Object to sustain,
> Or from my side subducting, took perhaps
> More than enough.

> (8.529–37)

And so Adam reposes the question of woman, obtaining woman as an eye in which to behold himself, only to fear that he will be held fast in "Beauty's powerful *glance.*" The name of the partaker adds "wo" to "man"; the part taken is "perhaps more than enough."[8] The introduction of difference (sex) within the same (my Self) changes things. The excess that is Eve, "more than enough" because she discloses the self by being another like the self, requires a reorganization of the economy of man, and the need of a peer, a partaker in "Collateral love," ironically, installs a hierarchy. The price of the subjectification of Adam is to be the subjection of Eve. In the economy of Milton's Eden, Eve is to be *for* Adam; she becomes excessive when she is *for* herself.[9] But, within the chronology of Milton's telling, she is for herself and speaks for herself before Adam speaks for her.

Eve's version of the story, given, in Book 4, not to Raphael but to Adam, who was there to witness the events himself (or was he dreaming?), supplies a crucial episode that Adam pointedly omits: the story of an initial, narcissistic engagement with her own image. In Milton's myth of the origin of difference, the episode of the image in the pool, suppressed in Adam's account, dislcoses what it means to be "Manlike but different sex." Because he is created first, Adam requires an image. Eve is created to be an image for him but, unlike him, she first encounters her own image. And, to her delight, this image, which she is, partakes with her:

> A Shape within the wat'ry gleam appear'd
> Bending to look on me, I started back,
> It started back, but pleas'd I soon return'd,
> Pleas'd it return'd as soon with answering looks
> Of sympathy and love.
>
> $(4.461-65)^{10}$

Eve's version of her creation thematizes the scandal of Adam's desire for himself by discovering Narcissus at the "origin" of "collateral love" and the necessary interplay of subjectification and subjection that attends it. Milton's universe requires Eve's complicity in her own decapitation. To fulfill Adam's need for conversation she must remain an empty place in which he finds himself:

> O thou for whom
> And from whom I was form'd flesh of thy flesh,
> And without whom am to no end, my Guide
> And Head.
>
> $(4.440-43)$

This submission is neither simple nor simpleminded.

What promise induces Eve to embrace this subjection? A new name. Eve admits she would have remained enraptured of her image in the pool and "pin'd with vain desire" had not a voice warned her that the image lacked the requisite difference, was the shadow of herself and not its other. The voice draws her from her image with a compensatory offer:

> but follow me,
> And I will bring thee where no shadow stays
> Thy coming, and thy soft imbraces, hee
> Whose image thou art, him thou shalt enjoy
> Inseparably thine to him shalt bear

> Multitudes like thyself, and thence be call'd
> Mother of the human Race.
>
> $(4.469-75)^{11}$

The name is "Mother," and it is delivered as a style, a title.[12] Having been generic woman, "Manlike, but different sex," Eve is now to be something generically unique, styled "Mother of the human Race." In return for this style, she must defer the sterile pleasure of her self-possession in the pool and invest her desire in Adam, whose image she is. The promised return on this investment is to be "Multitudes like thyself."[13] It is in view of Adam's role in the future productivity of her "different sex" that Eve confers upon Adam the title Adam had conferred upon God, and which interestingly enough the young Milton had, in view of his future productivity, appropriated to himself, "Author" (4.634).

So, the need for another like the self provokes difference, subjectification requires subjection; "collateral love" installs hierarchy, and the recompense for hierarchy is a multitudinous repetition of an originary image. Where else in the system of differences that is *Paradise Lost* may we follow this curious path? If Eve's sexual difference generates the human race in time, what generates Milton's text?[14] What is its originary event?

In Book 5, Raphael recounts the earliest event in the chronology of *Paradise Lost*. The chain of events that is Milton's plot begins when the Father, having called the angels into plenary session, announces the regency of the Son:

> This day I have begot whom I declare
> My only Son, and on this holy Hill
> Him have anointed, whom ye now behold
> At my right hand; your Head I him appoint:
> And by my Self have sworn to him shall bow
> All knees in Heav'n, and shall confess him Lord:
> Under his great Vice-gerent Reign abide
> United as one individual Soul
> For ever happy.
>
> $(5.603-11)$

The similarities between the exaltation of the Son *for* the angels and the creation of Eve *for* Adam are striking. The Son whom the angels "now behold" makes the divine glory visible not only to them but to the Father himself: "Son, thou in whom my glory I behold / In full resplendence" (5.719-20). This visible glory is offered to the eyes of the spiritual angels to perfect their collateral love by partaking with them "United as one individual Soul," much as corporal Adam perfects his collateral love by partaking with Eve as "one flesh, one Soul." To confirm and implement this union the angels are to submit to the Son and accept him as their "head."[15]

Abdiel's explanation of the submission by which the angels are to rise to closer union makes explicit the paradox of difference:

> And of our good, and of our dignity
> How provident he is, how far from thought
> To make us less, bent rather to exalt
> Our happy state under one Head more near
> United. But to grant it thee unjust,
> That equal over equals Monarch Reign:
> Thyself though great and glorious dost thou count,
> Or all Angelic Nature join'd in one
> Equal to him begotten Son, by whom
> As by his Word the mighty Father made
> All things, ev'n thee.
>
> (5.827–37)

To increase the opportunities of conversation in Heaven, the Father offers a part of himself to the eye, but the equality of all "United in one Soul" can only be preserved through the recognition of a natural or prior difference, a transcendent and originary merit that, as it were, chooses the Son as the head of the angels and makes of them a *body* politic.

But if the Son is positioned toward the angels as Adam is toward Eve, he is also positioned toward the Father as Eve is toward Adam. He is the image in which the Father beholds his glory in "full resplendence." There is, however, a difference. Where the "I" of Eve becomes autonomous once outside the eye of Adam (in the separation scene for example), the Son always perfectly expresses the "I" of the Father, whose eye cannot be evaded. The incarnation may thus be looked to as the literal inscription of the Son's *embodiment* of the Father's "head." Complementing this all-important difference between Eve and the Son is a striking similarity between the creation of the Son and that of generic Man, whom he is to save through a painful renunciation of the mortality/immortality difference: paternal birth. The Son, like Adam and Eve, lacks a mother.

At first. Eve, though second in order of creation, taken from Adam as a part, is repaid for her submission to the paternal claim of "authority," with the belated priority of "Mother of Mankind." Through a similar reversal, her descendant, Christ, is to be twice begotten: once, through the masculine authority of the Father and later, as the second Adam, in the womb of Mary, who may be styled henceforth "Mary, mother of God."[16] At this point, we may return to Eve's encounter with her image in the pool. This image is rejected because its love is self-love and consequently sterile. To achieve her destiny as progenitor, she must submit to Adam. Adam, we remember, is the primal namer, and Eve is called into being to help him name himself. She transfers her desire from her image in the pool to Adam in return for the deferred multiplication of that image, "Multitudes like thyself." In the economy of this exchange, she surrenders her image to the intervention of he-who-names on the advice of a voice that promises, a voice that names not what is present before her but what is to come. Is not Eve bound on both sides by language, bound to embrace he-who-names so that she may, after a time, bear a daughter whose womb will bring forth the Father's Word? When Eve trades the image in the pool for the head of Adam, she leaves the image of herself to accept the male word or phallus and become the transmitter of his difference, that is to say, to become *literature.*

The difference between Eve and the Son is precisely the allegorical difference—the difference between Speech, the living Word whose presence guarantees the Father's being, and Writing, the (more or less) autononmous reproduction of a *historical* utterance. The swerve from Speech to Writing is thus recorded in the Miltonic text as a swerve into history. Milton celebrates in a powerful way the trace of difference belatedly constituting itself as an originary moment. The Mother becomes the deferred text in which a male image is reproduced just as Writing becomes the deferred transcription of a living speech that can only be found within it. The historical situation of *differance* within sexual difference cohabiting here with the formal situation of sexual difference within *differance* — as *differance* —emerges as an irreducible aporia, at the empty center of which hovers the tantalizing possibility that sexual difference functions historically as the paradigm for the naturalization of differences as such.

The insight into the mystery of Narcissus accorded Eve by her encounter with her image also marks a difference between her and Adam. She has a vision of herself before she sees another, a vision of her image, and this vision is her mother, the model on which an utterly self-contained conception of her subjectivity is formed. Thus Adam and the Father find their image in an other whom they recognize as different from themselves. But Christ and Eve are always endowed with a dual nature; they always know themselves as one combining parts of two, because they each have a mother. The questions of governance, of equality and hierarchy, of subject and subjection that resonate through Milton's work are all included in the question of woman. Woman styled as mother, the origin who is herself both primary and secondary, is the object of Adam's scopic drive, "a headless subjectification, a subjectification without a subject, a bone, a structure, an outline."

The antithesis of the Son and of Eve is Sin, mother not of multitudes but of parasitic and incestuous images. Sin is not a partaker with Satan but the image of his rebellious thought. She is formed not by a divine author but by Satan's autonomous fancy. When Satan engenders with her, he donates only thoughts, and so materializes only the phantasy products of primary process. Satan is unable to establish himself as subject because he is subjected to his own internal economy and is unable to give of himself to mother or Son.[17]

To say that the subject, in the modern philosophical sense, is born of a desire for the mother is not only to recapitulate Freud, but also to install this formation of the subject or ego within a specific temporality.[18] For the mother is here understood as the deferred origin of a subject that presupposes her and confers upon her, by the testimony of its being, the title Mother. The mother is the place the subject creates in order that he may issue from the interior space which is the outline of his own being and of which he is the visible testimony. One becomes an author ("Author of the Universe," "My author, my disposer") by appropriating the difference of the other as a representative of the same. Within the Miltonic dialectic of sexual difference, woman, as mother, is the means of the (re)production of the paternal image, the place on which and in which the father writes his name and reproduces his style. But she is refractory, possessed of her own style, the mother's style, which must be subordinated under one (paternal) head. The subject as ego installs itself on the objectified other under the promise and offer of a head, a reunification, which is always deferred, always to come, when the "single defect" is made up and difference has run its course: "Then thou thy regal Sceptre shalt lay by, / For regal Sceptre then no more shall need, / God shall be All in All" (3.339–41). The temporality of deferral that underlies the providential and apocalyptic view of history is the historical projection of the temporality of the mother and the ego's deferred appropriation of her origin.

2

Paradise Lost, by virtue of its exhaustive intention, discloses the suppressed and deferred authority of the Mother underlying the superimposition of subjectification and subjection in the Miltonic text. It is the epic of the origin of generic Man and could hardly not include within it the origin of sexual difference. In fact, one could say with justice that it is the necessary relation of subjectivity to subjection that is obscured in the "great argument." I should like at this point to turn to an earlier and much less ambitious text, *Eikonoklastes,* in which this foreground and background are reversed. Milton's attack upon the King's Book, or more precisely, the image of the king in the image of his book, his purloined style, deals explicitly with the dialectic of head and body, leader and citizen, service and freedom in the functioning of a body politic, the commonwealth. We find, however, that the author disposes his arguments against the *Eikon Basilike* in images that inscribe the problematic interdetermination of subjectification and subjection within what I have called the temporality of the Mother. The question of woman is thus raised along with the question of the persistence of the image of a king, who, like her, has surrendered his head. The juxtaposition of the two texts will therefore further illuminate the relationship of sexual and social difference in Milton's discourse.

Two of the principal issues of the *Eikonoklastes* are the king's authority over the book, which represents his image, and the negative voice he claimed to exercise over parliamentary legislation. The king's image in the King's Book is a purloined image, cobbled together by a ghostwriter and, in the notorious case of "Pamela's prayer," plagiarized from another author, an inappropriate genre, and a female speaker. Milton's tract consistently distinguishes the image and the reality of the king by presenting Charles with a choice of mothers: the Parliament (which Milton portrays as preceding the commonweath and thus providing the entity over which he rules) and three papistical women, his grandmother, Mary Stuart, his (in the roundhead view) overweening wife, Henrietta Maria, and her mother, Marie de Médicis. Within this economy of mothers, the true king is not Charles, but a role or style created by Parliament. Thus Milton divides the king's rule from his physical body and reassociates it with an originary Parliament, asserting that those "who fought for the King divided from his Parliament, fought for the shadow of a King" (3.530).

Examination of the passages in which Charles is shown to embrace one of his female mothers and thus to sacrifice his head to an inappropriate authority shows the temporality of the Mother underlying Milton's attempt to create the commonwealth as historical subject through the subjection of an emasculated king. In Milton's version of events, the king's uxorious submission of his head to a woman leads inexorably to the Parliament's literal reappropriation of the royal capital.

In the *Eikon Basilike,* the king (with the help of John Gauden, his clerical and posthumous ghostwriter) appropriates the style of royal martyr, portraying himself at his devotions before his execution;[19] but Milton warns that "the deepest policy of a Tyrant hath bin ever to counterfet Religious": "*Andronicus Comnenus* the *Byzantine* Emperor, though a most cruel Tyrant, is reported by *Nicetas* to have bin a constant reader of Saint *Pauls* Epistles; and by continual study had so incorporated the phrase & stile of that transcendent Apostle into all his familiar Letters, that the imitation seem'd to vie with the Original. Yet this availd not to deceave the people of that Empire; who notwithstanding his Saints vizard, tore him to peeces for his Tyranny" (p. 361). The dismemberment of the king is justified by his acts, which must be divided from the false divinity of his misappropriated style. Milton's method in *Eikonoklastes* is, in fact, to dismember the king's text by inserting hostile commentary into a string of always fragmentary quotations from the *Eikon Basilike;* he disrupts the king's style by dispersing the king's text and reinscribing it as a series of falsehoods, distortions, and thefts.

Once the king's royal style has been divided from his acts, those acts are attributed to the queen, whose shrewish machinations miscarry the king's policies into a hysterical pregnancy that delivers only sterile imaginings. Thus Charles enters Parliament with an armed force, attempting to arrest five members suspected of, among other crimes, plotting against the queen, because he resolved not *"To bear the repulse with patience,* which his Queen by her words to him at his return little thought he would have done" (p. 378), and the indictment of the five members for treason is called for on the basis of "pregnancies" and "just motives" that come to nothing: *"He mist but little to have produc'd Writings under some mens own hands.* But yet he mist, though thir Chambers, Trunks, and Studies were seal'd up and search'd; yet not found guilty. *Providence would not have it so.* Good Providence, that curbs the raging of proud Monarchs, as well as of madd multitudes. *Yet he wanted not such probabilities* (for his pregnant is now come to probable) *as were sufficient to raise jealousies in any Kings heart.* And thus his pregnant *motives* are at last prov'd nothing but a Tympany, or a Queen *Maries* Cushion" (p. 379)."[20] This unsavory intrusion into other men's "Chambers, Trunks, and Studies" is later recompensed when the "King's Cabinet" is captured and writings produced under *his own hands* reveal that "to sumn up all, they shewd him govern'd by a Woman" (p. 538), while the text he now presents as his own is shown to contain a word, *"Damagogues,"* "above his known stile and Orthographie" that "accuses the whole composure to be conscious of som other Author" (p. 393).

The king, whose words are not his own and whose text is conscious of some other author, fails to maintain authority over the commonwealth or over what purports to be his own text, in part because he fails to subject his wife: "how good shee was a Wife, was to himself, and be it left to his own fancy; how bad a Subject, is not much disputed" (p. 419). Failing to install a paternal authority that defers the woman's style to the male testimony of motherhood (that is to the accession of *her* son), Charles allows Henrietta Maria to continue the arc of an unsubjected matriarchy:

"it need be made no wonder, though shee left a Protestant Kingdom with as little honour as her Mother left a Popish" (p. 419).[21] Milton places Charles in a line of woman-governed governors that extends ultimately to Adam and makes it clear that Charles's devotion to his queen was at the expense of Parliament:

> He ascribes *Rudeness and barbarity worse then Indian* to the English Parlament, and *all vertue* to his Wife, in straines that come almost to Sonnetting: How fitt to govern men, undervaluing and aspersing the great Counsel of his Kingdom, in comparison of one Woman. Examples are not farr to seek, how great mischeif and dishonour hath befall'n to Nations under the Goverment of effeminate and Uxorious Magistrates. Who being themselves govern'd and overswaid at home under a Feminine usurpation, cannot but be farr short of spirit and autority without dore, to govern a whole Nation. (pp. 420–21)

The corrective to such a succession of "Vice-gerent" mothers is included as a repressed episode in Charles's family history: his father's quiet betrayal of Mary Stuart's head to the literal subjection of the sexually ambiguous Elizabeth.[22] But, unfortunately, Charles chooses to imitate not his father's but his grandmother's model:

> The rest of his discours quite forgets the Title; and turns his Meditations upon death into obloquie and bitter vehemence against his *Judges and accussers;* imitating therin, not our Saviour, but his Grand-mother *Mary Queen of Scots;* as also in the most of his other scruples, exceptions and evasions: and from whom he seems to have learnt, as it were by heart, or els by kind, that which is thought by his admirers to be the most vertuous, most manly, most Christian, and most Martyr-like both of his words and speeches heer, and of his answers and behaviour at his Tryall. (p. 597)

This exchange, in which Charles eschews the model of the paternal Word and instead confronts his execution in the style of his papist grandmother, is more thorough than may appear at first glance. On the one hand, Mary Stuart had stood precisely on the claim of indivisible majesty that Milton set out to undermine: "she made no exception against their [the judges' and commissioners'] persons, only stood upon her Majesty as a Queen and chose a thousand deaths rather than descend to the capacity of a subject."[23] On the other, Jesus descended to the capacity of a subject for the express purpose of at once affirming and transcending the paternal Law. While Mary took the occasion of her execution as an opportunity to excoriate her persecuters one last time, Jesus refused to extend the word of judgment, offering his accusers the cryptic response, "Thou sayst." Christ's voluntary humiliation, his submission of his body to the paternal death sentence, insures his deferred ascent to the Father and the ascent of generic Man: "thy Humilation shall exalt / With thee thy Manhood to this Throne" (*PL* 3.313–14). It also fulfills the promise made to Eve in return for her submission to Adam, a promise that bridges the covenants when it is rewritten, after the Fall, as the protevangelium. In *Paradise Lost,* the procreation of·a "race of worshippers" is first secured when the divine Word offers Eve the style "Mother of the human Race," and it is resecured when Adam and Eve are rescued from the despair of sin by memory of the promise of renewal the Son had delivered to Eve:

> calling to mind with heed
> Part of our Sentence, that thy Seed shall bruise
> The Serpent's head; piteous amends, unless
> Be meant, whom I conjecture, our grand Foe
> *Satan,* who in the Serpent hath contriv'd
> Against us this deceit.
>
> (10.1030–35)

After the Fall, the promise of/to the mother is clearly the promise of the text, the opportunity of allegorical interpretation. First Eve is "Mother of the human Race," but second Eve transmits the style of Providence, signifies the meaning of history and its transcendence.

Milton replaces the unpleasant historical model of James's acquies-cence in the judicial murder of his mother, the suppression of which is ironically weakened by Charles's refusal to follow it by palliating Parlia-ment with the offer of his queen, with the providential model of the Passion as the alternative Charles rejects. By doing so, Milton performs the very task he describes, for his allegorical reading of Charles and Henrietta as generic Man and Woman allows him to rewrite the story of Charles's refusal to emulate his father, James, as a refusal to emulate the heavenly Father's perfect Son, and, at the same time, to foreclose any scenario in which Charles and Parliament are reconciled. By the time of *Eikonoklastes,* the only issue in the king's life is his manner of leaving it. More important, the relations of king and parliament are rhetorically inscribed within the relations of man and creator, which, in turn, inscribe them within Milton's economy of sexual difference. We may note, in particular, that the analogy of Henrietta Maria's subversive position in a Protestant commonwealth to that of Marie de Médicis's position in a Catholic one makes clear that the issue of male subjection to the mother's rule precedes the issue of religious reformation. The fall of Charles I is prior to the definition or institution of any earthly church, because it is a ritual reenactment of the Fall of man, when Adam was "fondly overcome with Female charm" (*PL* 9.999). Within Milton's rhetorical economy, the monarchist's identification of the king's two bodies reiterates Eve's identification with her image in the pool. The disruption of that identification transforms woman from image to signifier and opens the text of history to providential meaning. It also divides the king's body from his style as it divides him from female control over the continuity of the male line and delivers him to what Milton identifies as the law of nature that installs that which is learned from the mother "as it were by heart, or els by kind." Milton's rhetorical surgery reverses the traditional claim of the king to speak the law (Rex Lex Loquens), replacing it with the claim that the law (the writ of Parliament) speaks the king.

The clearest view of this strange pre-oedipal struggle of the mothers appears in what is certainly the most astonishing passage in *Eikonoklastes*. Milton rebuts the king's contention that the Parliament had placed itself in the livery of public tumults with the assertion that the more urgent threat to Parliament was the king's "encroaching Prerogative." The king's mistrust of Parliament results from his "overdated minority" and "Pupillage under Bishops," who have failed to explain to Charles that the "Parlament had *that part to act* which he had fail'd in" (p. 466):

> Yet so farr doth self opinion or fals principles delude and transport him, as to think *the concurrence of his reason* to the Votes of Parlament, not onely Political, but Natural, *and as necessary to the begetting*, or bringing forth of any one *compleat act of public wisdom as the Suns influence is necessary to all natures productions.* So that the Parliament, it seems, is but a Female, and without his procreative reason, the Laws which they can produce are but windeggs. Wisdom, it seems, to a King is natural, to a Parlament not natural, but by conjunction with the King: Yet he professes to hold his Kingly right by Law; and if no Law could be made but by the great Counsel of a Nation, which we now term a Parlament, then certainly it was a Parlament that first created Kings, and not onely made Laws before a King was in being, but those Laws especially, wherby he holds his Crown. (p. 467)

Thus, and too late, Milton takes over and corrects the tutorship of the bishops, explaining the facts of life to the eternally pubescent king: The king is born of the commonwealth and the commonwealth is born of the law and the law is born of a parliament. Here then is the masculine line of descent obscured by Charles's refusal to subjectify the king by subjecting the queen. The king does not rule according to an image, neither the precedent image of his father's rule (which he has refused) nor the eternal image of his heavenly Father's rule (to which he is inadequate). The king rules, if he rules at all, according to the laws produced by the natural wisdom of Parliament.

The king thus stands to Parliament as Eve stands to Adam. He may subjectify himself by being subject to its always precedent laws. As the son of the law, he may be liberated from the scandal of female originality and execute the royal authority that has, because of his failure, been reassumed by Parliament. To stand on the prerogative of the king's "negative" is to mistake the *nature* of law and Parliament in a way that reinscribes, in deadly form, the king's adolescent malady: to account the Parliament "but a Female":

> He ought then to have so thought of a Parlament, if he count it not Male, as of his Mother, which, to civil being created both him, and the Royalty he wore. And if it hath bin anciently interpreted the presaging signe of a future Tyrant, but to dream of copulation with his Mother, what can it be less then actual Tyranny to affirme waking, that the Parlament, which is his Mother, can neither conceive or bring forth *any autoritative Act* without his Masculine coition: Nay that his reason is as Celestial and lifegiving to the Parlament, as the Suns influence is to the Earth: What other notions but these, or such like, could swell up *Caligula* to think himself a God. (p. 467)

If the Parliament be female and require his "Masculine coition" to "bring forth," then it is the king, himself, who is a "windegg." The *OED* defines "windegg" as "an imperfect or unproductive egg, esp. one with a soft shell, such as may be laid by hens and other domestic birds" and cites Milton's only other use of the word, in *Colasterion:* "From such a wind-egg of definition as this, they who expect any of his other arguments to be well-hatched [etc.]." The king, in his "outdated Minority," is soft-shelled and ill-defined, his boundaries fail to differentiate him from his mothers, in whom he attempts to engender paternal laws through an incestuous copulation. I risk this admittedly strong reading of Milton's allusion to Caligula because, in the context I have been developing, the transgression and maintenance of boundaries, the separation of the subject from its origin and its peers, is so much the point. Caligula failed the test that God administers to Adam before the creation of Eve in Book 8; he failed to distinguish the mortal from the divine and fell into incest (with his sister). Is not copulation with the mother the too-literal execution of a desire to be one's own original, "self-begot, self-rais'd / By our own quick'ning power" (*PL* 5.860–61)? A desire as literal as this, returning to the image of its origin without the displacement of figuration, looking for itself in the past rather than the future of "Multitudes like thyself," must, within the economy of Milton's text, be answered with the counter-literalization of decapitation: the dismembered king figures itself, too late, as the object of its own drive: "a headless subjectification, a subjectification without a subject, a bone, a structure, an outline," a "windegg," a woman. On and in the text of the king's body, reposed, as it were, in the King's Book, Milton writes a new masculine birth; the law, freed from the image of the king, brings forth the commonwealth. Failing to grasp that the Parliament created "both him, and the Royalty he wore," the king failed to recognize that he embodied the superimposition of the two senses of "subject." He refused Eve's bargain and, because he would not subjectify the commonwealth by subjecting himself to the universal reason manifest in parliamentary law, he lost his head in deed.

Milton figures the movement from fantasy to execution of the king's incestuous attempt to make Parliament accept his head, the movement from "presaging signe" to "actual Tyranny" as a verbal act. Charles's waking affirmation that the Parliament "can neither conceive or bring forth" laws "without his Masculine coition" is the affirmation of a falsity and thus the true image of the king's negative. The rhetorical movement from a dream of copulation to the sin of waking affirmation anticipates three crucial moments in *Paradise Lost:* Eve's refusal in Book 5 to affirm waking the dream of flight induced by Satan, Adam's waking from his dream of Eve to find it true, and, most clearly, Satan's parthenogenesis of, and incest with, Sin, after his denial of the Father's Word. In the first instance Eve refuses to execute the fantasy of autonomy that Satan's dream has offered. With the help of Adam and God, she chooses not to make the journey from "signe" to "sin." In the second instance, Adam accepts the loss of a part for the boon of a partaker and affirms waking the masculine genesis of the mother. In Satan's embrace of Sin, we see the self-engenderment that *Eikonoklastes* imputes to Charles, and we see, in the hell of *Paradise Lost* Book 2, the body politic that rises from it. Over against these three moments of textual repetition, we may place the originary and successful parthenogenesis that begins Milton's epic and has all human history as its consequence: "This day I have begot whom I declare / My only Son." The Father begets and declares, engenders and names. His Word restores the womb and gives God a mother. His style is "Author." The Word of the Father validates his style by accepting subjection to crucifixion and death. The Son is "by merit rais'd" because he perceives and acts out the superimposition of subject and subjectification to which Charles and his grandmother were blind.

3

What then is an author? The handmaiden and the sister of Truth:

> Truth indeed came once into the world with her divine Master, and was a
> perfect shape most glorious to look on: but when he ascended, and his
> Apostles after him were laid asleep, then strait arose a wicked race of

deceivers, who as that story goes of the *AEgyptian Typhon* with his conspirators, how they dealt with the good *Osiris,* took the virgin Truth, hewd her lovely form into a thousand peeces, and scatter'd them to the four winds. From that time ever since, the sad friends of Truth, such as durst appear, imitating the carefull search that *Isis* made for the mangl'd body of *Osiris,* went up and down gathering up limb by limb still as they could find them. We have not yet found them all, Lords and Commons, nor ever shall doe, till her Masters second comming; he shall bring together every joynt and member, and shall mould them into an immortall feature of lovelines and perfection. Suffer not these licencing prohibitions to stand at every place of opportunity forbidding and disturbing them that continue seeking, that continue to do our obsequies to the torn body of our martyr'd Saint. We boast our light; but if we look not wisely on the Sun it self, it smites us into darknes. (*Areopagitica,* *CPW,* 2:549–50)

Five years before the publication of *Eikonoklastes,* Milton addressed this plea to mother Parliament that she not interpose her prevenient law between authority and the limbs of truth. I quote the passage in full to linger over its peculiar vocabulary, its images of dismembering and remembering, the subtle interplay of genders—of masculine master and feminine Truth, of sisterly Isis and the company of (male) writers who reassemble the "torn body of our martyr'd Saint"—and because I want to read this passage as an allegorical pre-inscription of Eve's encounter with her image in the pool and the exchange she subsequently accepts for relinquishing that image. Truth came into this world once, with Christ, *embodied* in "a perfect shape most glorious to look on," the shape of the Son. But that shape was dismembered on a cross, broken, and finally purloined, removed from the eye of man and returned to heaven, leaving only its "written Records pure" (*PL* 12.513). The mangled body of Truth, indeterminate of sex (virgin), is fragmented and then reproduced infinitely, yet "with difference of sex" until the master's return, when we, Isis-like collectors of its dismembered limbs, will remember its torn face. But this memory of the future, this (re)membering of the truth of and in the body is deferred beyond the grasp of writers who must accept the fragmentary nature of their achievement until the master returns. We remember his torn visage that we might behold it, returned before our eyes. But we—whose authority is that of writers—play the female part, the part of Isis, lest "we look not wisely on the Sun it self" and "it smites us into darknes."

Like Oedipus, the writer brings what is dark to light, but unlike that unfortunate king of the city founded by that same Cadmus who brought the alphabet to Greece, he must not bring prematurely to light the Truth that smites and blinds, the truth of his own incestuous conjunction with the mother, his masculine appropriation of the mother's style: "For Books are not absolutely dead things, but doe contain a potencie of life in them to be as active as that soule was whose progeny they are; nay they do preserve as in violl the purest efficacie and extractions of that living intellect that bred them. I know they are as lively, and as vigorously productive, as those fabulous Dragon's teeth; and being sown up and down, may chance to spring up armed men" (*CPW,* 2:492). Oedipus too is reason's child, and reason sends him back into the dark place whence he came, and in the wake of his failure and his discovery "spring up armed men."

The writer, at least the prophetic writer Milton seeks to be, performs, with and through his text, the function performed for the angels by the begotten Son, for Adam by Eve, and for the human race by Christ; he puts before our eyes that which we cannot otherwise see or name—that Truth which is shrouded at once in the interior darkness of the heart and the excessive brightness of the Sun: "as good almost kill a Man as kill a good Book; who kills a Man kills a reasonable creature, God's image; but hee who destroyes a good Booke, kills reason it selfe, kills the Image of God, as it were in the eye" (*CPW,* 2:492). How is it that a text (be)holds the image of God in the eye, while its author avoids the fate of Oedipus?

In the self-exculpating preface to the second book of *The Reason of Church Government,* Milton records his anxieties over his use of his own talents and the purchase of "ease and leasure" for his "retired thoughts" "out of the sweat of other men," particularly the "ceaselesse diligence and care" of his father (*CPW,* 1:804, 808). In response to his perceived obligation to repay this paternal investment, he converts ease and leisure to "labour and intent study," which "joyn'd with strong propensity of nature" will enable him to "leave something so written to aftertimes, as they should not willingly let it die" (p. 810).[24] What will keep this something alive, what "potencie of life" will it offer to aftertimes? Milton bases his expectations in part on the opinion of his "sundry masters and teachers": "It was found that whether ought was impos'd me by them that had the overlooking, or betak'n to of mine own choise in English, or other tongue, prosing or versing, but chiefly this latter, the stile by certain signes it had, was likely to live" (p. 809).

Milton goes on to recount his efforts to perfect this "stile," to make of it a "violl" that it will carry into the "progeny" of his soul, "the purest efficacie and extractions of that intellect that bred them": "I apply'd my self... to fix all the industry and art I could unite to the adorning of my native tongue; not to make verbal curiosities the end, that were a toylsom vanity, but to be an interpreter & relater of the best and sagest things among mine own Citizens throughout this Iland in the mother dialect" (pp. 811–12).

This perfect conversation in the mother dialect, the presentation of a poem "doctrinal and exemplary to a Nation" (p. 815), is to remain latent some twenty-four years, during which time Milton will give himself to the "carelesse and interrupted listening of these tumultuous times," choosing a "manner of writing wherein knowing my self inferior to my self, led by the genial power of nature to another task, I have the use, as I may account it, but of my left hand" (pp. 807–8).

During this extended gestation, however, Milton's muse is not inactive. She goes up and down like the good Isis picking up, here and there, the limbs of Truth. She will not find them all, but those she finds will contribute, according to the time of the Mother, to the re-membering of the "torn body" of a "martyr'd Saint." When this re-membered body is complete, it will form a text in that life-preserving style that at once expresses the propensities of nature and the diligence of the father. This text will reveal not an imitation of the sensible past, but the sensible signifier of the intelligible future. It will be not the "toylsom vanity" of "verbal curiosities" but the reasoned image of Truth's master brought out of the darkness of interior and personal revelation into the womb of a text where it can educate a "race of worshippers" for the blinding light of that day when the Father returns as the exalted presence of his Son.[25] In the matured style of that text, Milton gives birth to himself as the author of a poem "doctrinal and exemplary to a Nation" and beholds before his eye the hidden part he had perceived in 1642 as an "inward prompting which now grew daily upon me" (*CPW*, 1:810).

The interplay of subjection and subjectification that marks the marriage of Adam and Eve, the Son's vicegerent reign over the angels, and the Parliament's violent appropriation of the king's head is (re)played in Milton's account of his own temporal deferral in favor of the commonwealth's appropriation of his right-handed style, his long gestation, and his submission to the muse's delivery of "unpremeditated verse," until he can behold in the text those "inward promptings" that mark the presence of his style, tracing along the intersection of history and desire, subjection and subjectification, the fragmented, yet remembering, image of a woman, a mother, always about to answer the question in the text. The answer, however, remains and will remain deferred, the purloined image of an appropriated origin, until the return of the Master, the visibly present and perfectly voiced Word of the Father, who, with his Virgin Mother, Truth, withdrew—for a time—to his heavenly throne, leaving behind only a "written record pure."

NOTES

1. The epigraph, taken from Freud's *New Introductory Lectures*, XXXI, may be regarded as a motto or manifesto of psychoanalysis. In the *Standard Edition of the Psychological Works of Sigmund Freud* (London, 1953–74, hereafter cited as SE), Strachey translates it "Where Id is Ego shall be," but a more literal rendering — "Where it was, shall I become" — is more to my purpose, because it both retains the scheme of chiasmus from the original and makes more clear the elements of estrangement and appropriation incurred in Freud's effort to bring the dark parts of the psyche to light. On the translation of the phrase, see Jacques Lacan, "La chose freudienne: ou Sens du retour à Freud en psychanalyse," in *Écrits* (Paris, 1966), p. 417.

2. Jacques Lacan, *The Four Fundamental Concepts of Psycho-Analysis*, ed. Jacques-Alain Miller, trans. Alan Sheridan (New York, 1978), p. 184.

3. All citations of Milton's poetry refer to *John Milton: Complete Poems and Major Prose*, ed. Merritt Y. Hughes (Indianapolis, 1957).

4. We may note the expedited "natural history" of sex in these verses (8.467–68): Adam is first made woman — "wide was the wound," — then impregnated through a kind of self-coition — "But suddenly with flesh fill'd up and heal'd." The rib is here the gamete which passes from the man to the woman whose womb (*in*-formed by God) fashions *for* the man an image or copy of himself.

5. In the seventeenth century "conversation" may have the sense of intercourse as well as discourse. Adam's reference to propagation makes clear that he intends both denotations. For a discussion of the relation of intercourse and discourse in the quoted passage, see my "Augustine, Spenser, Milton and the Christian Ego," *New Orleans Review*, 11 (1984), 9–17.

6. Lacan's "mirror stage" and Hegel's dialectic of lordship and bondage converge in Milton's depiction of Adam's encounter with another who is a subject like himself, suggesting the common ground of both discourses in the historical foundation of the modern subject at the chiasmus of intending subjectivity and political subjection. See Lacan, "The Mirror State as Formative of the Function of the I," in *Écrits: A Selection*, trans. Alan Sheridan (New York, 1977), pp. 1–7; Hegel, *The Phenomenology of the Spirit*, B,IV,A.

7. See Freud's paper, "On Narcissism: An Introduction," SE.14, p. 78: "The individual does actually carry on a twofold existence: one to serve his own purposes and the other as a link in a chain, which he serves against his will, or at least involuntarily. The individual himself regards sexuality as one of his own ends; whereas from another point of view he is an appendage to his germplasm, at whose disposal he puts his energies in return for a bonus of pleasure. He is the mortal vehicle of a possibly immortal substance — like the inheritor of an entailed property, who is only the temporary holder of an estate which survives him. The separation of the sexual instincts from the ego instincts would simply reflect this two-fold function of the individual."

8. The OED records the pseudo-etymological association of wo-man and woe-man as frequent in the sixteenth and seventeenth centuries: Woman: I.l.k.

9. See Milton's discussion of Genesis 2:18 in the *Doctrine and Discipline of*

Divorce, in *Complete Prose Works of John Milton,* ed. Don M. Wolfe et al. (New Haven, 1953–82), II, 245–46. (Subsequent citations of Milton's prose will refer to the this edition, cited as *CPW,* by volume and page number.) Adam's expressed fear that Eve may be "more than enough" concerns precisely his anxiety that Eve may be for herself and that the loss of the rib will not be recompensed, that he will be left with an interior emptiness.

10. For an extended discussion of the allusion to Narcissus in this passage, with a full review of the literature, see Diane McColley, *Milton's Eve* (Urbana, 1983) pp. 74–85.

11. Cf. William Kerrigan's explanation of the transfer of Eve's affection from her image in the pool to Adam in *The Sacred Complex: On the Psychogenesis of "Paradise Lost"* (Cambridge, Mass., 1983), p. 70.

12. OED, Style: II.b.18: "A legal, official, or honorific title, the proper name or recognized appellation of a person, family, trading firm, etc.; the ceremonial designation of a sovereign, including his various titles and the enumeration of his dominions." See, for example, *Paradise Lost* 2.312. A "style" is a proper name, but unlike the name "Eve" it is a hereditary surname, in practice, a patronymic. Eve receives her unique given name from Adam's as a verbal gift. The title, "Mother," which is her royal style, proclaiming the dominions and the legal status of her daughter successors, is also a gift of Adam's, but this time written on and in her body. As my argument develops, I hope the apparently disparate denotations of "style"—pen, phallus, title, literary mark of ownership and origin—will appear less distinct, the collection of signifieds under this signifier more motivated. For a related discussion of the semantic relations of the stylish and the feminine, see Jacques Derrida, *Spurs: Nietzsche's Styles/Eperons: Les Styles de Nietzsche,* trans. Barbara Harlow (Chicago, 1979).

13. On the deferral of Eve's image until she recognizes herself in her children, see James Earl, "Eve's Narcissism," *Milton Quarterly,* 19 (1985), 13–16.

14. The association of textual and sexual reproduction goes back at least as far as Augustine's curious reading of the biblical injunction to "increase and multiply" as pertaining to the generation of thoughts and words (*Confessions* XIII.xxiv). See "Augustine, Spenser, Milton and the Christian Ego," p. 10.

15. For a discussion of the begetting of the Son *for* the angels, see Albert C. Labriola, "'Thy Humiliation Shall Exalt': The Christology of *Paradise Lost,*" *Milton Studies* 15, ed. James D. Simmonds (Pittsburgh, 1981), pp. 29–42.

16. Cf. Maureen Quilligan's discussion of "cosmic femaleness" and the gender of Milton's muse. *Milton's Spenser: The Politics of Reading* (Ithaca, 1983), pp. 218–20.

17. For a phenomenology of the Satanic subject, see my *"Authors to Themselves": Milton and the Revelation of History* (Cambridge, 1987), chap. 2.

18. The OED records no uses of "subject" in the modern philosophical sense, "for the mind or ego considered as the subject of all knowledge," before the eighteenth century, but cites transitional uses from 1682 and 1697. The change in the use of the word "subject" is only one indication of a general shift toward understanding the self or mind as an interior space in which exterior objects are known, a conception already clear in the Cartesian "cogito." For a study of the

development of an English vocabulary with which to express this interiority, see Anne Ferry, *The "Inward" Language: Sonnets of Wyatt, Sidney, Shakespeare, Donne* (Chicago, 1983).

19. On the authorship of the *Eikon Basilike,* see Philip A. Knachel's introduction to his edition, *Eikon Basilike: The Portraiture of His Sacred Majesty in His Solitude and Suffering,* Folger Shakespeare Library (Ithaca, 1966).

20. OED: Cushion 2.b: "A swelling simulating pregnancy: sometimes called *Queen Mary's cushion,* after Mary Tudor."

21. Henrietta's mother, Marie de Médicis, notorious for the power she asserted as queen regent during the minority of her son, Louis XIII, was driven into exile by Richelieu. See *CPW,* 3: 419, n. 3.

22. On James's accession and his acquiescence in the execution of his mother, see Jonathan Goldberg, *James I and the Politics of Literature: Jonson, Shakespeare, Donne, and Their Contemporaries* (Baltimore, 1983), pp. 11–17.

23. The quotation is from *Historicall Collections of Ecclesiastick Affairs in Scotland* ... (1615), as cited in *CPW* 3: 597, n. 38.

24. Cf. William Kerrigan's view in *The Sacred Complex* of *Paradise Lost* as a sublimation of Milton's oedipal ambivalence toward his father.

25. Milton follows Tasso's notion of "icastic imitation" in understanding prophetic poetry as a sensible signifier of intelligible Truth. See Torquato Tasso, *Discourses on the Heroic Poem,* trans. with notes by Mariella Cavalchini and Irene Samuel (Oxford, 1973), p. 31. See also Paul Stevens, "Milton and the Icastic Imagination," *Milton Studies,* 20, ed. James D. Simmonds (Pittsburgh, 1984), pp. 43–73.

Milton's Portrait of Mary as a Bearer of the Word

DAYTON HASKIN

> Maries prerogative was to beare Christ, so
> 'Tis preachers to convey him. . . .
>
> — Donne, "To Mr Tilman after
> he had taken orders"[1]

ACTIVE interest in Milton's portraits of women has been directed to Eve, to Dalila, and to the Lady of the Ludlow *Mask*. His depiction of the mother of Jesus in *Paradise Regained* has rarely received serious or systematic attention.[2] But as he retold the biblical story of the temptations in the wilderness, Milton accorded to Mary a relatively large and unconventional role. He painted a distinctive portrait of her as the bearer, par excellence, of the Word of God. Avoiding both the riches and the potential crudities of medieval symbolism (whereby Mary was sometimes represented as the new ark containing the Word or as a tabernacle for the eucharistic Presence), Milton depicted a Mary who is her child's first and best teacher. Her experiences partly anticipate those of her son; and as the poem unfolds we can infer that it was she who initiated him into the process that *Paradise Regained* dramatizes: the task of discovering and creating a fit between one's reading experience and the rest of one's life.

Milton's treatment of Mary may be thought surprising in that it had been one of the most dramatic successes of the Reformers that they managed, within the ninety years or so between Luther's first protests and Milton's birth, nearly to eradicate the cult of Mary from mainstream Protestantism. For this reason the neglect of Mary in writing about Milton's poetry could be thought appropriate: it is in keeping with the persistent polemic against vestiges of popery that runs through Protestant literature of the sixteenth and seventeenth centuries. Moreover, it

befits the fact that in his theological writings there is no indication that
Milton took an interest in Mary in her own right.[3] By Milton's time
aversion to "unwritten traditions" had taken sufficient hold in England
for nonbiblical features of Christian piety to have been largely suppressed.
In the case of Marian devotion in particular, the apocryphal legends met
with derisive scorn. Aversion to popular superstition issued into vocifer-
ous objection when it came to the doctrines of Mary's immaculate conception and bodily assumption. And while the biblically warranted doctrine
of the virgin birth remained intact, stories about the Virgin's apparitions
and miracles met with downright hostility.[4] Milton, for his part, never
deigned to write about superstitious abuses of the Marian variety.[5]

Though many Reformers were willing to grant the saints "due praise
and honour" insofar as this meant imitating their "faith" and "good
vertues,"[6] most Protestant writers on the subject thought that the evidence for Mary's sanctity is rather scanty. There are after all only four or
five relevant biblical passages, and as one writer put it they "make not
much for her greatness."[7] Against Catholic claims for allotting a special
place to the Mother of God, Protestants often quoted the words of Jesus
when he was informed that his mother and brothers had come to speak
with him, "Who is my mother, or my brethren?" (Mark 3:33); or the
words that Jesus addressed to Mary at the wedding feast in Cana, "Woman,
what have I to do with thee?" (John 2:4).[8]

Because the New Testament has little to say about Mary, and because
much of what it says seems demeaning, it is surprising that Milton
bestowed upon Mary, without obvious biblical precedent, a role in a
poem about the temptations of Jesus.[9] Given the poet's tendency to be
abstemious throughout the narrative, to get along with a plain style and
to celebrate a hero who triumphs in obscurity as he rejects wealth and
power and even learning, if he wished to include Mary, Milton might
very well have made Satan's temptations include the comforts of domestic life. In the companion poem in the volume of 1671, both Dalila and
Manoa invite the hero to retire from a public role in the service of God to
enjoy private pleasures. The Gospels provide ample warrant for suppos-
ing that Jesus had to resist similar temptations: "The foxes have holes,"
says Jesus to a would-be follower, "and the birds of the air have nests; but
the Son of man hath not where to lay his head" (Matt. 8:20). Similarly, in
the striking passage that lies behind Christian's departure from his
family at the start of The Pilgrim's Progress, Jesus declares that he is "come
to set a man at variance against his father, and the daughter against her
mother. . . . He that loveth father or mother more than me," he concludes,
"is not worthy of me" (Matt. 10:35, 37). All this is in keeping with the
synoptic picture of Mary and the brothers of Jesus as outsiders during

the course of the public life. But in Milton's poem, despite the emphasis on the single hero relying upon God alone, there is no rejection of family, nor any of the apparent discourtesy that the Jesus of the Gospels displayed to his mother.

From the Gospels of Matthew and Mark a glimpse of Mary as an outsider emerges. Mark, now commonly thought to have been the first gospel, presents Jesus' mother only briefly; she is as an uncomprehending obstacle to her son's work (3:31–35). Matthew largely follows Mark in this (12:46–50), adding however the story of the virgin birth told from Joseph's point of view. But the fourth gospel, unique in this matter as in many others, places Mary at the foot of the cross and shows that she was included in the community at the last moment of her son's life, when Jesus entrusted her to the beloved disciple (John 19:25–27). This scene suggested the sort of maternal tenderness that has inspired paintings and sculptures on the theme of the Pietà. In the seventeenth century Grotius drew on this material for his depiction of Mary in Act V of his tragedy, *Christs Passion*.[10] At last abandoning an emphasis on the sorrow and grief of the *Mater Dolorosa*, Grotius gives to Mary the final lines of the play, an apostrophe in which she addresses a vision of her Son leading the blessed into felicity. It is at once a biblical and a flattering portrait of Mary, and in this respect it anticipates something of what Milton would do in *Paradise Regained*.

Although Matthew, Mark, and John all treated Mary, Luke was the only evangelist to provide an ample verbal portrait. Long before Milton's time, this had the effect of joining Luke and Mary closely in the imaginations of Christians. By the sixth century, there were effigies of the *Mater Amabilis* in the Greek churches; and not long afterwards the idea was going round that Luke the physician and evangelist had also been a painter.[11] After the tenth century, in the West hundreds of statues and paintings were ascribed to Luke, and he was said to have converted people by showing them his portraits of Christ and the Virgin.[12] But it was not until the twelfth and thirteenth centuries that Mary became a major subject for artists generally; and the legend of Joachim and Anna became a familiar theme in the centuries that followed.[13] Another favorite subject, seen in paintings of the late Middle Ages and Renaissance by Hugo van der Goes, Rogier van der Weyden, and Jean Gossaert (Mabuse), was Luke painting the portrait of the Virgin.[14]

While Luke's gospel was the source of many images of Mary,[15] the numerous and nearly ubiquitous paintings and sculptures of the Christian centuries attest to the freedom that most artists have felt to handle their subject according to their own conceptions. If many artworks were spun by active imaginations working on Luke's stories of the Annunciation, the Visitation, and the Finding in the Temple, others owed a good deal to legends that were not grounded in the Bible.[16] The *Book of James* and the *Gospel of Pseudo-Matthew* had spread abroad the popular idea that as a girl Mary was brought up in the temple and nourished by angels. But they said nothing of her having received an education in Hebrew letters from her mother, a theme taken up only relatively late in the history of painting, by Rubens, Murillo, and Poussin.[17] The apocryphal writings were far more concerned with the circumstances of her engagement to Joseph; and they provided a number of other tales that passed into Jacobus de Voragine's *Golden Legend* (c. 1280) and became the basis for full-scale spiritual biographies to satisfy and stimulate the curiosity of the Madonna's devotees.[18] By the seventeenth century these were commonly spoken of in the language of art, and the Catholic Bossuet could be every bit as adamant about objecting to their extravagances as any Protestant: "Many portraits have been painted of Mary," he wrote, "by many artists, each painting her according to his own idea. There can, however, be only one true likeness of her: namely, a copy of her as shown forth in the Gospels, the account of which forms a portrait drawn, if we may venture so to say, by the Holy Spirit Himself." Bossuet goes on to say that the "essence of Mary's character" as it emerges from the Gospels "is her modesty and self-restraint"; and he praises her as a model Christian in her pensiveness and her unselfishness.[19]

While the other three evangelists all contributed something toward a picture of the mother of Jesus, Luke provided the basis of the "one true likeness." His depiction of Mary seems to have been geared to revising Mark's and Matthew's misleading attempts. In the Acts of the Apostles (1:14), Luke suggests that Mary came to accept Jesus' work when he places her with the disciples on whom the Spirit descended at Pentecost. And already in his gospel he seems to have been at pains to explain Mary's tardiness in accepting her son's mission. While he retains the question that Jesus asks about who his mother and brethren are, Luke places it in a new context, one that suggests that Mary meets the criterion for inclusion in Jesus' real family, "these which hear the word of God, and do it" (8:21). In fact, he has prepared for his placing of Mary among the first believers by telling of the virgin birth in quite a different way from Matthew; instead of giving the story from Joseph's point of view and dwelling upon the miracle of virginal conception, Luke emphasizes Mary's response to the strange invitation. She was "troubled," he says, at the angel's greeting, "and cast in her mind what manner of salutation this should be" (1:29). This sort of response seems to be a natural prelude to her acceptance of the role of "handmaid of the Lord" when she declares "be it unto me according to thy word" (1:38).

Mary is the common thread that runs through the whole collection of stories that Luke tells in the first two chapters; and one might suppose that the evangelist refers especially to her when he says that he consulted "eyewitnesses and ministers of the word" who knew the story "from the beginning" (1:2).[20] In Milton's time, when Quakers and other radical women were taking an active role in religion, there seems to be a hint of an understanding, even among the conformists, that women can serve such a role. Jeremy Taylor, for instance, insisted that from the beginning, "in matters of salvation and common duty, the rule of the Church is, *Scriptura loquens in Masculino, procedit etiam in foeminino.*" Using the verb *procedere,* which means, besides "to go forward" or "advance," "to come forward as a speaker," the saying suggested something of the potential in evangelical Christianity for promoting women's speaking and writing. "There is no difference in sexes," Taylor continued, "and before God it is now as it shall be in the resurrection, *There is neither male nor female with him,* but all alike."[21] But of course the twelve apostles had been men; and Mary, though she had been with them at Pentecost, had not had her res gestae recorded in the Acts. Still, Luke's opening remarks in his gospel and his narratives about Jesus' infancy and childhood implied that he had got a good deal of his material from Mary.[22] To seventeenth-century Protestants, therefore, she could be seen as the mediator not of grace but of the scriptural Word. According to Anthony Stafford, the Virgin could be called "the vessell, but not the fountaine of Grace."[23] Mary was not, however, "the weaker vessell."[24] Rather she was, as John Taylor put it (borrowing the phrase that Luke had used of Paul),[25] a "chosen vessell" through whom God's Son came into the world.[26] Milton, who developed the idea that her heart was a storehouse of memories, understood that she was also the "earthen vessel" that holds a priceless "treasure."[27] More than any other writer of his age, he explored the implications of the evangelist's dependence for his story on the Mother of the Word. This Milton did by comparing and relating a variety of biblical texts.

Already in the Renaissance learned Protestants recognized that the Scriptures had a prehistory in oral storytelling. But since this might seem to give some point to the Catholics' attempt to ascribe authority to Tradition, they had worked out ways of explaining how authentic tradition worked. In his systematic account of the differences between the "Reformed and Romish" religions, for instance, Perkins puts the essential difference into clear focus. "Papists teach," he writes, "that beside the written word, there be certain unwritten traditions, which must be believed as ... necessary to salvation. ... We hold that the Scriptures are most perfect, containing in them all doctrines needfull to salvation."[28] The difference between, say, a legend about Mary's birth to Joachim and

Anna and the traditions about Jesus' birth in the stable is that the latter came to be written down by the "sacred penmen," just as Moses eventually recorded things that God had revealed long before to Adam and to the patriarchs.[29] To rule out the accretions of unwarranted postbiblical traditions, then, Perkins cites a host of texts to support the contention that the Scriptures are utterly sufficient. He begins with the locus classicus, Deut. 4:12, *"Thou shalt not adde to the words that I command thee, nor take any thing there from."* [30] Then he concludes the chapter by dismissing the objection that disagreements about interpretation make appeals to Scripture indecisive. Here he sets down the guidelines within which Protestant writers characteristically worked. Difficult matters are clarified, he says, by means of "the analogie of faith, which is . . . gathered out of the clearest places of Scripture," and by making "conference of place with place."[31] Such a "conference" was the method by which divines came to compile systematic treatises of divinity based upon "the Bible only." "I read and pondered the Holy Scriptures themselves," says Milton at the outset of *De Doctrina Christiana,* "with all possible diligence, never sparing myself in any way."[32] The process moved from a collation of the pertinent passages, to the storing up of a "treasure [*thesaurum*] which would be a provision for my future life."[33] The result was something that he called his "dearest and best possession."[34]

The high estimate which, according to his nephew, Milton had for *Paradise Regained* may also be a function of the painstaking way in which he had gathered, compared, and synthesized diverse biblical passages to make a coherent narrative. As its origin in the Latin *conferre* indicates, "conference of place with place" involved a series of interpretive activities. These are suggested in the range of meaning given for the word in the OED: the "action of bringing [various texts, loci] together" into a "collection," making a "comparison" of them, with a view to their then "supplying" for future uses. All this was the prelude to finding an essentially biblical narrative about "deeds, / Above Heroic, though in secret done, / And unrecorded left through many an Age."[35] The story was "Worthy t' have not remain'd so long unsung" because a more comprehensive version than any of the evangelists told could be pieced together on the basis of "conference of place with place." In this respect, the poem adds nothing nonbiblical to the object of Christian faith; and the interpretive work that stands behind it is of a piece with that which went into compiling a systematic Christian doctrine on the basis of the Bible alone. And it has been well illustrated, by Louis Martz, Stanley Fish, and others, that *Paradise Regained* involves for the hero and the reader alike a struggle to achieve, or to move toward achieving, a right interpretation of the Scriptures.[36] It is as the mother of this sort of interpretive quest, of the process of "conferring place with place," that Mary figures most importantly in the poem. But in this respect Milton's Mary stands apart from other depictions of the mother of Jesus in seventeenth-century England.[37]

There were of course some Protestants who wished a larger scope for Mary in Reformed piety, especially since, on the basis of the Magnificat, she was widely thought to have been a prophetess.[38] John Taylor's rhyming couplets of 1622 presented Mary as the "gratious paterne of a sex [otherwise] so bad" and praised the patience, zeal, constancy, and love that proved her the "very best of women."[39] Jeremy Taylor commended Mary for having nursed her son herself and took occasion to recommend the practice to modern women.[40] He also praised her along with Joseph for their response to the discovery of the twelve-year-old child in the temple: they "wondred at these things which were spoken, and treasured them in their hearts, and they became matter of Devotion, and mental Prayer, or *Meditation.*"[41] Mention of Mary's practice then served Taylor as a jumping off point for recommending to Protestants the benefits of the neglected art of meditation.

But among those who advocated the imitation of Mary perhaps none was more eloquent than Stafford, whose book of 1635 presents the Virgin to his "feminine reader" as "the prime President of femall Perfection" and the model for all her sex.[42] Stafford saw in Mary a learned reader of the Scriptures (p. 23); and when he speaks of her having come to maturity at age fifteen, he uses the phrase, "she began to write woman" (p. 27).[43] But intent as he was on depicting Mary as the model for all women, Stafford drew on the fact that the Scriptures allot her only a small speaking part, in order to recommend the "prudency" of her "opportune silence and caution of speech" (p. 54). And unlike the creator of the angry woman of the Ludlow *Mask* who gives vent to her outrage when Comus tenders his offer, Stafford singled his lady out for special praise because of her mildness in questioning the angel who announced that she was to conceive. "Some women," he remarks, "(though chast, yet curst, and hasty) having once heard their chastity brought in question, would have omitted all interrogations, and have given the Angell a sermon ... and have reviled his name" (p. 56). But Stafford's book presents a Mary who resembles Milton's Lady in other ways and anticipates the hero of *Paradise Regained* in her avoidance of luxury in food and clothing, in the value she places on privacy, and in her concern to use her learning for spiritually and socially beneficial ends.[44] Mary "knew well," Stafford says, "that the holy Ghost himselfe had dwelt with the Prophets and Apostles in Caves, Dens, and Dungeons, and there pen'd the all-saving Writ" (p. 34).

Milton's depiction of Mary in *Paradise Regained* shares some of the features of works like those of Stafford and the Taylors, especially the notion, based on Luke 2:19 and 51, that Mary meditated on her experience. But Milton's work betrays nothing of the agenda Stafford had in mind when he drew his portrait of Mary to serve as a "Mirrour of Femall perfection" (b3ʳ) that would show the "Deformities" of the women who looked in it (b4ʳ). While respecting Mary's characteristically maternal role with respect to Jesus, and suggesting the psychological and spiritual ways in which she had nourished her son, Milton depicted Mary as a model for all disciples, male and female. He saw in her a "minister of the Word," inferring, naturally enough in view of what Luke had said about his sources, that she was the primary source for the biblical stories about the savior's infancy. From the Son's first interior monologue in the poem, we learn that his mother had brought forth the Word *to* her child as well as *in* him.

In the first book of *Paradise Regained*, after Jesus has received his calling, he retreats into the desert, and he proceeds to "cast in his mind," we might say, "what manner of" saying had been pronounced at his baptism. He is doing what his mother had done when she received her calling, and he soon brings to mind that his mother had told him the story of his divine conception when she noticed that his noble aspirations required to be "nourish[ed]" and also to be properly challenged.[45] Then, in relation to the Father's sudden declaration of his favor, the Son reviews the rest of what his mother had taught him: about the virgin birth, the arrival of the shepherds and wise men at the manger, etc. In this way, as he gives us access to the Son's memory of his mother's actual words, Milton has Mary weave together various details that came down to him and his readers piecemeal, from Matthew and Luke.[46] He makes this dramatically functional in the story by showing that Mary had told Jesus all this at the right time and that Jesus now remembers it when he needs it. Mary has been a bearer of the Word, mediating to her son information that proved timely for his mission long before the penmen wrote it down for aftertimes. Beyond this, Milton suggests that Mary first taught Jesus the work of conferring place with place, since he now puts together the "texts" she had given him orally with the ones "Concerning the Messiah" that he found when he "revolv'd / The Law and Prophets, searching what was writ" (1.259–61). This work of conferring places then continues through the course of the temptations.

Milton's inference that Mary was not only the source of the details about Jesus' infancy that the evangelists only wrote down but that she also taught her son to confer places in his reading rests upon his own conference of place with place. When, for instance, Luke tells of the angel's announcement that Mary would conceive virginally, he shows her responding with a disposition simultaneously to search for its meaning and to accept it as a mysterious expression of God's will. Moreover, he extends his treatment of Mary into subsequent narratives to record other responses to events in her son's life. He tells of her reaction to the choir of angels and the visit by the shepherds: "Mary kept all these things, and pondered them in her heart" (2:19). Again, after remarking on her puzzlement when she and Joseph listened to the twelve-year-old in the temple going about his Father's business, Luke says that "his mother kept all these sayings in her heart" (2:51). Taken together the two statements mean that Mary remembered both events ("these things") and speech ("these sayings"); and the context suggests that, because she did not understand everything that was going on, more than mere retention is meant. Whether, as Jeremy Taylor thought, she practiced formal meditation Luke does not say. Just what Mary did "in her heart" is not immediately clear from Luke's word *symballousa* (2:19), rendered *conferens* in the Vulgate and "pondered" in the English versions.

The ambiguity of this verse seems to have suggested to Milton a series of roles for Mary in *Paradise Regained*. Literally, *sym* "with" and *ballein* "throw" (the root of our English word *symbol*) suggest a particularly active and creative role for Mary. The word hints that she "combined" what she saw and heard and remembered in her heart into the coherent collection of narratives that Luke later recorded.[47] Still, it is also possible that *symballousa* carries a less literal sense and one that implies less mastery and control on the part of Mary. In Hellenistic literature, the word typically "refer[s] to an interpretation of dark and difficult matters, the right meaning of which is often ascertained only by means of divine help."[48] But a more relevant context for understanding Milton's usage seems to be the Authorized Version.[49] Besides Luke 2:19, the word *ponder* appears only in Proverbs. The five instances there suggest that the experience of Solomon stands in the background of Satan's scorning of sexual temptation in *Paradise Regained* (2.172ff.) and of his proposing the temptation of learning (4.195ff.). Early in Proverbs, the writer recommends the activity of pondering (4:26) as a means of avoiding sexual temptation (5:6 and 5:21). Later, he speaks of it as a particularly divine activity: the Lord is said to "ponder . . . the hearts" of his creatures (21:2, 24:12).

In any event, Milton concluded that Mary's encounter with God's mysterious word, which began with the announcement of the virginal conception, continued through the course of her life. The puzzling over texts anticipated her son's experience and that of later Christian readers. Just as Mary did not fully understand all at once the meaning and implications of the text of her calling, so Jesus, having heard that he was the Father's "beloved Son," gradually works through the implications of his calling during the trials in the wilderness. He learns "the rudiments" (I.157) of his mission by trying experiences analogous to those that Mary went through during his childhood—the slaughter of the innocents, the flight into Egypt, the predictions of trouble by aged Simeon, the loss of the child in the temple.

Milton's inferences about the kinds of things that Mary had taught her son inform his portrait of her at the beginning of Book 2, where he shows her to be more adept at dealing with delays and disappointments than Andrew and Simon, who have only recently had their hopes raised. Mary's soliloquy there is exemplary not in that it shows a person exempt from "cares and fears" (for these are essential to the testing of a disciple) but in that it dramatizes the inner struggle of one trying to make sense of her experience in relation to what she had previously heard from God. She recalls the things she has lately heard about her Son—all of it matter drawn, as if by anticipation, from what will be recorded in the New Testament.[50] She weaves it together into a new synthesis, making as much sense of it as she presently can, putting into question her previous interpretations in light of new data: "O what avails me now that honour high / To have conceiv'd of God, or that salute, / Hail highly favour'd, among women blest!" (2.66–68).

The characteristic method of Mary's interior monologue, that is, of what Milton shows going on with the things that she has kept in her heart, is a comparison of texts. The narrator points out that she has been "pondering oft, and oft to mind / Recalling what remarkably had pass'd / Since first her Salutation heard" (2.105–7). In this way Milton projects into Mary's experience during Jesus' adult life both the method that she had practiced and something of the content that she had learned when Jesus was a boy. "But where delays he now?" she asks herself,

> some great intent
> Conceals him: when twelve years he scarce had seen,
> I lost him, but so found, as well I saw
> He could not lose himself; but went about
> His Father's business; what he meant I mus'd,
> Since understand; much more his absence now
> Thus long to some great purpose he obscures.
> But I to wait with patience am inur'd. . . .

> (2.95–102)

The word *mus'd* here is particularly rich, suggesting as it does an alternative to "ponder" as a translation for the Greek *symballousa*. By

Milton's time its older senses (OED, 5; 6) of "To wait or look expectantly" and "To murmur; to grumble, complain" were obsolete. But as a reminder of the two divergent responses to God's promises made by the Israelites during their wanderings through the wilderness, these meanings are part of the background to the activities of both mother and son. Another sense of the word (OED, 2) implies "be[ing] at a loss," and this perfectly befits the context in which Mary now finds herself. For her, unlike the new disciples, the experience of missing something turns out to be an inspiration; and Milton gives a longer speech to Mary here than she has in any of the canonical Gospels.

Pondering over the meaning of God's words in the way the writer of *De Doctrina Christiana* says he "pondered" over the words of Scripture, Milton's Mary emerges as a portrait of the responsible reader. She is, in the phrase that Luke uses later in his gospel to provide a way to reinterpret Jesus' definition of his true family, one who, "in an honest and good heart, having heard the word, keep[s] it, and bring[s] forth fruit with patience" (8:15). Perhaps even more to the point, she has understood by anticipation the saying that her son will pronounce before the crowds: "where your treasure is, there will your heart be also" (Luke 12:34).

Beyond this Milton ascribes to Mary greater interpretive powers and privileges, more in keeping with the notion that she exercised the power of symbol-making. There is already something of this activity in Book 1, when Jesus recalls what his mother had told him and how it sent him back to reread the Scriptures (1.259ff.). But this role is hinted at again and given a striking name at the close of Mary's speech in Book 2. There she says that her "heart hath been a store-house long of things / And sayings laid up, portending strange events" (2.103–4). This paraphrase of Luke 2:19 and 2:51, inserted at the end of the soliloquy in which she had demonstrated what she does with the things she keeps in her heart, makes it clear that Mary does what Milton does. More than a disciple who waits expectantly for further clarification of the texts that she does not understand,[51] Mary actively seeks out meaning. Her own heart serves as the reservoir of invention.

Some typical uses of the word *storehouse* in the Renaissance reinforce the notion that Milton looks upon Mary's heart as a writer's commonplace book. The *storehouse* served as the standard image in rhetorical treatises for the container in which the topics were kept. In his *Arte of Logique*, Thomas Wilson speaks of "the storehouse of places, wherin Arguments rest"; and he recommends that one "conferre" there matters that are to be "put to the profe," insisting meanwhile that this will require "a very diligent labourer."[52] Ralph Lever, in *The Art of Reason*, enumerates ten storehouses and spells out their uses.[53] Moreover, translators of commonplace books often enlisted the word *storehouse* to render the Latin *thesaurus*, emphasizing more than they might by the word *treasury* the functional aspect of the collection.[54] Other writers related the storehouse to the religious use of books. Robert Cawdray, in *A Treasurie or Store-house of Similes*, spoke of the Word as a mine to be searched into and from which readers could draw out "whatsoever is requisite and necessarie for the salvation of our soules."[55] Closer to Milton's time, Henry Jessey presented his cases-of-conscience book, *A Storehouse of Provision*, as a "storehouse of various kinds of spiritual food."[56] In any event, the storehouse and treasury which is Mary's heart makes her akin to the writer whose method Milton describes in the opening chapter of *De Doctrina Christiana*, where he cites Matthew 13:52, "every scribe who has been instructed in the kingdom of heaven, is like a householder who brings out of his treasure new and old possessions."[57] This assimilation of Mary's heart to a thesaurus, upon which the scribe then draws to produce a work at once old and new,[58] makes a sort of signature in Milton's poem, even as it validates the storyteller's method. The words *symballousa, conferens,* and *pondered* apply to the activities of Milton and Mary alike, as they collect, compare, and recombine texts in a continuing search for meanings that cannot be permanently fixed. All this suggests why, at the end of Milton's poem, the victor returns to his mother's house; and it gives some indication of what he will do there.

Paradise Regained shows then that Mary nurtured Jesus at some times and learned from him at others. Without in any way implying that the papists had reason to see in her a mediatrix of divine grace, Milton presents a Mary who mediates the Word—first to Jesus himself, then to the New Testament writers, and ultimately to Christians in every age. Beyond this, he has painted in her a portrait of the artist. She exercises the authorly roles of preserving, interpreting, and combining diverse texts into a unique personal synthesis. In this way Milton's Mary anticipates the activity of other bearers of the Word, that is, of both the evangelists like Luke and latter-day poets like Milton himself.

It is important to recognize, finally, that Milton has not painted a portrait of the Madonna by herself. Mary is a figure in a larger portrait; and her significance remains, as Protestant writers insisted that it should, a function of her relation to her son. This should not obscure, however, the degree to which Milton has painted the son to resemble his mother. The hero of *Paradise Regained* learns from his mother a whole range of virtues, including the ability to ponder texts patiently and persistently, searching out their implications for life. This family resemblance between mother and son places an unmistakable emphasis on the right uses of reading and of learning; and it tends to blur one of the distinctions between male and female roles that we have been accustomed to associating with the English seventeenth century.

NOTES

1. *The Complete Poetry of John Donne,* ed. John T. Shawcross (New York: New York Univ. Press, 1968), p. 386.

2. For brief treatments of the subject, see Carolyn H. Smith, "The Virgin Mary in *Paradise Regained,*" *South Atlantic Quarterly,* 71 (1972), 557–64; Walter MacKellar, *A Variorum Commentary on the Poems of John Milton, Vol. IV: "Paradise Regained"* (New York: Columbia Univ. Press, 1975), pp. 31, 108–11, 251–52; and Burton Jasper Weber, *Wedges and Wings: The Patterning of "Paradise Regained"* (Carbondale: Southern Illinois Univ. Press, 1975), pp. 69–71. Cf. also Dayton Haskin, "Matthew, Mary, Luke, and John: The Mother of the Word in Milton's Poetry," *Proceedings of the PMR Conference,* 11 (1986): 75–86.

There are several comments about Mary in the eighteenth-century editions of Newton and Dunster. See *The Poetical Works of John Milton. With Notes of various Authors,* ed. Thomas Newton, 3 vols. (London: Tonson, 1761), 3:24, 49, 55–57, and "Paradise Regained, a Poem in Four Books, by John Milton. A New Edition, with Notes of Various Authors," by Charles Dunster, in *Milton's "Paradise Regained": Two Eighteenth-Century Critiques by Richard Meadowcourt and Charles Dunster,* facsimile reproductions with an introduction by Joseph Anthony Wittreich, Jr. (Gainesville: Scholars' Facsimiles and Reprints, 1971), pp. 60, 71–72. As an index of the general neglect of Mary in recent Milton criticism, note that Barbara Kiefer Lewalski barely mentions her in *Milton's Brief Epic: The Genre, Meaning and Art of "Paradise Regained"* (Providence: Brown Univ. Press, 1966) or in the article on *Paradise Regained* in *A Milton Encyclopedia,* vol. 6, gen. ed. William B. Hunter, Jr. (Lewisburg, Pa.: Bucknell Univ. Press, 1979). There is no entry on "Mary" in *A Milton Encyclopedia.*

3. On references to Mary in Milton's prose, see Smith, p. 562.

4. For a summary account, see Hilda Graef, *Mary: A History of Doctrine and Devotion,* 2 vols. (London: Sheed & Ward, 1965), 2:1–16, 62–67.

5. The most telling reference to Mariolatry in Milton's prose appears almost as an obiter dictum in the course of an attempt to discredit the authority of Irenaeus in *Of Prelatical Episcopacy,* in *Complete Prose Works,* gen. ed. Don M. Wolfe, 8 vols. (New Haven: Yale Univ. Press, 1953–82), 1:642.

6. See William Perkins, *A Reformed Catholike,* in *Workes* (London: John Legatt, 1612), 1:601. Here and in other quotations from early printed sources, *i, j, u, v,* and *w* are brought into conformity with modern usage.

7. See William Fleetwood, *An Account of the Life and Death of the Blessed Virgin, According to Romish Writers* (London: H. Clark, 1687), p. 2.

8. Unless otherwise indicated, biblical quotations are from the Authorized Version.

9. See Smith, who observes that there are no precedents in the apocrypha, the mystery cycles, standard Renaissance commentaries, or the poems of Vida

and Fletcher, for the emotional struggles that Milton gives to Mary after the baptism of Jesus (p. 557).

10. Hugo Grotius, *Christs Passion. A Tragedie. With Annotations* [trans. George Sandys ?] (London: John Legatt, 1640).

11. See Adolfo Venturi, *The Madonna,* trans. Alice Meynell (London: Burns & Oates, 1902), pp. 1–8.

12. See G. A. Wellen, *Theotokos: Eine Ikonographische Abhandlung über das Gottesmutterbild in Frühchristlicher Zeit* (Utrecht: Uitgeverig Het Spectrum, 1961), pp. 177, 213–24; and John Beckwith, *Early Christian and Byzantine Art* (Harmondsworth: Penguin, 1970), pp. 38–39. Cf. Marina Warner, *Alone of All Her Sex: The Myth and the Cult of the Virgin Mary* (New York: Knopf, 1976), pp. 291–92.

13. See Gilbert Cope, *Symbolism in the Bible and the Church* (London: SCM, 1959), pp. 164–70; and G. G. Coulton, *Art and the Reformation,* 2d ed. (Cambridge: Cambridge Univ. Press, 1953), pp. 293–302, 558.

14. See Clara Erskine Clement, *Saints in Art* (Boston: Page, 1899), pp. 60–66.

15. See Gertrud Schiller, *Iconography of Christian Art,* trans. Janet Seligman, 2 vols. (1966; 1st American edition: Greenwich, Conn.: New York Graphic Society, 1971), 1:33–52, 55–56, 124–25. Cf. Jean Guitton, *The Madonna* (New York: Tudor, 1963), p. 4.

16. See Coulton, p. 300.

17. See Sir Charles Holmes, Introduction on the Madonna in art, in *The Madonna: An Anthology,* ed. Sir James Marchant (London: Longmans, Green, 1928), pp. xxv–xxvi. Cf. Louis Réau, *Iconographie de l'art chrétien,* 3 vols. (Paris: Presses Universitaires de France, 1955–59), 2, 2:168–69.

18. The second-century *Protevangelium Jacobi* came to be known in Europe only in the sixteenth century; see Montague Rhodes James, *The Apocryphal New Testament* (Oxford: Clarendon Press, 1924), p. 38.

19. Quoted in *The Madonna: An Anthology,* pp. 89–90. For the original, see the sermon for 9 December 1669 in *Œuvres oratoires de Bossuet,* ed. J. Lebarq, 7 vols. (Paris: Desclée de Brouwer, 1926–27), 5:616.

20. On the centrality of Mary in the opening chapters of Luke's gospel, see Paul S. Minear, "Luke's Use of the Birth Stories," in *Studies in Luke-Acts,* ed. Leander E. Keck and J. Louis Martyn (1966; rpt., Philadelphia: Fortress, 1980), pp. 111–30. For a recent estimate of the idea that Mary is the source of the materials in Luke 1–2, see Raymond E. Brown, *The Birth of the Messiah: A Commentary on the Infancy Narratives in Matthew and Luke* (Garden City, N.Y.: Doubleday, 1977), pp. 238–39, 244–45.

21. Jeremy Taylor, *Ductor Dubitantium, or The Rule of Conscience...In Four Books,* 2 vols. (London: Richard Royston, 1660), Book III, Chap. 4, Rule 12, section 6.

22. See Matthew Poole's *Synopsis Criticorum,* 4 vols. in 5 (London: J. Flesher & T. Roycroft, 1669–76), 4:844.

23. Anthony Stafford, *The Femall Glory: or, the Life, and Death of our Blessed Lady, the holy Virgin Mary, Gods owne immaculate Mother* (London: John Waterson, 1635), p. 10.

24. Antonia Fraser discusses this phrase from I Peter 3:7 in some detail in her study of women in the seventeenth century, *The Weaker Vessel* (New York: Knopf, 1984), pp. 1–6. Margaret Homans presents a rather crude caricature of Christian beliefs about Mary in *Bearing the Word: Language and Female Experience in Nineteenth-Century Women's Writing* (Chicago: Univ. of Chicago Press, 1986), pp. 158ff.

25. Acts 9:15.

26. John Taylor, *The Life and Death of the most blessed among women, the Virgin Mary Mother of our Lord Jesus* (London, 1622), A8ᵛ.

27. 2 Cor. 4:7: "But we have this treasure [the knowledge of the glory of God in the face of Jesus Christ] in earthen vessels, that the excellency of the power may be of God, and not of us."

28. Perkins, *A Reformed Catholike*, in *Workes*, 1:581.

29. Perkins, *Workes*, 1:580.

30. Perkins, *Workes*, 1:581.

31. Perkins, *Workes*, 1:583.

32. Milton, *De Doctrina Christiana*, vol. 6 of *Complete Prose Works*, ed. Maurice Kelley, trans. John Carey (New Haven: Yale Univ. Press, 1973), p. 118.

33. Here I have cited the translation of Charles Sumner (rather than Carey's), because it better suggests the sense of Milton's Latin. See *The Works of John Milton*, gen. ed. Frank Allen Patterson, 18 vols. in 21 (New York: Columbia Univ. Press, 1931–38), 14:8–9.

34. Milton, *De Doctrina, Complete Prose Works*, 6:121.

35. Quotations from the verse are from *The Poetical Works of John Milton*, ed. H. C. Beeching (Oxford: Oxford Univ. Press, 1922).

36. See Louis Martz, "*Paradise Regained:* The Meditative Combat," *ELH*, 27 (1960), 223–47; revised in *Poet of Exile: A Study of Milton's Poetry* (New Haven: Yale Univ. Press, 1980), pp. 247–71. Cf. Stanley Fish, "Things and Actions Indifferent: The Temptation of Plot in *Paradise Regained,*" *Milton Studies*, 17, ed. Richard S. Ide and Joseph Wittreich (Pittsburgh: Univ. of Pittsburgh Press, 1983), pp. 163–85; Mary Ann Radzinowicz, "*Paradise Regained* as Hermeneutic Combat," *Univ. of Hartford Studies in Literature*, 15–16 (1983–84), 99–107.

37. For the standard contrast made between Eve and Mary, see Linda Woodbridge, *Women and the English Renaissance: Literature and the Nature of Womankind, 1540–1620* (Urbana: Univ. of Illinois Press, 1984), passim. I have been unable to obtain a copy of H. H. Petit's "The Second Eve in Paradise Regained," *Papers of the Michigan Academy of Sciences, Arts, and Letters*, 44 (1958), 365–69.

38. Cf. Cedrenus, *Annales, sive Historiae ab Exordio mundi ad Isacium Comnenum usque Compendium* (Heidelberg, 1566), p. 153; Perkins, *Reformed Catholike*, in *Workes*, 1:601; Richard Baxter, *A Paraphrase on the New Testament* (1685), 3d ed. (London: T. Parkhurst, 1701), glosses on Luke 1:41–45, 67–71.

39. John Taylor, *Life and Death*, C4ʳ.

40. Jeremy Taylor, *The Great Exemplar of Sanctity and Holy Life according to the Christian Institution. Described in the History of the Life and Death of the ever Blessed Jesus Christ* (London: Francis Ash, 1649), pp. 33–39.

41. Jeremy Taylor, *Great Exemplar*, p. 82. Cf. the discourse "Of Meditation," pp. 83–95.

42. See Anthony Stafford, "The Epistle Dedicatory," n.p.

43. Stafford's use of this phrase to indicate arrival at maturity thus anticipates by twenty-five years the earliest citation of this usage in the OED.

44. Stafford, *Femall Glory*, pp. 26, 34, 49–50.

45. See *Paradise Regained* 1.227ff.

46. Of course, long before Milton many writers and painters had effected a fusion of the accounts by Matthew and Luke. But in the time scheme of Milton's poem, Mary is using words and phrases—and Jesus is remembering them—some years before Matthew and Luke will set them down in the Scriptures.

47. See *Mary in the New Testament*, ed. Raymond E. Brown et al. (Philadelphia: Fortress, 1978), p. 149. Cf. Joseph A. Fitzmeyer's commentary in the Anchor Bible, *The Gospel According to Luke (I–IX)* (Garden City, N.Y.: Doubleday, 1981), p. 413.

48. See Brown, *Mary*, pp. 149–50. Cf. W. C. van Unnik, "Die rechte Bedeutung des Wortes treffen, Lukas 2,19," in *Verbum: Essays on Some Aspects of the Religious Function of Words: Festschrift for H. W. Obbink*, ed. T. P. van Baaren et al. (Utrecht: Kemink, 1964), pp. 129–47.

49. I owe this suggestion to Geoffrey F. Nuttall, who commented on an earlier version of this paper.

50. When he treats this phenomenon in *The Bible in Milton's Epics* (Gainesville: Univ. of Florida Press, 1962), James Sims seems to have things the wrong way round. He misses what Milton is doing with the biblical language when he says that Mary "uses the very language . . . recorded by Luke" (p. 52).

51. Cf. the excellent commentary by Sanford Budick in *The Dividing Muse: Images of Sacred Disjunction in Milton's Poetry* (New Haven: Yale Univ. Press, 1985), pp. 128–29, which reached me after I had written this article.

52. See Thomas Wilson, *The Rule of Reason Conteinying the Arte of Logique* (1551), ed. Richard S. Sprague (Northridge, Calif.: San Fernando Valley State College, 1972), p. 89.

53. Ralph Lever, *The Arte of Reason, rightly termed Witcraft, teaching a perfect way to argue and dispute* (London: Bynneman, 1573), pp. 7ff.

54. See Sister Joan Marie Lechner, *Renaissance Concepts of the Commonplaces* (New York: Pageant, 1962), pp. 147–51.

55. Robert Cawdray, *A Treasurie or Store-house of Similes* (London: Thomas Creede, 1600; facsimile ed., New York: Da Capo, 1971), p. 853.

56. Henry Jessey, *A Storehouse of Provision* (London: T. Brewster & G. Mould, 1650), A2r.

57. See *Complete Prose Works*, 6:127–28.

58. Cf. also John Spencer, *KAINA KAI PALAIA. Things New and Old. Or, A Storehouse of Similes, Sentences, Allegories, . . . Collected and observed from the Writings and Sayings of the Learned in all Ages to this present* (London: W. Wilson and J. Streater, 1658). I wish to thank Anne Ferry for this reference, and for guiding me into the terrain of Renaissance rhetorical treatises.

"Incident to All Our Sex": The Tragedy of Dalila

JOHN C. ULREICH, JR.

WHILE it no longer seems very fruitful to talk about Milton's "Turkish contempt for females," his idea of woman remains problematic. Without always acknowledging the force of Dr. Johnson's objection, traditional criticism has, more or less implicitly, accepted Milton as a spokesman of patriarchal values, "echoing and reaffirming the paternalistic ethos and values of the Judeo-Christian tradition." Recently, however, feminist critics like Sandra Gilbert have attacked Milton's vision on precisely those grounds, as a conspicuous embodiment of "a long misogynistic tradition."[1] More recently still, Diane McColley has challenged both the traditional and revisionist positions by questioning whether Milton is, in Gilbert's sense, a patriarchal poet. McColley's persuasive attempt "to extricate Eve from a reductive critical tradition, as Milton sought to redeem her from a reductive literary and iconographic tradition,"[2] has refocused the debate in a way that promises to redeem Milton himself once again from the reductive tendency of critical orthodoxy.

Further regenerative work remains to be done, however, especially in connection with the problematic, and apparently misogynistic, image of Dalila. Indeed, Dalila becomes problematic precisely to the degree that McColley's case for Eve is successful, inasmuch as Milton's portrait of Dalila seems to suggest a deliberate perversion of just those qualities which make Eve attractive. For if Eve is, indeed, "imaginative and rational, sensuous and intelligent, passionate and chaste, and free and responsible ... a pattern and composition of active goodness and a speaking picture of the recreative power of poetry itself" (pp. 3, 4), Dalila has appeared to be imaginative but irrational, more sensual than sensuous, less intelligent than cunning, enslaved by her own lust and in proportion recklessly irresponsible. As a composition and pattern of the worst and basest in female human nature, Dalila becomes an embodiment of energies wholly destructive in their operation, a speaking picture of those "common female faults" that tradition had regarded as "incident to all [her] sex."[3] Even Mary Ann Radzinowicz's massively generous reading of the play as a compendium of humanistic values is less than kind to Dalila's flawed humanity: as "a recognizable psychopathic personality," Radzinowicz argues, Dalila wants both to "love" Samson and to "defeat" him, "to master him sexually and demean him" while at the same time continuing "to enjoy him."[4]

Rather than submit to what might seem remediless, however, I should like to reopen the case of Dalila, in an attempt to rescue her from a hostile critical tradition. I shall argue (1) that Dalila is sincere in her professions of loving concern for Samson; that she is the victim of a mutual failure of charity rather than simply of her own mortal weakness; and that she is therefore more deserving of compassion than condemnation; (2) that the case of Dalila becomes especially poignant when we compare her failure to regain Samson's love with the more fortunate fall of Eve; when the two reconciliation scenes, comic and tragic, are placed side by side, in terms suggested by Rosalie Colie's discussion of genre-theory in the Renaissance, they appear as "countergenres, twinned yet opposite,"[5] and Dalila herself becomes a genuinely tragic figure, not irredeemable though finally unredeemed; and (3) that when Dalila is seen in that perspective, as tragic failure rather than mere woman-serpent, she becomes an ironic type of salvation, whose potential for redemptive love is frustrated as much by Samson's demonic impulses as by her own.

In attempting to see Dalila dramatically, as Milton presented her, I hope to do for Dalila what McColley and others have done for Eve.[6] And by occasion, following Milton's example in tackling the worst possible case, I may hope also "by raising pity and fear, or terror, to purge the mind of those and such like passions, that is to temper and reduce them to just measure with a kind of delight" ("Of . . . Tragedy," p. 549). The resulting image of Dalila—"gravest, moralest, and most profitable"—should prove somewhat more generous than the one afforded by received opinion, at once more radiant and more complex, more distinct in itself and richer in dramatic possibility.

I

I begin with an assumption: that Dalila means what she says.[7] The appropriateness of this assumption is strongly suggested by Milton's concept of decorum, inasmuch as it implies two critical principles that are vital to an interpretation of *Samson Agonistes*. The first is a firm insistence that Dalila speaks for herself, "not the poet's opinion but what is appropriate for [her] person."[8] We are thus instructed to regard Dalila's arguments, not as a reflection of Milton's beliefs, but as the decorous expression of her own dramatic character. And character, as Aristotle observes, "is that which reveals moral purpose, showing what kind of things a [wo]man chooses or avoids."[9] The second principle defines Dalila's role in the larger drama, her suitability to the "cause and purpose [Milton] hath in hand": that purpose is most fully revealed by an analysis of Dalila's character, not as an expression of abstract ideas, but as a concrete imitation of action in Aristotle's sense.

For the sake of argument, then, and still more for the sake of decorum, let us suppose that Dalila's visit is inspired, not by cruelty or malice, nor yet by a desire to prove her power over Samson, but by genuine "conjugal affection" (l. 739). If we accept this dramatic motivation, much that has seemed obscure to previous critics becomes clear and persuasive. Let us attempt to discover, then, so far as possible without prejudice, what Dalila has to say for herself.

Prompted by her love for Samson, Dalila has overcome her natural doubts and fears and comes to seek his forgiveness, "though [her] pardon / [is] No way assur'd" (l. 740). She acknowledges that she is "without excuse" (l. 734), but she desires to "expiate" (l. 735) her fault by "penance" (l. 738). By offering to "light'n" his suffering (l. 744), she hopes to make "what amends" might be in her power (l. 745) and "in some part to recompense / [Her] rash but more unfortunate misdeed" (ll. 746–47). When Samson rebuffs her with an accusation of "feign'd remorse" (l. 752), Dalila attempts to persuade him of her sincerity. Without attempting "To lessen or extenuate [her] offense" (l. 767), she asks forgiveness. Acknowledging her own weakness (l. 773), she reminds Samson of his: "Ere I to thee, thou to thyself wast cruel" (l. 784). Although they have typically been regarded as a piece of deliberate malice, Dalila's pointed remarks on Samson's self-betrayal seem more likely intended to recall him to himself in an effort to compel his acknowledgment of their mutual humanity:

> Let weakness then with weakness come to parle
> So near related, or the same of kind,
> Thine forgive mine.
>
> (ll. 785–87)

It is perhaps true, as Samson says, that "All wickedness is weakness" (l. 834), and that Dalila's argument is "relativistic,"[10] but it is also true that all human beings are wicked, and the way to genuine forgiveness is not through "uncompassionate anger" (l. 819), but through "Charity, the soul /

JOHN C. ULREICH, JR.

Of all" the Christian virtues (*PL* 12.584–85). When Dalila begs for Samson's "pity or pardon" (l. 814), "Thine forgive mine," she founds her argument upon the rock of Christian ethics: "For if ye forgive men their trespasses, your heavenly Father will also forgive you: But if ye forgive not men their trespasses, neither will your Father forgive your trespasses" (Matt. 6:14–15).[11]

If we can avoid the temptation to justify Samson at her expense, as so many critics have joined the Chorus in doing,[12] we may allow Dalila's arguments to speak for themselves, and for herself. Her rhetorical situation is complex; her self-admission is delicately balanced against her accusation of Samson: "I saw thee mutable / Of fancy" (ll. 793–94). Given her circumstances—as a wife now rejected and perhaps never greatly cherished—her claim that love, not hatred, caused her betrayal seems perfectly sincere, and her arguments are neither unreasonable nor inhumane. Her jealousy is by no means admirable, but her confession of it is at least candid, and her retrospective lament, "Wailing [Samson's] absence in [her] widow'd bed" (l. 806), is genuinely moving.

Though selfish, and in the event destructive, Dalila's desire to keep Samson "Whole to [her]self, unhazarded" (l. 809) is neither unnatural nor unsympathetic.[13] Nor does she lack compassion for Samson's suffering. And whatever conclusions we might wish to draw about its theological validity, Dalila's final, eloquent appeal for mercy seems both morally reasonable and passionately sincere: "Love hath oft, well meaning, wrought much woe, / Yet always pity or pardon hath obtained" (ll. 814–15). So far from being reductive, as most critics have argued,[14] her appeal to "Love's law" (l. 811) points obliquely to the principle of Christian charity. For did not Jesus say to the woman taken in adultery: "Neither do I condemn thee: go, and sin no more" (John 8:11); and to the Pharisees: "Ye judge after the flesh; I judge no man" (8:15)?

Given the harshness of Samson's response to her appeal—"Impartial, self-severe, inexorable" (l. 827)—Dalila's brief lapse into self-justification is at least dramatically comprehensible. Her appeal to religious and civil duty (ll. 843–70) does not carry conviction; indeed, she implies some skepticism herself regarding "maxim[s]" that are "rife and celebrated in the mouths," if not necessarily in the actions, "Of wisest men" (ll. 865, 866–67). Were it not for her subsequent attempt to seek refuge in patriotism (ll. 960–96), we should probably not take Dalila's argument here too seriously. At worst it seems an ill-judged attempt to appeal to Samson's "better," public self: If you showed yourself willing to betray me for the sake of *your* God, why should I not betray you for *mine?*

Dalila should not have descended to Samson's level. When she discovers that she has been "quite mistaken / In what [she] thought would

188

have succeeded best" (ll. 907–8), she returns quickly to her initial plea for "forgiveness" (l. 908) and offer of "recompense" (l. 910). Wisely counseling Samson not "to afflict [himself] in vain" (l. 914), she offers "solace" (l. 915) for his wounds, in the futile hope "That what by me thou hast lost thou least shalt miss" (l. 927). Dalila acknowledges Samson's loss and offers such recompense as might lie within her power: "though sight be lost, / Life yet hath many solaces, enjoy'd / Where other senses want not their delights" (ll. 914–16). She speaks directly to Samson's condition, and in terms that powerfully suggest her desire to find an effective remedy for his suffering through "nursing diligence" (l. 924). And her promise of "redoubl'd love and care" (l. 923) seems genuinely compassionate, even selfless.

Dalila's final appeal, reducing all argument to the bare essential of her deeply human need, perfectly typifies her vulnerable passion: "Let me approach at least, and touch thy hand" (l. 951). Beneath all her elegant finery, Dalila is a woman desperately seeking love, struggling to find means by which to communicate her feeling to the man who hates her.

One of the most striking qualities of Milton's closet drama is the apparent absence of any human connection between the actors; they are always speaking against rather than to one another, at cross-purposes and at a great distance. And the distance is as much physical as spiritual; with the exception of the disembodied "guiding hand" (l. 1) that he grasps in the opening, Samson touches no one, and no one touches him. When he does, finally, reach out to others, it is only to destroy. When Manoa asks, "What glorious hand gave *Samson* his death's wound?" (l. 1581), the Messenger replies: "Unwounded of his enemies he fell . . . By his own hands" (ll. 1582, 1584). Dalila's pathetic desire to touch Samson is meant not to rouse his passion but to inspire compassion; juxtaposing her weakness to his strength, she seeks to mitigate his suicidally destructive rage. Her failure is a profound symbol of their mutual tragedy, immixt, inevitable.

II

Had the confrontation ended here, with Samson's distant forgiveness and Dalila's silent departure, "somewhat crestfall'n" (l. 1244), little more would need to be said in vindication of Dalila's character. As a genuinely penitent wife struggling to recompense Samson for the injury she has done him, she has acquitted herself nobly. At this point, however, something seems to go horribly, finally, and fatally wrong—so much so that Dalila's probable immixture with the ruined flower of Philistine nobility (l. 1654) has seemed to most readers less tragic than poetically just. In her final response to Samson's rejection, she manifests all the faults of which her critics have accused her: cruelty and malice, spiteful pride, complacent hypocrisy, cynical relativism, and a nihilistic lust for power.

Descending once again to Samson's level of self-preoccupation, Dalila indulges her sense of injured merit in an orgy of self-justification. Rather than continue to expose herself to his "repulse and hate" (l. 966), she seeks refuge in the self-righteous approval of her own "concernments" (l. 969). Her willingness to triumph over Samson suggests present complacency and past hypocrisy—precisely the "feign'd Religion" (l. 872) of which Samson had accused her. And her next, self-aggrandizing attempt to undermine his integrity sinks her even more deeply into a quagmire of relativism. It may be, she insinuates, that Samson's people will revile her as a proverbial instance "Of falsehood most unconjugal traduc't" (l. 979), but her own people, whose praise she most desires (l. 980), will name her "among the famousest / Of Women" (ll. 982–83); among the Philistines (had they but lived to tell the tale) she would have been celebrated in story and song, just like the infamous Jael.[15] Still worse, her self-justification is couched in terms of deliberate malice toward her (supposedly helpless) victim, whom she cruelly portrays as "a fierce destroyer" (l. 985) rendered impotent by her heroism.[16]

Do we not see at last "where all [her] circling wiles must end" (l. 871)? "Bare in [her] guilt how foul must [she] appear?" (l. 902). Samson's patient investment in hatred is amply rewarded by Dalila's answerable malice; she is apparently ready to take his advice: "to satisfy [her] lust" (l. 837) by "Cherish[ing her] hast'n'd widowhood" (l. 958).

Having failed to achieve any measure of genuine, personal satisfaction, she accepts, perforce, a merely public success, as she allows the fancy of her ex post facto piety to nourish the delusion of herself enshrined "among the famousest / Of Women" (ll. 982–83). Her smug self-complacency, leaving Samson to his lot and liking her own (l. 996), will deserve its inevitable reward, the very "public marks" (l. 992) left by Samson's destructive rage. "Discover'd in the end" (l. 998), Dalila bids fair to justify the harshest condemnations of her critics, inasmuch as she suggests that "she has always willed exactly his present condition— weakness, imprisonment, blindess."[17] Whether or not Jon Lawry is correct in that assessment of her original motivation, Dalila's choice now has apparently destroyed her: consumed by her voracious lust for power, she becomes wholly identified with the Chorus's image of her as "a manifest Serpent" (l. 997).

The question of character development is crucial, however: does Dalila merely reveal what she has been all along? or does she rather become, now for the first time, the "specious Monster" (l. 230) that Samson has all along wanted her to be? Most of Milton's readers have agreed with Samson and the Chorus that Dalila simply manifests her essentially serpentine nature: Samson's "despotic power / Over his female" (ll. 1054–55) compels her to reveal the truth that had been "till now conceal'd" (l. 998). But Samson's reading of Dalila's motives is at least arguably perverse, especially in view of the obtuse theological rationalization to which it gives rise: "God sent her to debase me" (l. 999). And the Chorus is equally disposed to regard Dalila in the worst possible light. But a more disinterested reading of her character allows us to suppose that Dalila's professed motives are essentially genuine: she loves Samson, according to her (admittedly less than perfect) lights and wishes to atone for her treachery. When she fails to make Samson hear her, she becomes what she appears to be in the end; her love degenerates into hatred, so that she seems to justify Samson's rejection, as though that were in some sense her intention from the first. Her actual intention, however, was redemptive: "Let me approach at least, and touch thy hand" (l. 951).

In order to maintain this line of defense, however, one is obliged to give some account of what went wrong: Why and how is (putatively) redemptive love transformed into irremediable hatred? One natural place to search for an answer is in a comparison of Dalila's degeneration with Eve's regeneration in Book 10 of *Paradise Lost.* Radzinowicz has explored this comparison in considerable detail, and though I draw rather different conclusions from the same evidence, I find her exposition extremely suggestive. She argues a radical antithesis between the "'natural' renovation...shown in Eve" and the "'hardening of the heart'...shown in Dalila."[18] Both women "are dramatizations of the struggle to achieve true freedom and virtue after a fall" (p. 167); Dalila's failure parodies Eve's success.

So far I am in essential agreement with Radzinowicz. I disagree sharply, however, with her assertion that Eve "wills the good," whereas "Dalila wills her own not Samson's good" (p. 179). The nature of that disagreement can perhaps best be suggested by a question: If, as Radzinowicz rightly insists, we must not suppose that Dalila's "past treason...has determined her character absolutely" (p. 168) any more than Eve's betrayal of Adam has, and if "the possibility of moral regeneration is fundamental" to Milton's belief (p. 181), how do we account for the appalling moral and spiritual distance between "the rehabilitation of Eve and the hardening of Dalila's heart" (p. 181)?

The answer to that question is obviously *choice.* But at what point does each woman elect her destiny? The obvious answer in Dalila's case is: when, and only when,[19] she prefers her "lot" (l. 996) to Samson's. But our insight into that crucial decision really depends on our understanding of the relation between each woman and her husband. And when we look at them from this dramatic point of view, we see at once that the destinies of the two women diverge precisely at that point when Adam's response to Eve changes from rejection to compassion.

Both Eve and Dalila come initially as penitents, seeking to console their husbands and to atone for the injuries they have inflicted, and as suppliants for the love and affection they have deservedly lost. Beholding Adam "afflicted" and "Desolate" (*PL* 10.863, 864), Eve assays "Soft words to his fierce passion" (l. 865); just so does Dalila come to Samson, submissive and weeping (*SA* 727–29), offering "to light'n" his suffering (l. 744) and to make "amends" (l. 745).

Both meet with emphatic rejection: "Out of my sight, thou Serpent" (*PL* 10.867); "Out, out Hyaena" (*SA* 748). Adam accuses Eve of "inward fraud" (*PL* 10.871), "false / And hateful" (ll. 869–70), and blames her "pride / And wand'ring vanity" for his fall (ll. 874–75). Inasmuch as all her "imagin'd" virtue (l. 881) was "but a show" (l. 883), she must have been corrupt in her very creation, "a Rib / Crooked by nature" (ll. 884–85). Adam then goes on to generalize Eve's fault as a "fair defect / Of [Feminine] Nature" (ll. 891–92) and closes with a misogynist lament for "infinite calamity . . . / To Human life" (l. 907–8) — by which he means exclusively masculine life. Samson's initial response to Dalila enacts, in condensed form, a closely analogous movement from specific accusations of her to a generalized rejection of his own sexuality as embodied in women: "these are thy wonted arts. / And arts of every woman false like thee" (*SA* 748–49). Like Adam, he accuses his mate of reiterated falsehood and "feign'd remorse" (l. 752); he sees woman not as helpmate but as adversary, "a pois'nous bosom snake" (l. 763); and he ends on a note of generalized execration that echoes Adam's curse: "to Ages an example" (l. 765).

"Not so repulst" (*PL* 10.910), both Eve and Dalila struggle to close the distance between themselves and their estranged husbands. Humbly embracing Adam's feet and bathing them with her tears (ll. 910–12), Eve begs him not to forsake her (l. 914). She professes the sincerity of her "love . . . and reverence" (l. 915) and claims that her offense was unintended and unfortunate: "unweeting" (l. 916), she was herself "Unhappily deceiv'd" (l. 917) before she deceived him. Appealing to Adam as her "only strength and stay" (l. 921), she pleads for "peace" (l. 924) and unity "Against a [common] Foe" (l. 926). She wisely urges Adam not to "exercise / [His] hatred" (ll. 927–28) upon her,[20] who is already twice miserable in having sinned against him as well as God (l. 931). Generously, albeit foolishly, she accepts more responsibility for their joint misery than is actually hers; she is *not* "sole cause to [him] of all this woe" (l. 935). With equal generosity and perhaps greater folly, she offers to lighten Adam's suffering by deflecting God's curse from Adam to herself: "that all / The sentence from thy head remov'd may light / On me . . . Mee mee only just object of his ire" (ll. 933–36).

Since Dalila has already been absolutely forsaken, she cannot draw close enough to touch Samson, and her tone is correspondingly (and, I believe, consequently) less reverential. Nonetheless, her plea for a *hearing* (*SA* 766) plays eloquent variations on the major themes of Eve's entreaty. Both the motive of Dalila's fall and her proposed remedy become archetypal by virtue of her filial association with the Mother of Mankind. For just as Dalila's curiosity reenacts Eve's, and as her desire for power over Samson (ll. 790–810) recalls Eve's wish to render herself "more equal" or "Superior" (*PL* 9.823, 825) to Adam, so her proposed remedy for Samson's distress—"That what by me thou hast lost thou least shalt miss" (*SA* 927)—specifies Adam's suggestion that fallen human beings should "strive / In offices of Love" to "light'n / Each other's burden in our share of woe" (*PL* 10.959–61).

These broad, structural analogies are worked out in minute detail, in ways that play one character against the other, contrapuntally: Eve's naiveté is set against Dalila's disillusioned worldliness, Dalila's corrupted self-honesty against Eve's honest self-delusion. Like Eve, Dalila affirms the sincerity of her love (ll. 39–42) and insists that her offense, essentially her "infirmity" (l. 776), was unintentional and fortuitous—"rash but more unfortunate" (l. 747). Although she cannot identify Samson as her "only strength" (*PL* 10.921), Dalila does suggest, implicitly, that as his weakness inspired hers (*SA* 784), so his superhuman strength (ll. 817–18) might also be hers—if he would exercise it constructively, in the form of "pity or pardon" (l. 814), rather than vent his suicidal rage against her. And her suit for peace is similarly grounded in her conception of mortal "frailty" (l. 783): There being no (other) serpent to blame, Dalila internalizes the common foe as human "weakness" (l. 785), which is to be overcome not by united opposition to an external threat but by mutual self-understanding.[21]

This essentially spiritual perception of their common predicament informs her plea that Samson not vent upon her his "uncompassionate anger" (l. 818) against himself. And it is on these realistic terms, rather than from any idealized notion of self-sacrifice, that Dalila accepts responsibility for her own "offense" (l. 767). Her proposed remedy for Samson's suffering is correspondingly practical. Her intention to intercede with her Philistine lords (l. 920) is a diminished version of Eve's notion that she might appropriate God's curse to herself. Dalila's idea is less exalted than Eve's, but it is workable, and it would entail a real self-sacrifice in the form of "nursing diligence" (l. 924).

Given the very doubtful odds between Eve and Dalila,[22] the crucial difference between comedy and tragedy must arise from the choices of the male protagonists, the one to yield up, the other to yield to, his anger. So far as Adam's and Eve's joint salvation is concerned, the essential responsibility is Adam's—just as he had been primarily responsible for their fall. In the same way, insofar as Dalila's damnation is the consequence of Samson's suicidal rage, the responsibility for their mutual ruin must be primarily his. The way in which Adam and Samson are distinguished, as compassionate life-giver and impervious death-dealer, informs the generic relation between the two works, which interpenetrate as comedic and tragic aspects of a single dramatic whole, a tragicomedy of Redemption. In the end, however, Samson insists on his tragically masculine destiny, and so far as his relation to Dalila is concerned, the crucial choice of life or death belongs to him.

Criticism of Samson's confrontation with Dalila has usually been concerned with Samson's psychological development, to the virtual exclusion of any interest in Dalila's psychology. Readers who wish to discover evidence of Samson's "steady, upward progression" from "self-centeredness [and] wounded pride" to "penitent humility, renewed faith," and "untroubled exaltation of Spirit"[23] have naturally relegated Dalila to the role of more or less demonic adversary, sent by God to "debase" Samson (l. 999). From this point of view, she is simply a temptress, to be staunchly resisted, and her dramatic function is to provoke Samson's spiritual revival, to purify him by trial.[24]

Now, one immediate advantage of looking at things from Dalila's point of view is that she forces us to question Samson's spiritual progress—as a number of recent critics have done—by calling attention to his persistently violent and suicidal impulses. Indeed, the Chorus more than validates Dalila's judgment when it refers to the Philistines in words that have a profoundly ironic relevance to Samson himself, "Among [his] slain self-killed" (l. 1664):

> So fond are mortal men
> Fall'n into wrath divine
> As their own ruin on themselves to invite
> Insensate left, or to sense reprobate,
> And with blindness internal struck.

> (ll. 1682–86)

Samson's "uncompassionate anger" (l. 818) is thrown into particularly sharp relief by Adam's life-affirming compassion for Eve's suffering. Even before he learns to hope, Adam is willing to face "A long day's dying to augment our pain" (*PL* 10.964); Samson desires only "speedy death" (*SA* 650). Adam might almost be counseling Samson when he advises that a desire for "self-destruction" implies not "contempt of life and pleasure," but "anguish and regret / For loss of life and pleasure overlov'd" (*PL* 10.1016, 1013, 1018–19). Life seeks to have life, but Samson cannot answer his own riddle: "as for life, / To what end should I seek it?" (*SA* 521–22).

The purport of this thematic contrast becomes clear when we contemplate the generic relation between the two episodes. For there is at least one other advantage of looking at things from Dalila's point of view: when we regard her as an agent rather than a mere instrument, we can see much more deeply into the dramatic complexity of this crucial episode. For what Milton has given us is, essentially, a play within a play, a *Passionsspiel* that reenacts the tragedy of Samson's squandered virtue and a domestic tragedy that counterbalances the domestic comedy of *Paradise Lost.*

The intergeneric, tragicomic relation between the reconciliation scene in *Paradise Lost* and the fruitless confrontation in *Samson Agonistes* embraces both their thematic continuity—"the tenor of man's woe" (*PL* 11.632)—and their archetypal identity: mankind fallen is always falling and struggling to rise. The countergeneric relation between the two episodes, however, articulates the structural antithesis between comedy and tragedy, salvation and damnation. Adam and Eve, each yielding to the other, provide the model for salvation: weakness complementing weakness and being redeemed by supernatural strength. Samson and Dalila are the recipe for damnation: self-righteousness disguising itself as moral rigor, weakness pretending to be strength, and strength reducing itself to Satanic violence.

A line from "The Canonization" neatly characterizes the generic antithesis between the two episodes: "love was peace, that now is rage."[25] The reaffirmation of their love enables Adam and Eve to achieve reconciliation and a hope of redemption: Eve says "Let there be peace" (*PL* 10.924), and there is "peace" (l. 938). The rejection of love by Samson and Dalila breeds only "much woe" (*SA* 813) so that love itself is ultimately reduced to "furious rage" (l. 836) and "inexpiable hate" (l. 839). And when "wounds of deadly hate have pierc'd so deep" (*PL* 4.99) that love becomes inexorable rage, the whole Christian scheme of salvation falls apart. When charity becomes impossible, a potential comedy of redemption is reduced into a tragedy of damnation.

That, I believe, is the real point of what many critics have castigated as Dalila's moral relativism: the ambiguity of her arguments reflects a dialectical equivalence between her and Samson which, like the imagistic associations explored by John Carey, tends to draw Dalila and Samson "into an implied and disturbing parallelism."[26] That parallelism intensifies and complicates the dramatic tension between Dalila and Samson; and by making her character more sympathetic in contrast with Samson's, dramatic ambiguity renders their mutual ruin more fully tragic.

The word *mutual* is crucial here, not because it mitigates but because it intensifies the individual responsibility of each for the injury done to the other. Notwithstanding Samson's assertion that he and Dalila "Long since are twain" (*SA* 929), they are inescapably necessary to one another, "Each to other like, more than... is thought" by either, "of kind the same" (*PL* 4.573–74, 490; cf. *SA* 786: "the same of kind"). For just as Adam and Eve are Everyman and Everywoman inextricably bound together in a marriage embrace that is ultimately redemptive, Samson and Dalila are the archetype of "wedlock-treachery" (l. 1009), whose "dire necessity" (l. 1666) seals their mutual doom.

Even if Dalila were as corrupt as Samson believes her to be, her falsehood could not justify his absolute rejection. As the case actually stands, his distinction between his folly and her wickedness is meanspirited and, if "All wickedness is [truly] weakness" (l. 834), question-begging. Unable to pardon himself, Samson has no thought to spare for, or compassion to give to, anyone else. His spiritual condition is, in fact, precisely as Manoa had described it: "self-rigorous... argues overjust, and self-disples'd / For Self-offence, more than for God offended" (ll. 513–15). And so his final, violent rejection of Dalila—"lest fierce remembrance wake / My sudden rage" (952–53)—forebodes his final rejection of life:

> So *Sampson* groap'd the Temples Posts in spight,
> The World o'rewhelming to revenge his Sight.[27]

III

Having sought to extenuate Dalila's trespass by implicating Samson in her moral and spiritual destruction, I must now struggle to make clear precisely what I have tried to claim in Dalila's defense and (briefly) what I take to be the implications of that claim for an understanding of her character. Were I content merely to balance ruthless judgments of Dalila with mercy, I should be inclined to accept David Daiches's judicious suggestion "that she may well... represent something evil" and yet "be sincere."[28] I am persuaded, however, that what she represents is *not* simply, or even primarily, evil. In the beginning, before she has fallen victim to Samson's wrath, she is no more evil than any other fallen human being—and, of course, no less. And if that is true, then her destiny is not merely pathetic but genuinely tragic.

The assertion of Dalila's relative innocence and tragic virtue is, manifestly, a direct challenge to received readings of the tragedy. In my view, the traditional argument, that Samson is purified by his encounter with Dalila, lacks both inherent plausibility (how has Samson improved?) and evidential support. The only change that we can discern in Samson is a disposition to take a more active role in his own destruction. And if Samson's moral regeneration is something that we must apparently take (or leave) on faith, as Stanley Fish and some others have argued,[29] then his spiritual regeneration is at least equally problematic. His desire to exercise the violence of his self-hatred upon Dalila is no more edifying than his earlier despair. Coming from one "Who tore the Lion, as the Lion tears the Kid" (l. 128), Samson's threat "to tear [Dalila] joint by joint" (l. 953) is no idle boast. The lion's death produced at least a honeycomb, and a riddle; Dalila's *sparaggmos* is unlikely to prove equally fruitful. If he cannot deliver himself from Dalila by peaceful means, Samson's strength will not serve any life-giving purpose.

In the apparent absence of any clear moral or spiritual growth in Samson, we must look elsewhere to discover the meaning of this crucial episode. As it happens, Milton has provided a very clear sign of his intention by making Dalila Samson's *wife*. The marriage of Samson and Dalila has the simultaneous effect of complicating their moral and spiritual relationship and of endowing their sexual relation with symbolic significance. Therein, I believe, lies the heart of Dalila's mystery: having been one flesh with Samson, she prefigures the central Christian mystery of the Incarnation, especially as an expression of God's charity: "For God so loved the world that he gave his only begotten Son, that whosoever believeth in him should not perish, but have everlasting life" (John 3:16).

In brief: (1) As the central episode of *Samson Agonistes,* the tragedy of Dalila explores the possibility of charity between fallen human beings, in particular as that virtue is (or is not) expressed in marriage. Moreover, (2) as the ideal of mutual love engendered and sustained by Christian marriage is an image of Christ's redemptive love for those united in his body, so Dalila's frustrated love of Samson becomes an ironic type of salvation—a symbol of the nurturing Mother as well as of the Great Whore. Finally, (3) that symbolism is itself *incarnated* in the dramatic complexity of her character.

1. As Radzinowicz has shown,[30] Milton's conception of marriage as a *spiritual* union implies a standard against which Dalila's actions ought to be measured—and, I would add, against which Samson's actions must also be measured. According to *The Christian Doctrine*, "Marriage ... is a most intimate connection of man with woman, ordained by God" (I. x; p. 994b); "the *form* of marriage consists in the mutual exercise of benevolence, love, help, and solace between the espoused parties" (p. 1000b), and the end of marriage is "conjugal affection" (p. 1004b).

Conjugal affection is precisely the central point at issue between Dalila and Samson. She claims that she had loved him and that her unfortunate treachery was essentially a response to his lack of corresponding affection: "I saw thee mutable / Of fancy" (ll. 793–94). He replies that her love was only "furious rage / To satisfy [her] lust" (ll. 836–37) and that he had truly loved her, not wisely but "Too well" (l. 879). She urges her continuing love and her desire to recompense his injury; he counters by insisting that they "long since are twain" (l. 929). A man should cleave to his wife, but because Dalila's enforced separation from him mirrors his separation from himself, her most intimate relation to him is only as "A cleaving mischief" (l. 1040), *clinging* to him like Deianira's tunic and *dividing* him from himself like the sorb-apple in the parable of Aristophanes.[31]

The traditional conception of this episode as Samson's triumphant resistance to temptation and consequent purification by trial is simply not supported by the evidence. The evil that Dalila is supposed to represent is merely putative, and even if she were attempting to seduce him, Samson shows absolutely no inclination to succumb.[32] When we look at this episode dispassionately, we do *not* see an heroic male resisting the blandishments of a corrupt female. What we do see is a man and a woman speaking tragically at cross-purposes, without much right on either side and a great deal of wrong on both. Of the two, however, it is Dalila, not Samson, who speaks largely to, rather than at, the other person, and who more nearly embodies the spirit of charity. The traditional belief that Samson's rejection of her is justified contradicts the dramatic evidence, which clearly manifests Dalila's frustrated desire to mitigate Samson's "inexpiable hate" (l. 839). Even if one is predisposed to believe that Samson ought to reject Dalila, one ought to see that his motive in doing so is plain hatred. Conversely, our disapprobation of Dalila's treachery and consequent partiality for Samson cannot excuse our rejection of "The penitent" (l. 761). On the most fundamental level, according to the plain evidence of their words and actions, Samson merely hates, whereas Dalila at least tries to love.

The true form of marriage is an ideal according to which fallen men and women must reshape themselves by struggling "to temper them[selves] and reduce them[selves] to just measure with a kind of delight" ("Of Tragedy," p. 549). Just as the image of Adam and Eve "Imparadis't in one another's arms" (*PL* 4.506) symbolizes Edenic marriage, by embodying the essence of Paradise, so Adam's advice to Eve during their reconciliation articulates the way in which fallen human beings may struggle to regain Paradise: "rise, let us no more contend . . . but strive / In offices of love, how we may light'n / Each other's burden in our share of woe" (10.958–61). Adam's conception of conjugal affection, of *lightening* suffering by sharing, captures the essence of charity in its practical application to human affairs: "Bear ye one another's burdens, and so fulfill the law of Christ" (Gal. 6:2).

It is to this principle that Dalila implicitly appeals, and whose proper form she expresses, albeit obliquely and at a distance, when she offers to "light'n" Samson's suffering (*SA* 744). Conversely, in rejecting her, Samson also rejects the principle of charity: for "Charity suffereth long, *and* is kind" (1 Cor. 13:4), and "he that loveth another hath fulfilled the law" (Rom. 13:8). And Samson rejects truth deliberately, "Against his better knowledge, not deceiv'd" (*PL* 9.998), for it is he, not Dalila, who invokes the Pauline ideal: "That wisest and best men . . . With goodness principl'd [do] not . . . reject / The penitent, but ever [do] forgive" (*SA* 759–61).

The essential art required for the lightening of burdens is forgiveness: the recognition that weakness in others is "the same of kind" (l. 786) as our own enables our mercy toward them and ourselves. With nothing to gain from Samson except his misery, and the hope of alleviating it, and with everything to lose in terms of self-esteem, Dalila nonetheless humbles herself to accept the Pauline burden of shared affliction:

> I to the Lords will intercede, not doubting
> Thir favorable ear, that I may fetch thee
> From forth this loathsome prison-house to abide
> With me, where my redoubl'd love and care
> With nursing diligence, to me glad office,
> May ever tend about thee to old age
> With all things grateful cheer'd, and so supplied
> That what by me thou hast lost thou least shalt miss.
>
> (ll. 920–27)

Indeed, Dalila's desire to *lighten* Samson's suffering (l. 744) bespeaks a deeper charity than either of them can quite fathom. Implicit in the Pauline conception of suffering as purification (Gal. 5:24: "they that are Christ's have crucified the flesh") is a belief that sharing burdens is liberating (lightening) because it is enlightening: through our suffering, vicarious as well as actual, we come to the knowledge of Christ. Milton does not allude directly to the Pauline conception of charity here, as he does in *Paradise Lost*. He does not need to, because Samson's insistent blindness ensures that we will grasp the significance of his unenlightenment. In the context of *Samson Agonistes,* where the word "light" occurs some dozen times, the word "light'n," which occurs only here, must mean not only 'alleviate' (as Dalila intends) but also 'illuminate' (as Milton intends). Dalila implicitly hopes to redeem the darkness of Samson's mind as well as the affliction of his blindness; figuratively speaking, at least, her charity offers him a true liberation.

2. When the relation of Samson and Dalila is seen from this perspective, as a failure of conjugal love, and thus as an instance of charity offered and rejected, traditional readings of this episode undergo a sea change. So far from representing a revival of Samson's spirit, his confrontation with Dalila suggests an actual regression—at least to the extent that hatred is more actively morbid than apathy. In particular, Samson's distant forgiveness of Dalila, supposed by some to be a measure of his regeneration, is in fact a sign of his implacable self-severity—as the "sudden rage" (l. 953) of his subsequent execration, "Cherish thy hast'n'd widowhood" (l. 958), makes clear. Forgiveness "At distance" is no forgiveness at all, and Samson's absolute separation from Dalila measures the distance between himself and his agony; his rejection of her is also self-rejection.

St. Paul urges "men to love their wives as their own bodies" (Eph. 5:28). This analogy presses directly upon Samson's self-divided psyche, especially as expressed by his desire to tear Dalila "joint by joint" (l. 953). "He that loveth his wife loveth himself" (5:28), but Samson loves neither the one nor the other. If his putative divorce had in fact freed him from Dalila's influence, he would not need to hate her so violently.[33] Conversely, Dalila's ability to articulate her passion constructively, to shape her feelings according to her understanding, and in the direction of compassion for Samson, suggests that she has partially succeeded in achieving a harmonious reintegration of her appetitive and rational natures.

In itself, the practice of charity fulfills the law of Christ, "For all the law is fulfilled in one word, *even* in this; Thou shalt love thy neighbour as thyself" (Gal. 5:14; cf. Matt. 22:39). But Dalila's passion for Samson also betokens a deeper mystery, for she is Samson's wife, an emblem to him of lost conjugal affection and to us a sign of divine love, according to the Pauline symbolization of charity as the fulfillment of sexual love. Working within, and beyond, the long allegorical tradition associated with the Song of Solomon, St. Paul reinterprets the Edenic covenant of marriage, flesh of flesh, as a symbol of Christ's love for His church.

> The husband is the head of the wife, even as Christ is the head of the church, and [as] he is the saviour of the body. . . . Husbands, love your wives, even as Christ also loved the church, and gave himself for it. . . . So ought men to love their wives as their own bodies. He that loveth his wife loveth himself. For no man ever yet hated his own flesh; but nourisheth and cherisheth it, even as the Lord the Church: For we are members of his body, of his flesh, and of his bones. For this cause shall a man leave his father and mother, and shall be joined unto his wife, and they two shall be one flesh.
>
> This is a great mystery: but I speak concerning Christ and the church. (Eph. 5:23, 25, 28–32)

According to the vision of Saint Paul regarding the true form of human marriage, the relation of husband and wife is, or ought to be, redemptive: "As Christ . . . loved the church, and gave himself for it . . . So ought men to love their wives."[34] Ironically, and of course tragically, it is Dalila rather than Samson who attempts the necessary work of redemption. She acknowledges the burden of marital obligation that Samson refuses. Even if unmerited, the forgiveness that she seeks from him would make it possible for her to nourish and cherish him. If he will not love her as his body, she will love him as hers; even if her natural affection has been corrupted by possessive lust, she does in some measure love herself and seeks to love Samson as herself. His duty, as husband, is to redeem that perverted natural affection (his own as well as hers). Samson's failure to do so seals their mutual doom and, as it were, repeats the original sin of Adam and Eve by inverting it: where Adam fell through loving Eve only as himself, an extension of his ego, Samson falls again by hating Dalila as himself: "Such pardon . . . as I give my folly" (l. 825).

Perhaps the most significant consequence of comparing Samson with Adam, or Dalila with Eve, is a heightened sense of lost possibility; for where *Paradise Lost* points toward the self-creation of Paradise within, *Samson Agonistes* seems to represent only a "Holocaust" (l. 1702) of self-destruction, "Among thy slain self-kill'd" (l. 1664). The difference between Adam's salvation and Samson's "heroic" damnation measures the distance between comedy and tragedy. At the same time, however, the likeness between Eve's redemptive self-sacrifice and Dalila's marks the interpenetration of comic with tragic form. When Adam joins Eve in sin rather than attempt to redeem "what seem'd remediless" (*PL* 9.919), his "mortal taste" (1.2) seals their mutual doom. Eve initiates their recovery from the immediate consequences of their sin when she offers to take the whole burden of their mutual guilt upon herself; venturing to invoke God's curse upon herself—"On me, sole cause to thee of all this woe, / Mee mee only just object of his ire" (10.935–36)—she mysteriously invokes His blessing: "Behold mee then, me for him, life for life / I offer, on me let thine anger fall; / Account me man" (3.236–38). In this way, Eve opens Adam's eyes, and ears, and heart to the way of salvation, through "offices of Love" (10.960).

In the same way, Samson has betrayed himself by submitting to Dalila's importunity, and she likewise struggles to show him the path to redemption, by the example of her willingness to share his burden and through the "glad *office*" of her "nursing diligence" (*SA* 924). Samson, it seems, cannot learn this lesson; he *will* not be enlightened because he insists on bearing his burden alone: "Thou and I long since are twain" (l. 929). Nonetheless, Dalila struggles to love him as her own body: "Let me approach at least, and touch thy hand" (l. 952). By attempting to lighten Samson's suffering, Dalila seeks, implicitly, to fulfill the Adamic and Pauline conception of practical charity: "Bear . . . one another's burdens" (Gal. 6:2). Dalila not less than Eve, though more obscurely, is an incarnation of heavenly Love. By virtue of the Pauline symbolization of Christ's love as the fulfillment of conjugal love, both Eve's natural affection and Dalila's sexual passion are transfigured, flesh of flesh, into shadowy types of charity, so called "By name to come" (12.984).

Dalila is by no means simply loving, any more than Samson's hatred is untouched by the "amorous remorse" (l. 1007) which he struggles to repress. Her "conjugal affection" (l. 739) is tainted by self-love—as all merely natural affections are. Nonetheless, the genuineness of her affection is attested by the practical form in which it seeks to embody itself; Dalila's offer to "intercede" with the Philistine lords (l. 920) and to solace Samson's diminished old age is necessarily sincere because only a genuine affection would contemplate such humble and self-sacrificing means for its expression. For "greater love hath no [wo]man than this, that [she] lay down [her] life" for her husband (John 15:13). However ineffectual it may prove, Dalila's attempt to repair the ruin of her first trespass manifests the depth of her natural affection for Samson.

And conjugal affection is both an end in itself, as the true form of human marriage (and thus an image of all social obligation), and as a means to (as well as an image of) the fulfillment of charity; for "true Love . . . is the scale / By which to heav'nly Love [we] may . . . ascend" (*PL* 8.589, 591–92). By marrying Dalila to Samson, Milton creates a structure in which Dalila herself can remarry, in one flesh, the archetype of the Mother, at once heavenly and earthly, creator and destroyer, spirit and flesh. As a symbol, Dalila represents to Samson, and to Milton's fit audience, not merely an image of his own "effeminate slackness" (11.634), but the vulnerable *body* of his, and our, passion: "The wife hath not power of her own body, but the husband: and likewise also the husband hath not power of his own body, but the wife" (1 Cor. 7:4). According to the use we make of it, that corruptible body may become either corrupt or incorruptible, as we descend to mere passion (lust and loathing are the same of kind) or ascend to genuine compassion.

The mystery of the body is that it may become either because it is already both: selfish desire and selfless affection, that which consumes and that which nourishes—like Samson's riddle of the lion and the honeycomb. And that is also Dalila's mystery: that she may fall (again) into Satanic lust or rise to saintly charity. St. Paul speaks of a time when we shall know even as we are known (1 Cor. 13:12), in corruptible flesh that has been sanctified by the incarnate Word. For charity "is sown a natural body [as conjugal affection inmixed inevitably with sexual desire]; it is raised a spiritual body" (15:44). And with it is also raised the natural compassion which gave it birth: "For this corruptible [affection] must put on incorruption, and this mortal [desire] *must* put on immortality" (15:53). Of such stuff is charity made.

3. This complex feminine symbol of charity is all the more powerful for being dramatically embodied in the character of a real woman. There are at least two, apparently opposite, sources of that power. On the one hand, dramatic realization renders the representation of the archetype fully symbolic, rather than merely emblematic. On the other hand, the embodiment of the symbol in the doubtful motives of a real psychology renders the symbol far more complex even than it had been in its mythic configuration.

Although its consequences are profound and far-reaching, the first point is rather easily made: The archetype of the Great Mother is not merely figured forth in such an allegory as might represent life and death to Samson's imagination. The polarities of the archetype are actively symbolized because they are incarnate in Dalila's character. Samson and the Chorus abstract from that concrete reality a type of the Great Whore—as many critics have also done. But the real presence of Dalila frustrates such reductive simplicities: because she is an actual instance of the archetype, participating in the reality that she represents, she embodies the whole range of its possibility. Eve and Dalila are real women in whom the polarity of life herself, creating and destroying, is embodied, "She all in every part" (*SA* 93).

The second point is equally consequential but more complicated in its operation. Because the archetype is embodied in a real woman of less than exemplary character, the figure of charity is "clowdily enwrapped"[35] in self-love. Dalila's natural affection, more distant from its first original than fallen Eve's, can be only a shadowy type of disinterested love; her compassion for Samson is clouded by passions that have ugly names—lust, greed, self-interest, a desire for vainglory. Milton is too wise a poet to deny these motives in any fallen human being, let alone in one whom he seeks to portray as struggling to rise above the afflictions of perverted love. Where we go wrong is in imitating Samson's attempt to reduce Dalila to these motives. Where we go right is in seeking to discern the way in which our organic passions, "if not [wholly] deprav'd from good" (*PL* 5.471), are—or may be, or might have been—disciplined by Right Reason, as matter is disciplined by form, until "body up to spirit work" (l. 478). That such a gradual sublimation is not realized in Dalila characterizes the fundamental tragedy of the play. As one who struggles to repair the ruins of her first treachery by regaining to know Samson aright, and out of that knowledge to love him and serve him (*Of Education*, p. 631a), Dalila commands our respect. As one who fails of that charitable purpose, she inspires, or ought to inspire, compassion.

If, as I have tried to show, Dalila is a genuinely tragic figure, fatally flawed rather than radically corrupt, and if her purpose in coming to Samson is not to seduce him into a further self-betrayal but to redeem his suffering, then she is, or ought to be, an object of sympathy rather than of Samson's "inexpiable hate" (*SA* 839). And if Dalila is to be pitied rather than despised, then her dramatic function in Milton's tragedy of salvation becomes highly significant—the more so when we see her as an agent rather than as a mere instrument of God's mysterious purpose toward Samson. Because she is more fully open to us, more vulnerable and more transparent in her motives, she can inspire both pity and terror even more powerfully than Samson, who repels our efforts to approach him: "Let her not come near me" (l. 725). She invites our pity because, although she appears to get what she deserves, things are not always as they seem, and with a little love from Samson, and a little mercy, she might have deserved much better. She compels our terror because her tragic flaw is simply the common weakness of ordinary humanity, the frailty of all mortal flesh. In Dalila, more intimately than in Samson, we behold the "mirror of our [own] fickle state" (l. 164).

The climax of her tragedy occurs when she offers Samson her hand and is finally rejected. In all of Milton's poetry, the occasion that most resembles this moment occurs in the twenty-third sonnet when Milton's "late espoused Saint" reaches out to embrace him, only to compel her own disappearance by precipitating his awakening into darkness. In precisely the same way, Dalila's attempt to embrace Samson forces her departure and intensifies his blindness. Dalila is no saint, certainly; "Love's not so pure, and abstract, as they use / To say, which have no Mistresse but their Muse."[36] And the redemptive archetype of *Sonnet XXIII* is radically disfigured in *Samson Agonistes*, dismembered by Samson's blinding rage, who reaches out only to destroy. But the essence of the symbol, as a type of charity, is preserved, even enhanced, by the pathos of Dalila's self-sacrificial gesture; she comes within a hand's breadth of becoming a scapegoat for her countrymen. The quality of Dalila's mercy, and the depth of her compassion for Samson, is powerfully suggested by the figurative association between her and Milton's espoused saint: one is radiant in her virtue, the other obscured by her corruption, but both are veiled by their husbands' blindness. Each offers herself as a gift to heal that blindness.

Dalila is superficially unlike Milton's saint in the impurity of her love but profoundly like her in expressing the true form of marriage, which is conjugal love. And the distance between her incorruptible spirit and Dalila's corrupt flesh adumbrates the way in which the mortal body of Dalila's passion struggles to become immortal by incarnating the love of God. Dalila's love is not of that perfect order which casts out fear (1 John 4:18); nevertheless she lives, yet not she, but Christ lives in her (Gal. 2:20). She has not yet been crucified with Christ; nonetheless, "Her sins, which are many, are forgiven; for she loved much" (Luke 7:47). In part by virtue of the Pauline symbolization of Christ's love as the fulfillment of sexual love, in greater part by virtue of her own struggle to redeem Samson, Dalila's sexual passion is transfigured into a shadowy type of charity, so called "By name to come" (*PL* 12.584).[37] But this is a great mystery.

Discovered in the End

Samson Agonistes is mysterious in essentially the same terms, "much like [Samson's] riddle" (*SA* 1016). So far as the immediate outcome of their conflict is concerned, we can be quite certain that Dalila has failed to awaken Samson's compassion; he forgives her only "At distance" (l. 954) and remains to that extent himself unforgiven and unredeemed. On the surface at least, Dalila's twisted preoccupation with mere mortal fame and her frustrated, self-justifying intention to tend her own "concernments" (l. 969) would seem to bode ill for both of them.

Her ultimate destiny remains mysterious, however, as Samson's does. If she has failed to lighten what Samson suffers, if both she and Samson remain tragically unredeemed by her compassion, we have at least been able to glimpse the possibility of salvation through the dark glass of her natural affection. If, on the other hand, divine charity somehow wrought mysteriously to achieve her redemption as well as Samson's, so much the more cause have we to rejoice, wiping the tears from our eyes:

O felix culpa! O felix peccatum Dalilae!

JOHN C. ULREICH, JR.

NOTES

1. Barbara K. Lewalski, "Milton on Women—Yet Once More," *Milton Studies,* 6 (1974), 4; Lewalski's critique of feminist criticism remains firmly traditional in its attempt to "read Milton for what is of enduring importance rather than what is historically conditioned in his conception of man and woman" (p. 19). Sandra Gilbert, on the other hand, in "Patriarchal Poetry and Women Readers: Reflections on Milton's Bogey," *PMLA,* 93 (1978), 368–82, has shown how oppressive "Milton's myth of origins" (p. 368) can seem when it is conceived in strictly patriarchal terms.

2. Diane Kelsey McColley, *Milton's Eve* (Urbana, 1983), p. 4. McColley quotes Samuel Johnson's notorious dictum from *The Lives of the English Poets* (Dublin, 1926), p. 199. More recently still, William Shullenberger, in "Wrestling with the Angel: *Paradise Lost* and Feminist Criticism," *Milton Quarterly,* 20 (1986), 69–85, has urged the case for "a feminist re-vision of Milton" (p. 81) by arguing that "the subtext of *Paradise Lost* encourages and supports feminist reading" (p. 70).

3. *Samson Agonistes,* ll. 777, 774. All quotations of Milton's poetry and prose, unless otherwise noted, are taken from Merritt Y. Hughes, ed., *John Milton: Complete Poems and Major Prose* (Indianapolis, 1957), and are hereafter cited parenthetically in the text.

4. Mary Ann Radzinowicz, *Toward "Samson Agonistes": The Growth of Milton's Mind* (Princeton, 1978), p. 42. Despite repeated reminders that "we should consider not so much what the poet says, as who in the poem says it" (*A Defense of the People of England,* in *The Complete Prose Works of John Milton,* ed. Don M. Wolfe et al. [New Haven, 1953–], IV, pt. 1, 439), Milton's critics have almost unanimously accepted Samson's vision of Dalila as a "cunning . . . sorceress" (l. 819) and have repeatedly reaffirmed the Chorus's condemnation of her as "a manifest Serpent" (l. 997).

5. This formulation of the generic relation between *PL* 9.845–1104 and *SA* 710–1009 is adapted from Rosalie Colie's discussion of *genera mixta* in *The Resources of Kind: Genre-Theory in the Renaissance,* ed. Barbara K. Lewalski (Berkeley, 1973), p. 67.

6. William Empson (*Milton's God,* rev. ed. [London, 1965], pp. 211–28) is virtually the only critic to have attempted a sustained defense of Dalila's character. His argument makes at least three points that bear directly on the central moral paradox of the drama, the problem of regeneration: (1) The question of Dalila's sincerity is at least problematic: "it would be wilful to doubt that she still loves [Samson] and wants to help him, because we are given no other reason for her visit" (p. 221). (2) Her apparent moral relativism is not obviously greater than her husband's: Samson claims that "gods unable To acquit themselves . . . But by ungodly deeds . . . Gods cannot be" (896–99), but "Samson's own God admittedly needs to be helped by deeds which are at least unlawful and such as Dagon would call ungodly" (p. 215). In the light of this dilemma, (3) the *marriage* of Samson and Dalila one of the central mysteries of the drama—in Empson's terms, "a peculiarly shocking moral paradox" (p. 219): "We do not hear of any political use that

[Samson] made of his wife, but that he could do so is his defence for having married her" (p. 219).

7. We have, after all, no reason to doubt her sincerity. Moreover, as Virginia Mollenkott has shown ("Relativism in *Samson Agonistes*," *Studies in Philology*, 67 [1970], 95), the dramatic effect of this episode depends heavily on the genuineness of Dalila's professed love for Samson: "Unless we are willing to accept Dalila's reason for coming to Samson, we are forced to assume with certain critics that the whole episode is doubtfully motivated and dramatically weak."

8. Milton, 1 *Defence, CPW,* 4, pt. 1: 439. Decorum is, of course, "the grand masterpiece to observe" (*Of Education,* p. 637a) because it "teaches what the laws are of a true . . . dramatic [poem]."

9. Aristotle, *Poetics* VI.17, in *Aristotle's Theory of Poetry and Fine Art,* trans. S. H. Butcher, 4th ed. (New York, 1951), pp. 27, 29.

10. Critics have not been slow to seize on these words as evidence that Dalila's moral standards are "relativistic and self-regardful, disconnected from reality" (Radzinowicz, *Toward "Samson Agonistes,"* p. 39). But I am unable to conceive of any other basis for a genuine reconciliation between fallen human beings: "Judge not, that ye be not judged. For with what judgment ye judge, ye shall be judged: and with what measure ye mete, it shall be measured to you again" (Matt. 7:1–2). If we choose to sanction Samson's rejection of Dalila, we may accept Radzinowicz's judgment that Dalila's "argument of weakness . . . implies not simply forgiveness but reenactment of weakness" (p. 38). But I do not believe that we are compelled to any such conclusion.

11. Unless otherwise noted, all quotations of the Bible are taken from the Authorized Version of 1611.

12. Even J. B. Broadbent, *Milton: "Comus" and "Samson Agonistes"* (Great Neck, 1961), p. 48, seems anxious to justify Samson (and God) at Dalila's expense: her "simple selfishness condemns her. . . . Samson's treatment of her is justified and his vulnerability to her in the past excused." Anthony Low, *The Blaze of Noon: A Reading of "Samson Agonistes"* (New York, 1974), p. 155, agrees that "Samson . . . is thoroughly justified" in rejecting Dalila.

13. Her chosen metaphor—"Mine and Love's prisoner" (l. 808) is unfortunate, certainly, in its suggestion of motives darker than she is yet capable of confessing, but it is, after all, a metaphor, a figurative suggestion of her desire rather than the literal expression of her will into which Samson transforms it: "This Gaol I count the house of Liberty / To thine" (ll. 949–50).

14. We may allow Thomas Kranidas, in "Dalila's Role in *Samson Agonistes,*" *Studies in English Literature,* 6 (1966), 125–37, to speak for the majority: "The argument from Love" is only a "sentimental generalization" that reduces "Law . . . to Love's law." Notwithstanding its superficial appeal, Dalila's "argument [is] selfish at its root and her claims for the history of that argument [are] false" (pp. 129–30).

15. The ambiguity of Dalila's diction belies the apparent straightforwardness of her confession: does *traduc't* mean 'justly censured' (as she seems to imply) or (as she really intends) 'falsely vilified'? Her allusion to the "inhospiable guile" (l. 989) of Jael is brilliantly "double-mouth'd" (l. 971). Seeking to goad Samson by

insisting on the tenuousness of his own moral position, she does not so much acknowledge as boast of her superior treachery: more exquisite (blindness rather than the speedy death given to Sisera), more elaborately subtle (Dalila did not herself drive nails through Samson's temples [l. 990]), more intimate (a violation of "wedlock" [l. 986] rather than of mere hospitality), more glorious (more richly celebrated by "public marks of honor and reward" [l. 992]), and more profitable.

16. Her chosen epithet for Samson's people, "Circumcis'd" (l. 975) is even nastier than its conventional antonym. For although Dalila's term of endearment is less openly contemptuous than Samson's earlier racial slur upon "the un-circumcis'd" (l. 260; so also the Chorus at line 640), her allusion to his manhood carries with it the sting of "a pois'nous bosom snake" (l. 763); she knows Samson intimately, in the depth of his flesh, even in the seal of his violated covenant with Yahweh. Like Samson's unshaven hair, circumcision was established as "a token of the covenant": "my covenant shall be in your flesh for an everlasting covenant" (Genesis 17:11, 13). Playing thus exquisitely upon Samson's agony, Dalila reminds him at once of lost pleasures (she will have him, one way or the other) and of his failed vocation.

17. Jon S. Lawry, *The Shadow of Heaven: Matter and Stance in Milton's Poetry* (Ithaca, 1968), p. 379.

18. Mary Ann Radzinowicz, "Eve and Dalila: Renovation and the Hardening of the Heart," in *Reason and the Imagination: Studies in the History of Ideas, 1600–1800,* ed. J. A. Mazzeo (New York, 1962), p. 159.

19. Any other supposition begs the question by prejudging Dalila's character; thus, for example, the conventional argument, that Dalila is not truly penitent, renders the question of her regeneration merely trivial. The whole line of reasoning entailed by this approach—that Dalila selfishly seeks power over Samson—is precisely analogous to the exploded argument that Eve had already fallen before she ate the fruit.

20. Eve says: "On me exercise not / Thy hatred for this misery befall'n" (*PL* 10.927–28). The relative abstractness of "this misery," reinforced by the unspecified participial adjective ("befall'n" how?) and by the emphatic contrast between *me* and *Thy,* suggests a rather pointed reaing: "Do not vent your self-hatred, *your* 'misery . . . / On me already lost.' " This implicitly accusatory note, at once abrasive and genuinely compassionate, becomes explicit in Dalila's references to Samson's self-afflicting anger (ll. 818, 914).

21. This internalization—*we* are the serpent—represents, I believe, a major point in Dalila's favor as far as the question of responsibility is concerned. Whereas Eve tends to project her crime onto the serpent, Dalila's foreordained identification as "pois'nous bosom snake" (l. 763) precludes her from any such ready and easy self-exculpation; she must come to terms with her own treachery.

22. Radzinowicz, "Eve and Dalila," sees Eve as accepting, Dalila as rejecting, grace: "Dalila's growth into a hard-hearted taunter" occurs in a series of "step-by-step rejections which match Eve's affirmations" (p. 168). It is not obvious to me, however, that Dalila is ever given an opportunity to reject anything. If Milton had really wanted to represent a dogmatic contrast between Eve's regeneration

and the hardening of Dalila's heart, he might have contrived circumstances in which salvation and damnation were more clearly merited—and more sharply distinguished from each other by the moral character of the agents.

23. Douglas Bush (ed., *Complete Poetical Works of John Milton* [Boston, 1965], p. 514) speaks for the general tendency of Christian humanist critics, who see Dalila as simply a means to Samson's regeneration.

24. See, for example, Ann Gossman, "Milton's Samson as the Tragic Hero Purified by Trial," *JEGP*, 61 (1962), 528–41.

25. Donne, "The Canonization," l. 39; *The Complete Poetry of John Donne,* ed. John T. Shawcross (New York, 1967), p. 98.

26. John Carey, ed., *Milton: Complete Shorter Poems* (London, 1971), p. 338.

27. Andrew Marvell, "On Mr. Milton's Paradise Lost," ll. 9–10; *The Poems and Letters of Andrew Marvell,* ed. H. M. Margoliouth (Oxford, 1963), I, 131. In order to conform Marvell's syntax to my purpose, I have silently altered his punctuation in line 9, which is parenthetical in the original.

28. David Daiches, *Milton* (New York, 1957), p. 243; he argues that Dalila "wanted Samson at home and in her power. That was her way of loving him. It was a wrong way, but she is not lying in her account of it" (p. 244).

29. Stanley Fish ("Question and Answer in *Samson Agonistes,*" *Critical Quarterly,* 11 [1969], 237) asks, "What is the relationship between Samson's spiritual regeneration . . . and the act of pulling down the temple?" and answers: "None, necessarily."

30. Radzinowicz, *Toward "Samson Agonistes,"* pp. 36–50. She suggests that, "Of the various proffered answers to the question of why Milton made Dalila Samson's wife and not his harlot, one obviously important one is that the relationship of marriage is the relationship he had particularly studied in connection with the balance of reason and the passions and in connection with the paradox of freedom and responsibility" (p. 37).

31. Plato, *The Symposium,* in *The Republic and Other Works by Plato,* trans. Benjamin Jowett (Garden City, 1960), pp. 335–36: According to Aristophanes, "the original nature was not like the present, but different. . . . the primeval man was round and had four hands and four feet, back and sides forming a circle, one head with two faces, looking opposite ways. . . . [To protect the gods from their terrible assaults] Zeus . . . cut the [original man] in two . . . like a sorb-apple which is halved for pickling. . . . After the division the two parts of man, each desiring his other half, came together, and threw their arms about one another eager to grow into one. . . . [And so it is that] Each of us . . . is always looking for his other half."

32. John Carey, in *Milton* (London, 1969), p. 143, suggests that Samson is "terrified of feeling her body against his." In my view, however, Samson's concern for Dalila's safety suggests a degree of genuine self-knowledge; the temptation here is to destructive violence rather than to lust.

33. Radzinowicz, *Toward "Samson Agonistes,"* argues—more persuasively, I think, than any other critic has done—that by rejecting Dalila, Samson has achieved within himself a "balance of reason and imagination, of [his] love and [her] obedience, of freedom and responsibility." I really do not see, however, how Samson's divorce from Dalila can possibly signify a reintegration of feeling,

thinking, and willing. Indeed, Samson's rejection of Dalila, as of his own feeling, would seem to imply, dramatically as well as allegorically, a ruthless rejection of his own passionate nature — or rather, the ruthless suppression of passion which aggravates (l. 1000) affection into hatred.

34. The most conspicuous Old Testament embodiment of this redemptive archetype — and the one that bears most poignantly upon the "wedlock-treachery" (l. 1009) of Samson and Dalila — is the prophet Hosea's parabolic marriage to the harlot Gomer. As Samson had been impelled to marry a daughter of the Philistines, so Hosea is commanded by God to marry "a wife of whoredoms" (Hosea 1:2). As Dalila betrayed Samson, Gomer falls into adultery, playing the harlot with her many lovers (2:5), and so Hosea divorces her. The intent of this separation is penitential, however, rather than merely punitive. Chastened by her trial, Gomer becomes capable of salvation, "as in the days of her youth" (2:15). Commanded by God once again, and inspired by his own compassion, Hosea redeems Gomer and betroths her to him again "in rightousness, and in judgment, and in loving kindness, and in mercies" (2:19).

35. Spenser's "Letter . . . to Sir Walter Raleigh," in *Spenser's Faerie Queene*, ed. J. C. Smith (Oxford, 1961), II. 485.

36. Donne, "Loves Growth," ll. 11–12, in *Complete Poetry*, p. 121.

37. Insofar as a figurative reading of Dalila can be separated from the defense of her character, my interpretation of her earthly love as a shadow of heavenly charity receives considerable support from Heather Asal's argument, in "In Defense of Dalila: *Samson Agonistes* and the Reformation Theology of the Word," *JEGP*, 74 (1975), 183–94, that Dalila's symbolic role in the drama is implicitly redemptive, that "as a spokesman for the paradox of forgiveness and the ironies of the Word" (p. 190), Dalila is both "the cause of Samson's fall and the agent of his regeneration" (p. 183).

Intestine Thorn:
Samson's Struggle with
the Woman Within

JACKIE DiSALVO

HISTORY as it appears in *Samson Agonistes*—one nation under the heel of another, its would-be liberator displayed in torment as a threat to would-be followers—would be tragedy enough, but Milton would heap melancholy upon melancholy by forcing our simultaneous contemplation of the anguished relationship between man and woman. That microcosm of the larger war is seen here as a disastrous encounter between enemy camps, with tortures all its own, the "secret sting of amorous remorse" (l. 1007), and a strife so deep within the self, a "Thorn / Intestine" (l. 1038),[1] that even its expelling tears the innards. I will focus here on that introjected conflict to suggest that in Samson's betrayal by an enemy woman, Milton has also dramatized the horror of woman as enemy, an enemy, moreover, "far within defensive arms," within the agon of masculine identity itself.[2]

Samson has been read as interior drama since Parker first called it a drama of regeneration, based upon "the hero's recovery and its results." Allen found the "genesis and cure of despair"; Mary Ann Radzinowicz sees Milton "in the role of physician to the soul" and Samson "a heroic mind battling with itself and achieving true integration." Particularly germane to my endeavor is Arnold Stein's view of Milton as "strikingly modern, an understanding practitioner of the new art of psychiatry."[3] Samson's mental state is described as suffering a "lingring disease" whose "maladies innumerable . . . must secret passage find / To th'inmost mind" (ll. 618, 608–11). Both the poem's medicinal imagery and its concept of a catharsis through a homeopathic use of negative experience to cure a negative state suggest the psychoanalytic process. Nor is it merely the theme that does so, but the dramatic form itself, imitating or inventing a therapeutic method which is itself psychodrama, a confrontation with objects through which one might reexperience conflicts in the psyche, conflicts invariably with the objects of childhood emotions.

Of course, *Samson* immediately calls to mind such psychodynamics by its associations with the classic psychological script, the story of Oedipus. *Oedipus at Colonus* has been found by Woodhouse and others to be the most relevant Greek analogue, its opening paralleling that of Milton's play, and its heroes sharing the fate of having been blinded through sexual transgression.[4] William Kerrigan suggests that we read the play within the final oedipal simile of *Paradise Regained*,[5] and Samson, like Oedipus, solves riddles and is brought down by the self-revelation of a critical secret. In the notorious Freudian reading of Sophocles, the secret, of course, is incest and patricide, the wishes of the oedipal child who wants to sleep with his mother and slay his father but shudders before the threat of castration, symbolically displaced to the gouging of Oedipus's eyes. For Freud this conflict, once repressed, creates the unconscious which psychoanalysis must uncover by bringing about the reliving for relieving of the repression and displacement.

Kerrigan's brilliant study, *The Sacred Complex*, leaves us with little doubt that there are psychogenetic processes at the heart of Milton's poetry, but his reading of "the oedipal complex [as] the generative center of his character and art" rests upon Freudian assumptions that feminist psychology has come to challenge.[6] Kerrigan, moreover, invents for Milton a rather un-Freudian triumph over that complex, reading the later poems as a testimony to Milton's personal triumph over and artistic transcendence of that human malaise. In order to establish the divine comedy of his sacred complex, he must avoid any thorough consideration of *Samson*, where some of the more disturbing aspects of Milton's poems, notably their misogyny, are less mitigated. In this most blatantly Freudian of Milton's visions, the triumphant affirmation of the ego in the face of castration is rendered ironic both by the woman-hatred endemic to the process and the self-destruction which is its inherent end. Samson, it appears, must destroy his male identity in order to save it.

The worst problem with the Freudian concept of the oedipus complex was its application to woman; she became an "homme manqué" her character determined not by what she is, in her maternal potential, erotic existence, or daughterly relations, but by what she lacks, i.e., a male organ, the "genital deficiency" which comes to account for all her female predilections: her desire for motherhood, heterosexual passion, alleged dependency, masochism, narcissism, and inferiority. But such suggestions go back to Genesis, and Milton, pondering her emergence from Adam's rib, has Adam call her "a fair defect of nature." But Milton, marvelously, always contradicts himself, always, that is, gives us the whole contradiction and not just his preferred stance on it, and so here threatens to subvert his own male supremacist views when Adam speculates upon his own fragmentary nature, "in unity defective," seeking his completion in what appears to him a far more all-inclusive female being "that what seem'd fair in all the world, seem'd now / . . . in her contain'd" (8.472–73). Within his Genesis myth of origins he can only presume that "from my side subducting" the Creator "took perhaps / More than enough" (8.536–37).

Under the tutelage of his masculine analysts, angelic and divine, Adam has fallen victim to an inadequate theory of psychogenesis. He might have benefited from the insights of feminist psychology. Recent theorists, such as Nancy Chodorow and Dorothy Dinnerstein, have attempted to build upon Freud while correcting his patriarchal biases. They do so by affirming the following premises: (1) the primary influence of the bond with a primary caretaker over later oedipal relations, (2) the significance of the female monopoly of that mothering role; and thus (3) a substitution for Freud's biological determinism of a socially constructed psyche defined by the different relationships males and females will have with parents in different gender roles. Thus, psychic conflicts will not merely reflect the resolution of libidinal drives, but also the asymetrical growth of a selfhood intertwined with the development of gender in male and female.[7]

Milton, like Samson, his outer sight "extinguish't" "with inward eyes illuminated" (l. 1689) had, it seems, extraordinary access to the unconscious, and in telling its truths he undermines and expands his own conscious ideologies. In *Samson Agonistes,* I propose, while endorsing the goals of male psychogenesis, Milton also presents its agonizing contradictions and terrible costs, both to the male Samson, who overcomes mutilation and inward festering only to be outwardly destroyed, and the female Dalila, who must be viciously denigrated in the process, as both are "tangl'd in the fold / Of dire necessity" (ll. 1165–66) which is the interpersonal and intrapsychic web of our gender dynamics.

In this reading, Milton's narrative, once attacked as arbitrary and episodic by Samuel Johnson, reveals another dimension of its integral and inevitable logic. Samson's "regeneration" requires a painful reliving of the primal traumas of his masculine development, primarily through his encounter with Dalila. But this encounter with her in the plot, the events dramatized before us, doubles his earlier experience with her in the story which he reconstructs for us through flashbacks, the plot serving as an undoing of that story or, almost literally, a divorce from their earlier marriage. The connection with Dalila is then the pivot around which both aspects of the narrative turn in a kind of inverted symmetry, propelling us alternately back into Samson's past and forward to his future. On the psychoanalytic level, moreover, Dalila herself substitutes for the suppressed figure of Samson's mother, as generally in adult heterosexual relations a man invariably encounters the repressed object of childhood desire, now become an internalized object of loathing and love. Consequently, the story reveals a Samson who, through dependence on Dalila, has regressed to his almost infantile vulnerability at the play's opening, while the plot which begins there enacts his reemergence from that state by rejecting his bond to her and other related regressive temptations. That "divorce" is an objective correlative for his severance from interior bonds, for his therapeutic de-cathexis.

Such is the psychoanalytic logic of the plot, with the resemblances between narrative and therapy observed by structuralist critics, who have noted the analogy between analysis and detective-story-like narratives which begin in medias res and must go back and discover the germinal events and between the significance of the telling of stories in fiction and therapy.[8] In reconstructing his own story, Samson liberates himself from its hold. Once he has opened up the regressive, circular logic of the story of his relations with women, he recovers his masculine vigor and can proceed to challenge Harapha and fulfill his militant vocation against the Philistines. Both movements in the drama, backward and forward, must, therefore, be seen as well within another enveloping narrative; the contrary narratives of regression and recovery both occur within the more comprehensive story of Samson's vocation in which we find the earliest and last events, a beginning rooted even before his conception in its prophecy, and a consummation achieved in his dying act and its projected celebration. Prophecy and celebration emphasize, therefore, that the drama of Samson's vocation is coterminous with his psycho-biography, the narrative of his male psychogenesis, with its evolutions, fixations, regressions, and restorations described in the mutual implications and enfoldings of these narratives, with their births and rebirths, marriages and divorces, relapses and recoveries. The story of Samson's vocation, which one would expect to find within the story of his biological life, here contains that biography, and both are narratively contained within the plot of Samson's therapeutic storytelling which they also enclose. Similarly, the story of his regression exists within the plot of his recovery which undoes it, by recapitulating an invisible narrative of uncompleted maturation.

The consequence of this implicated structure is to place Samson's social, and especially gender, relations within his psyche, and vice versa, thus unveiling its fundamentally social construction. The centrality of his embrace and divorce of Dalila to his own psychological integration reveals that for Samson, as for other mothers' sons, maleness, selfhood, and misogyny are essentially the same, all psychic defenses, as we shall see, against the external and internal "temptation" of femininity.

Recent feminist psychology has turned to the object-relations school in order to interpret psychosexual development within the social context of family and gender. Unlike Freud, who emphasized instinctual drives, and those ego psychologists, followed by Kerrigan, who added the active modifying role of an ego itself composed of quasi-physiological apparatuses, the object-relations school of D. W. Winicott and Margaret Mahler emphasizes, in addition, social relations and their objects.[9] These are seen as becoming psychologically internalized in the construction of the psyche, and since these objects are gendered, the psyche is also constructed by gender relations, rather than being, as Freud would have it, the reflex of biology and of purely compensatory responses to the libidinal oedipus complex. Following Mahler, a greater emphasis is given to the pre-oedipal relation to the mother, and maternal pathology is given primacy over the paternally oriented oedipus complex in explaining adult neurosis. Thus too, penis envy and identification with the father are seen as secondary formations, created by the access maleness gives to power in a patriarchal society.

In *The Reproduction of Mothering*, Nancy Chodorow stresses that the first and determining crisis for all human beings is the difficult process of separation-individuation from the original primal unity of symbiosis in which mother was inseparable from self. In this "narcissistic relation to reality" the infant "cognitively and libidinally" "experiences itself as merged and continuous with the world in general and with its mother or caretaker in particular," or, as Norman O. Brown once put it "Reality is its mother; . . . infantile sexuality affirms the union of the self with a whole world of love and pleasure."[10] The essential task of early development is "differentiation," "the development of ego boundaries (a sense of personal psychological division from the rest of the world) and of a body ego." This process, fraught with anxiety and pain, occurs "through experiences of the mother's departure and return, and through frustration which emphasizes the child's separateness and the fact that it doesn't control all its experiences and gratifications."[11] Hence, all human psyches carry within them memories of unitary bliss and fearful dependency whose siren song, heard from psychic depths, may continue to feel profoundly seductive and dangerous.

In a culture where gender is defined by a monopoly over or exclusion from mothering, this process is complicated by the demands of gender formation. Since both sexes acquire their earliest sense of self in relation to the mother whom they imitate and internalize as her attentions reflect back an evolving sense of selfhood, Robert Stoller argues that both basic core gender identity and basic morphology is female for both sexes, and the boy is obliged to become a kind of "femme manqué."[12] If, as his studies of transsexuals indicate, gender is not decided merely by sexual characteristics, then its social construction involves a process in which girls are led to identify with and boys against this maternal being with all her relational and nurturant associations. For a boy, this experience will be especially contradictory, for, as Nancy Chodorow argues, "A boy must learn his gender identity as being not female or not mother . . . learning what it is to be masculine comes to mean learning to be not-feminine." Girls can develop their femininity through identification and continuity, as one self in relation to another, but boys must define their selves by disidentifying in an exaggerated assertion of separation, required by the demands, not of selfhood but of male difference.

Hence, as Chodorow explains, it "becomes important to men to have a clear sense of gender difference, of what is masculine and what is feminine and to maintain rigid boundaries between these." But mothers' functions are emotional, sensuous and erotic; a child associates her with its feelings, desires, physical needs, and sensuous pleasures, with intimacy and communication. Thus, in disidentifying with her, "Boys come to deny the feminine identifications within themselves and those feelings they experience as feminine: feelings of dependence, relational needs, emotions generally."[13] Such an identity, however, must always be precarious, for, as Robert Stoller writes: "The whole process of becoming masculine is at risk in the little boy from the day of birth on; his still-to-be-created masculinity is endangered by the primary, profound, primeval oneness with the mother, a blissful experience that survives, buried but active, in the core of one's identity as a focus which, throughout life, can attract one to regress back to that primitive oneness. That is the threat lying latent in masculinity."[14]

From this view, the oedipus complex merely extends and completes the repression of a boy's attachment to his mother. It might be said, moreover, that it is not that the father competes with the son over the mother so much as that he competes with the mother over the son's gender allegiance. Similarly, the son's jealousy may be directed at the father's possession of an intimacy which he now denies the developing boy with threats of castration not only for sex but for "feminine" attachments and behaviors. The boy, to avoid such mutilation of his genitals, accepts the mutilation of his psyche as he becomes severed irrevocably, if imperfectly, from his infant self.

Since this arrangement for a boy, more than for a girl (in whom Freud observed the oedipus complex was far weaker), postpones emotional gratifications deemed inappropriate to his gender and since his return to intimacy involves contact with a female being resembling the one who dominated his infancy, adult sexual relationships are likely to renew for a man, as they do not for a woman, these childhood traumas. A woman with whom a man resurrects that buried life of emotional and erotic desire is, thereby, likely to appear as a reincarnation of his mother and, thus, to resurface original conflicts and threaten him with regression. Hence, the paranoia men often express about emotional relationships.

Samson appears to be caught up in just such a conflict, as he oscillates drastically between two extremely contrary mental states, an infantile helplessness and a supermasculine aloofness and aggression. Furthermore, this oscillation seems to arise from his connection to or separation from a woman, Dalila.

At the opening of the poem, paralleling the blind Oedipus led by his daughter's hand, Samson appears childlike, unable to walk, in an excruciating state of almost infantile contingency and vulnerability. We are, in addition, immediately confronted with allusions to birth; the reviving breeze "with day-spring born" (l. 11) signals Samson's need for psychic rebirth but also points to his recounting of his own "birth from Heaven foretold" (l. 24). His blindness, furthermore, his hairlessness, and even his soiled weeds, all evoke early infancy. Moreover, both blindness and bondage involve deprivations of the two preconditions of autonomous selfhood, sight and mobility. Vision, unlike the other senses which internalize experience, distinguishes the self as a body ego from those other "objects of delight" which for Samson are now "Anull'd" (ll. 71–72). Mobility, a self-propelling and self-determining power, has been linked to a child's "maintenance of proximity" as a stage in differentiation: "To separate and return physically to its mother permits it to gain feelings of independence through mastery of its environment and greater equality of relationship."[15] Samson, by contrast, lies, infantlike, in complete passivity, "carelessly diffus'd / With languish't head unpropt" (l. 119), totally dependent (etymologically: to hang from) "in power of others, never in my own" (l. 78).

He is, besides, in danger of an even more total regression. Freud identified the tendency toward an unchecked regression as "the Nirvana principle," an attempt to return to boundless unity with the mother through obliteration of the ego, ultimately through death itself, precisely the condition Samson will reach in that oxymoron of death and gestation, the phoenix in its "ashy womb" (l. 1703). But his blindness is already a living death, as he finds "Myself my Sepulcher, a moving Grave" (l. 102). For Freud the regressive Nirvana principle was also a form of thanatos or death wish, as it is with Samson, plunged into an undifferentiated darkness "*Inseparably* dark" (l. 154), yearning, furthermore, to "yield to double darkness" (l. 593) of "death's benumbing Opium" (l. 630), literally to surrender consciousness in "faintings, swoonings of despair" (l. 631). This desire for self-extinction which recurs in the poem is, psychologically, a desire for extinction of the self. Such regressive impulses have been seen to reveal an underlying "fixation," a state of arrested development in which anxiety has prevented a person's advance to a later psychic stage. So Samson comes to understand the full psychological significance of the Chorus's lament that "thou art become (O worst imprisonment) / The Dungeon of thyself" (ll. 155–56) and his own complaint of "living death." And so, as the fixated individual often becomes trapped in a compulsive repetition of his original conflicts, we find Samson bound to the wheel of his mill, his only movement a hopeless circle of torment.[16] But in his biography that critical repetition has occurred with regard to women, replicating the errors of his first marriage in his second, exactly what we would be led to expect both from the theoretical connections between fixation and separation anxiety and the hints of infantile dependency already observed.

If, therefore, we read Milton's poem as a drama of "regeneration," understood as recapitulation of Samson's male psychogenesis, the first act presents us with his recognition and active feeling of his agonizing state of fixation and regression and his beginning reconstruction of a still superficial and external narrative of its origins. The ensuing psychodrama will provide, in the "provocative incidents" recognized by criticism, two crucial moments of transference in which he attempts to overcome those neurotic conditions.

Within this psychic replay, the appearance of his father is also to be expected, for Manoa provokes Samson's recovery of his sense of masculine vocation. In both Freudian and feminist theory, it is the father who enforces separation, either directly and personally or through cultural interventions. However, where Freud emphasizes the father's sexual prohibitions, feminists tend to stress the primacy of gender identifications which Freud thought merely compensatory. The boy relinquishes his mother, more totally than the girl does, in order to become an exalted male rather than the poor, castrated, and disparaged thing he has learned his mother to be. His father proffers the carrot and the stick of male gender perquisites: the threat, on the one hand, of castration, or more accurately, emasculation, which in Samson's case has been imposed by a punitive divine father, and the promise, on the other hand, of access to the world of male privilege which grants to the aspiring male autonomous activity, enterprise, and social renown as well as the domination of women.[17] The drama of vocation, of a social role intimately connected to gender role, in Milton's play, therefore, as feminist theory predicts, encompasses the drama of psychic development, beginning with the earliest event alluded to being the divine sanction for Samson's entirely masculine mission and culminating in the acts of its completion and proposed social commemoration.

Underlying the split in male and female roles is a social and economic division of home and work, reproduction and production, domestic and social labor, the private and the public sphere. The subordination of woman is the subordination of the domestic to the world of enterprise dominated by men. In Milton's play this dichotomy is affirmed by Samson's insistence that he "was no private but a person rais'd" for public achievement (l. 1211). Dalila's claim that for herself as well "to the public good / Private respects must yield" (ll. 867–68) is, on the contrary, dismissed contemptuously for she should have been bound to domestic duties, "being once a wife thou wast to leave / Parents and country" (ll. 885–86). The poem dramatizes a conflict between marriage and vocation, emotion and duty, between conflicting allegiances to a loved woman and a revered heavenly Father and demonstrates the replication of the gender split in the male psyche itself.

Merely by dropping his question mark, we can read the vocation which Manoa recalls to Samson as simply a vocation to manhood itself, to being "a Son . . . / Who would now be a Father in my stead" (l. 355). This masculine identification is reinforced by the endorsement of an idealized heavenly father figure who chose Samson before birth for exemplary masculinity. Since Manoa's marriage was barren before divine intervention, that Almighty Father is actually implicated in Samson's paternity. His mother, on the other hand, is almost completely suppressed in this narrative, only once included in a reference to the prophetic vision granted his "Parents." This contrasts directly with the biblical account, moreover, where it is explicitly said that Samson's mother was barren and that she was the one twice addressed by the angel announcing Samson's birth. The whole incident with Manoa and the issue of Samson's relationship to his father is, of course, a Miltonic invention. In addition, God seems to usurp the maternal function, for Samson asserts "I was his nursling once . . . / His destin'd from the womb" (l. 634), as if Samson was generated by a double-sexed god, or by two fathers, one divine and one human. His heavenly Father exacted from him a vow of renunciation of a *Nazarite* (literally meaning to separate) and his "breeding order'd and prescrib'd / As of a person separate to God / Design'd for great exploits" (ll. 30–32). Thus, the heavenly Father becomes the guarantor of Samson's autonomy by mandating a socialization disengaged from maternal dependencies and marked for masculine conquests.

Consistent with such supersuppression of the mother is Samson's exaggerated masculinity and self-sufficiency as "he who stood aloof . . . insupportably" (ll. 135–36). Related to this identity is Samson's obsession with renown, when, as he himself admits, "like a petty God / I walk'd about admir'd of all (ll. 529–30) and "swoll'n with pride" (l. 532). Such pursuit of public approval, the essence of the hero-Chorus relationship in the play, has been found endemic to male role development in which boys, unlike girls, must reject personal emulation of the mother for an imitation of more abstract cultural stereotypes in acquiring a male identity which is consequently less secure and more dependent on social confirmation.[18]

Also connected to this syndrome is the physical aggression which is one of the few traits consistently found to differentiate males and females.[19] Samson's hypermasculinity is particularly seen in the very personal and sadistic violence in which he repeatedly gloats. Samson is "himself an Army" (l. 346) "Who tore the Lion, as the Lion tears the Kid" (l. 127). Numerous psychological explanations have been given for such aggression. Melanie Klein stressed the frustrated infant's rage at its mother, a rage mitigated in a girl's later identifications.[20] Dorothy Dinnerstein has seen male repression of feelings of dependence on a seemingly omnipotent nurturer countered in acts of domination, as well as a transformation of desires for the mother into the compensatory aggression of male enterprise.[21] Milton evokes the childhood eroticism in Samson's violence when with "his sword of bone / A thousand foreskins fell" (ll. 143–44) and its origins when he reveals, as the counterpart of Samson's military violence, a wild hatred of Dalila and the "fierce rememberance," on one level, of the mother she reincarnates, which wakes his "sudden rage to tear thee joint by joint" (ll. 951–52).

If nothing else, Samson's hypermasculinity would unveil its infantile source in its identification with a Father who appears, as always to a child, all-mighty. But such inflated masculinity has also been seen as an indication of the contrary, of the insecurities of a male identity presuming a power adequate to overthrow its maternal identifications. The "invincible Samson" (l. 340) up until his final confrontation with Dalila has, in fact, found all his prowess inadequate to the task. Paradoxically, Manoa assists his separation, not only by bringing painfully into focus the contrast between Samson's exalted ego-ideal and his passive condition, but by negative reinforcement. When Manoa proposes to exchange his function as paternal validator of his son's male autonomy for a maternal acceptance of his emasculation and regression to the "household hearth" (l. 566), his vocation abandoned, to be nurtured passively, Samson's weakened ego is threatened with almost total dissolution.

It is at this moment, apparently "helpless . . . hopeless . . . remediless" (ll. 644, 648), in opposition to this overwhelming menace, that Samson begins to mobilize the resistance which he expresses in his assertion of his maleness against Dalila. Relations with women are viewed by Samson as a combat in which he has been previously "overpowr'd" (l. 880) by an enemy whose emotional initiatives, described in military terms, have been more than a match for his masculine prowess. The woman of Timna "wrested" from Samson his riddle; Dalila "assay'd with . . . amorous reproaches" "With blandisht parleys, feminine assaults / Tongue batter-ies . . . / To storm me overwatch't" (ll. 403–5). Karen Horney has attributed a man's "dread of woman" to his memories of apparent maternal omnipo-tence which endow women with a seemingly magical power.[22] Thus, Dalila's "wonted arts / And arts of every woman," her "wiles" and "snares" reveal her (pagan, after all) to be a "sorceress" through whose "fair enchanted cup and warbling charms" (l. 934) are "wisest and best men full oft beguil'd" (l. 759).

This power of women, associated as it is with love, stems from a projection in which male desires are disowned by their attribution to female emotional and erotic manipulations, Dalila's "venereal trains" (l. 533). (By contrast, no sympathy is wasted on the women Samson married to exploit politically.) The trope of "bondage" is reiterated so often that one can hardly avoid hearing the simple "bond" within it, an emotional bonding perceived through a male paranoia. Dalila was only able to cause his imprisonment because he was already "enslav'd with dotage" (l. 1042). Dalila is made to confess a plot to keep him undistracted from her boudoir by perilous adventures, "Mine and Love's Prisoner" (l. 808). His subsequent mutilation allows her to anticipate his becoming completely dependent upon her, chained not to his prison but to her bed.

Again, a kind of negative reinforcement occurs, as Samson revolts against the suggestion that he live "uxorious to [her] will / In perfect thraldom" (ll. 945–46), insisting that "This Gaol I count the house of Liberty" (l. 949) compared to such a love nest. He recognizes explicitly at this moment that his real fear is erotic regression, though he can only blame it on Dalila, whom he sees trying to reduce him to childish dependency "now blind, And thereby / Deceivable in most things as a child / Helpless, thence easily contemn'd and scorn'd, / And last neglected" (ll. 941–44). The regressive element is dramatized here by the sense of repetition in the attempt to draw him back into a relationship barred by their alienation and his lost virility for, as he reproves, "thou and I are long since twain" (l. 929), but his claim to exemption from the "secret sting of amorous remorse" (l. 1007), a powerful romantic analogue for infantile nostalgia, is belied by his unrelinquished anger. There is also a

note of poignancy in his sadder fear of neglect, which recalls his possessive plaint at Dalila's abandonment "Thou mine, not theirs" (l. 888).
Nevertheless, his regeneration, such as it is, only proceeds once he repudiates that primal paradise regained which Dalila would create through
her "*redoubl'd* love and care / With nursing diligence" (ll. 923–24) "where
other senses want not their delights" (l. 916).

Such rehabilitation has required that he first recognize that his
maturation, as defined by his vow of separation, had been incomplete
and thus easily undone whenever he regressed in a woman's arms. When,
alluding to this vow, the Chorus celebrates his oral asceticism, the sobri-
ety in which "desire of all delicious drinks . . . / Thou couldst repress"
(ll. 541–43), we find that such satisfactions had been replaced (or displaced)
by a "clear milky juice" (l. 550). Samson then asks "what avail'd this tem-
perance, not complete / Against another object more enticing" (ll. 558–59);
he had, as it were, shut out the maternal foe "at one gate" (l. 560)
or organ of pleasure, only to admit her "Effeminately vanquish't" (l. 562)
at another. The association of genital eroticism with emasculation here
would be inexplicable except in an oedipal context. Samson's love for
Dalila involves his loss of potency through a symbolic castration because
it is a regressive oedipal attachment.

This subtext also explains the contempt for eroticism which pervades
the poem, so unlike Adam and Eve "Imparadis't in one another's arms"
(*PL* 4.506), but so like the incestuous triad in Milton's Hell. Dalila is
condemned for her "furious rage / To satisfy [her] lust" (ll. 836–37),
Samson for violating his "vow of strictest purity" with "that fallacious
Bride / Unclean, unchaste" (ll. 320–21). When Samson becomes "Soft'n'd
with pleasure and voluptuous life; / At length to lay my head and
hallow'd pledge / Of all my strength in the lascivious lap / Of a deceitful
Concubine who shore me / Like a tame Wether . . . ridiculous, despoil'd"
(ll. 534–39), the associations are with castration and oedipal taboos. Love
is an entanglement with a life-threatening snake which must "by quick
destruction [be] soon cut off" (l. 764). The "Gaol" Samson fears as a
bondage to Dalila is the fixation of incest, an arrest at the "household
hearth" which would bar all other relationship and enterprise. The
image of the mill which symbolizes his repetition complex had, moreover,
had sexual connotations for Milton elsewhere, in *The Doctrine and Discipline of Divorce,* when he expressed his aversion to grinding in the "mill
of servile copulation."[23]

The centrality of the castration theme in this story is underlined by
the symbol's doubling in the twin motifs of Samson's loss of his hair and
his eyes, and emphasized by Milton's lament for "such a tender ball"
(l. 93). For Freud, castration anxiety arose from the oedipal taboo and

prompted a boy to sacrifice his maternal attachment for identification with his father, but, as in feminist theory, in Milton the problem of emasculation and gender role is prior, for "effeminacy" is given as the cause as well as the consequence of Samson's fall into Dalila's "Spousal Embraces" (l. 359). Dalila is able to overpower Samson only through collaboration by that enemy within through which "She sought to make me Traitor to my self" (l. 401). Complaints of a foe within the household are expressed in images of one within Samson himself, for woman "once join'd . . . proves, a thorn / Intestine far within defensive arms" (ll. 1037–38) and man becomes "Entangl'd with a pois'nous bosom snake" (l. 763). Samson's debasement derives from an overthrow of the sexual hierarchy, simultaneously without and within, for, in his attachment to Dalila, whom "degenerately I served" (l. 419), he fell into "true slavery and that blindness" (l. 418) to the antifeminine requirement of his identity. Thus, "With a grain of manhood well resolv'd" Samson "Might easily have shook off all her snares / But foul effeminacy held me yok't / Her Bondslave" (ll. 408–11). His ultimate crime has been an "impotence of mind" (l. 52) whose punishment by rendering him infantile and "Unmanly, ignominious, infamous" (l. 417) has been itself, "the servile mind / Rewarded well with servile punishment" (ll. 412–13). Femininity is "ignominious" and translated simply as "woman's frailty" (l. 783) which Dalila offers as her excuse and Samson's, "Let weakness then with weakness come to parle" (l. 785), but femininity is also identified with emotional attachment, with love which, to invert Milton's line, like all weakness, is wickedness. In summary then, a female, infantile, emotional, and erotic strata of Samson's psyche, insufficiently repressed, has been punished with the humiliation of an infantile and female vulnerability and powerlessness, experienced both in his external condition and on the level of the emotions themselves.

Such realities dictate that Samson's secret is, in fact, more than a secret from God, the "secrets of men" (l. 492) and of manhood itself. His "shameful garrulity" (l. 491) might, like Eve's oral indiscretion, appear, on the surface, too slight a fault on which to rest so great a tragedy. However, as Sidney Jourard indicates, studies of gender difference have revealed that in addition to physical aggression, the most consistent psychological disparity between the sexes lies in the far stronger taboos on male self-disclosure; even Dalila admits "curiosity . . . importune of secrets" (l. 775) "a weakness . . . incident to all our sex" (ll. 773–74).[24] Nowhere has the male prohibition been more profoundly explored than in Milton's tragic depiction of a Samson who "gave up my fort of silence to a woman" (l. 236). The initial image of Samson in a blind "Dungeon of [him]self" (l. 156) turns out ironically to be identical to that of the virtue he violated by abandoning the mute defenses of a male identity barricaded within its own character armor.

Secrecy is, however, intimately linked to repression, and what it protects a man from is an unmasking of the artificiality and precariousness of his masculinity. Even Samson remarks about his virile powers that God "to show withal / How slight the gift was, hung it in my Hair" (l. 59) (a substitution, no doubt, for another appendage likely to remind a man of his vulnerability). A man who discloses himself to a woman may fear that she will turn out to be too much like that woman who once knew him as a helpless child before his masculine defenses were constructed. The self-knowledge he is likely to discover when he abandons secrecy and sees himself through a woman's eyes is precisely that primal identification with woman against which such masculinity is an inevitably inadequate protection. When Samson "unlock'd her all my heart" (l. 407), he risked just this exposure to the woman without of the woman within. Within these dynamics, as Milton makes painfully clear, disclosure is identical with castration. In such a world a man like Samson must undergo the inner agon, expressed in the militarized psychological imagery of the drama, against "Thoughts my Tormentors arm'd with deadly stings" (l. 623). That "black mortification" (l. 622) which "must secret passage find / To th'inmost mind" (ll. 610–11) was the torment of an unresolved psychogenesis, that awful abyss of lethargy and paralysis into which he was flung, while unable to embrace either his lost feminine attachments, so severely punished, or his masculine ego-ideal and vocation.

To overcome this "living death" Samson had to become a warrior against himself and his own inner impulses. His weapon in this battle is misogyny. Freud seemed to presume as natural and legitimate "what we have come to consider the normal contempt for women," noting the resolution of the oedipus complex in "the contempt felt by men for a sex which is the lesser."[25] But it is because a boy must free himself from his own femininity that he, unlike a girl, generalizes his hostility toward his mother to the whole female sex. Furthermore, female psychologists have traced such misogyny earlier. Karen Horney finds it a strategem through which a male wards off his own infantile fear of maternal power by projecting his own fears onto woman, so "it is not . . . that I dread her; it is that she herself is malignant, capable of any crime, a beast of prey, a vampire, a witch, insatiable in her desires."[26] Samson hurls all these charges at Dalila, a subhuman "Monster," "viper," "Hyaena," "Adder," "manifest Serpent," allegedly guilty of malice, greed, hypocrisy, sacrilege, idolatry, falsehood, and betrayal, accused of both traitorous rejection and the insatiable possessiveness of a demonized lust. Dalila's vices are generalized by the Chorus to all women, "One virtuous, rarely found" (l. 1047), which establishes an apology for patriarchal domination on this alleged need for defense against woman's apparently overwhelming psychic power:

> Therefore God's universal Law
> Gave to the man despotic power
> Over his female in due awe,
>
> . . . .
>
> So shall he least confusion draw
> On his whole life, not sway'd
> By female usurpation . . .
>
> (ll. 1053–60)

These words provide an ideological consolidation of the rejection of woman that violently rose from Samson's gut as he threatened to tear Dalila apart with his bare hands, and it is that rage which brings the revival of male bravado with which he then immediately defies Harapha. The source of his aggression could not be more clear, and presumably he does slaughter his once-loved wife along with the other Philistines. *Samson Agonistes* is a tragedy, a tragedy of gender of which there is almost none greater. Milton apparently concludes here that Samson could either have a world to love with women or a world to conquer with men; he cannot have both.

This presents a certain critical complexity. Samson resolves his paralysis not through love but through hatred, but that paralysis resembles nothing more in Milton's works than the image of the "root-bound" lady of *Comus,* her "nerves all chain'd up in Alabaster" (ll. 662, 660), so incisively analyzed by Kerrigan. Kerrigan reads that masque as reflecting a crisis in Milton's adulthood in which he was unable to move either toward love or a vocation as a result of a psychological fixation in which castration anxiety fused with separation anxiety, a neurosis expressed in the erotic revulsion of its conception of virginity. This stasis was resolved, according to Kerrigan, by his mother's death and the release of blocked aggression in the "licensed rage" of his political tracts. Milton's ultimate psychological breakthrough allows him to move from this inert repression to the healthy sexuality and fecundity of *Paradise Lost* with its apotheosis of married love and copulating angels. In his mature epic, moreover, Milton, according to Kerrigan, also celebrates a poetic vocation embued with eroticism and inspired by a positive regression in blindness to reunion with the pre-oedipal mother, and recovery through that Muse-mother of the poet's own feminine powers. What does it mean then that Samson, celibate in the end, recapitulates so closely the psychic stasis of the aspiration to "defensive stainlessness" in *Comus.*[27]

In Samson, only a total rejection of woman can end his immobility.

In the final acts of the play, Samson is finally liberated for action. Having repudiated feminine attachments, he feels "Some rousing motions" (l. 1382) of masculine vigor, returns to combat and proceeds to fulfillment of his vocation, which is not to generation, however, but destruction. Ending the anguish of his gender ambivalences, he culminates those experiences of being "cut off" (ll. 764, 1157), from his community, his wife, and his own feminine characteristics, which echo through the poem. Renouncing all residual desire for pleasure or relationship in an act so brave, so horrible as that last, his identity is restored, and "Samson has quit himself like Samson" (l. 1710).

We cannot, however, simply celebrate with Manoa, but rather, forced to contemplate such an ending, must wonder whether the cure has not been more horrible than the disease. With helpless awe we watch a Samson, now so dreadfully alone in his potency and mission, devoid of all human contact, departing for a world entirely of enemies. Committed to his male enterprise of total asceticism, he has exchanged his body of pleasure for a body of aggression, desire for "inexpiable hate" (l. 839) and "anger unappeaseable" which "still rages / Eternal tempest never to be calm'd" (ll. 963–64), and, ultimately, a body of sacrifice. The intimations of suicide in the text cannot, moreover, be entirely silenced by the Chorus's reassurances of a Samson "self-kill'd / Not willingly" (ll. 1664–65), because his earlier yearnings for death, for extinction of the self, have only been conquered by their partial satisfaction, in the strangling of desire and the obliteration of a good part of his humanity. How can we help but share Manoa's wail at Samson, "O lastly overstrong against thyself" (l. 1590)? Are we not, like the Chorus, drawn into the tragic empathy of a primal interior cry wrenched from us by the spectacle of a drama we know too well and the anguish of the inherent inner heroism, that "plain heroic Magnitude of mind" (l. 1279) which we demand of masculinity? For such is the awful sacrifice imagined when Samson, bound in those cords of "dire necessity" (l. 1665), willingly mounts the altar of his own immolation to bring the pillars of his masculine destiny horrendously down upon himself.[28]

But is it necessary? Kerrigan seems to think so. His profound insights into the psychodynamics of Milton's poetry are firmly wedded to an individualistic and ahistorical Freudian revisionism whose consequence is a tragic liberalism and resigned optimism with its celebration of the compromises of maturity. Accepting as inevitable and universal the fundamentally asocial necessities of the oedipus complex and its requisite denials, Kerrigan must revert to an un-Freudian religious transcendence of those psychic contradictions which even his own reading of the bleak last books of *Paradise Lost* finds it difficult to sustain. What could he say about *Samson*, what optimism does it offer for life as it is in the world as it is? Kerrigan balks at the apocalyptic hope of Milton's ending in *Paradise Lost*, finding it merely otherworldly. Milton and Freud were both more radical in presenting civilization and its discontents in which the psychology of fallen history is defined by neurosis and original sin.

If criticism has been unable to resolve what our attitude should be in the face of Samson's tragedy, and we remain uncertain whether or not to join with "calm of mind" in the Chorus's commendation, the reason, I suspect, is that the drama has exposed too nakedly and has, unconsciously, rebelled too emotionally at the exactions of gender. Samson himself goes with as much rage as resignation to his fate, and we bring to his recognition of necessity a resistance that has been fortified by the historical hindsight with which we view the psychic costs of modern patriarchy. Milton's radicalism lies in facing the tragedy of individual existence within those constraints, but history, not the afterlife, which offers no escape for the Hebrew Samson, history has its comedy, its apocalypse. Samson exists preeminently in history; thus, despite Milton's tendency toward absolutizing gender, so does the masculinity he represents. So too then that male identity has its apocalyptic historical potential which Milton cannot describe but only symbolize as something which, though the individual is destroyed, "revives, reflourishes" and "survives" for the future, "A secular bird of ages" (ll. 1704–7). And that bird must be an androgynous bird, uniting the masculine eagle with his "cloudless Thunder" (l. 1696) and the feminine phoenix, whose femininity has been recovered from "her ashy womb" (l. 1704) in which it was sacrificed when man made that "holocaust" (l. 1702) of himself, recovered now amid images of teeming fecundity a "self-begott'n bird" (l. 1609), a *self* begotten, beyond all contraries of gender, a fully human self.

NOTES

1. Quotations from Milton's poetry are from *John Milton, Complete Poems and Major Prose*, ed. Merritt Y. Hughes (Indianapolis: Odyssey, 1957).

2. After completing this article, I found some conjunction with Miecke Bal's psychoanalytic reading, "The Rhetoric of Subjectivity," *Poetics Today*, 5 (1984), 337–76.

3. William Riley Parker, *Milton's Debt to Greek Tragedy in "Samson Agonistes"* (Baltimore: Johns Hopkins, 1937) and "The Date of *Samson Agonistes*," *PQ*, 28 (1949), 145–66; Don Cameron Allen, *The Harmonious Vision* (Baltimore: Johns Hopkins, 1954), p. 83; Mary Ann Radzinowicz, *Towards "Samson Agonistes": The Growth of Milton's Mind* (Princeton: Princeton Univ. Press, 1978), pp. 55, 66;

Arnold Stein, *Heroic Knowledge: An Interpretation of "Paradise Regained" and "Samson Agonistes"* (Mineapolis: Univ. of Minnesota Press, 1953), p. 210.

4. A. S. P. Woodhouse, "Tragic Effect in *Samson Agonistes,*" in *Milton: Modern Essays in Criticism,* ed. Arthur E. Barker (New York: Oxford Univ. Press, 1965).

5. William Kerrigan, *The Sacred Complex: On the Psychogenesis of "Paradise Lost"* (Cambridge: Harvard Univ. Press, 1983). I am using psychogenesis to refer to evolution of the psyche itself, not, as Kerrigan, of the poem.

6. Kerrigan, *Sacred Complex,* p. 6.

7. Nancy Chodorow, *The Reproduction of Mothering: Psychoanalysis and the Sociology of Gender* (Berkeley: Univ. of California Press, 1978); Dorothy Dinnerstein, *The Mermaid and the Minotaur: Sexual Arrangements and the Human Malaise* (New York: Harper and Row, 1976); Luise Eichenbaum and Susie Orbach, *What Do Women Want: Exploding the Myth of Dependency* (New York: Berkley Books, 1984); Judith Lorber, Rose Laub Coser, Alice S. Rossi, and Nancy Chodorow, "On *The Reproduction of Mothering:* A Methodological Debate," *Signs,* 6 (Spring, 1981), 482–514; Mary Brown Parlee, "Psychology and Women," *Signs,* 5 (Autumn, 1979), 121–33; for an orthodox Freudian feminist approach, see Juliet Mitchell, *Psychoanalysis and Feminism* (New York: Pantheon, 1974).

8. For narrative structures, Gerard Genette, *Narrative Discourse* (Oxford: Oxford Univ. Press, 1980); for psychoanalytic aspects, Shoshana Felman, ed., *Literature and Psychoanalysis* (Baltimore: Johns Hopkins, 1982) and Christian Metz, *The Imaginary Signifier: Psychoanalysis and the Cinema* (Bloomington: Indiana Univ. Press, 1982).

9. D. W. Winicott, *The Maturational Processes and the Facilitating Environment* (New York: International Univ. Press, 1965); Margaret Mahler, *On Human Symbiosis and the Vicissitudes of Individuation* (New York: International Univ. Press, 1968); W. R. D. Fairbairn, *An Object Relations Theory of Personality* (New York: Basic Books, 1952).

10. Chodorow, "Gender Relation and Difference in Psychoanalytic Perspective," in *The Future of Difference,* ed. Hester Eisenstein and Alice Jardine (Boston: G. K. Hall, 1980), p. 5; Norman O. Brown, *Life against Death* (Middletown, Conn.: Wesleyan Univ. Press, 1959), p. 45.

11. Chodorow, "Gender Relation," pp. 5–6.

12. Robert Stoller, *Sex and Gender: The Development of Masculinity and Femininity,* vol. 1 (New York: Jason Aronson, 1968).

13. Chodorow, "Gender Relation," p. 13.

14. Stoller, "Facts and Fancies: An Examination of Freud's Concept of Bi-Sexuality," cited in *Women and Analysis,* ed. Jean Strouse (New York: Grossman, 1974), p. 358.

15. Chodorow, *Mothering,* p. 72.

16. I owe this and other insights in this paper to Michael Strong.

17. Dinnerstein, *Mermaid and the Minotaur,* pp. 160–97.

18. Chodorow, *Mothering,* pp. 176–77.

19. James A. Doyle, *The Male Experience* (Dubuque, Iowa: Wm. C. Brown, 1983), pp. 122–23; Eleanor Maccoby and Carol Jacklin, *The Psychology of Sex Differences* (Stanford, Calif.: Stanford Univ. Press, 1974).

20. Melanie Klein, *Envy and Gratitude* (London: Free Press, 1957).

21. Dinnerstein, *Mermaid and the Minotaur,* pp. 93–98, 124–30; see also Jessica Benjamin, "The Bonds of Love: Rational Violence and Erotic Domination," in *The Future of Difference,* ed. Eisenstein and Jardine, pp. 41–70.

22. Karen Horney, "The Dread of Woman," *International Journal of Psychoanalysis,* 13 (1932), 348–60.

23. I owe this observation to Marshall Grossman.

24. Sidney Jourard, *The Transparent Self* (New York: Van Nostrand, 1964).

25. Sigmund Freud, *Some Psychical Consequences of the Anatomical Differences between the Sexes,* in *The Standard Edition of the Complete Psychological Works* (London: Hogarth Press, 1925) vol. 19, p. 253.

26. Horney, "Dread of Woman," p. 155.

27. Kerrigan, *Sacred Complex,* pp. 22–72, 53, 63, 185–89, 259.

28. There are apparent discrepancies between my reading here and the historical one presented in " 'The Lord's Battells': *Samson Agonistes* and the Puritan Revolution," *Milton Studies,* 4 (1972), 32–62, where Samson is a revolutionary hero. The text sustains both readings; I wrestle with the contradictions in a subsequent article on gender and war in *Samson* and Brecht.

Female Autonomy in
Milton's Sexual Poetics

JANET E. HALLEY

THE early feminist critics of *Paradise Lost* read Eve as a product of Miltonic misogyny: she is a purely derivative being, a "defect / of Nature,"[1] the rebellious ally of Satan.[2] Their essays initiated a vigorous controversy, in which women critics have rebutted the early feminist analysis. Barbara K. Lewalski wrote a sharp retort to Marcia Landy; Joan Malory Webber rebutted Sandra Gilbert in a posthumously published article; and Diane Kelsey McColley countered the feminist critique of Milton in a book-length defense of his Eve.[3] In the process of this debate, the term "feminist" as a descriptor of Milton criticism has become multivalent, referring both to critics who see Eve as the object of Milton's patriarchal imagination and to others to whom she is the image of a genuine female subjectivity not created but recognized by a progressive, liberal Milton. At least one of the things at stake in this controversy is the involvement of the critics themselves in a history of subjectivity in which, most participants can agree, Milton played an important role.

Lewalski, Webber, and McColley alike charge that the application of contemporary feminist thinking to Milton is ahistorical. And they propose, as a historically more accurate strategy, that we link the poem with the development of what Lawrence Stone has called the "companionate marriage."[4] In Eve, they argue, Milton gives poetic expression to the new and improved position of woman in Puritan marriage: as the companion and helpmeet ordained for man by God, she may still be her husband's civil inferior, but she has become his spiritual equal. Milton's epic represents Adam and Eve as free, they argue, both in electing marriage and in continuing to love one another. It thus reflects the historical innovation of the progressive bourgeois marriage, in which even brides were freed from the economic constraints of parental prearrangement, and instead voluntarily entered into marriage as autonomous individuals.[5]

These critics of early feminist essays on Milton argue convincingly that his Eve, far from being a mere image of deficiency and perversion, is endowed with a subjectivity as genuine as Adam's. But paradoxically, in proposing this reading as more truly historical than the feminist ones they oppose, they offer it as a means of transcending history altogether: as Lewalski writes in her conclusion, "great poets have a way of rising like phoenixes from whatever ashes are left in the wake of social and intellectual revolutions, so no doubt it will not be long before we can all again read Milton for what is of enduring importance rather than what is historically conditioned in his conception of man and woman."[6] This double attitude to history—it is both the ground of all valid critical argument and the clog that great art and good readings must shed—is part of an effort to make the female subjectivity historically created by bourgeois marriage as transcendent and enduring as the poem that represents them purportedly is.

The prominent academic women who have taken on this liberal effort in Milton studies attribute to themselves, then, the same autonomy they read in Milton's Eve. Their work is part of a widespread effort, in which antifeminist and liberal feminist work by women has been important, to construct an ideology of professional women's "academic freedom" appropriate to a "postfeminist" era.[7] But feminists cannot merely dismiss their challenge—for it raises a question that has become urgent throughout the feminist community in vitally important debates over the place of heterosexuality and marriage in the feminist movement, over dominance and submission in sexual relations, over pornography and censorship. At its most general, that question might be phrased, "Is autonomous female subjectivity possible?"[8] If the first wave of feminist criticism of Milton, regarding Eve as an object of male imagination and desire, neglected the problematics of her subjectivity, its opponents—not only in their scholarly polemics but also in propria persona—have made that question inescapable. Their reading of Eve reminds us that real women actively participate, with widely varying degrees of consciousness and irony, in forms of subjecticity and desire prepared for us by a history dominated by patriarchal power. Their challenge calls for a reformulation of the feminist project in Milton studies.

History and Heterosexual Reading

The arguments offered by Lewalski (1975), Webber (1980), and McColley (1983) range from the conservative to the liberal, from humanist to humanist-feminist—a gradient that may reflect the growing ability of mainstream academic feminism to assimilate originally conservative analyses. For they share a great deal, most notably a finding that the freedom of Eve applies to the reader of *Paradise Lost* as well. Lewalski commends *Paradise Lost* to us as a profound exploration of "a basic human predicament," the conjoining of "full individual responsibility" in each of our first parents with the experience of "the need for the other, the inescapable bonds of human interdependence."[9] In the course of the poem, Adam and Eve discover their sameness and equality as well as a structure of differences that makes each the incomplete part of a hetero-sexual pair that is the only whole. Lewalski provides a model for Webber and McColley not only in proposing this analysis of the relationship between Adam and Eve, but also in basing an aesthetic for the poem on it: she offers heterosexual interdependence as a strategy for reading *Paradise Lost*. While acknowledging that "our perceptions of art are necessarily affected in important ways by race, class, or sex," Lewalski nevertheless "affirm[s] the capacity of great art to transcend these lesser categories of human experience and speak to our common humanity"[10]—to speak, that is, precisely to that shared posture of individual moral respon-sibility and inescapable heterosexual interdependence that founds the bourgeois marriage.

Webber extends Lewalski's analysis of the social life of Adam and Eve to a description of the heterosexual constitution of Milton's universe itself. The "two great Sexes [which] animate the World" (*PL* 8.151), like all conflicts and oppositions in the created cosmos, proceed from the fundamental universal principle that opposites coincide in God but are necessarily divorced in his creation. Marriage figures forth both the harmony of differences in the created cosmos and the anticipated apoca-lyptic assimilation of all differences into God.[11] Webber concludes that "For [Milton] the epic goal was the wholeness that marriage offers, figured also in every part of the universe that grows through its many opposites, and figured ultimately in the visionary time when 'God shall be all in all.' The challenge that confronts us now is whether it is possible to retain that ideal, perhaps the only remaining idea that makes poetry out of life, while reaching beyond the particular poetry that seems to promote male dominance."[12]

In this difficult paragraph, Webber leaves intact the suggestion that transcendent reading may not be possible. Against the pull of actual experience ("life" itself) and of "particular poetry," though, Webber hopes that readers will aspire to an ideal: indeed, they will make *poetry* out of their lives by seeing *Paradise Lost* only in terms of the ideal that it offers. The language of transcendence here masks the material conditions Webber silently posits for reading: the ideal reader of *Paradise Lost* is a married heterosexual, someone who seeks "the wholeness that marriage offers" not only in poetry but also in life. The "inescapable bonds" of heterosexual "interdependence" are applied here to the reader herself (or himself), whose married transcendence provides both a very practical and an aesthetic enactment of Milton's *coincidentia oppositorum*.

McColley's book presents a decidedly Christian version of this correspondence between transcendence in reading and in life. This study proposes that "redeeming" Eve from the reductive readings offered in "our own incoherent and friable age" will result in a "regenerative reading of her role," an understanding of Eve as "a speaking picture of the recreative power of poetry itself."[13] This power is figured, tellingly, in Eve's conscription into heterosexuality in Book 4 of *Paradise Lost.* There, Eve relates to Adam how, newly created, she was transfixed with the admiration of her own reflection in a lake. Called first by God and then by Adam, she turned from the contemplation of her own image to the husband in whose image she was created. McColley argues that Milton represents here "a pattern of response that is a mimetic model, both for the art of marriage and for the art of reading"—and, she later adds, "for a regenerate reading of the poem."[14] Free choice is at the center of that pattern: "the method of Eve's creation . . . requires for its completion the free and deliberate choice that Eve's decision, after she knows whose face is in the lake, supplies. . . . Her moment of hesitation marks her discovery that her will is free."[15] Only because Eve *wills* her acceptance of Adam, only because she freely *responds* to his call to heterosexual love, can she be a model for marriage and for reading.

This aesthetic of transcendence rests on an ideology that woman autonomously, freely elects not only heterosexuality and marriage, but even, McColley holds, the subordination these institutions have historically demanded of her. It is no accident that Lewalski, Webber, and McColley are able to build convincing arguments about Eve's subjectivity—its creation was one of the major ideological projects of the seventeenth century in England, and of Milton himself after his own disastrous first marriage. Milton's antifeminist and liberal feminist readers repeatedly charge that it is ahistorical to approach his work with reading assumptions invented after the seventeenth century—Webber even asserts that the modern reader of Milton should study his representation not of woman but of humanity, because seventeenth-century women did not see their interests as distinct from men's.[16] Against this charge we may observe that a poetic ideal of transcendence, though ideologically loaded, represents itself as historically "objective" by virtue of its congruence with the codes of the poem, by virtue of its own historical continuity with seventeenth-century sexual ideology.

Feminist thought and action have broken this continuity, making visible something that Lewalski, Webber, and McColley do not see because, for all the three hundred years that separate them from Milton, they share it with him—a particular moment in the historical construction of the female subject. By opening the gap between (biological) sex and (learned) gender, and by studying the systematic ways in which a "sex/gender system" socially transforms the former into the latter,[17] feminists have shown that female heterosexuality is not natural but socially constructed. Indeed, Adrienne Rich, asking "why such violent strictures should be found necessary to enforce women's total emotional, erotic loyalty and subservience to men," has argued that female heterosexuality is not a "sexual preference" but compulsory.[18]

In a powerfully revisionist essay, Gayle Rubin has argued that human females are "engendered" as women in a system of exchange that requires their heterosexuality not because it is natural to them but because it articulates relations among men. The pattern of interaction she describes was first outlined by Claude Lévi-Strauss in *The Elementary Structures of Kinship:* Lévi-Strauss argues that the exchange of women between men is a basic form of gift-giving, orchestrating relations of trust and rivalry between men and so articulating the social relationships that constitute culture. As Rubin points out, "if it is women who are being transacted, then it is the men who give and take them who are linked, the women being a conduit of a relationship rather than a partner to it. . . . [I]t is men who are the beneficiaries of the product of such exchanges—social organization."[19] The paradigm offered here has profound resonance for the study of male interrelationship, as Eve Kosofsky Sedgwick has demonstrated in her powerful book, *Between Men: English Literature and Male Homosocial Desire.* Sedgwick defines her term "male homosocial desire" very carefully:

"Homosocial" is a word occasionally used in history and the social sciences, where it describes social bonds between persons of the same sex; it is a neologism, obviously formed by analogy with "homosexual," and just as obviously meant to be distinguished from "homosexual." In fact, it is applied to such activities as "male bonding," which may, as in our society, be characterized by intense homophobia, fear and hatred of homosexuality. To draw the "homosocial" back into the orbit of "desire," of the potentially erotic, then, is to hypothesize the potential unbrokenness of a continuum between homosocial and homosexual—a continuum whose visibility, for men, in our society, is radically disrupted.[20]

Along the continuum of male homosociality, then, active heterosexuality is only one of the forms in which the partnership and rivalries of men can take shape. In such a dynamic, the heterosexuality enjoined upon women is a mechanism of male identity and interrelationship, not a vehicle of female will.

This context makes it clear that the voluntary participation of seventeenth-century bourgeois women in marriage is ideological in the sense suggested by Louis Althusser: it "represents the imaginary relationship of individuals to their real conditions of existence."[21] For women, those real conditions required marriage—in this they do not differ from earlier forms of arranged marriage—but they required it with the super-addition of desire. The bourgeois form of compulsory heterosexuality "interpellates" woman, as Althusser would say, calls upon her to assume the subjectivity of a *fully assenting* heterosexual, a free agent in the sexual marketplace. We do not know—and *Paradise Lost* cannot tell us—how fully real women of the seventeenth century entered into this subjectivity. Even for ourselves we may not be able to answer this question, so problematic is the issue of consent that it raises. But we can examine Milton's own relationship to the ideological formation of the female subject, and trace in his writing the contradictions that invest the apparently simple notion of heterosexual reading.

Milton's Homosocial Poetics

Milton's great narrative poems—*Comus, Paradise Lost, Paradise Regained, Samson Agonistes*—present us with single women enmeshed in male worlds. They establish sex "triangles" composed of two men and a woman in which the isolated woman is the pivot between two male powers, social groups, or ethical value which can be understood to participate in a homosocial relation through her. In *Comus,* the Lady becomes lost as she travels with her brothers to their father's house: the plot traces her capture by Comus and her restoration to her (motherless and sisterless) family. In *Paradise Lost,* Sin links Satan and Death—one her father and mate, the other her son, brother, and mate—in an incestuous triangle; and Eve articulates the relationship of God and Adam by being the offspring of them both (in another motherless family), while her subservience to Adam and God is intended to model Adam's filial obedience to his father.[22] Further, she links these two triangles—the depraved and the righteous family—when she allows Satan to tempt Adam through her. In *Paradise Regained,* Mary is the medium through which a divine father begets a human son. And in *Samson Agonistes,* Dalila is an object of exchange through whom Samson and the Philistines conduct their national conflict.

Women bear relation to *other women* in only one kind of Miltonic scenario: the poet's own invocations to sister Muses. In *Paradise Lost,* Milton invokes the obscure figure Urania:

> ... for thou
> Nor of the Muses nine, nor on the top
> Of old *Olympus* dwell'st, but Heav'nly born,
> Before the Hills appear'd, or Fountain flow'd,
> Thou with Eternal Wisdom didst converse,
> Wisdom thy Sister ...

(7.5–10)

In *Lycidas,* he invokes the "Sisters of the sacred well, / That from beneath the seat of *Jove* doth spring," to "Begin, and somewhat loudly sweep the string" (ll. 15–17). And *At a Solemn Music* begins:

> Blest pair of *Sirens,* pledges of Heav'n's joy,
> Sphere-born harmonious Sisters, Voice and Verse,
> Wed your divine sounds ...

(ll. 1–3)

By inviting these sisters to "wed" their divine sounds, Milton apparently counters the entire strategy of the traffic in women, by acknowledging a primary and sufficient relationship between two female figures. Whereas the more typical male-female-male triangle establishes the relatedness of its male members, these passages situate the isolated male poet before two women, making him a petitioner who asks that his poetic identity be established on *their* using *him* as a conduit for *their* voice. The traffic relationship has been inverted.

Oddly, it is inverted only when Milton petitions for a perfect language, for "lucky words" (*Lycidas,* l. 20), an "answerable style" (*PL* 9.20). In a single anxious figure, Milton associates a challenge to male primacy and autonomy with a recognition that his poem's language will not necessarily be perfectly referential. His poetic construction of the traffic relationship gives special resonance to Lévi-Strauss's evaluation of woman's problematic situation in culture: "For a woman could never become just a sign and nothing more, since even in a man's world she is still a person, and since insofar as she is defined as a sign she must be recognized as a generator of signs."[23] As a genuinely autonomous generator of signs, the Muse threatens to disrupt the very fullness of meaning that her exchange makes possible.

Milton illuminates this sexual poetics when he recasts a complex topos by invoking a "blest pair of Sirens, Voice and Verse." From Homer, Vergil, Horace, and numerous other classical poets, Milton inherits the familiar tradition that the Muses, daughters of Jove and Mnemosyne, inspire creators in the various arts. From a quite distinct classical tradition—originating in Pythagoras, evidently, and repeated in Plato's *Republic* X—Milton inherits the fable of the music of the spheres. Plato places eight Sirens on the world's great spheres: each perpetually sings a single note as she rides along, and the harmony of the eight notes produces a song that perfectly renders the cosmic harmony. These are Sirens, not Muses: Plato makes a distinct reference here to the fatal enchantresses of Homer's *Odyssey*. There, of course, Circe warns Odysseus to have his men plug their ears with wax and to tie him to the mast, for only these precautions would make it safe for him to listen to the irresistible song of these temptresses.

The "music of the spheres" motif that plays such an important role in Renaissance iconography does not take shape until the late antique period. The Pythagorean mythographers who crafted it excised the latent and presumably threatening allusion to the Homeric Sirens.[24] They place nine *Muses,* each associated with a particular genre and musical mode,[25] on the spheres of a mathematically harmonic universe. In *At a Solemn Music,* Milton accepts this fusion of two distinct traditions—but he does not submerge or delete the allusion to Homer's Sirens. Those Sirens, powerful female figures capable of fascinating and destroying the men who hear them, take on the roles of the Muses, riding the spheres and creating a divine and ravishing music. The suggestion of their erotic power over the poet implies an association of the power of language and female sexual power to deflect the male poet from his own course.

Milton's *Second Prolusion,* too, associates the bewitching power of sister Siren/Muses with the entrancing power of language. In *Republic* X, Plato embeds the Siren fable in his notorious repudiation of poetic imitation. Milton's prolusion is a playfully ironic defense of Plato's extravagant fable of the music of the spheres—so that it is also an ironic defense of poetry. In the myth of the music of the spheres, Milton tells his audience, Pythagoras "seems to have followed the example of the poets—or, what is almost the same thing, of the divine oracles—by which no sacred and arcane mystery is ever revealed to vulgar ears without being somehow wrapped up and veiled." Milton then defends poetic fiction against an implicit Platonic attack by appealing to Plato's own figure: "The greatest of Mother Nature's interpreters, Plato, has followed him [that is, Pythagoras], for he has told us that certain Sirens have their respective seats on every one of the heavenly spheres and hold both gods and men fast bound by the wonder of their utterly harmonious song."[26] In grounding his authority on Plato's, Milton makes an alliance between himself and the philosopher, a male bond established by their shared relationship to a single fable.[27] We may observe as well that Milton would have Plato interpreting "Mother Nature" into the Siren figure: the male reads a prior female and thus creates a female *figure* without any great distortion of the prior "reality." But "Mother Nature" is itself a metaphor. Milton's text alludes to the possibility that figural language is present even at the outset of, and indeed prior to, poetic figuration. And in doing so it represents figural language *as a female* who may be not merely the object of male creativity but an uncontained and prior subject in her own right. If Plato presents a contradiction between his logical proof that poetry is false and his use of a poetic fable to advance that proof, Milton concentrates the conflict in the seemingly ubiquitous female figure. The threatening possibility of her autonomy erupts in the pointed emphasis on Homer's Sirens: poetic fiction and the Siren sisters together "hold gods and men fast bound by the wonder of their utterly harmonious song." Like *At a Solemn Music,* the prolusion registers anxiety that feminine textuality, as autonomous and prior to the male poet's expression, will undermine his efforts to construct a referential language—to control the meaning of his own words.

Evading the Sirens, escaping textuality and the female figure at once, is the goal of transcendent visions that conclude three important early poems. All three, moreover, examine the relations between male friendship and the practice of poetry: *Elegy VI,* a Latin epistle to Milton's friend—also a poet—Charles Diodati; the *Epitaphium Damonis,* a Latin elegy on Diodati's premature death; and *Lycidas,* Milton's great English elegy on the premature death of a poet and male friend. Taken together, these poems suggest that male poetic power and autonomy are most perfectly achieved not through a traffic in the female figure but through her complete banishment from a homosocial sexual poetics.

Elegy VI provides the sharpest example of this strategy. This Latin epistle to Milton's friend Diodati intitially praises poetry that relies on the Muses, but it then moves with diagrammatic clarity to extol a poetic mode that replaces female sources of inspiration with a male one. The business of the poem is to praise Diodati's lyric identity while demonstrating the superiority of Milton's epic persona. Milton apologetically praises Diodati's indulgence in feasting and wine, arguing that "the chorus of the Nine has often mingled with the rout of Thyoneus" (that is, of Bacchus) (l. 18), and predicting that "through a maiden's eyes and music-making fingers Thalia will glide into full possession of your breast" (ll. 47–48). The Muses' erotic relationship to Diodati will be one of possession: the lyric song that will emerge from his lips will in fact be theirs. Against the erotic elegy, then, Milton sets the epic: "But he whose theme is wars and heaven under Jupiter in his prime, and pious heroes and chieftains half-divine, and he who sings now of the sacred counsels of the gods on high, and now of the infernal realms where the fierce dog howls, let him live sparingly, like the Samian teacher; and let herbs furnish his innocent diet. Let the purest water stand beside him in a bowl of beech and let him drink sober draughts from the pure spring. Beyond this, his youth must be innocent of crime and chaste, his conduct irreproachable and his hand stainless" (ll. 55–64).

The generic requirements of epic include sexual abstinence, not only in the poet's physical appetites but also in his poetic ones. Milton calls up the example of Homer, "the spare eater and water-drinker," whose abstemiousness enabled him to carry Odysseus through "vada foemineis insidiosa sonis," through seas made treacherous by female song. Whereas the lyric poet passively yields to Siren/Muses, deriving his voice from the divine yet fatal sisters who inspire him, the epic poet will transcend feminine influence altogether. There is no mention of the Muses in the "epic" section of <i>Elegy VI:</i> rather, the epic poet's "hidden heart and his lips alike <i>spirat...Iovem,</i> breathe out Jove" (l. 78). Epic poetry will be purified of the female: the poet, <i>in</i>spired by a male god, will <i>ex</i>pire a poem that is the God himself. This equation of the inspiring male God with the poem indicates that, once the epic poet is freed of the female figure, he is simultaneously liberated from the referential failures of language.

Transcendence is decidedly homosocial here, though any homoeroticism is denied by the assertion of epic abstemiousness.[28] The <i>Epitaphium Damonis,</i> on the other hand, transcends both the female figure and the threat of homoerotic alliance by envisioning a linguistic paradise that is entirely genderless. Milton mourns Diodati in the persona of the shepherd Damon, concluding: "Because you loved the blush of modesty and a stainless youth and because you did not taste the delight of the marriage-bed, lo! the rewards of virginity are reserved for you. Your glorious head shall be bound with a shining crown and with shadowing fronds of joyous palms in your hands you shall enact your part eternally in <i>the immortal marriage where song and the sound of the lyre are mingled in ecstasy with blessed dances,</i> and where the festal orgies rage under the heavenly thyrsus" (ll. 212–19; emphasis mine). Because Diodati has foregone sexual union with women in his mortal lifetime, he can participate in a marriage free of the female figure. The poem displaces eroticism first from heterosexual union to the male friends, and then from the male friends onto language. The ecstatic partners here are song, the lyre, and the dance: these are <i>"mista,"</i> mingled or, significantly, engaged in sexual intercourse. Language unites with itself in the apocalyptic <i>cantus</i> of the <i>Epitaphium Damonis,</i> giving us a transcendence as free from referential failure as it is from gender.

Lycidas proposes three different solutions to the problem posed by At *a Solemn Music,* and seriatim it discards all of them. Milton first associates the female not only with the Muse but also with a natural world that mediates male friendship and its expression in verse. As the poem begins, the "Sisters of the sacred well" are invoked as a benign influence, but the speaker proceeds:

> Hence with denial vain, and coy excuse,
> So may some gentle Muse
> With lucky words favor my destin'd Urn,
> And as he passes turn,
> And bid fair peace be to my sable shroud.
>
> (ll. 18–22)

The bold shift to a Muse who might "as *he* passes turn" explicitly breaks the sister bond and sets in motion a series of related analogical shifts. Milton recasts the Muse as a poet whose "lucky words" might, in future, favor his destined urn: that is, the relationship he hopes to bear to Lycidas, he also hopes a male "Muse" may later have to him. But Milton does not remove the female figure by appropriating its role: in fact, the crucial point that he would establish a network of brotherhood between poets becomes clear only when the female figure is reintroduced in a new form:

> For we were nurst upon the self-same hill,
> Fed the same flock, by fountain, shade, and rill.
>
> (ll. 23–24)

Because she nurtured both Lycidas and the poet, a maternal nature established their brotherhood and, in some obscure way, supplies the reason ("*For* we were nurst") another poet should similarly claim brotherhood with the speaker after *his* death. At this early point in the poem, effective masculine verse depends on the mediating presence of a female figure, here identical with the poem's pastoral setting.

But, as Samuel Johnson objected in his life of Milton, "We know that they never drove afield, and that they had no flocks to batten; and though it be allowed that the representation may be allegorical, the true meaning is so uncertain and remote that it is never sought because it cannot be known when it is found."[29] Far from resisting Johnson's interpretation, *Lycidas* repeatedly discloses and repudiates the very artificiality of its own pastoral setting and mode that Johnson inveighs against here. Further, because it associates these with the female, particularly with sister nymphs and sister Muses, it repeatedly finds *both* to be false. The figure of the mediating female, itself an effort to resolve tensions built into the sister-Muse construction, remains unstable because of its female member. As the poem oscillates between invocations of pastoral Muses and the "dread voice" of male deities, it seeks to establish a stable discursive triangle and a perfectly indicative language.

The next solution offered by *Lycidas* is identical in sexual structure to the rapture of *Elegy VI:* the destabilizing female figure is banished altogether, and the language of transcendence is spoken by male voices. Soon after introducing the accustomed furniture of the pastoral setting, the poet asks in perfectly conventional form:

> Where were ye Nymphs when the remorseless deep
> Clos'd o'er the head of your lov'd *Lycidas?*
>
> (ll. 50–51)

He soon discovers that he has become trapped in a poetic fiction:

> Ay me, I fondly dream!
> Had ye been there—for what could that have done?
> What could the Muse herself that *Orpheus* bore,
> The Muse herself, for her enchanting son
> Whom Universal nature did lament,
> When by the rout that made the hideous roar,
> His gory visage down the stream was sent,
> Down the swift *Hebrus* to the *Lesbian* shore?
>
> (ll. 56–63)

Orpheus is traded from female figure to female figure—the Mother-Muse, the violent "rout that made the hideous roar," Lesbos—each part of an ensemble associating the female voice, sisterhood, betrayal, and destructive eroticism. The entire configuration reveals the male speaker betrayed, too, by the fiction of the nymphs. This section of the poem appears to find a resolution—often called the "first consolation"—in the vocal intervention of Phoebus Apollo, the inspiring voice of the male god of poetry himself. Immediately after that, however, the speaker invokes the "fountain *Arethuse*" and "Smooth-sliding *Mincius*" (ll. 85–86), involving himself in the highly problematic pastoral once again. The poem repeatedly follows this sequence, positing and then disestablishing the purely male discursive world envisioned at the close of *Elegy VI.*

The penultimate verse paragraph of *Lycidas* breaks out of this oscillation by proposing a third solution: a simultaneous transcendence of language's fictions and of gender itself very much like the one that concludes the *Epitaphium Damonis.* In an apocalyptic vision, the speaker sees Lycidas in "the blest Kingdoms meek of joy and love," where he hears what he calls "the unexpressive nuptial Song" (ll. 176–77). An "unexpressive" language would sustain no division between word and

JANET E. HALLEY

meaning, no "*expression*": here as in the elegy for Diodati, reference would disappear in language's union with itself. Further, Milton tells us that "all the Saints above, / In solemn troops, and sweet Societies / ... sing, and singing in their glory move" (ll. 178–80), suggesting by the pun on "move" that this linguistic paradise erases all distinction between the angels' physical movement and its emotional effect. In this beatific utterance, language, meaning, and understanding are to coincide precisely; speaker and audience are to be one. Unlike the rapture concluding the *Epitaphium Damonis,* this one lacks gender marks altogether, and so is even more precipitous. But the absent sign does not therefore become irrelevant: instead, its removal forces itself on our awareness. Just as the homoeroticism repressed by the conclusion of the *Epitaphium Damonis* is not actually transcended but rather masked by the poem's image of transcendence, so the strictly polarized gender arrangement of *Lycidas* is repressed in an apparently genderless transcendence that is, covertly, homosocial.

Milton's vision of a transcendent union, leaving far behind the struggles of sexual difference and linguistic reference, has proven profoundly attractive to critics of his poetry: it may be one of many historical sources for Lewalski's conviction that great poets rise like the phoenix from the ashes of history. But in *Lycidas* Milton sternly denies any equation between the wished-for "nuptial song" and the poem before us. The poem ends with the sudden introduction of its pastoral speaker:

> Thus sang the uncouth Swain to th'Oaks and rills,
> While the still morn went out with Sandals grey....

(ll. 186–87)

This *repoussoir* figure helps us gauge important relations—as he is to the poem, so Milton is to him—and so reminds us of the presence of an artificer. It is true that the escapist vision has removed explicit mention of gender from the poem. But it has not replaced a pastoral discourse in which gender is profoundly problematic. The problem of woman's autonomy, of her power to generate signs, silently reenters the poem in its final lines.

Milton's Heterosexual Poetics: The Doctrine and Discipline of Divorce

Milton did not figure poetic transcendence in heterosexual terms in the early poems examined here: instead, transcendence is a strategy for evading dangers imposed by the female figure, and is represented in entirely male and even in genderless terms. The Milton who wrote those poems might well have cried out with his Adam, "O why did God, / Creator wise, that peopl'd highest Heav'n / With Spirits Masculine ... / ... not fill the World at once / With Men as Angels without Feminine?" (*PL* 10.889–93). But *Paradise Lost* as a whole rebukes this form of misogyny, insisting instead on the incorporation of woman into its picture of social and poetic harmony. It constructs a sexual poetics that can accommodate rather than eliminate the female subject.

If the problem posed by the Siren/Muse is the ability of woman to produce her own signification and so to disrupt the traffic in which she is the sign of male interrelationship, Milton's strategy in *Paradise Lost* is to incorporate into the traffic relationship woman *as a generator of signs*, a "genuine subject." As Sedgwick's analysis of male homosocial desire makes clear, the heterosexual bonds that result from such a move do not eliminate but rather reformulate male homosocial relations: thus, the heterosexual transcendence offered in *Paradise Lost*, even though it includes woman as a desiring and speaking subject, repeats the homosocial forms of transcendence found in the early poems.

The social implications of this new sexual poetic are displayed most clearly in the *Doctrine and Discipline of Divorce*. Here, Milton develops for the first time his argument that husband and wife are not merely "one Flesh" but also "one Heart, one Soul" (*PL* 8.499); that God's purpose in instituting marriage was to provide Adam not with relief from lust or a source of progeny, but with intellectual and emotional companionship; that in God's eyes a marriage without affection was no marriage at all. This first divorce tract advances the scandalous thesis "That indisposition, unfitnes, or contrareity *of mind*, arising from a cause in nature unchangable, hindring and ever likely to hinder the *main benefits of conjugall society, which are solace and peace,* is a greater reason of divorce then naturall frigidity, especially if there be no children, *and that there be mutuall consent.*"[30] Milton innovates profoundly both in insisting on the wife's full subjective participation in marriage, and in recognizing the concept of her consent in divorce. Her autonomy, far from being an object of dread, has been welcomed into Milton's pattern for sexual love. As Lewalski points out, Milton here progresses beyond any simple view of women as "either sex objects or mother figures."[31]

Webber goes further, asserting that the title of the first divorce tract—*The Doctrine and Discipline of divorce Restor'd to the good of both sexes* ... —and the drift of all the tracts make it "apparent ... that Milton addresses himself to both men and women." She sees in Milton's pattern for marriage a profound recognition of the rights and subjectivity of women, and cites with admiration Milton's speculation in *Tetrachordon* that the natural rule of the husband may be abrogated when the wife is the wiser: "then a superior and more naturall law comes in, that the wiser should govern the lesse wise, whether male or female."[32] But Webber fails to note that the wife's ascendency depends on the husband's prior consent: in practice, her wisdom and power — indeed, her subjectivity — originate in his. This is not to say that, in Milton's vision of marriage, she has not got wisdom, power, and subjectivity; rather, it is to observe that her very autonomy is required of her.

The wife's discursive autonomy amounts to an essential property of marriage. Milton insists that God's promise of "a meet help" must be fulfilled for a relation to be a marriage (p. 309), and defines a "meet help" as "an intimate and speaking help," a "fit conversing soul" (p. 251). When he argues, then, that "shee who naturally & perpetually is no meet help, can be no wife; which cleerly takes away the difficulty of dismissing such a one" (p. 309), he requires her voluntary participation in married love and makes her refusal the grounds for her involuntary dismissal.

The degree to which a wife's autonomy is subsumed in a husband's becomes clear when Milton stipulates the procedures that should dissolve marriage. "If [God] joynd them not," he argues, "then is there no power above their own consent to hinder them from unjoyning" (p. 328). But insisting on the totality of the husband's private authority, Milton's libertarian argument leaves the law no role in protecting a woman who does not share in this "their own consent." In fact, such a woman cannot exist: "The law can only [appoint the just and equall conditions of divorce, and is to] look whether it be [how it is] an injury to the divorc't, which in truth it can be none, as a meer separation: for if she consent, wherin has the law to right her? or consent not, then is it either just and so deserv'd, or if unjust, such in all likelihood was the divorcer, and to part from an unjust man is a happines, & no injury to be lamented" (p. 349).[33] That is to say, if she does consent, then the law has nothing to do; but if she does not consent, she either gives proof of her unconversible spirit and so of the justice of her husband's will — or she gives proof of his injustice to her, in which case her true intent must be to divorce him.

These passages help to explain the shift from Milton's stipulation in his introductory *propositio* "that there be mutuall consent" to a divorce, to his later insistence that the civil power refrain from interfering with a divorce "against the will and consent of both parties, or of the husband alone . . . " (p. 344). In divorce, the wife's will is the inevitable product of her husband's; she is understood to consent when and because he does.

Female subjectivity is equally complex within marriage. Perhaps remembering his own courtship of Mary Powell, Milton resents the "bashfull mutenes of a virgin," which may deceive her suitor into "hoping well of every sociall vertue under that veile," when in fact he "may easily chance to meet, if not with a body impenetrable, yet often with a minde to all other due conversation unaccessible . . . " (p. 249). By associating and almost confusing a discursive with a sexual right of access, Milton requires that, in conversation as in bed, the groom's desire must be mirrored in the bride's. The function of a woman's speech—of her advance to the status of "an intimate and speaking help," a "fit conversing soul"—is to enable the suitor or husband to read the derivation of her will from his. She does not fail to achieve the status of subject; but, as Althusser would suggest, she is constrained, or subject-ed, to it.[34]

Under these conditions, male autonomy will not resemble its female counterpart. Instead, it establishes male identity on the basis of heterosexual potency. Milton promises that his doctrine of divorce would restore to spouses a "native liberty, and true manlines" (p. 227) that can belong only to men, and asserts that, confronted with the alternatives of divorce and adultery, the "agrieved *person* shall doe more *manly*" by divorcing, (p. 247; emphasis mine):[35] "to constrain him furder were . . . to unman him . . . " (p. 353). Moreover, when Milton images a man's conversation in courtship and marriage as phallic and female silence as emasculating, he constructs masculine freedom as an ability both to penetrate the bride's body and to determine her meaning. The husband's production of his wife's meaning, even though it requires her subjective cooperation, is a function of heterosexual male potency: to be unable to produce the meaning of the feminine text is to be castrated.

The problem of feminine textuality vexes the *Doctrine and Discipline of Divorce* just as it troubles the Diodati poems and *Lycidas*. In the poems, it is solved by resort to homosocial linguistic paradises. But here, Milton privileges masculine interpretation as free from the feminine text. The crux of this new construction is the tract's great blocking passage in Matthew (19:3–9), where Christ rebukes the Pharisees for arguing that Deuteronomy 24:1–2 authorizes husbands to divorce their wives. Christ's response—"What therefore God has joined together, let not man put asunder"—seems to make divorce under the gospel impossible. In response, Milton attacks literal interpretation as an unwarranted constraint of Christian liberty. He threatens the reader who holds fast to a "pretious literalism": "let some one or other entreat him but to read on in the same 19. of *Math.* till he come to that place that sayes *Some make themselves Eunuchs for the kingdom of heavns sake*. And if then he please to make use of *Origens* knife"—Origen is supposed to have castrated himself on the strength of a literal reading of this text (Matt. 19:12)—"he may doe well to be his own carver" (p. 334).[36] Unlike his opponents, Milton will not deprive himself of an interpretive authority he figures as both phallic and heterosexual. The subversive textuality that Milton associates with

245

the figure of woman in the early poems, and that he attempts to control there by evading the female altogether, is controlled here by the power of masculine interpretation.

This potency, far from being a merely private matter between husband and wife, functions as a determining element in male political inter-relationships by circulating through the wife her husband's rivalries with other men. What makes this difficult to see is that these homosocial relations are the libertarian ones of bourgeois privacy. Milton dates the English Reformation from Henry VIII's decision that he would (and Parliament's decision that he could), on his own authority, divorce Anne of Cleves—a wife so incompatible that she made him impotent. This act restored to the king his potency, and to the English paterfamilias his absolute domestic rule: "For ev'n the freedom and eminence of mans [sic] creation gives him to be a Law in this matter to himself"; in matters marital he must not "be forc't . . . to hear any judge . . . above himself" (pp. 347–48). The doctrine of divorce, by authorizing husbands to create the will and consent of their wives by acts of interpretation, establishes domestic privacy as a form of power that defines the relations among men in the public sphere as those of autonomous individuals. Where the reciprocal interactions of male identity require a woman's subjectivity, as they do here, we might say that she is not precisely an object, but rather a subject, of exchange.

Milton's Heterosexual Poetics: Paradise Lost

As the work of Lewalski, Webber, and McColley would suggest, *Paradise Lost* incorporates female subjectivity into its most gorgeous descriptions of harmony, both in the relationship of Adam and Eve and in the poet's intimacy with his Muse. But the result is a newly heterosexual form of transcendence that closely echoes the relations of male and female subjectivity in the *Doctrine and Discipline of Divorce,* incorporating the female voice and the female will only by subsuming them in male intention. Far from abandoning history, then, the epic's formulation of sexual poetics belongs to the history of the liberal self. Modeling his relation to the Muse on the husband's proper relation to his wife—for Adam and Eve represent the perfect marriage envisioned in the *Doctrine and Discipline of Divorce* —Milton creates an intersubjective heterosexual encounter that is, nevertheless, the product of his own autonomous mind. And again, the homosociality of this transcendence is disguised by the privacy of the nuclear family and of the solitary poet.

The epic repeatedly figures married love as a harmony. Adam adds to Scripture when he rejoices that he and his wife are "one Flesh, one

Heart, *one Soul*" (8.499; emphasis mine): they spontaneously sing a prayer in perfect unison, "unanimous" in the root sense of the term (4.736). Commenting on their harmony, Adam praises

> . . . all [Eve's] words and actions, mixt with Love
> And sweet compliance, which declare unfeign'd
> Union of Mind, or in us both one Soul;
>
> Harmony to behold in wedded pair
> More grateful than harmonious sound to the ear.
>
> (8.602–6)

Though Adam had originally asked God for an "equal," he realizes by the time he says these lines that the living harmony of married action depends on Eve's "sweet compliance," on her derivation of her will from his.

This asymmetry of male and female will in heterosexual harmony has been the subject of grateful rumination on the part of some male critics,[37] and the target of stern critique by feminist readers like Landy and Gilbert. To Lewalski, Webber, and McColley it is an historical accident which the harmony itself, and the heterosexual reading it invokes, transcend. But the poetics of transcendence in *Paradise Lost* places female participation in a far more complex dynamic than any of these analyses would suggest. Perhaps the poem's most concise rendering of that dynamic occurs when Eve herself defines the terms on which she participates in heterosexual harmony.

The poem allows Eve to voice the story of her conversion to heterosexual love. She relates how, in her first moments of consciousness, she bent down to see and interact with "A Shape within the wat'ry gleam," the image of her own face:

> . . . there I had fixt
> Mine eyes till now, and pin'd with vain desire,
> Had not a voice thus warn'd me, What thou seest,
> What there thou seest fair Creature is thyself,
> With thee it came and goes: but follow me,
> And I will bring thee where no shadow stays
> Thy coming, and thy soft imbraces, hee
> Whose image thou art, him thou shalt enjoy
> Inseparably thine, to him shalt bear
> Multitudes like thyself, and thence be call'd
> Mother of the human Race: what could I do,
> But follow straight, invisibly thus led?
>
> (4.466–76)

Does Eve's question about her induction into heterosexuality—"what could I do, / But follow straight"—reflect her sense that she has been compelled to turn to Adam or that she has engaged in a reasoning interaction with a persuading voice? And when she goes on to relate how she then spurned the sight of Adam, fleeing to "that smooth wat'ry image" (4.480) until she was called back by him, does her narration of the crisis—"with that thy gentle hand / *Seiz'd* mine, I *yielded*" (4.488–89; emphasis mine)—emphasize his violent appropriation of her or her willing compliance? The ostensible function of her speech is to confirm to Adam her voluntary participation in heterosexual love, but what meaning can be given to her repeated references to male compulsion in this crucial scene? Or conversely, the clear subtext here is Eve's resentment of the force under which she has acted: what meaning can we give, then, to her repeated affirmations of her active, reasoning assent to it? Adam's interpolation of Eve as his "individual solace dear" (l. 486) suggests that the contradictions that structure female autonomy in the *Doctrine and Discipline of Divorce* reappear here, making any simple answer to these questions untenable. For Adam's term creates Eve both as an autonomous individual in the liberal tradition, and as a being in-dividual, indivisible from the husband whose speech provides her with her true identity.

A failure to accommodate this dilemma characterizes two of the strongest feminist analyses of this scene—one offered by Christine Froula, working with great theoretical sophistication in the feminist tradition exemplified by Landy and Gilbert, and the other proposed by McColley in her liberal-feminist defense of Eve and her creator(s). Froula focuses on God's words, "What there thou seest fair Creature is thyself": "The reflection is not *of* Eve: according to the voice, it *is* Eve." God defines her as a "substanceless image" and invites her to mirror not her own face but that of Adam, that of the man "Whose image thou art." In response, Eve internalizes the utterance of the "voice" and of Adam: her "indoctrination into her own 'identity' is complete at the point at which her imagination is so successfully colonized by patriarchal authority that she literally becomes its voice."[38] The sequence Froula sees here is exactly what we would expect from the *Doctrine and Discipline of Divorce*—except that Froula's conclusion, that "Eve does not speak patriarchal discourse; it speaks her,"[39] obscures Milton's historically innovative insistence on female conversation. At least part of the importance of Eve's speech is that she *does* speak patriarchal discourse, *as* an autonomous subject. McColley, on the other hand, studies this autonomy without acknowledging its embeddedness in a social relation structured by male power. Observing that the scene as Eve relates it follows an educational sequence which activates her free will, McColley provides a needed corrective to Froula's analysis by emphasizing the salience of Eve's autonomy. But her argument ignores not only Eve's references to the constraints she encountered, but also its own language of compulsion: "Eve's narrow escape from narcissism . . . *requir[es]* her to lose herself in order to find herself while leaving her full freedom to fail. . . . [T]he method of Eve's creation is part of what Milton believes to be God's way in creating all things, and *requires* for its completion the free and deliberate choice that Eve's decision, after she knows whose face is in the lake, supplies. . . . It is *important to Milton's concept of domestic liberty* that Eve should respond spontaneously yet preparedly to Adam, . . . in full knowledge of who she is."[40]

McColley's language quite properly points to the backstage presence of a mastermind whose intentions require Eve's autonomy. *Pace* Lewalski, it is this figure who enjoys the only transcendence actually represented in *Paradise Lost*. The poet's invocations of the Muse repeat the sexual harmonics of Adam and Eve: just as Eve's creation remedied Adam's "single imperfection" (8.423), the Muse rescues the poet from "solitude": he is "not alone," he says in the invocation to Book 7, "while thou / Visit'st my slumbers Nightly" (7.28–29). And by incorporating that harmonic's adaptation of the politics of domestic meaning expounded in the *Doctrine and Discipline of Divorce*, these invocations reformulate the terms of transcendence. Milton's strategy is no longer to transcend female textuality by driving the Muse from the poem. In the four invocations of *Paradise Lost*, he never abandons his appeal to a female Muse. Instead, a prior masculine understanding or meaning both incorporates and transcends the mere imagery of the female figure.

The clearest model for this transcendence appears in the invocation to Book 1, where Milton calls on the "Heav'nly Muse" but soon revises his appeal:

> But chiefly Thou O Spirit, that dost prefer
> Before all Temples th' upright heart and pure,
> Instruct me, for Thou know'st; Thou from the first
> Wast present, and with mightly wings outspread
> Dove-like satst brooding on the vast Abyss
> And mad'st it pregnant. . . .
>
> (1.17–22)

Exactly when maternal brooding becomes paternal impregnation, the female figure of the "heav'nly Muse" is displaced by a male spirit.[41] Milton has finally reached the origin—"Thou from the first / Wast present"—that he has sought throughout the invocation. But the female is not utterly transcended in the invocations of *Paradise Lost* as she is in the raptures of the Diodati poems: the shift in address—"But chiefly Thou"—rather than abandon the female Muse, incorporates her into the prior, higher, and more inclusive person of the male spirit.

The invocation of Urania in Book 7 suggests how this new form of transcendence resolves the problems that *At a Solemn Music* concentrates in the sister-Muse figure. For here Milton invokes Urania as one of a pair of sisters whose identity is clearly subsumed in that of their father:

> Thou with Eternal Wisdom didst converse,
> Wisdom thy Sister, and with her didst play
> In presence of th' Almightly Father. . . .

$$(7.9–11)$$

It is no accident that, in juxtaposition with this super-real "Father," the sister Muses assume the texture of fable. For Milton has already carefully delimited Urania to the status of a sign profoundly remote from its divine signification:

> Descend from Heav'n *Urania,* by that name
> If rightly thou art call'd. . . .
> The meaning, not the Name I call. . . .

$$(7.1–5)$$

Textuality and the female are again associated here, but now they are clearly subordinated to and controlled by a phallocentric "meaning" whose powers resemble those of the husband envisioned in the *Doctrine and Discipline of Divorce.* Moreover, it is almost certain that the meaning Milton actually invokes here is the spirit he invoked in Book 1: it knows, and Milton knows it. Milton establishes here a traffic in the female "Name" that orchestrates the relationship between two male signifying powers. Its heterosexual design should not blind us to its homosocial function.

This semiotic transcendence expresses in Christian terms the union of the epic poet with the male God figured in the *Elegy VI.* And it repeats the simultaneous elision of woman and of textuality that Milton envisions in the *Epitaphium Damonis.* But unlike the earlier poems, this invocation continues to address the "Name" of Urania through its thirty-nine lines. At its close, Milton presents a key revision of *Lycidas.* He asks the Muse to drive far off not the "rout that made the hideous roar," the Thracian women who destroyed Orpheus in the earlier poem (l. 61)—but their "barbarous dissonance" and "savage clamor." It is not the women but their unharmonious noise that must be driven off: Urania, Eve, the female figure must participate in this text, as a harmonic "other half" whose "meaning" originates in male intention. The truly transcendent element in this aesthetic is not the heterosexual couple that it requires, but the male mind that defines both its members.

NOTES

1. *Paradise Lost,* in *John Milton: Complete Poems and Major Prose,* ed. Merritt Y. Hughes (Indianapolis: Odyssey Press, 1957), ll. 891–92, p. 427. All subsequent quotations of Milton's poems, and all translations of them, will be from this edition, and will be noted by book and line number as necessary in the text.

2. See, for example, Marcia Landy, "Kinship and the Role of Women in *Paradise Lost,*" *Milton Studies,* 4, ed. James D. Simmonds (Pittsburgh: University of Pittsburgh Press, 1972), pp. 3–18, and " 'A Free and Open Encounter': Milton and the Modern Reader," *Milton Studies,* 9 (1976), 3–36; Sandra K. Gilbert, "Patriarchal Poetry and Women Readers: Reflections on Milton's Bogey," *PMLA,* 93 (1978), 368–82. A useful bibliography is provided by Marilyn R. Farwell, "Eve, the Separation Scene, and the Renaissance Idea of Androgyny," *Milton Studies,* 16 (1982), 17, n. 1.

3. Barbara K. Lewalski, "Milton on Women — Yet Once More," *Milton Studies,* 6 (1974), 3–20; Joan Malory Webber, "The Politics of Poetry: Feminism and *Paradise Lost,*" *Milton Studies,* 14 (1980), 3–24; Diane Kelsey McColley, *Milton's Eve* (Urbana: University of Illinois Press, 1983).

4. Lawrence Stone, *The Family, Sex and Marriage in England,* 1500–1800 *(New York: Harper & Row, 1977).*

5. In addition to Stone's study, works on the development of Puritan or bourgeois marriage include: Roland Frye, "The Teachings of Classical Puritanism on Conjugal Love," *Studies in the Renaissance,* 2 (1955), 148–59; William Haller and Malleville Haller, "The Puritan Art of Love," *Huntington Library Quarterly,* 5 (1942), 235–72; William Haller, "Hail Wedded Love," *ELH,* 13 (1946), 79–97; James Johnson, *A Society Ordained by God: English Puritan Marriage Doctrine in the First Half of the Seventeenth Century* (Nashville: Abingdon Press, 1970); Joan Larsen Klein, "Women and Marriage in Renaissance England: Male Perspectives," in *Topic 36: The Elizabethan Woman,* intro. Anne Paston (Washington, Pa.: Washington and Jefferson College, 1982), pp. 20–37; Levin L. Schucking, *The Puritan Family* (New York: Schocken, 1970); and Eli Zaretsky, *Capitalism, the Family, and Personal Life* (New York: Harper-Colophon, 1976). Studies specifically focusing on Milton's position in this development include Jackie DiSalvo, "Blake Encountering Milton: Politics and the Family in *Paradise Lost* and *The Four Zoas,*" in *Milton and the Line of Vision,* ed. Joseph Anthony Wittreich, Jr. (Madison: University of Wisconsin Press, 1975), pp. 143–84; Cheryl H. Fresch, " 'And brought her unto the man': The Wedding in *Paradise Lost,*" *Milton Studies,* 16 (1982), 21–33; Allan H. Gilbert, "Milton on the Position of Women," *MLR,* 15 (1920), 240–64; John Haklett, *Milton and the Idea of Matrimony: A Study of the Divorce Tracts and Paradise Lost,* Yale Studies in English, 173 (New Haven: Yale University Press, 1970); and Edward Le Comte, *Milton and Sex* (New York: Columbia University Press, 1978).

6. Lewalski, p. 19.

7. For an analysis of "postfeminist criticism," see Elaine Tuttle Hansen, "Saving Chaucer's Good Name," in *Feminist Criticism of Chaucer*, ed. S. Tomasch (forthcoming).

8. The radical feminist critique of female consent within political systems that make sex an arena for male power is best represented, perhaps, by Adrienne Rich, "Compulsory Heterosexuality and Lesbian Existence," *Signs*, 5, no. 4 (1980), 631–60, and by Catharine A. MacKinnon, "Feminism, Marxism, Method, and the State: Toward Feminist Jurisprudence," *Signs*, 8, no. 4 (1983), 635–58 (see esp. p. 637, n. 5 and pp. 646–55). These and other works helped to spark a debate over sexuality in which many feminists have argued that modes of female desire and consent can—or, *faut de mieux*, must—be found within the cultural forms of dominance and submission: see *Heresies #12*, 3, no. 4 (1981), the "Sex Issue"; *Powers of Desire: The Politics of Sexuality*, ed. Ann Snitow, Christine Stansell, and Sharon Thompson (New York: Monthly Review Press, 1983); and *Pleasure and Danger: Exploring Female Sexuality*, ed. Carole S. Vance (New York: Routledge & Kegan Paul, 1984).

9. Lewalski, p. 5.

10. Lewalski, p. 4.

11. On this point, see also Don Parry Norford, "'My Other Half': The Coincidence of Opposites in *Paradise Lost*," *MLQ*, 36 (1975), 21–53.

12. Webber, p. 15.

13. McColley, pp. 4, 16.

14. McColley, pp. 75–76.

15. McColley, pp. 81–82.

16. Webber, p. 5.

17. The quoted term is Gayle Rubin's; see "The Traffic in Women: Notes on the 'Political Economy' of Sex," in *Toward an Anthropology of Women*, ed. Rayna R. Reiter (New York: Monthly Review Press, 1975), p. 159.

18. Rich, pp. 637–48.

19. Claude Lévi-Strauss, *The Elementary Structures of Kinship*, rev. ed., trans. James Harle Bell, John Richard von Sturmer, and Rodney Needham (Boston: Beacon Press, 1969); Rubin, p. 174.

20. Eve Kosofsky Sedgwick, *Between Men: English Literature and Male Homosocial Desire* (New York: Columbia University Press, 1985), pp. 1–2.

21. Louis Althusser, "Ideology and Ideological State Apparatuses (Notes toward an Investigation)," in *Lenin and Philosophy and Other Essays* (London: New Left Books, 1971), pp. 121–73, esp. p. 153.

22. On Eve's mediation of Adam's relation with God, see Kathleen M. Swaim, "'Hee for God only, shee for God in him': Structural Parallelism in *Paradise Lost*," *Milton Studies*, 9 (1976), 121–49.

23. Lévi-Strauss, p. 496.

24. Ernst Robert Curtius, *European Literature and the Latin Middle Ages*, trans. Willard A. Trask (New York: Harper & Row, 1953), p. 234. See Chapter 13, "The Muses," pp. 228–46.

25. See Edgar Wind, *Pagan Mysteries in the Renaissance,* rev. ed. (New York: W. W. Norton, 1968), Appendix 6, "Garurius on the Harmony of the Spheres," pp. 265–69.

26. Hughes, *John Milton,* p. 603.

27. See Stella P. Revard, "Milton's Muse and the Daughters of Memory," *English Literary Renaissance,* 9, (1979), 432–41, for another analysis of Milton's method of establishing relationship with his classical predecessors through the Muse.

28. John Shawcross has explored the correspondence of Milton and Diodati, finding evidence of Milton's homoerotic experience of masculine friendship: see "Milton and Diodati: An Essay in Psychodynamic Meaning," *Milton Studies,* 7 (1975), 127–63.

29. Samuel Johnson, *The Life of Milton,* in *Johnson's Lives of the Poets: A Selection,* ed. J. P. Hardy (Oxford: Clarendon Press, 1971), p. 94.

30. *The Doctrine and Discipline of Divorce,* in *Complete Prose Works of John Milton,* vol. 2 (New Haven: Yale University Press, 1959), p. 242. In the original, this passage is entirely in italics; emphasis here is mine. All subsequent quotations from this tract will be from this volume, and will be cited by page number in the text.

31. Lewalski, p. 11.

32. Webber, pp. 14 and 23, n. 36; *Tetrachordon* in CPW 2, p. 589.

33. Brackets enclose phrases added to the 1644 edition of the *Doctrine and Discipline of Divorce;* in the second case Milton has changed his wording.

34. See Althusser, p. 169.

35. David Aers and Bob Hodge, " 'Rational Burning': Milton on Sex and Marriage," *Milton Studies,* 13 (1979), 17–18, provide a useful analysis of Milton's contradictory individualism here.

36. The report of Origen's castration is to be found in Eusebius, *Ecclesiastical History;* see CPW 2, p. 334n.

37. See Northrop Frye, "The Revelation to Eve," in *Paradise Lost: A Tercentenary Tribute,* ed. Balachandra Rajan (Toronto: Toronto University Press, 1969), pp. 18–47; and Norford, " 'My Other Half.' "

38. Christine Froula, "When Eve Reads Milton: Undoing the Canonical Economy," *Critical Inquiry,* 10 (December 1983), 328–29.

39. Froula, p. 329.

40. McColley, pp. 75, 81–82.

41. For an argument that the Muse here is androgynous, see Virginia R. Mollenkott, "Some Implications of Milton's Androgynous Muse," *Bucknell Review,* 24 (Spring, 1978), 27–38.

Notes on Contributors

RICHARD CORUM, educated at Harvard and the University of California at Berkeley, teaches Renaissance literature and creative writing at Dartmouth College, and has recently finished a book on the Donne controversy, entitled *Memory, Trope, Donne.*

JACKIE DiSALVO teaches at Baruch College, City University of New York. She has published one ideological study of Milton, *War of Titans: Blake's Critique of Milton and the Politics of Religion,* and is writing the Milton volume for the Harvester Press Feminist Readings series. Her articles on Milton have appeared in *Milton Studies* and various anthologies. She received her Ph.D. from the University of Wisconsin, Madison.

LYNN ENTERLINE is writing her dissertation, "Renaissance Men: The Politics of Self, Gender, and Poetic Language," in the Department of English of Cornell University. She has received a Woodrow Wilson Research Grant in Women's Studies for the project. Another of her essays, "The Mirror and the Snake: The Case of Marvell's 'Unfortunate Lover,'" will appear in *Critical Quarterly* (Fall, 1987). Ms. Enterline studied at Vanderbilt University and at Oxford University as a Rhodes Scholar.

NOAM FLINKER studied English at Haverford College, Columbia University, and New York University. He has published articles on seventeenth-century poetry (Milton, Donne, and Herbert) and prose as well as on poetry in America (Frost and Cummings) and Israel (Bialik and Amichai), and is now writing a book about canticles in seventeenth-century England. Flinker is a senior lecturer at Ben-Gurion University of the Negev in Israel, and has taught at the University of Haifa, the University of Texas at Austin, Dickinson College, and the University of Pennsylvania.

MARSHALL GROSSMAN teaches English and comparative literature at Fordham University (Lincoln Center). Educated at Harpur College (SUNY–Binghamton) and New York University, he is the author of *"Authors to Themselves": Milton and the Revelation of History* and numerous articles on literary criticism and Renaissance literature.

JANET E. HALLEY will graduate J.D. from the Yale Law School in 1988. She has published numerous articles on the conflict of orthodox and heretical discourses in sixteenth- and seventeenth-century England, and is co-editor, with Sheila Fisher, of *The Lady Vanishes: Feminist Contextual Criticism of Medieval and Renaissance Writings.*

DAYTON HASKIN was born in Ann Arbor, studied at the University of London and at Yale, and teaches English at Boston College. He has written on Milton's *De Doctrina Christiana* in the *Heythrop Journal* and on *Samson Agonistes* in *ELH,* and is now at work on a book on Milton and Bunyan. In connection with his research as a contributing editor for the *Donne Variorum* project, he has begun to write about the revival of interest in Donne's poetry in the nineteenth century.

LEAH MARCUS is Professor of English at the University of Wisconsin-Madison. She is the author of *Childhood and Cultural Despair, The Politics of Mirth: Jonson, Herrick, Milton, Marvell, and the Defense of Old Holiday Pastimes,* and *Shakespeare and the Unease of Topicality,* in addition to numerous articles. She has held NEH and Guggenheim fellowships, and received her Ph.D. from Columbia University.

DIANE McCOLLEY, author of *Milton's Eve* (University of Illinois Press, 1983), is an Associate Professor of English at Rutgers University, Camden College of Arts and Sciences. She was educated at the University of California at Berkeley and at the University of Illinois at Urbana-Champaign. Her book-in-progress is "A Gust for Paradise: The Arts of Eden in the Age of Milton."

JOHN C. ULREICH, Jr., was educated at Hamilton College and Harvard University. He is a Professor of English at the University of Arizona, where he teaches in the English Renaissance (chiefly Milton and the seventeenth century), the Bible, humanities, and modern fantasy. He has published on Milton, Spenser, Sidney, the Old Testament, C. S. Lewis, and Owen Barfield.

JULIA M. WALKER, educated at the University of Tennessee and Purdue University, is an Assistant Professor of English at the State University of New York at Geneseo. Her articles on Donne have appeared in *Studies in Philology,* the *John Donne Journal, Review of English Studies,* and other journals; she has also published on Milton and Spenser. In addition to her contribution to the *Donne Variorum,* she is working on a study of mirror images of women in Renaissance texts.

KATHLEEN WALL was educated at the University of Michigan and the University of Manitoba. She is an Assistant Professor at the University of Manitoba, in an affirmative-action program designed to train inner-city teachers and social workers. She has published poems in *Queens Quarterly, Antigonish Review, minnesota review and Contemporary Verse II.* Her study of the Callisto myth in literature from the Middle Ages to the twentieth century is forthcoming.

SUSANNE WOODS is Professor of English and Associate Dean of the faculty at Brown University. She is the author of *Natural Emphasis: English Versification from Chaucer to Dryden,* numerous articles on Renaissance poetry and poetics, and a forthcoming book, tentatively titled *Freedom and Tyranny in Spenser and Milton.* The article in this volume is one of several debts to an NEH fellowship year at the Huntington Library.

Index